THE LURE OF THE NORTH WOODS

Cultivating Tourism in the Upper Midwest

AARON SHAPIRO

UNIVERSITY OF MINNESOTA PRESS
Minneapolis · London

The University of Minnesota Press gratefully acknowledges financial assistance provided for the publication of this book by Auburn University.

Portions of this book were previously published in "'Air Conditioned by the Cool Breezes of Lake Superior': Vacationing in Michigan's Copper Country after World War Two," in Kim Hoagland, Terry Reynolds, and Erik Nordberg, eds., *New Perspectives on Michigan's Copper Country* (Hancock, Mich.: Quincy Mine Hoist Association, 2007), reprinted with permission of the Quincy Mine Hoist Association; and in "Up North on Vacation: Tourism and Resorts in Wisconsin's North Woods," *Wisconsin Magazine of History* (Summer 2006): 2–13, reprinted with permission of the Wisconsin Historical Society. Portions of chapter 1 were previously published in "Promoting Cloverland: Regional Associations, State Agencies, and the Creation of Michigan's Upper Peninsula Tourist Industry," *Michigan Historical Review* 29 (Spring 2003): 1–37.

Original maps were created by Philip Schwartzberg, Meridian Mapping, Minneapolis

Published by the University of Minnesota Press
111 Third Avenue South, Suite 290
Minneapolis, MN 55401-2520
http://www.upress.umn.edu

Design and production by Mighty Media, Inc.
Interior/text design by Chris Long

Library of Congress Cataloging-in-Publication Data

Shapiro, Aaron.
The lure of the north woods : cultivating tourism in the upper midwest / Aaron Shapiro.
Includes bibliographical references and index.
ISBN 978-0-8166-7792-4 (hc : alk. paper)
ISBN 978-0-8166-7793-1 (pb : alk. paper)
1. Tourism—Middle West—History. 2. Outdoor recreation—Middle West—History. 3. Outdoor life—Middle West—History. 4. Middle West—Social life and customs. I. Title.
G155.U6S44 2013
338.4'79177—dc23

2012043825

Printed on acid-free paper

In memory of my father, Jack Shapiro

Contents

Abbreviations

ASA	Arrowhead Sportsmen's Association
BIA	Bureau of Indian Affairs
BWCA	Boundary Waters Canoe Area
C&H	Calumet and Hecla
CCC	Civilian Conservation Corps
CCVL	Copper Country Vacationist League
FOW	Friends of the Wilderness
FWP	Federal Writers' Project
IRRRB	Iron Range Resources and Rehabilitation Board
MAA	Minnesota Arrowhead Association
MECC	Minnesota Emergency Conservation Committee
MTC	Michigan Tourist Council
MUCC	Michigan United Conservation Clubs
NCOR	National Conference on Outdoor Recreation
NMDA	Northern Minnesota Development Association
NORGLAC	Northern Great Lakes Area Council
OAU	Outdoor America United
OBCA	Outboard Boating Company of America
ORAP	Outdoor Recreation Act Plan
ORRRC	Outdoor Recreation Resources Review Commission
UP	Upper Peninsula
UPDB	Upper Peninsula Development Bureau
WPA	Works Progress Administration; Work Projects Administration after July 1, 1939

INTRODUCTION

A North Woods Transformation

For centuries, Ojibwe people enjoyed dense green forests, abundant wildlife, and waters teeming with fish on land that the United States later labeled northern Minnesota, northern Wisconsin, and Michigan's Upper Peninsula. By the end of the nineteenth century, mining and logging had stripped this land of much of its natural wealth and splendor. Today, it is again recognized for its forests and lakes as well as its history of extractive industry that attracted immigrants and capital to the region. For many residents and visitors, it offers a natural paradise with more wildlife than people. While Ojibwe continue to call this land home, it is a changed place.

During the twentieth century, vacationers arrived at housekeeping cabins, state parks, and family-owned resorts like northern Wisconsin's Ross' Teal Lake Lodge, where they discovered "not city conditions, but the pleasingly novel conditions attending sojourns in the North Woods" and "an ideal vacation for all the family." For the Tobin family, paved roads led them north from Illinois to Teal Lake Lodge, where rustic cabins lacking running water reinforced the escape from city life. The family enjoyed hay fever relief in the crisp air and explored lakes and forest trails. Writing during winter in Illinois, L. M. Tobin recalled the benefits of summer days in a place called the North Woods. Another Teal Lake Lodge visitor, B. A. Claflin, praised the accommodations and food as better than other area resorts. He also noted the previous destruction of the region's trees and how a new forest emerged to offer an appealing and scenic landscape for tourists. Teal Lake Lodge promotional materials, Claflin's remarks on forest regeneration, and Tobin's reflections on his family vacation demonstrate how the North Woods was increasingly viewed and experienced from a consumer perspective.[1]

The North Woods that Tobin, Claflin, and many other vacationers enjoyed was a new creation. Geographically and ecologically, the North Woods describes a forested landscape encompassing northern Wisconsin, northern Minnesota, and Michigan's Upper Peninsula, which is also one of the most concentrated lake regions in the world. In this sense, it is a place that can be marked on a map. During the interwar and postwar years, the North Woods moniker came to define the broad region, although places within it emerged with distinct names. Today, vacationers to the Upper Peninsula still discuss visiting the "UP," and residents often call themselves Yoopers; whereas in Minnesota, a commonly heard refrain involves being "up at the lake" or "up north." Minnesota's Arrowhead is part of the North Woods and includes Carlton, Cook, Lake, St. Louis, Aitkin, Itasca, and Koochiching Counties. But counties bordering the Arrowhead also developed as important North Woods destinations and are included in this story. Today, the North Woods moniker resonates most strongly in northern Wisconsin. But perhaps more than geography and labels, the North Woods also describes an abstract idea and conceptual realm forged by a range of actors during the twentieth century. This book tells the story of how this particular place came to be known and experienced as the North Woods.

Far more complicated than simply a story of outsiders imposing their will, this book shows how vacationers at places like Teal Lake Lodge interacted with local tourist providers and residents, private and public tourism advocates, and fellow consumers to create the North Woods. Hunters and anglers formed organizations to advocate for limits on logging and improved fish and game propagation. Ojibwe challenged policies that conflicted with their subsistence hunting and fishing practices, but they also provided for tourists at places like northern Wisconsin's Lac du Flambeau reservation. Local boosters viewed the forested landscape as a commodity to sell to consumers seeking escape from daily life. Timber and mining companies valued trees and minerals, while state conservation agencies managed natural resources and promoted recreation. The U.S. Forest Service pursued Gifford Pinchot's conservation vision, which grew to include outdoor recreation aided by Civilian Conservation Corps (CCC) young men carving trails, building campgrounds, and planting trees on public lands.

While numerous studies exist on how other industries changed the region, tourism's influence in transforming cutover forests into the North Woods remains less understood. This story thus contributes to both a broader understanding of the region as well as the history of American tourism and its connections to consumer society and modern environmentalism.[2] The market's intrusion into the nineteenth-century countryside established urban-rural connections that exploited natural resources, altered lives, and transformed the landscape. By promoting vacations as a consumer item that improved health and productivity while providing an escape to a supposedly more natural environment, twentieth-century advocates hoped tourism could diversify the economy and address land-use concerns. Like earlier lumbermen, they also saw profit in nature. But unlike those lumbermen, who often cut and ran after felling the forest, they relied on nature's regenerative forces to provide a new cash crop, a forested and lake-dotted countryside offering outdoor recreation for the masses.[3]

Experiencing deindustrialization earlier than the Rust Belt cities to which it sent natural resources, North Woods residents participated in transforming a landscape of production into one of consumption. Familiar with the boom-and-bust cycles of extractive industry directed by outside capital, they wanted a more secure future, and a growing market of vacationers boosted such aspirations.[4] Promoted and experienced as a haven from the industrial world despite the North Woods' intimate connection to it, vacationing offered a respite in the place that had provided resources to build cities. But this time, the consumers—tourists—traveled to enjoy the landscape rather than having nature's resources shipped to them. As a result, the North Woods came to be viewed and experienced as a place of leisure instead of labor, as a retreat from urban life rather than an economic storehouse of timber, iron, and copper. Places across the North Woods became worthy of admiration for their scenery as residents and vacationers recognized that play instead of production offered economic and spiritual benefits.

The ascription of aesthetic values to natural places commoditized nature in new ways, privileging tourism and outdoor recreation over previous industrial uses. As this book demonstrates, such shifts highlight modern American environmentalism's interwar origins, when people increasingly realized that consuming nature for pleasure demanded new approaches toward natural resources. While Rachel Carson's 1962 *Silent Spring* is often seen as marking the birth of modern American environmentalism, average Americans came to view and experience nature differently in places like the North Woods during the interwar years. Vacationing with the family at a rustic lakeside cabin, embarking on mental journeys by reading Works Progress/Work Projects Administration (WPA) guides, enjoying summer camp, and hiking trails constructed by the CCC, they increasingly redefined the natural world in consumerist terms through leisure.[5]

While vacations provided escape from daily toil, they also created opportunities for local providers of goods and services. Former miners and lumbermen entered the tourist business, reshaping work as well as their understanding of nature. From accommodation to outfitting, tourists depended on the work of others. Tourism fit a seasonal labor tradition that saw workers alter the region as vacationers and by providing for tourists. This book also illustrates, therefore, how shared rural work and leisure experiences contributed to a new regional identity.[6]

The North Woods story challenges the traditional narrative of mass tourism as solely a post–World War II phenomenon and explores tourism's place in modern American culture. North Woods advocates appealed to the masses, recognizing that tourists made choices about their journeys. As they read promotional materials and traveled to the North Woods, they contributed to a vacation experience that shared similarities with other regional transformations in North America, but also diverged from them due to factors such as nearby large cities with middle- and working-class vacationers, pioneering land-use initiatives, the proliferation of mom-and-pop tourist operations, and an activist political tradition with a strong union presence. Historian Hal Rothman characterized western tourism as a devil's bargain because it provided economic benefits but vested decision-making power with outsiders and contributed to a loss of uniqueness that made places worth visiting. North Woods tourism attracted nonresident interest and surely altered the landscape, but residents exerted greater control and experienced tourism as less of a devil's bargain than their western counterparts. In the North Woods, they helped create a more democratic experience in terms of opportunities for vacationers and local providers than under earlier industry.[7]

Although scenic beauty helped make the region a destination, tourism is not a natural product but rather is managed and packaged by people and organizations with often competing interests. For some residents, tourism offered survival in a changing economy. Others who worked and vacationed in the North Woods saw it as a means to preserve connections to place, conserve nature, or capitalize on its economic potential. Together, they transformed the North Woods and helped change attitudes about nature, work, and leisure.

As an important element of an expanding consumer culture during

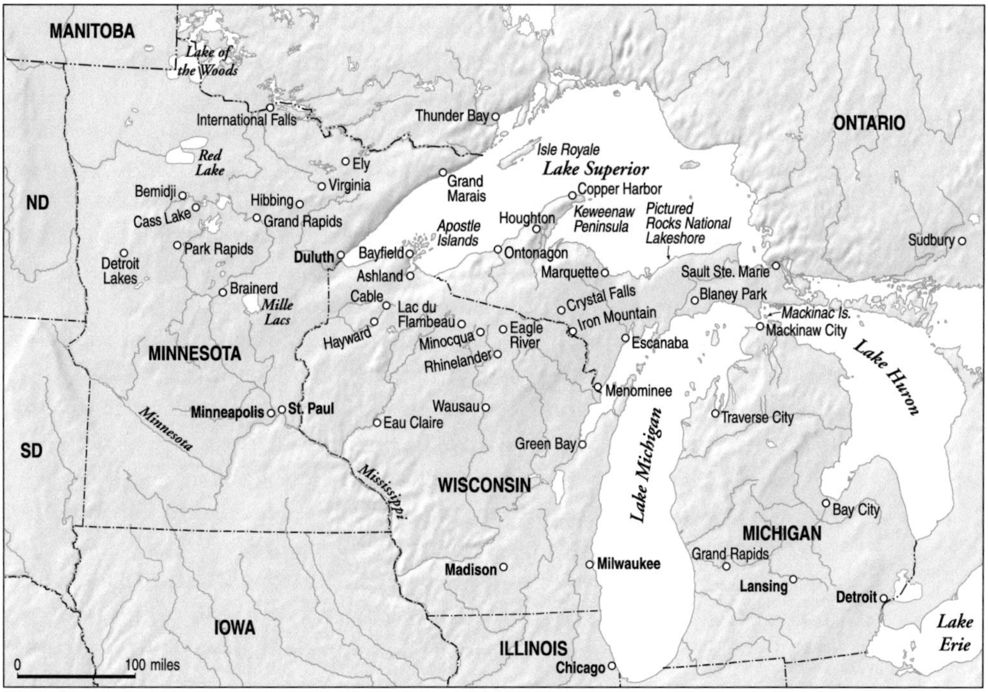

The North Woods.

the twentieth century, tourism linked regional developments to national debates. The creation of the U.S. Forest Service in 1905 and the National Park Service in 1916 led states to develop additional parks and forests to conserve natural resources and provide recreation. Minnesota played a pioneering role in this effort, establishing Itasca State Park at the Mississippi River's headwaters in 1891. While many rural residents expressed concerns about outside interference in local affairs, they looked to participate in consumer society on their own terms. According to historian Hal Barron, consumer culture also brought expanded state power and professional expertise to the nation's countryside. As the preeminent symbol of that culture, the automobile democratized travel and increased access to the North Woods, where visitors joined more than half of American families who vacationed away from home during the 1920s.[8]

Revealing how local and state activities to develop North Woods tourism and manage land use presaged 1930s federal government efforts, this book focuses on the deeper roots of New Deal conservation and land-planning programs. Thus, tourism underscores the changing role and activity of the state before, during, and after the New Deal.[9] Nationally, rural land-use policies emerged within the context of an urban industrial society, and conservation efforts were increasingly connected to urban consumer needs, from early-twentieth-century fights over access to water in California's Hetch Hetchy and Owens Valleys to growing urban desires to enjoy leisure in nature. Ultimately, the activity of local residents cooperating with and contesting government conservation regulations proved crucial in the North Woods.[10] Government at all levels facilitated tourist development—through promotion, conservation, and construction efforts—becoming a vital player and stakeholder in the tourist industry. Minnesota promoted itself as the Land of Ten Thousand Lakes, while Wisconsin's Conservation Department produced billboards and promotional literature with the slogan, "Relax in Wisconsin: Where Friends and Nature Meet." States established tourist offices and attended outdoor shows in midwestern cities. As more Americans recreated in the outdoors, they increasingly demanded that government ensure it had places to do so.

During the interwar years, private interests and the state looked to tourism to diversify a region suffering from industrial decline and an inability to successfully farm cutover northern lands. Working within the region's environmental benefits and constraints, they looked to remake a deforested landscape and establish a new regional identity. North Woods promotional literature presented a menu of options that contributed to changing residents' and vacationers' perceptions. Historian Robert Gough suggests that during the 1930s northern Wisconsin farmers lacked the necessary political and social capital to succeed and that government policies encouraged agriculture's demise.[11] But the reality of agricultural problems and changing understandings of natural resources proved to be more serious obstacles, leading Wisconsin and its neighbors to forge a different path. As this book demonstrates, that new direction—the creation of a tourist North Woods—was fueled by the region's engagement with a modern consumer culture in which changing technologies and expanding market relationships helped transform land, labor, and leisure during the interwar and postwar years.

Chapter 1 analyzes the role of local, regional, and statewide organizations, as well as state and federal government, in creating the North Woods. Declining mining and lumber industries along with failed agricultural promotion and settlement before World War I led to the emergence of a new perspective in which tourism emerged as a means to improve and diversify the region. New tourism organizations discovered a partner in state government. Examining the relationship that developed between private enterprise and the state, the chapter describes the political and organizational groundwork necessary for transforming the region. Across the North Woods, land planning initiatives generated conflict as well as compromise. Focusing on experts who offered plans for remaking the region and residents who shaped land-use initiatives on the ground, chapter 2 explains the contested nature of conservation efforts and their importance for tourism. North Woods tourism was a product of industrialization just as much as agriculture, forestry, and mining. While tourism developed alongside these industries, it emerged as the key response when the region experienced the environmental and economic realities of a denuded and infertile landscape.

Chapter 3 explores the people involved in developing tourist facilities, the vacationers who frequented these places, and the workers who provided for people's leisure and helped shape experiences and views of the North Woods. It is a story of consumption as well as production, leisure as well as work. Transforming the North Woods into a tourist destination also involved the movement of people and goods. Along with the activities of tourist operators and vacationers, the trade in vacation-related commodities and the experiences provided by workers fostered a service economy in which conveying a positive vacation message remained essential. Chapter 4 analyzes the North Woods image as portrayed in promotional literature and compares it with actual vacation experiences. Promotional materials show the nature of the tourist pitch in a consumer culture that commoditized nature for human enjoyment. These items changed how people viewed the region and, along with existing organizational structures, helped create the North Woods as both idea and place before World War II.

Chapter 5 examines North Woods transformations after World War II. Drawing on previous chapter themes, it analyzes the connections between conservation, land use, and tourism initiatives, how and where people vacationed, increased private-public cooperation, and the language of postwar promotion. A section on Michigan's Copper Country illustrates policy and development shifts across the North Woods from the interwar to the postwar years. For example, Canadian and American officials increasingly advocated for cooperative tourism and conservation programs. Such efforts built on the foundation established in Minnesota and Ontario's Quetico-Superior area during the interwar years and added a new wrinkle to government's role in the tourist landscape.

Chapter 6 considers the North Woods within the larger outdoor recreation debates spearheaded by the Outdoor Recreation Resources Review Commission (ORRRC) chaired by Laurance Rockefeller in the late 1950s and early 1960s. Samuel T. Dana, the first dean of the University of Michigan's School of Forestry, and Chester Wilson, Minnesota's Conservation Commissioner from 1943 to 1955, served as two of the ORRRC's six members. ORRRC recommendations urged setting aside recreational areas for a growing population seeking access to the outdoors and placed government in a stronger position to manage recreation assets. Along these lines, the chapter explores controversies regarding Indian reservations and tourism, summer cottages, and wilderness recreation in which residents, nonresidents, and the state fiercely debated the area's future. Recognizing that the North Woods tourism story does not end with the 1960s outdoor recreation crisis or the 1964 Wilderness Act, the chapter briefly discusses how a tourist industry with roots dating back to the late nineteenth century now generates billions as visitors flock north.

Whether in the 1920s, 1960s, or today, tourism has never offered a simple panacea for addressing problems associated with regional economic decline. Since the early twentieth century, changing conceptions of land use along with increased leisure time have contributed to a growing appreciation for outdoor recreation in the North Woods. A variety of interests have engaged government at the local, state, and federal levels to ensure spaces will be available for all. Today, tourism is regularly used in attempts to revitalize rural areas and declining downtowns. While tourist landscapes can help reclaim extractive resource landscapes by embracing recreational and aesthetic conceptions of nature, they can also foster new forms of exploitative labor and land use just like earlier industry. Integrating places like the North Woods into the larger story of American society suggests that leisure, and tourism particularly, remains essential for understanding modern America.

The North Woods and its residents were far from alone in shifting from extractive industry to tourism in the twentieth century. But the region and its people offer an instructive example of the forces at work (or, one might suggest just as appropriately, at play) in such a situation and the elements that created a vacation destination for the masses. Diverse tourist destinations have encountered similar issues, albeit with varying levels of distinctiveness. Bend, Oregon, according to historian William Robbins, moved "from milling lumber to mining tourists," and "the town that once prospered through sending the products of nature to the city is now surviving in a weird kind of exchange."[12] That "weird kind of exchange" has roots in the North Woods and has become typical of many regions formerly dependent on resource extraction. It is a story of conflict and compromise, labor migration and leisure travel, local versus outside control, resource use as well as preservation. Like Robbins's Oregon folk, those who worked and vacationed in the North Woods, including the Ross and Tobin families, believed tourism was the right crop to cultivate and offered a landscape of promise. But promise for whom and with what effect on the people and land remained questions at the heart of the region's development and growth as a tourist destination.

CHAPTER 1

A Crop Worth Cultivating: Creating the North Woods

Depicting a farmer holding a hoe with "publicity" emblazoned on the bottom, looking at a bush full of moneybags denoting $450 million in tourist expenditures since World War I, a 1920s cartoon captured tourism's growing impact on Minnesota's economy, people, and landscape. Beside the farmer is a watering can with "hospitality" in prominent letters and a scarecrow telling him, "Seems to me this is one crop worth cultivating." During the interwar years, residents and organizations across the North Woods, some avidly and others reluctantly, helped tourism replace farming as the crop to cultivate. The lingual link to agriculture was no mistake. In the battle to transform the region from a cutover landscape to one marked by lakes and reemerging forests, state and federal government, quasi-public agencies, organizations, and residents increasingly looked to tourism to improve land and life.[1]

In the late nineteenth century, state immigration boards recruited farmers to northern lands. Upon arrival, individuals discovered stump-filled lands needing dynamite for removal and tilled rocky soil with hopes of improved farming. After several decades of unsuccessful immigration board efforts, organizations like the Upper Peninsula Development Bureau (UPDB), Minnesota Arrowhead Association, Paul Bunyan Playground Association, and Wisconsin Land O' Lakes Association emerged as regional tourism advocates. Ultimately, these organizations turned to the state for support, where they found a partner. In backing these organizational efforts, governments in Michigan, Minnesota, and Wisconsin committed to tourism to help redevelop northern lands. The area did not initially offer an aesthetically pleasing landscape, so tourism advocates supported a program of reimagining it, conserving and even reconstitut-

—*Foley in the Minneapolis Daily Star*

As this cartoon from the *Minneapolis Daily Star* attests, tourism emerged as big business in Minnesota in the 1920s.

ing its natural scenery in order to sell North Woods charms to urban dwellers. Advertised as untouched and natural, the reality was that the land had experienced the imprint of human hands through farming, lumbering, and mining. With a decreased supply of mining and lumber products and agricultural difficulties, tourism emerged as a sustainable alternative. By the end of the 1930s, Michigan's tourism industry placed second to automobiles in revenue generated, while tourist expenditures in Minnesota and Wisconsin each totaled over $100 million.[2]

As this chapter points out, organizations across the North Woods believed tourism would diversify the economy, but their composition and goals led to diverse methods and varying levels of success. Michigan's UPDB initially advocated a program stressing agriculture and industry over reforestation and tourism. Wisconsin resort owner associations emphasized attracting customers and proved less concerned with using tourism as a development tool. In northern Wisconsin, public and private entities also hoped to capitalize on the area's agricultural potential. Faced with a landscape transformed by mining and lumbering, they suggested that farms followed forests, and crops followed the axe. But this would not be the case, as recipients of such messages realized rhetoric did not match reality. Tourism emerged as the best hope for reversing the region's fortune, and residents, vacationers, and eventually the state backed the cause.[3]

At the turn of the twentieth century, much of the region lacked trees. State immigration boards published booklets like *Michigan: Agricultural, Horticultural, and Industrial Advantages* or focused on specific areas in *Northeastern Minnesota: Land of Certainties* and *Northwestern Minnesota: A Wonderful Agricultural Section* to encourage settlement.[4] In 1896, William A. Henry, dean of University of Wisconsin's School of Agriculture, worked with the state to produce *Northern Wisconsin: A Hand-Book for the Homeseeker*. Its images of agricultural bounty suggested farming followed lumbering, but descriptions hinted at other possibilities. Highlighting diversions for potential settlers, it suggested life in northern Wisconsin entailed hard work but also promised outdoor recreation. Settlers and visitors could enjoy the outdoors, with readers reminded that northern Wisconsin lakes offered solitude amid "primeval forest." Farmers could hunt and fish, while those looking to escape urban life would discover a refreshing change. The private Northern Wisconsin Development Association later drew on Henry's vision by emphasizing security, independence, and community life in its efforts to transform northern Wisconsin into a land of farmers.[5]

While Henry's *Hand-Book* proposed that farming replace lumbering on cleared land, others envisioned reforestation as the solution. Wisconsin's first state forester, Edward Griffith, advocated setting aside large portions of northern Wisconsin as a state forest reserve but encountered opposition from those who believed Henry's vision held the key to prosperity. Labeling Griffith a "man with a vision . . . who knew the possibilities of reforestation," a local newspaper editor received a lashing from readers for pointing out agricultural problems and supporting Griffith's approach. Several resort owners backed Griffith's plan, seeing it as a boon for tourism

Farm family with copious produce: Matthew H. Stephenson, his wife, Julia Hebert Stephenson, and their son, William Clinton, pose with produce samples from the Menominee River Boom Company garden near Marinette, Wisconsin. This photograph is one of many created for *Northern Wisconsin: A Hand-Book for the Homeseeker*, 1896. COURTESY OF THE WISCONSIN HISTORICAL SOCIETY, WHS IMAGE ID 1979.

generally. In the process, they forged an alliance between tourist operators and foresters best expressed by resort owner and former Chicago railroad worker Angus McDonald, who suggested, "This land as a Federal Forest is going to be worth more to Wisconsin than the few struggling farms that may locate there in years to come."[6] Griffith believed forests remained northern Wisconsin's most productive land use. Despite support from McDonald and other operators, Griffith's plans would have to wait until after World War I, as states and private entities first focused on farming.

In Wisconsin, the *Hand-Book for the Homeseeker*'s message of a prosperous land where settlers reaped benefits continued. Ben Faast's Wisconsin Colonization Company received support from Harry Russell, who followed William Henry as dean of Wisconsin's School of Agriculture. Russell shared Faast's conviction that the "plow would follow the axe in northern Wisconsin." Faast employed agents in cities and advertised in the ethnic press to attract settlers, who gradually realized that establishing an agricultural paradise remained elusive.[7] Struggling to meet basic needs, they made do in a seasonal economy by hunting, fishing, and working in the growing number of local resorts. Tourism conformed to seasonal work patterns that often divided along gender lines. Women tended to small farms, accepted boarders, and worked in tourist establishments, while men served as guides.[8]

Competing visions contributed to tension between forestry and agriculture advocates, although farming slowly yielded to reforestation policies benefiting tourism after World War I. Wisconsin's Board of Immigration first warned potential settlers in 1911 of the need for sufficient capital, knowledge, and endurance to farm the northern cutover. University of Wisconsin economist Richard T. Ely was among the experts calling for efficiency and social stability. In the 1890s, Ely backed state programs for agricultural settlement but later came to believe the state must limit such settlement since agriculture would not provide a solid economic foundation on northern lands.[9]

As the regional economic situation worsened, Griffith's forest reserve idea gained momentum. Professional forestry's growth, reflected in the establishment of the U.S. Forest Service, forest fire prevention initiatives, and academic programs at the University of Michigan and Yale, aided the effort. While Wisconsin had set aside land for forests in the late nineteenth century, effective management remained elusive. Minnesota Forest Commissioner Christopher C. Andrews gathered Michigan, Wisconsin, and Minnesota representatives in 1910 to address forest fire pre-

Cutover and stump-filled landscapes dominated the region in the early twentieth century. This photograph is from the Upper Peninsula of Michigan, April 18, 1908. FOREST SERVICE, U.S. DEPARTMENT OF AGRICULTURE, EASTERN REGION PHOTOGRAPH COURTESY OF THE FOREST HISTORY SOCIETY, DURHAM, NORTH CAROLINA, USFS NEGATIVE 75111.

vention and regeneration. Andrews was not new to the fight. In 1898, he called on the federal government to reserve forests in portions of northern Minnesota's Cook and Lake Counties and, like Griffith, experienced opposition.[10] During the 1910s, Griffith's belief that reforestation offered a better solution to regional problems than farming found support among the country's growing cadre of professional foresters. Residents also saw reforestation as key to tourism. Buttressed by this support and responding to agricultural failure, regional organizations and states helped foster a new vision of productive northern lands that relied on attracting tourists rather than settlers.

During the interwar years, tourist competition intensified as public involvement in Michigan and Minnesota outpaced Wisconsin. Each state looked to develop tourism, with private and public entities framing the region as a vacation destination. Due to a minimal National Park Service presence in the region, the rivalry between the U.S. Forest Service and Park Service was limited. Michigan's Isle Royale was one exception, although the Forest Service did not fight efforts to make it a national park. Instead, the agency focused on the region's national forests, emphasizing

Federal lands and reservations in Minnesota.

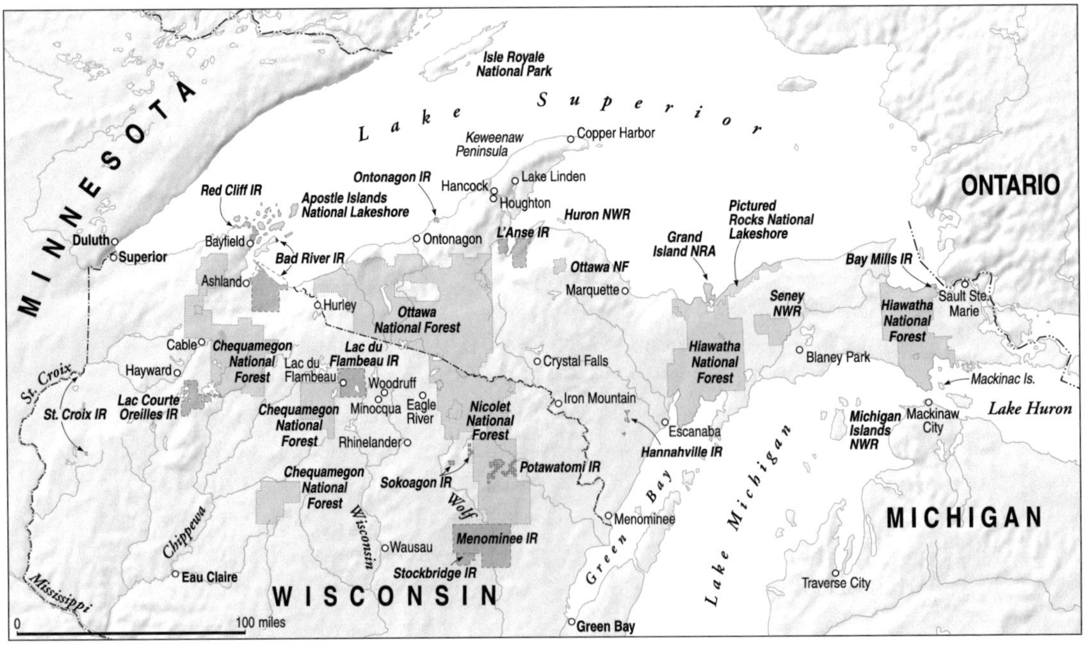

Federal lands and reservations in northern Wisconsin and the Upper Peninsula of Michigan.

recreational opportunities and working with states to transform northern lands. This proved helpful in fashioning the North Woods during the 1930s, when new national forests in Wisconsin and Michigan joined New Deal programs in bolstering the earlier local and state initiatives, to which we now turn.

From *A Hand-Book for the Homeseeker* to "The Sunny Side of Cloverland": Organizing the North Woods

Early-twentieth-century concerns about declining mining and lumber industries in Michigan's Upper Peninsula (UP) led to a focus on diversification. Building on efforts by railroads to attract settlers, the UPDB suggested, "No state offers better inducements to homeseekers," and promoted the UP as Cloverland with "Seven Million Fertile Acres." Given the land and short growing season, the Cloverland moniker gradually came to suggest a healthy retreat for urban dwellers seeking respite in nature rather than a land of agricultural bounty. The state immigration and public domain commission supported UPDB efforts and began pushing tourism's potential. Its 1914 *Michigan: Agricultural, Horticultural, and Industrial Advantages* suggested Michigan was one big summer resort where visitors spent five million dollars annually and provided a market for farm products.[11]

Pre–World War I efforts to attract settlers hinted at the UP's tourist potential. Published in 1910, *The Story of Cloverland* described I. Stephenson Company's efforts to sell 400,000 acres to homesteaders by promising ideal climate, rainfall, and soils for agriculture in "the sunny side of Cloverland." Railroads connected farmers and their goods to market, while offering tourist transportation to the UP. Rather than focus on the short growing season, the company promoted outdoor recreation and hay fever relief as benefits of UP living, all of which might draw tourists. The western UP's Porcupine Mountains and Ontonagon River also proved attractive. Ontonagon County's Board of Supervisors suggested, "Come to us in summer, if you would get well and strong—if you would rest from your labors for a while." Invoking scenery, health, and the outdoors, organizations linked agriculture, tourism, and settlement in hopes of deriving economic benefits from the land.[12]

In 1911, the same year Wisconsin's Board of Immigration first warned potential settlers about northern farming, the UPDB published *Homes and Farms in the Upper Peninsula of Michigan* to advertise the UP's farming potential while also suggesting tourist possibilities. U.S. Secretary of Agriculture James Wilson remarked in the publication, "There is every reason why profitable agriculture can be conducted on what your people call the Upper Peninsula." *Homes and Farms* pointed to other regions with bountiful agriculture in a similar climate and emphasized connections to urban markets. It also appealed to people's senses, describing the UP as offering an escape from polluted cities to a place "where the milk is pure, the butter sweet, the air invigorating, the chance to romp and play limited only by the sturdiness of the little legs and lungs of city-bred children to hold out." Promoting family togetherness and linking it to a language of antimodern purity and a life rooted in the land, the UPDB emphasized health benefits and outdoor activities. It posited the UP as a haven for those seeking escape, hoping not only to attract tourists but also to convince people of a better life if they made the UP home. While *Homes and Farms* was not a tourist booklet, it presented the region in terms potential vacationers might find appealing.[13]

Even though tourism was not part of its initial goals, the UPDB ultimately led UP tourism efforts. Formally established in 1911 after *Menominee Herald Leader* editor Roger Andrews commented, "The upper peninsula of Michigan, rich beyond telling in the possibilities of agriculture, forestry, mining, fruit, cattle raising and diversified manufacturers stands before the country today a confessed pauper," the UPDB prodded businesses and residents to diversify.[14] Andrews moved to Menominee in 1901, published *Northwestern Farmer*, which was renamed *Cloverland*, and initially pushed farming. Like many boosters, Andrews, according to one observer, "presented the Upper Peninsula as an agricultural paradise surrounded by hungry markets, and praised it as a drought-free area where farmers plowed in January, and where the fertility of the soil insured bumper crops every year."[15] But this vision was not rooted in reality, and Andrews and others came to realize that farming held limited promise. Hopes for prosperity lay instead in developing and conserving the forest and marketing scenery. Within three decades of his initial pronouncement, Andrews praised the UP as a tourist paradise, labeling it a "vest pocket edition of almost every resort region on the globe."[16]

The UPDB's early contributors, which included industrial enterprises, county boards, and individuals, reflected the organization's initial focus on agriculture. It worked with the state to attract farmers, supported legislation to establish county extension services, and promoted farming with literature and exhibits at the Michigan State Fair and Chicago livestock shows. In 1913, the UPDB campaigned for five thousand one-dollar memberships, hoping to move away from relying on business and local government contributions. The following year it authorized a representative to travel the region, generate publicity, and enroll members. Throughout the 1910s, the UPDB cooperated with the Michigan Packers Association for better highways, aiding the good roads movement. It also encouraged sheep and cattle grazing, but housing and feeding problems quickly ended this experiment.[17] Contradicting as it did the realities of land and climate, agricultural boosterism failed to convince people that farming in the UP was the ticket to economic revitalization. But the UPDB remained concerned with land-use questions, turning to reforestation and conservation to develop tourism.

Realizing that agriculture could not solve the region's economic woes and that farms did not always follow forests, the UPDB appropriated $3,000 in 1917 for tourism initiatives. Drawing on outdoor recreation and health themes present in agricultural promotion, it published its first tourist booklet, *Cloverland in Clovertime: Touring through Picturesque Upper Peninsula of Michigan*. New roads and better transportation allowed the UPDB to highlight accessibility even though the area was farther from major cities than northern Wisconsin and Lower Michigan. Despite legacies of mining and logging, the UPDB also suggested the UP offered a wilderness experience that could not be found elsewhere in the North Woods. The UPDB faced numerous challenges, including working with residents and industry to demonstrate tourism's advantages and developing an adequate infrastructure to support additional visitors. Until the Mackinac Bridge connected the UP with Lower Michigan in 1957, travelers ferried across the Straits of Mackinac to reach the UP. While the UPDB did not ignore tourists from the Lower Peninsula and Cleveland, it more easily tapped Chicago, Milwaukee, and the Twin Cities markets, whose vacationers avoided the straits.[18]

The UPDB came to believe tourism could provide work for residents and aid existing industries. Roads built for mining and logging offered infrastructure for cars carrying tourists. To justify additional roads, the 1917 guide reported increased tourist traffic over the previous two years. Appealing directly to Chicago travelers, the UPDB provided a detailed itinerary from Menominee, where Chicago motorists would enter the UP, to the tip of the Keweenaw Peninsula in the Copper Country. The UPDB asked potential tourists, "Did you ever realize that some day you might be worn out and need a rest 'just somewhere' in fresh, invigorating, rest-

The Upper Peninsula Development Bureau issued its first tourist publication in 1917, *Cloverland in Clovertime: Touring Through Picturesque Upper Peninsula of Michigan.* COURTESY OF THE MICHIGAN TECHNOLOGICAL UNIVERSITY ARCHIVES AND COPPER COUNTRY HISTORICAL COLLECTIONS.

ful air?" The answer was that the UP offered the proper "somewhere." It was accessible, affordable, and provided wonderful scenery. The UPDB emphasized uniqueness, claiming, "Where is there a place in the Middle West that motorists can find farms, copper and iron mines, ranches, forests, lakes, rivers, mountains, valleys, and cities within one day's travel? That answer is—in Cloverland." It described the Copper Country, Pictured Rocks, Lake Superior fishing, waterfalls, and Indian lore. If vacationers desired, industrial sights also awaited them.[19]

In 1919, Michigan and Minnesota tourism leaders met in St. Paul, marking the first cooperative effort emphasizing the North Woods as a vacation destination. UPDB head John Doelle discussed the shift from Cloverland as an agricultural paradise to a tourist one, claiming, "the tourist traffic is self-advertising" and adding, "Our actual tourist campaign is over, I think that here is one instance where we can almost sit back, smile and say: 'Well, there's ONE job done.'"[20] Upon leaving the UPDB two years later, Doelle recognized that developing tourism involved substantial effort. Writing Traverse City author Harold Titus, who later served on the Michigan Conservation Commission and as *Field and Stream* conservation editor, Doelle hoped to convince him to move north and promote the UP through his fiction, remarking that such an endeavor "would be worth five times the amount we are spending for publicity today."[21] When George Bishop assumed the UPDB leadership in 1921, the organization chose not to follow Doelle's earlier declaration that the tourist campaign was complete. Under Bishop, the UPDB advertised regionally and nationally, distributed its *Development Bureau News* to residents, and established an information bureau to respond to tourist inquiries. The *Development Bureau News* proclaimed, in language dramatically different from Doelle's in 1919, "The tourist business isn't a passing fad, a flickering something which goes to return no more. It is a definite, actual, paying and growing industry which must be fostered by all the means in our power."[22] The UPDB worked to convince members of tourism's long-term benefits by positing it as an alternative to the often land-exhausting practices of earlier extractive industry.

The UPDB heralded its efforts by citing an increase in UP car-ferry crossings from 700 in 1918 to 9,236 in 1922. Northern Wisconsin's *Vilas County News* reported tourism generated $5 million annually for the UP, resulting in businesses benefiting from this "profitable annual crop." Farmers did too, as tourists purchased items along the roadside. The UPDB distributed twenty-five thousand copies of its *Cloverland* booklet in 1923. By 1925, the UPDB claimed additional success, with 52,000 tourists crossing via ferry. With its agricultural connotation, the Cloverland moniker was dropped in favor of "Land of Hiawatha," recalling Longfellow's "The Song of Hiawatha."[23]

Other Michigan organizations joined the UPDB in the state's tourism cause. The Northeastern Michigan Development Bureau initially encouraged agriculture in the Lower Peninsula but also sponsored the Huron Shore Road Association. Formed in late 1922, the Huron Shore Tourist Association grew out of the Road Association and became the East Michigan Tourist Association in 1924. As in the UP, northeastern Michigan boosters and residents realized cutover land was more suitable for forestry and recreation than farming. The Michigan Tourist and Resort Association, later renamed the West Michigan Tourist Association, was established in 1917 after Arthur Stace authored a series in the *Grand Rapids Press* urging Michiganders to capitalize on the state's natural resources and develop tourism. Stace witnessed this in Colorado and argued Michigan must follow suit or risk losing vacationers. Like the UP's Andrews, Stace's articles suggested tourism could increase local opportunities, and the state later adopted West Michigan's slogan as the "Playground of the Nation."[24]

Michigan State geography professor Edward Prophet recognized regional tourist association accomplishments but called for further changes. Suggesting that they have "provided information to prospective visitors and have tried to improve the 'tone' of the services rendered by their members," Prophet believed the biggest issue remained the attitude of those who provided for tourists. He expressed concerns about operators who did not charge a fair price or withheld information on good hunting and fishing areas. Adamant that "the viewpoint must be changed to that of service to the visitor and a fair living in return rather than promotion and exploitation and the faint hope of getting rich quick," Prophet urged organizations to broaden enforcement activities to address unfair practices. While the UPDB aimed to spur tourist development, Prophet insisted that organizations assist operators with service and facility improvements.[25] At a 1938 event honoring West Michigan Tourist Association leadership, organizers reflected on the foresightedness of those who saw tourism's ability to change the physical and economic landscape:

> Following the lumber era in Michigan it was thought that agriculture would be the state's big industry. Gradually the truth developed that while the regions served by these bureaus possessed large areas of splendid farming lands that could be utilized with profit to their owners and to the state, they contained still vaster areas that Nature claimed for itself—to grow woods and wild life and facilities for healthful recreational enjoyment.[26]

Michigan tourist boosters were well aware of agricultural difficulties. They realized remaining timber and copper resources limited industrial development and viewed tourism as having limitless potential. During the interwar years, regional organizations like the UPDB helped plant the seeds of a new North Woods tourist industry.

As the UPDB entered the tourist arena after World War I, Minnesota responded to the competition. One longtime resort owner and founding member of the Minnesota Resort Association recalled that by 1912, "Michigan and Wisconsin were beginning to advertise their vacation resources in newspapers and magazines in the Midwest; especially the Chicago area."[27] Rather than rely solely on private efforts, in 1918 Minnesota appropriated funds for the Land and Lakes Attractions Board to direct the Ten Thousand Lakes of Minnesota Association's activities. In language equating tourism with a cash crop, the *St. Paul Pioneer Press* suggested the state was now "officially interested in the exploitation of its natural scenic resources" but declared Minnesota had not fully capitalized on these assets. Mindful of the state's funding commitment, the newspaper encouraged conservation and policy initiatives that viewed tourism as a benign and feasible land use.[28]

The Ten Thousand Lakes of Minnesota Association marketed Minnesota to potential visitors and encouraged residents to back its efforts so that "the outdoor wealth of Minnesota can be advertised and sold at a profit to the entire State."[29] Relying heavily on state appropriations, its efforts proved successful on many fronts. Inquiries poured into the association, including many echoing the sentiments of Des Moines resident Charles Parker, who labeled Minnesota "the most wonderful summer resort state in America." In 1918, the organization handled 3,088 inquiries. In 1919, it received 4,953, and by 1920, nearly 10,000 people requested information about Minnesota vacations.[30] It initially believed people would come to Minnesota as tourists and choose to settle and develop land. By 1923, with tourists depositing money in state and local coffers, the organization viewed tourism as a solid industry in its own right.[31]

Regional organizations like the Northern Minnesota Development Association (NMDA) increasingly backed the efforts of the Ten Thousand Lakes Association. During the 1910s, the NMDA encouraged agriculture, but northern Minnesota farming offered limited opportunities, and, like Michigan's UPDB, the NMDA began emphasizing tourism's potential. Supporting "progressive and forward looking policies with respect to the preservation and propagation of fish in our Ten Thousand Lakes; creating in the pure cool waters of this state a continuing industry and one of growing recreational and commercial importance," it advanced a conservation agenda tied to tourism.[32]

By organizing the NMDA and the Minnesota Scenic Highway Association and as a member of the Cass Lake Commercial Club, Mathias Koll aided diversification efforts. Koll encouraged the state to publicize attractions, pointing to a spike in summer sales as evidence that tourists helped local businesses and provided a market for farm products. Like earlier agricultural advocates, Koll initially viewed tourists as potential settlers rather than spenders. In 1917 and 1920, he distributed questionnaires on behalf of the Scenic Highway Association to promote northern Minnesota travel and solicit funds for a tourist booklet. Respondents categorized tourism as one of northern Minnesota's principal industries and cited the need for additional lodging. By 1920, the focus turned to attracting vacationers who spent money in the North Woods.[33] At the same time, the Minnesota Board of Immigration began integrating tourism into its program by highlighting northern Minnesota's natural and built environment, while suggesting extractive industry had not devastated the land. The board assured vacationers of a pleasant time in Minnesota's lake-dotted north, where woods and waters offered fishing and hunting opportunities along with lodging options.[34]

The NMDA, Ten Thousand Lakes Association, and Board of Immigration were not alone in believing tourism could provide employment, return abandoned land to the tax rolls, and diversify the region's economy. In Minnesota, federal agencies aided local efforts by providing for outdoor recreation on public lands. While the Minnesota (now Chippewa) and Superior National Forests were initially established for timber and watershed protection, beginning in 1916 the U.S. Forest Service faced competition for the recreational dollar, as well as its lands, from the National Park Service. The Forest Service's Term Permit Act allowed for cottage construction on national forests and extended leases for up to thirty years with subsequent renewal options. Acknowledging recreation's economic potential, the Forest Service leased potential sites starting at ten dollars annually. Promoting North Woods remoteness while also noting that cars spurred tourist access to the Superior, the agency proposed, "The lake region north of Grand Marais will no doubt be a mecca for people in search of ideal summer-home sites upon the completion of the automobile road now being built into that region."[35] The presence of two national forests, along with agency interest in recreational resources, aided residents and organizations interested in developing the tourist trade.

During the 1920s, tourism emerged as a key element of northern Minnesota's physical and economic landscape. Minnesota's resorts grew from a few hundred to nearly fourteen hundred as roads opened previously inaccessible areas to automobiles. Both the Ten Thousand Lakes Association and Minnesota Arrowhead Association (MAA), established in 1924, capitalized on people's desire to vacation in nature. Like other advocates, MAA publicity director M. I. Stewart initially hoped tourists would settle and become producers for a new industrial economy, commenting, "The industrial development of the Arrowhead can be accomplished, and one of the greatest factors in bringing this about will be the proper type of tourists, attracted first for pleasure and later, for permanency." But the MAA quickly realized tourism was tied to transience rather than permanence, so the goal became attracting tourists as consumers who would contribute to the local economy and sustain businesses.[36]

Like Michigan's UPDB, the MAA drew institutional members from area towns. It encouraged reforestation and new highways, promoted vacations in the Arrowhead, and received tourist inquiries from the Ten Thousand Lakes Association. In 1926, the MAA garnered national publicity with a naming contest for the organization, which had been known as the Northeast Minnesota Civic and Commerce Association. Pittsburgh's Odin MacCrickart, who coined the Arrowhead term because the region's boundaries appeared as such, emerged as the winner from among thirty thousand entries. After visiting, MacCrickart commented that he would "never forget the beautiful views of island-dotted lakes that passed before my eyes as I traveled through the Arrowhead Country." The Arrowhead name stuck, broadcasting an image of adventure to tourists. In 1933, the MAA reminded members that while efforts to develop tourism were a priority, it continued to advocate a balanced program that included other industry.[37]

While the MAA was private and regional in scope, the Ten Thousand Lakes Association affirmed its position as the state's tourist organization. In 1926, the state adopted a citizen's suggestion that it emblazon "Land of Ten Thousand Lakes" on Minnesota license plates to garner publicity. With Minnesota closing its Immigration Department in 1927, attracting settlers fell to the Ten Thousand Lakes Association. It published tourist guides and merged with the Greater Minnesota Association to integrate industrial development into its agenda.[38] One mark of tourism's increasing prominence involved Governor Floyd Olson informing visitors in 1931 that Minnesota was "not only an ideal vacation-land, but also a state wherein agricultural and industrial activities may be advantageously pursued."[39] No longer viewed merely as a means to attract settlers, tourism had developed to the point where the governor felt the need to reinforce the state's commitment to agriculture and other industry.

While statewide initiatives and regional organizations contributed to northern Minnesota tourist development, local entities also aided the process. Founded in 1908, the St. Louis County Club and Farm Bureau Association called for a diverse economy. Its efforts helped attract tourists and spur demand for lakefront property.[40] In the state's northeast corner, the Gunflint Trail Association enticed vacationers by promoting rustic resorts along a sixty-three-mile dirt road into the Superior National Forest. During the Depression, Gunflint resort owners cooperated to achieve a modicum of success. Justine Kerfoot, who moved to the trail to operate Gunflint Lodge after completing college in Illinois, recalled that the initial association meeting took place at a trail resort, where owners "found out we'd all been suckers" and "agreed that we could earn a living, or at least an honest return, at a certain figure." Agreements on rates contributed to further resort owner cooperation on phone service, electricity, and road improvements.[41]

Gunflint operators joined other northern Minnesota resort owners in organizing during the Depression. Merrill Cragun, Max Ruttger, and W. J. Madden established the Paul Bunyan Playground Association to develop the Brainerd Lakes area with Brainerd and Bemidji as anchors. Cragun's background in the newspaper business helped the organization develop effective promotional materials. It encouraged local membership and emphasized specific attractions while working with the state tourist bureau to develop public areas. During the 1930s, signs, games, maps, and guides, like *Come to Paul Bunyan's Playground*, helped propagate the Bunyan legend. Beginning in 1922 and continuing throughout the 1930s, the *St. Paul Pioneer Press* annual vacation section, *Call of the Open*, broadcast northern Minnesota to Twin Cities' residents, while federal agencies and regional organizations produced literature to attract visitors to northern Minnesota's nature-filled paradise. Together, they marketed nature and leisure to urban vacationers and, along with those who visited, helped establish Minnesota's North Woods as a land of ten thousand lakes.[42]

While Michigan and Minnesota organizations initially viewed tourism as a means to settlement, Wisconsin's early associations were primarily comprised of resort owners and outfitters interested in luring sportsmen north. The Fish and Game Protective Association of Northern Wisconsin combined conservation with tourism, heralding "the beauty and advantages for sport and outing offered to the vacationist and tourist" and appealing directly to the "office worker or city dweller who can spare only a week or 10 days for an outing." Established in 1916 with thirty members, the Resort Owners Association of the North Wisconsin Lake Region urged recreational land use. Its early initiatives included marking a road from Chicago to Eagle River as the "Big Fish Auto Route," establishing an information bureau headed by *Vilas County News* editor D. C. Menefee, and placing cooperative advertising in city newspapers.[43]

Citing reports that Minnesota garnered $10 million annually from two hundred thousand tourists and the UP netted $5 million in 1922, Wisconsin resort owners proposed national advertising in addition to distributing literature directly to potential visitors. While Wisconsin had the facilities, scenery, and climate to compete with Michigan and Minnesota, it lagged behind in public-private cooperation. Founded in 1922, the Wisconsin Land O' Lakes Association, which was initially named the Northern Wisconsin Resort Association, promoted resorts and urged improved services. By 1925, it was advocating for conservation. The following year it advertised lakefront cottage sites and helped Connor Land and Lumber Company promote recreation on its harvested timberlands.[44] Its Chicago office received thirty-three thousand inquiries during its first season. Since 80 percent of Wisconsin's tourist business came from Illinois, the office provided proximity to a key population, promoted visits outside summer, and helped counter Michigan competition. Still, many expressed the need for greater statewide cooperation, including the *Wisconsin Land of Lakes Magazine*, which connected conservation and tourism with three goals: "To develop more faith and pride in the resources and possibilities of this state, to stimulate interest in the development of this state as a great recreational playground, and to commend and exploit every genuine effort toward conservation of Wisconsin's natural resources."[45] Chicago Outdoor Life Exposition organizer Milo Westbrooke wrote the magazine's editor to suggest Michigan's program "constitutes a menace to the tourist industry of the Badger state" and encouraged Wisconsin to seek state support, which was not forthcoming.[46]

With state government on the sidelines in Wisconsin, opportunities existed for individuals like Joseph Handlos, who moved to the Wisconsin-Michigan border in 1908 and worked as a millwright and guide and in construction. In 1929, he established the U.S. Highway 45 Association to promote this tourist route north and served as the organization's president for thirty years. While Handlos promoted tourism in the UP and Wisconsin, calls for tristate cooperation proved more difficult in the wake of tourist competition. More often, cooperation involved local residents or public and private organizations within a single state.[47] During the interwar years, private and public entities no longer highlighted bountiful agricultural possibilities. Rather, people looked for vacation and outdoor recreation opportunities in the North Woods. As the next section describes, new state and federal initiatives supported these messages, building on the work of local and regional organizations.

The State of the Tourist Industry

North Woods vacationers increasingly looked for a brief escape from their daily lives. Organizations and the state told them it was possible, reminding them of pine-scented air, cool summer breezes, lakes teeming with fish, and woods filled with wildlife. But in many ways, the escape was far from complete. During the interwar years, vacationers were immersed within a web of actors that regulated the experience, influencing how and where they vacationed. Realizing the economic benefits that accrued from such efforts, state governments accepted tourism as an industry on par with others in terms of creating jobs, and tourist competition increased in the 1930s across the North Woods. In 1940, Governor Harold Stassen welcomed Minnesota visitors, stating:

> May you enjoy with our people the great recreational areas that crown our state, studded with thousands of jewel-like lakes, fringed with beautiful forest lands, alive with game and fish, ribboned by thousands of miles of modern highways, and dotted with hundreds of cabins and campsites. Spend your vacation with us in a manner "as you like it," simple or luxurious, primitive or modern. Our tourist bureau is at your service; our highway patrol will cheerfully help you; our people will be gracious hosts. Our only request of you, help us maintain our outstanding safety record and cooperate in conserving our natural resources.[48]

The governor's message was clear. Tourists should come enjoy Minnesota's outdoor opportunities amid natural beauty, where citizens offered cordial service and lodging while the state ensured a safe and pleasant experience.

Officials from other states joined Stassen. Michigan suggested it provided "a haven of contentment" where "climate, scenery, lakes, streams, abundant wildlife, and an excellent system of highways satisfy any taste." Wisconsin reminded visitors to "Relax in Wisconsin, Where Friends and Nature Meet." Across the North Woods, government helped organize disparate efforts as the tourist industry came to depend on public-private cooperation. Vacations involved spending time with friends and family while enjoying nature. Boosters and the state increasingly managed and crafted these escapes, taking an active role in developing a new tourist landscape. Heeding calls from the likes of Michigan Highway Commissioner Grover Dillman, who argued it was the state's responsibility to preserve natural beauty for the public's enjoyment, state governments also laid a foundation for environmental action through tourism.[49]

As concerns arose about the future of northern lands, state conservation and highway departments helped facilitate tourism. Michigan's High-

Road signage promoted and developed tourism across the region. Here resort and hotel owners gather in front of a Wisconsin tourism sign in Rhinelander in the 1930s. COURTESY OF THE WISCONSIN HISTORICAL SOCIETY, WHS IMAGE ID 37927.

way Department issued a free road map in 1912, and in 1919, the legislature authorized it to publish and sell a tourist map. By 1922, the map included all state parks, and the following year added campsites, recreational sites, and ferry schedules. After Herbert Larson, an engineer for the UP's Iron County Road Commission, had difficulty finding a picnic location while vacationing in northern Wisconsin in 1919, Michigan introduced roadside parks and rest areas to facilitate tourist travel. Larson worked with mining and lumber companies to donate land to the state for these facilities. Responding to good roads advocates urging transportation enhancements to assist commerce and trade, Highway Department projects under commissioners Grover Dillman and Murray Van Wagoner improved tourist and local resident access. State agencies also helped determine how people used and experienced the outdoors. Michigan established a Park Commission in 1919 and a Department of Conservation in 1921. Abolished in 1923, the Park Commission and its program were moved to the Department of Conservation. States mediated encounters with nature and influenced vacations through licensing, mapping, managing parks and forests, fish and game laws, and land-use policies.[50]

Sign maps, like this one from 1941 covering the western portion of Michigan's Upper Peninsula, aimed to help motoring tourists find their way. LOCAL IDENTIFIER USFS NEGATIVE 414012, RECORDS OF THE FOREST SERVICE, RECORD GROUP 95, THE NATIONAL ARCHIVES AT CHICAGO.

During the early 1920s, Michigan's UPDB worked with government officials to establish state parks. In 1922, P. J. Hoffmaster, who served as parks superintendent in the 1920s and as Department of Conservation director from 1934 to 1951, visited the UP to inspect proposed park sites and assured the UPDB of approval. Despite a reduction in funding and staff and the transfer of Hoffmaster's position to the Department of Conservation, the UP had four state parks the following year.[51] Reflecting on Hoffmaster's accomplishments, a Michigan parks brochure said:

> He knew the importance of hunting and fishing to the thousands of Michigan workers who need these releases from industrial routine. He knew the special pleasure which comes to the true nature lover, the family finding a state park for a picnic, the people who enjoy "just looking," studying the moods and beauties of nature, preserving their memories with cameras.[52]

State parks offered conservation opportunities as well as vacation destinations for people with a range of interests. Parks were affordable recreation spots, but as crowds increased, they experienced overuse. By 1925, Michigan had the second most state parks in the nation, and Minnesota's Itasca State Park joined the state's newer parks in attracting visitors. Minnesota's expansionary park vision prompted Iowa conservationist and park proponent Louis Pammel to question, "Do we want to send these people to Minnesota? I am told on good authority . . . that the state of Minnesota plans to catch all of the tourists from Iowa by establishing a system of state parks across the southern part of that state." Without a sound park program, Pammel feared Iowa would lose visitors.[53]

Although tourism's economic benefits motivated state action, Michigan also proffered a civic rationale. Michigan's Department of Conservation promoted state parks and forests as democratic spaces, suggesting there was "no class distinction" in terms of who could enjoy them.[54] Parks offered "places of retreat for human beings" and "refuges where the masses may obtain rest and a change of scene."[55] As it added UP parks to its roster, the department also limited the ideal of "equal access," claiming the goal was to "attract not the rough element, but rather the middle or better classes."[56] While parks offered attractive destinations for the growing vacationing public, the department's policies also defined the types of leisure available and the nature of the public it sought to benefit through public lands management. The goal of creating a better citizenry through outdoor recreation did not, however, extinguish the state's desire to recoup economic benefits from park vacationers. From 1922 to 1930, Michigan state park attendance increased from 220,000 to nearly 9 million, demonstrating tourism's growing importance along with the state's investment in new parks. Across the UP, state parks offered tourist destinations and generated local employment.[57]

Given these developments, Michigan's public and private interests increasingly recognized tourism's benefits, culminating in direct state promotional support in 1929. The UPDB's George Bishop used the 1927 Chicago Outdoor Show to call on Michigan to "join with its individuals, corporations, municipalities and county boards in the work of increasing tourist volume to a point commensurate with its great possibilities."[58] Over the subsequent two years, Senator Herbert Rushton of Escanaba and Representative Gus Hartman of Houghton, sons of the Upper Peninsula, shepherded a tourist promotion bill through the state legislature. The UPDB's *Development Bureau News* supported passage, stating, "Its adoption will afford an opportunity for the increased development of another of Michigan's industries, and it will decidedly augment the returns from the tourist business to the people of the Upper Peninsula."[59] Hartman-Rushton placed lawmakers in accord with organizations that saw tourism as a wise state investment.

Upon passage, Hartman-Rushton provided the UPDB and the state's three other regional tourist associations a boost in competing for vacationers. For Hartman and Rushton, the legislation offered their home region a chance to further develop tourism while providing funds for others across the state to do likewise. The act placed private interests and state agencies under a broad umbrella and allotted funds to the four regional associations through the Conservation Department. Balancing the regional interests involved, the state appropriated up to $25,000 in matching advertising funds to each association. The act was renewed in 1931–32, revised in 1937, and eventually superseded by new legislation that created the Michigan Tourist Council after World War II.[60] In 1931, Michigan Governor Wilber Brucker extolled the act's benefits, stating, "I am glad that army [of tourists] is coming for it justifies Michigan's confidence in our four resort associations of the state."[61] Two decades of work by the UPDB and fellow organizations led the governor to regard them as vital to the tourism effort.

In conjunction with Hartman-Rushton, state agencies updated their efforts to attract vacationers. Michigan's Highway Department built roads and published maps, while the Conservation Department focused on reforestation and state parks. Its education and public relations division provided information on Michigan's natural resources. This division also oversaw Hartman-Rushton expenditures, including those by regional organizations, which spent one-third on tourist literature, one-third on newspaper advertising, and the remaining third on personnel, advertising, and a Chicago office. The department celebrated partnership possibilities, reporting, "It would seem that expenditures from the public treasury to make Michigan better known, appreciated and utilized, especially when matched by like amounts of private funds, take on much of the nature of intelligent investments." Even the Conservation Department viewed tourism in economic terms, referring to the potential cash value of a scenic landscape.[62]

Official state recognition of tourism contributed to efforts to study the industry's contributions. State universities provided expertise and offered programs connecting public and private interests. Michigan State professor Edward Prophet coordinated a UP tourist survey and authored studies on Michigan's tourist industry. The Conservation Department used such studies to determine tourism's economic impact and whether providers met tourist needs. This research contributed to citizen support by fostering cooperation between regional organizations, chambers of commerce, communities, faculty, and state officials.[63]

State agency activities aided tourism in northern Minnesota and Wisconsin as well. In 1924, Minnesota increased its annual promotional appropriation from $15,000 to $20,000. In 1931, it established a State Tourist Bureau within the Department of Conservation to direct this effort. In its second biennial report, the bureau outlined its function "as an advertising agency and publicity agent for the corporation that is Minnesota" and emphasized tourism's economic significance. Under directors George Bradley, who coined the phrase "Marvelous Minnesota," and former newspaper writer Ed Shave, the bureau oversaw Minnesota's tourist campaigns and assisted regional organizations. Bradley stressed educating the public on "what we have to offer in competition with other states if we are to share equitably the income that comes from tourist trade." One of the bureau's first projects involved inviting out-of-state newspaper writers and editors on a tour, recognizing their ability to encourage Minnesota tourism.[64] The state's Highway Department addressed infrastructure and scenic roads, while its Planning Board encouraged city dwellers to visit, hoping such efforts would create jobs.[65]

Regional organizations contributed to statewide efforts by focusing on areas like the Arrowhead and generating local support. Throughout the 1930s, the MAA distributed literature to prospective vacationers, launched campaigns to extend the tourist season, and promoted visits to Lake Superior's Isle Royale, hoping people would stay in the Arrowhead on their travels. In its 1931 annual report, the MAA focused on regional tourist competition, emphasizing the UP's $42,000 promotional expenditure and noting a similar movement afoot in Wisconsin. Despite a presence at outdoor shows, national advertising, and official state recognition of tourist promotion twelve years before Michigan, Minnesota still lagged behind in attracting tourist dollars.[66]

As in Michigan, the Wisconsin Conservation Commission's administration of public lands benefited the tourist industry. It promoted good roads to increase state park patronage and established the Northern Highland and American Legion State Forests in 1925 and 1929, respectively. Wisconsin state parks and forests offered respite to those who "live among congested conditions and in the high pitch of industrial and commercial activities." Officials claimed state parks democratized travel so that "the tourist driving the Cadillac as well as the man driving the Ford will be provided for either at the regular hotels or resorts along the way or in his own tent."[67] Working- and middle-class automobile tourists increasingly enjoyed public amenities while spending money on a Wisconsin vacation.

While Conservation Commission efforts aided tourism, Wisconsin waited longer than Michigan and Minnesota to use public funds on promotion. In 1929, Assemblyman Charles Lacy, who represented northern Wisconsin's Vilas and Oneida Counties, proposed a $150,000 appropriation. Calling for Wisconsin to respond to Michigan's commitment, his bill met defeat. Lacy blamed the failure on legislators' desire to have every bill aid their district. Urging an end to political squabbling, he called for unity and cooperation. The *Wisconsin Land of Lakes Magazine* championed Lacy's efforts to "advance the recreational and outdoor interests of Wisconsin and help build sentiment to conserve Wisconsin's natural assets." Decrying Wisconsin's lack of promotional funds, the magazine feared Michigan and Minnesota would lure tourists. Michigan's decision to divide promotional funding equally among regional bureaus mitigated squabbling, but Wisconsin legislators were unable to develop a program satisfying all.[68]

Despite the lack of promotional funds, other state agencies entered the tourist arena. The Wisconsin Board of Health began inspecting hotels and collecting license fees in 1932, increasing the state's regulatory role. Just as Governor Stassen assured Minnesota tourists of a safe and enjoyable vacation, Wisconsin took steps to ensure lodging met certain standards. These efforts also boosted business by helping reduce complaints from vacationers frustrated with substandard facilities.[69]

In 1936, Wisconsin finally designated state promotional funds and established a recreational publicity department within the Conservation Commission. Convinced the appropriation would help draw tourists, the commission predicted "a banner tourist year" in which tourists would leave "many times the amount of the $50,000 appropriation within the borders of the state." The state suggested everyone stood to benefit from a future cash infusion, although one local paper warned residents and tourist entrepreneurs to "treat our summer visitors more like guests and less like gold mines that can be worked indefinitely." Without proper hospitality, the tourist industry would suffer.[70]

State appropriations facilitated several new ventures. Illinois and Iowa governors joined Wisconsin Governor Philip La Follette on a fishing trip in September 1937 that the state promoted as "Battle of the Muskies." The state distributed photos of the governors and their catches, hoping publicity would draw tourists to northern Wisconsin. The new appropriation helped produce newspaper material and roadside signage. To compete with Minnesota and Michigan, Wisconsin promoted year-round vacations in state parks and marketed nature as a consumer item; one brochure informed readers to "Follow the Birds to Vacation Land, Wisconsin."[71] The State Planning Board reported on rehabilitating northern lands and Vilas County recreational land use. By the end of the 1930s, Wisconsin's state agencies had entered the tourist arena. When Walter Fisher ran successfully for state assemblyman from northern Wisconsin in 1942, he reported that tourism was the state's second most profitable industry and "ample funds should be at hand every year to attract this business into the state." Fisher supported renewing the $50,000 recreational advertising appropriation when the war ended, and noted tourism provided benefits to local businesses.[72]

Rather than sit back and wait for tourists to arrive, state support brought the rustic North Woods to Midwesterners. The UPDB, MAA, and other regional bureaus and state agencies presented displays and distributed literature at urban outdoor shows and at the 1933 Century of Progress Exposition. These shows helped build a critical mass interested in experiencing the North Woods, often drawing over two hundred thousand visitors, and witnessed destinations outdoing each other with displays.[73] Chicago residents like Ned Colby expressed delight with their

VACATION
The perfect

States used displays at outdoor shows, meetings, and conventions, like this illustrated panel advertising Minnesota in 1937, to attract potential tourists.
PHOTOGRAPH BY FRANK C. ZAC. COURTESY OF THE MINNESOTA HISTORICAL SOCIETY.

North Woods vacations and believed the shows helped plan trips. Despite some minor problems with transportation and roads, Colby stated, "We fell in love with the north country and are going back for a longer, more leisurely vacation at the first opportunity."[74] At the Century of Progress, states appealed to tourists to vacation amid natural beauty. Since many were tourists to Chicago, states hoped to draw them their way on future trips, by suggesting, for example, they add a North Woods stop to their Chicago visit.[75]

Michigan's regional associations used state support to distribute literature and answer questions at offices in Chicago, Detroit, and Cleveland. The UPDB received eighteen thousand inquiries at the new Chicago office in 1930 and believed Chicago and Detroit residents saw the UP as a "logical summer playground."[76] In addition to being present at information offices and outdoor shows, the UPDB responded to inquiries and collated them in a bulletin distributed to members. Eugene Nowacki of Chicago asked about cottages, swimming, and fishing for a party of nine that included three children, and O. J. Scott of Detroit wanted a cottage for his family to enjoy the outdoors. Frederick Meyer of Chicago informed the UPDB that its materials enticed him to vacation in the UP. Tourist entrepreneurs used the bulletins to send information to potential guests like Nowacki, Scott, and Meyer.[77]

During Michigan's first decade of promotional appropriations, the UPDB and Conservation Department found ways to cooperate. In 1931, the state established the Isle Royale National Park Commission to help Isle Royale, an island seventy miles from Houghton in Lake Superior, become a national park. The idea was conceived ten years earlier when a Conservation Department official raised the possibility and an editorial in the *Detroit News* proclaimed "the State of Michigan is now facing an opportunity to preserve this bit of Nature's wonderland for its children." *Detroit News* conservation editor Albert "Pete" Stoll Jr. spearheaded the campaign and was joined by the department and the UPDB. In 1922, conservation commissioner John Baird emphasized his preference for federal rather than state ownership of the island, even if the state had to acquire land first. The following year, the UPDB's George Bishop claimed that developing the UP's four new state parks would provide greater benefits than an Isle Royale park and hoped publicity generated by the Isle Royale campaign would draw visitors to the parks.[78] As UP parks garnered notice in the 1930s, Bishop and the UPDB reversed course, backing the national park initiative as an opportunity for recovery and claiming it could prove "a lodestone that would draw into Michigan thousands of new visitors every year."[79] Bishop hoped government's presence combined with Depression-era federal relief projects would increase the UP tourist trade.

Isle Royale National Park proponents increasingly focused on regional economic benefits. Michigan Senator Arthur Vandenberg believed the proposal offered the "greatest development opportunity in the history of the Upper Peninsula and would add immeasurably to the economic well-being of that section by attracting hundreds of thousands of tourists."[80] Vandenberg argued it would relieve Depression conditions in the UP and boost Michigan tourism. In 1935, with difficulties raging over securing land on Isle Royale, Vandenberg wrote Stoll, "I continue to believe that the development of Isle Royale as a National Park would pour as much money back into the Upper Peninsula as the miners have taken out."[81] Stoll originally sought to preserve Isle Royale as a game refuge and preserve in the 1920s, but by the mid-1930s, both he and Vandenberg hoped tourism could reshape the landscape and provide work for UP residents. Conflicts over land acquisition and the advent of World War II delayed formal national park designation until 1946, but the effort to create the park resonated across the UP and Michigan in the 1930s. Like the Hartman-Rushton bill, the Isle Royale effort united public and private interests behind the tourist cause.

In 1932, the UPDB called for a new advertising initiative using state matching funds and encouraged member cooperation to retain tourist interest. Concerned about growing tourist competition, it advocated a program that included paving highways, continued cooperation with state and federal agencies, improving fish and game propagation, and expanding recreational areas and facilities. George Bishop believed the UP's future depended on tourism and stressed the need to meet middle-class tourist expectations, agreeing with a colleague's comment that "to them [middle-class tourists] the annual vacation from the noise and hum-drum of city life is the big event of the year." In assessing regional competition, the UPDB conceded that northern Wisconsin and the northern Lower Peninsula might have better accommodations but not necessarily better attractions.[82]

With Bishop's vision in mind, the UPDB stopped publishing the *Development Bureau News* in 1933. Assured that residents understood tourism's importance, the UPDB shifted resources to attract more tourists by using state funds to publish its *Lure Book* filled with colorful images of vacation possibilities. By 1936, it distributed fifty thousand *Lure Books* annually, and people responded to its appeal. Typical was the reaction of A. M. Royce, president of the State Teacher's College in Platteville, Wisconsin, who wrote, "Thanks for the Lure Book. I am going to pass it around and see if it won't whet the appetites of a number of my friends for your splendid north country." During this era, which the UPDB labeled the "Lure Book Epoch," the organization appealed for federal funds to improve facilities, witnessed local tourist bureaus and chambers of commerce publish tourist literature, saw its membership shift from mining, land, and lumber companies to tourist and resort interests, and convinced local transportation companies, motor clubs, and resort interests to advertise. Approximately twenty-five years after its establishment and with state backing, the UPDB devoted itself fully to tourism.[83]

While efforts initially focused on summer tourism, North Woods winter vacations gradually garnered attention in an economic climate that saw tourism emerge as the region's key industry. In 1928, Chicago outdoor show exhibitors included winter activities. In cooperation with Eagle River's Jack O' Lantern Lodge, the Chicago and North Western Railway pioneered northern Wisconsin and UP winter tourism in the early 1930s. Railroads provided transportation for those unable to traverse snow-covered roads, and lodges offered guests snowshoeing and cross-country skiing. In 1929, the northern Lower Peninsula town of Grayling established a winter sports park with toboggan runs, and visitors arrived on weekend snow trains. In 1938, Michigan's Conservation Department assumed management and made it a state park. The following year the park attracted 16,500 people, raising awareness of winter vacationing and helping spur additional development across the North Woods.[84]

In the UP, Iron Mountain completed the world's highest artificial ski jump in 1939. Though limited by the height of the UP's hills, downhill skiing and ski jumping developed as attractions that flatter areas in the region could not match. In 1939, twenty years after the region's first cooperative tourist conference, the UPDB sponsored the Tri-State Winter Sports Conference at which representatives from Michigan, Minnesota, and Wisconsin gathered to discuss winter tourism. Minnesota's B. G. Schroeder enthused, "I am here as a learner and would like to go back to Duluth with more ideas of just how you folks in Wisconsin and Michigan are attacking this problem." Michigan Conservation Department director P. J. Hoffmaster hoped to inculcate in children a love for winter sports and also looked to establish the western UP's Porcupine Mountains as a state park, seeking to preserve a wilderness area for people to enjoy year-round.

Winter recreation increasingly drew vacationers to the North Woods. The residents of Bemidji, Minnesota, erected these statues of logging folk hero Paul Bunyan and Babe the Blue Ox during the town's first winter carnival in 1937. PHOTOGRAPH COURTESY OF THE FOREST HISTORY SOCIETY, DURHAM, NORTH CAROLINA, FHS778.

Promoters produced artistic images to attract winter vacationers, including these scenic winter vistas along North Shore Drive near Lake Superior in Minnesota Arrowhead Country, circa 1930. COURTESY OF THE MINNESOTA HISTORICAL SOCIETY.

Michigan emerged as a winter playground with facilities and activities for tourists and local residents developed by rural communities and the state. A more reliable snow cover and bigger hills compared to Wisconsin and Minnesota aided the UP, although the onset of World War II brought a temporary halt to this developing enterprise.[85]

The Tourist Crop Cultivated

During the 1920s and 1930s, the establishment and growth of public recreational lands encouraged travel and helped residents develop the tourist industry. Federal New Deal programs built upon these local and state efforts to create the North Woods. The President's Research Committee on Social Trends surveyed Americans' leisure activities, concluding that outdoor recreation and travel were vital in modern society and recommending initiatives to increase such opportunities. Federal funds for roads, conservation, and the Federal Writers' Project's (FWP) American Guides promoted travel as a means to unity, recovery, and nation building. At a fundamental level, these programs offered work during the Depression. But they also provided people with a new understanding of the nation's landscape and people. Whether traveling with a guidebook, working in a CCC camp, or building roads to facilitate travel, Americans rediscovered their country's past and looked toward a better future.[86]

Minnesota's state guide and its Arrowhead guide reported on the history of logging and iron mining, which attracted immigrants. Both guides reinforced the notion of far northeastern Minnesota as a wilderness enclave for visitors. For example, the Superior National Forest section described fifteen canoe trips along the international border. The Arrowhead guide mentioned those who helped shape the region and informed readers about national forest recreation opportunities. Readers of Minnesota's guides discovered a place filled with outdoor adventure and learned how the region's industrial history shaped the landscape.[87]

While Minnesota's Arrowhead guide emphasized wilderness experiences, the Wolverine State guide portrayed the UP as a rustic outpost where tourism helped transform northern lands. As Michigan's second largest industry, the guide suggested of tourism, "Villages are sustained by it; small cities thrive on it; metropolitan areas remain prosperous because of its ramifications." Readers learned it had not always been that way. But with forest resources depleted by 1910, "the summer visitor was quickly recognized as a new source of income" and helped reframe thinking about the forest. The guide suggested Michigan "became a tourist state with a vengeance" after World War I due to improved transportation as well as higher wages, increased leisure, and a growing appreciation of wildlife, scenery, and solitude among urban visitors.[88]

Like other FWP state guides, Wisconsin's offered tours and informed readers that the land of farmers' despair now offered a vacationer's paradise. Tourism was not always presented in glowing terms, however. The guide reminded readers that making a living from it was difficult and warned of commercialization stripping towns of institutions crucial to preserving people's sense of place. Concerns about loss informed the guides, which sought to preserve the past and make it available for visitors. Readers of Wisconsin's guide learned that Hurley, which had a bawdy reputation as the sister city for Ironwood miners, promoted itself as a tourist center and that Iron, Vilas, and Oneida Counties formed Wisconsin's Northern Lakes Region. Vacationers discovered that 3,000 summer homes, 218 resorts, and 32 children's camps existed within forty miles of Minocqua in 1931. Farther west, in Hayward, visitors had numerous lodging options in an "elastic" community that widened its belt to cater to visitors. Wisconsin's guide captured both the promise and pitfalls of tourism while aiming to convince readers to visit the state's northern vacationland and explore its history.[89]

Along with FWP guides, additional relief efforts facilitated federal involvement in North Woods tourism. Built during the early years of FDR's presidency on a plateau overlooking Lake Superior south of Copper Harbor, the Keweenaw Mountain Lodge and golf course demonstrated how federal funds could be used locally for tourism projects addressing unemployment. In addition to the lodge and course, unemployed miners erected three stone boats in the Copper Country and constructed Brockway Mountain Drive into Copper Harbor. Geared toward sightseers and providing an additional route to the lodge, the drive offered scenic views of Lake Superior and the Keweenaw. Promoted and overseen by Ocha Potter, the road and lodge project were originally labeled "Potter's Folly" by one newspaper. But Potter remained undeterred, securing federal funds for construction and a power line from Eagle River to serve the resort. Potter advocated tourism as a member of the county road commission, as a Calumet and Hecla (C&H) mining company official, and as president of the Copper Country Vacationist League. He directed relief projects employing over five hundred jobless miners and believed public tourist development would spur private investment.[90]

Keweenaw Mountain Lodge, built in the 1930s. COURTESY OF THE MICHIGAN TECHNOLOGICAL UNIVERSITY ARCHIVES AND COPPER COUNTRY HISTORICAL COLLECTIONS.

Potter had not always been a tourism advocate, expressing reservations in 1924 that "the expensive road system beyond Mohawk in this county was not required for anything except tourist or pleasure traffic." He continued, "To burden the state or the mining companies in this district to maintain roads for tourist traffic or for pleasure riding except to a very limited extent is unreasonable." At the time, Potter saw little need for either to be saddled with developing roads for tourists. But depression on the Copper Range forced a change of heart. Nearly a decade later, Potter called on C&H and the state to aid tourist development. Assuaging local fears about a short season, distance from population centers, and cold lake waters, he bemoaned the meager efforts to develop the Copper Country tourist trade and argued the region was a comfortable day's drive from major cities and people would be attracted to Lake Superior.[91]

In a speech to a local chamber of commerce, Potter remarked on the initial skepticism he encountered among many fellow residents who expressed concerns about the "short season, lack of attractions, lack of suitable accommodations, fear that if successful there would be no spots in which local nature lovers could find privacy, and a general disbelief in the idea that a tourist trade could help local business conditions."[92] Sensing that initial worries faded as residents came to understand the opportunities, Potter believed tourism could cushion the impact of mine closings and "become the future principal source of income to Keweenaw County."[93] He stressed public over private values, suggesting Brockway Mountain Drive and the six new public parks on Lake Superior assured tourists that Lake Superior views "will not be obstructed by refreshment stands or advertisements or the back yards of private cottages." Recognizing the region's lack of farms and mining's decline, he looked to develop and promote a scenic escape away from hot and humid cities so that Copper Country residents could "become again independent self-respecting citizens." Potter worked with the county road commission and state relief administrator to carry out tourist development at the tip of the Keweenaw. The golf course and lodge transformed the landscape, as workers felled pine and spruce to create the course and used the logs to build the lodge and cabins. By 1938, Keweenaw County, with a population of five thousand, received eighty thousand visitors. Communities throughout Michigan's northernmost county benefited from the tourist industry, mitigating initial local skepticism. While the federal government provided unemployment relief, Potter knew tourism's success depended on local initiative.[94] As a UP resident, Potter drew on his experience and utilized government support to develop tourism in a way that met local needs.

Ocha Potter helped spearhead Copper Country tourist development in the 1930s. COURTESY OF THE MICHIGAN TECHNOLOGICAL UNIVERSITY ARCHIVES AND COPPER COUNTRY HISTORICAL COLLECTIONS.

During the interwar years, competition and political considerations influenced tourist development in Minnesota, Michigan, and Wisconsin. Despite some differences in the nature of earlier extractive industries, the states found themselves connected by their history and geography and a desire to attract tourists. While each state traveled its own course, the work of individuals, regional organizations, state agencies, and the federal government helped transform barren agricultural lands and depressed mining areas into the North Woods. By the mid-1930s, Michigan had developed a coordinated program to reach tourists. With certain areas of the state benefiting more than others, some residents still questioned the approach. James R. Snody wrote the East Michigan Tourist Association, claiming, "tourists were not spenders and that the object ought to be to get settlers."[95] Such a view expressed an earlier attitude that viewed tourists as transients who did not contribute to local communities. As someone who had shifted his position to support tourism in the 1930s, Ocha Potter found himself vindicated after fellow residents voiced support. Facing limited options, public and private interests increasingly looked to tourism as the answer for the region's future.

The UPDB's Bishop enunciated a new vision for the UP when he suggested in 1925, "We have attractions that have cash values and are appre-

Recently constructed Brockway Mountain Drive offered scenic views of Copper Harbor, Michigan, and Lake Fanny Hooe in the 1930s. COURTESY OF THE MICHIGAN TECHNOLOGICAL UNIVERSITY ARCHIVES AND COPPER COUNTRY HISTORICAL COLLECTIONS.

ciated by tourists."[96] Regional organizations like the UPDB pioneered Michigan's tourism efforts, attracting vacationers and urging state funding. The organization shaped a dialogue about what a UP vacation offered and helped develop a tourism infrastructure rooted in promotion, good roads, conservation, and diversification. The UPDB's efforts from the 1910s through World War II, in conjunction with regional and local organizations and state agencies, created an environment wherein Michigan became a pioneer in advocating tourism as a means to recovery. In 1937, the National Automobile Chamber of Commerce declared Michigan the nation's leading tourist state, and 1938 tourist expenditures amounted to nearly $400 million. Looking past the wartime interruption in tourism, former highway commissioner Grover Dillman, who became president of the Michigan College of Mining and Technology (now Michigan Tech), expressed optimism, stating, "No Upper Peninsula industry of comparable significance offers as much possibility for rapid expansion and development during the transition period immediately following the war." Dillman called for municipal associations to assist in postwar planning focused on advertising regional attractions, providing modern and attractive lodging, improving transportation, and developing seasonal lures to attract more visitors. He suggested the UPDB was well positioned to continue working with public and private entities to develop UP tourism. Much had been accomplished in the interwar years, but Dillman hoped for further growth and cooperation.[97]

Michigan's 1929 Hartman-Rushton Act provided a new beginning for public-private cooperation. Michigan's regional tourist associations played a pioneering role, and the state joined Minnesota by 1932 as one of six spending public funds to promote tourism. With the FWP's publication of *Michigan: A Guide to the Wolverine State* in 1941, vacationers could learn about nine tours of the UP as well as suggestions for hikes on Isle Royale. But this information was nothing new for UP vacationers, as the UPDB, tourist entrepreneurs, and state and federal government had spent the previous decades cultivating tourism. This became a model for other jurisdictions, and beginning in 1938, Wisconsin and Minnesota sent delegates to the UPDB's annual meeting. Minnesota was first to establish a state park and provide promotional funds, while Michigan's program offered a regional model for public-private cooperation. To promote tourism and ease travel, Wisconsin banned heavy trucks from highways on Saturday afternoons and most of Sunday during summer. That Wisconsin took such action underscored tourism's growing importance. Differences existed regarding government's role across the states, but all eventually determined tourism offered citizens more than economic benefits and deserved public support.[98]

Across the North Woods, tourism advocates turned to the growing urban middle class, capitalizing on their desire to enjoy leisure in nature. Despite some voices of protest, tourism developed as a major industry that altered the region's physical and economic landscape just as mining and logging left their imprints. State and federal government, regional associations, residents, and private interests made tourism central to the region's economy and identity. While they were convinced tourism was a crop worth cultivating, they had to actually reforest the landscape, maintain fish and game populations, and make waters accessible to attract tourists—they had to conserve, manage, protect, and sustain those natural elements so essential to the North Woods tourist landscape.

CHAPTER 2

Tourists Do Not Deplete Our Soil: Interwar Land Conservation

In 1920, author, professor, and Michigan Land Economic Survey organizer Parrish Lovejoy arrived in Michigan's Upper Peninsula, where he marveled at the devastation of "brushy wastes of scrub, fire-weed forests, bleached snags and charred stumps" as well as the potential of Michigan's northern lands.[1] The lumberman's ax had cleared land and left stumps, but Lovejoy viewed reforestation as a possibility through appropriate forestry and conservation measures. His travels led to a series of articles in *Country Gentleman* capturing conditions in the Upper Peninsula, and he concluded, as many settlers realized, that "very large areas of the cut-over lands are not well-suited to any existing form of agricultural practice."[2] Lovejoy's vision was not necessarily of a tourist paradise. His concerns were with profitable and sustainable land use, and he believed forestry provided a better alternative than farming cutover lands. Years later, Wisconsin conservation official J. H. H. Alexander proclaimed tourism benefited residents financially and vacationers spiritually, the latter returning to daily life "tan and refreshed, re-created in body and in spirit and wearing a little bit of our Wisconsin in their hearts." Having "inoculated their silver dollar corpuscles liberally into our state's financial blood stream," Alexander claimed that "except for the fish they catch, they do not deplete our soil."[3]

Lovejoy and Alexander were among the many people connecting conservation and tourism during the interwar years, helping transform the North Woods into a landscape of reemerging forests and serene lakes packaged and managed by private and public entities to attract vacationers. Competing interests viewed forests and other natural resources as vital to their respective goals, creating a situation wherein strange bedfellows often supported policies benefiting tourism. Government officials, wilderness advocates, land-use experts, writers, sportsmen, and residents had distinct yet often overlapping agendas. By zoning land, developing recreation plans and activities, and mobilizing community support, they helped create a tourist landscape.

The region's shift from a timber and mineral producer to tourist provider reflects the development of an American consumer society that saw some individuals oppose industrialization's environmental impacts and look to protect and package nature to meet consumer desire. Scenery and outdoor recreation filled the void left by the declining supply of raw materials and changed how people thought about and acted upon the land. Beginning in the Progressive Era, state efforts merged tourism and nature conservation both ideologically and in practice, helping regenerate the region's forests and ensuring people's access to nature. As the number of people hiking, fishing, and hunting grew, states appointed forest wardens and established forestry and public domain commissions before World War I, placed responsibility for outdoor recreation under departments of conservation after the war, and passed zoning plans in the early 1930s designating land for agriculture, reforestation, recreation, and wilderness. By the New Deal era, federal officials could look to the North Woods for recreation, land-use, and conservation ideas.[4]

Increased state regulation contributed to a more democratic and accessible interwar tourist landscape. In creating and experiencing the North Woods, residents and visitors also developed a new nature consciousness. Enmeshed in the industrial order, North Woods residents sought to harness tourism's potential while gaining control over the transformation. Tension emerged over changes tourism wrought, including increased state regulations, a growing influx of visitors, and new work opportunities. Despite these concerns, many residents embraced surrounding land and lakes for recreational use and helped establish a landscape that supposedly diverged from the urban industrial order despite its clear connection to it. In doing this, local people and the popular imagination fueled policies that fostered both nature conservation and consumption, reinforcing connections between consumerism and environmentalism. Far more complex than a story of outsiders against local residents or utilitarian conservation versus wilderness preservation, tourist development combined the work of efficiency-minded experts like Lovejoy with organizations and local resource users who conceived and sometimes challenged land-use policies and programs to help establish the North Woods.[5]

Fighting for Minnesota's Wilderness

As the nation's urbanization proceeded apace—the 1920 census famously defined America for the first time as more urban than rural—the idea of preserving natural resources emerged more forcefully among wilderness advocates, government officials, and North Woods residents. In his 1921 essay "The Wilderness and Its Place in Forest Recreational Policy," Aldo Leopold suggested large numbers of tourists could devastate an area and defined wilderness as "a continuous stretch of country preserved in its natural state, open to lawful hunting and fishing, big enough to absorb a two weeks' pack trip, and kept devoid of roads, artificial trails, cottages, or other works of man." A former U.S. Forest Service employee who became the University of Wisconsin's first professor of game management, Leopold believed wilderness had social value, and his vision permitted hiking, fishing, and camping but not commercialization.[6] For those charged with developing recreation for the masses, he suggested that it was "a job, not of building roads into lovely country, but of building receptivity into the still unlovely human mind." Leopold's emphasis on outdoor recreation's intellectual and emotional benefits resonated in places like northern Minnesota's boundary waters, where he traveled in 1924. While private

Aldo Leopold, February 1911. PHOTOGRAPH COURTESY OF THE FOREST HISTORY SOCIETY, DURHAM, NORTH CAROLINA, USFS NEGATIVE 92605.

landowners were crucial to his conservation ideas, Leopold's work on Wisconsin's 1927 Conservation Act establishing a conservation department demonstrates his belief that government also played a key role.[7]

Born in Chicago in 1899 and raised in northern Wisconsin, Sigurd Olson called northern Minnesota home beginning in the 1920s. A naturalist, writer, and educator, Olson viewed wilderness as both physical place and ideological concept. As a salve for the overworked urbanite, wilderness allowed those escaping their everyday lives to return, in Olson's words, with "a wealth of memories that will help him tide over the times when the stress of city life bears too heavily upon him."[8] Noting the confluence of capitalism and wilderness for people living near such areas, he reflected on interwar transformations, suggesting, "Economically, wilderness is becoming an important resource to communities dependent for their existence on the development of recreation facilities."[9] Olson, who operated a canoe outfitting and guide service, believed wilderness experiences provided spiritual and financial returns while helping establish friendships between guide and visitor. But guides still worked for vacationers, providing information on fishing spots and maneuvering through the landscape in exchange for payment. Leopold and Olson both saw wilderness as an escape from the urban order, but that order clearly prescribed ways people experienced and thought about wilderness.

During the interwar years, Americans increasingly came to view the outdoors as a source of leisure rather than a place of labor. Such a transformation helps explain the emergence of the North Woods, where the recreational and aesthetic interests of vacationers and residents along with the economic interests of tourist operators often obscured deeper connections between work and nature. Justifying designating portions of Minnesota's Superior National Forest as roadless, Olson championed preservation over exploitation and believed wilderness areas allowed people to escape "to some wild part of the country which has not as yet been entirely caught up in some scheme of exploitation or development, that they would return to their friends and families strengthened and rejuvenated."[10] Olson also believed that industry should not ravage the forest for private gain and that wilderness areas in Superior National Forest remained a national question because Forest Service land belonged to all Americans. Elaborating on the region's uniqueness in 1929, Olson wanted people to experience it as voyageurs did, writing, "Nowhere else can such beautiful lakes be found. Nowhere else can you find them close together enough to make what is known as a canoe country, and nowhere else is there so much

Sigurd F. Olson, circa 1949. COURTESY OF THE MINNESOTA HISTORICAL SOCIETY.

A canoe is pulled from the warehouse loft at Sigurd Olson's Border Lakes Outfitting Company to outfit a party starting out on a ten-day canoe trip into the wilderness country on April 4, 1940. LOCAL IDENTIFIER USFS NEGATIVE 400545, RECORDS OF THE FOREST SERVICE, RECORD GROUP 95, THE NATIONAL ARCHIVES AT CHICAGO.

beauty concentrated in one spot as here. It is the last area of its kind in the country. Are we going to sacrifice it to the ogre of commercialism?"[11]

Both Leopold and Olson emphasized North Woods land-use questions. Through their activities and writing, they forced people to reconsider ideas about the natural world. With articles in the *Journal of Forestry* and the *Journal of Land and Public Utility Economics*, Leopold's professional community recognized his ideas. Olson remained active in northern Minnesota. While he emerged as a prolific writer after World War II, he had a profound impact on the region as an educator, activist, and entrepreneur during the interwar years. Leopold and Olson joined other regional voices that saw benefits in tourism and recreation, although not all viewed things similarly.

The U.S. Forest Service initially considered recreation a lesser use than timber production, but with automobile touring expanding demand, it responded by providing recreation opportunities to compete with the National Park Service. In 1918, landscape architect Frank Waugh's report for the agency declared recreational forest use equal to that of timber, grazing, and watershed protection. Arguing that recreation should take place alongside other forest functions, Waugh calculated an annual return of $7.5 million from recreational forest use. Noting its "substantial commercial value," he encouraged the agency to further develop recreation.[12] The Forest Service's first landscape architect, Arthur Carhart, crafted plans for Superior National Forest that called for keeping the area pristine while providing easier tourist access with backcountry lodges, marked canoe routes, and motorboat highways. Carhart's notion of constructing such a place differed from Leopold's vision of an area "devoid of roads, artificial trails, cottages, or other works of man," but both saw recreational value in the forest and said little about a working landscape.[13]

Leopold, Olson, Waugh, and Carhart were joined in the debate by Ernest Oberholtzer in his fight to preserve Minnesota and Ontario's Quetico-Superior. In 1927, Oberholtzer established the Quetico-Superior Council, which stressed a conservation program involving water, timber, wildlife, and recreation that brought together American and Canadian interests. Fighting industrialist Edward Backus's plan to build power-generating dams that would have flooded several thousand miles of international shoreline, Oberholtzer expressed outrage that private greed could destroy such a unique wilderness resource. Writing Secretary of Agriculture William Jardine, who oversaw the Forest Service, and asking for federal intervention to stop Backus, Oberholtzer opined, "no conceivable benefits from such a plan can justify the wholesale impairment of public values in so large and so unique an area."[14] He gathered support from local communities, supporting legislation like the Shipstead-Newton-Nolan bill to preserve shorelines and water levels in Minnesota's border lakes. Backing came from the local Arrowhead Sportsmen Association, which sought to protect its members' ability to hunt and fish, and tourist entrepreneurs like Wilderness Outfitters owner Joe Pluth, who remarked, "We will be only too willing to help out in any way we can to work against the Backus project."[15] But Oberholtzer needed more than the Shipstead bill for government to acquire additional property. To preserve scenic, recreational, and inspirational values, he advocated public control of the region's wilderness. Hoping to gain additional support, Oberholtzer, like Olson, pointed to spiritual and economic benefits, writing a colleague for "some figures on the economic value of the things we are trying to protect."[16] Oberholtzer was not without his critics, including the *Duluth Herald*, whose "complete lack of confidence in those who made huge sacrifices to prevent exploitation of the thing that most friends of the region

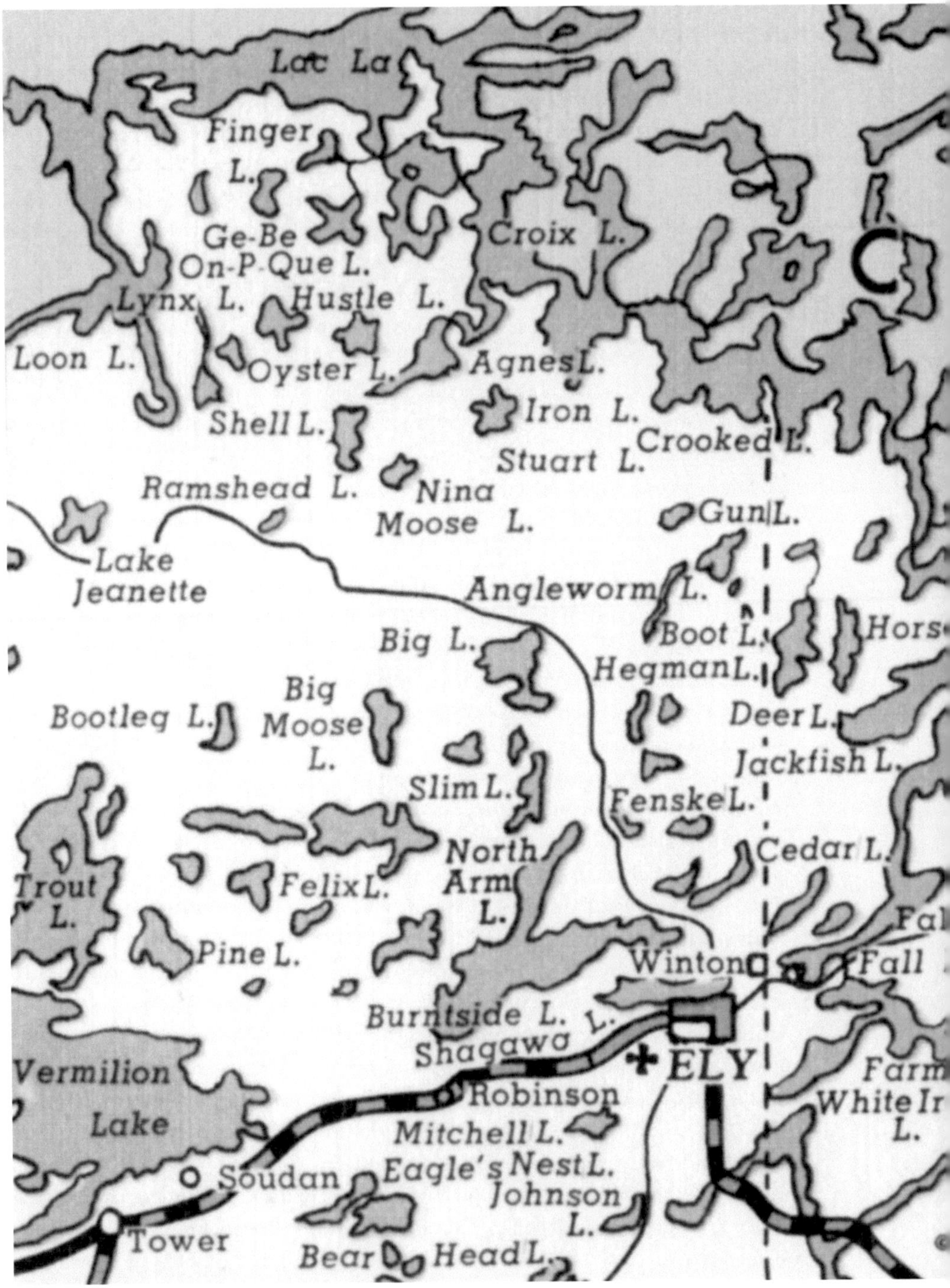

Minnesota border lakes, circa 1935. COURTESY OF THE MINNESOTA HISTORICAL SOCIETY.

E-12
N A D A
Saganaga L.
Alpine L.
Cypress L.
Knife L.
Basswood Lake
Ogish-Ke
Muncie L.
Prairie Portage
Cacaquabic L.
Ensign L.
Wind L.
Newfound L.
Snowbank L.
Moose L.
Little Saganaga L.
Thomas L.
Round L.
Insular L.
Minnesota Border Lakes
in Superior National Forest
8B-H1055

Ernest Oberholtzer poses with an Indian guide during one of his many Canadian canoe trips, circa 1915. COURTESY OF THE MINNESOTA HISTORICAL SOCIETY.

Making sure she is not left behind, a woman climbs on top of the Wilderness Outfitters bus, circa 1930, to embark on a tour. COURTESY OF THE MINNESOTA HISTORICAL SOCIETY.

would consider its most precious single resource" appalled him. Directors of the Naniboujou Club comprised of prominent Duluthians also opposed some council initiatives.[17]

Joining Oberholtzer was Chicago attorney Frank Hubachek, who first came to northern Minnesota in 1919 as a canoe tourist and returned annually with his children after purchasing property. The Ely Commercial Club, a group of business people convinced Backus's plan would harm Ely's economy, also offered support. When Joe Pluth drowned in 1932 and left his outfitting business and property without an owner, Hubachek worked with residents to revive the business and purchased an interest in it. Years later, in an open letter to Ely residents, he refuted charges that his wilderness advocacy was financially motivated and reflected on the history of the business, "It has never paid a dividend. It is a strictly local enterprise and a credit to Ely." Remarking that his total investment in Wilderness Outfitters was less than half his yearly payroll to Ely residents, Hubachek argued that tourism provided employment and the canoe wilderness was a unique resource deserving protection.[18]

Local, regional, and national conservation organizations joined the Quetico-Superior Council in opposing Backus's plan for hydropower dams. Not simply a case of outsiders as preservationists versus residents as resource users, this struggle saw local commercial clubs join sportsmen and wilderness advocates to fight industrial expansion and landscape despoliation. The Izaak Walton League was perhaps the most prominent of these sportsmen's groups. Established in 1922 at a meeting of fifty-four sportsmen in Chicago, its mission was "to save outdoor America for future generations." Taking its name from Izaak Walton, the seventeenth-century English angler-conservationist and author of *The Compleat Angler*, the organization quickly engaged northeastern Minnesota issues. On April 3, 1923, league president Will Dilg appeared at a Duluth public hearing, testifying that the Forest Service should abandon its forest road plans and telling those assembled, "Only God could make that forest and only man can destroy it. It must be preserved as wilderness for future generations of young Americans, and none of us have the moral right to destroy it as such." An *Izaak Walton League Monthly* article reported positively on the meeting, suggesting Dilg helped convince the Forest Service "that the biggest word in the Superior Forest dictionary is 'National'—that it is bigger than the forest itself." Despite the article's spin and Dilg's sense of accomplishment, the league continued to work diligently in support of the Quetico-Superior Council's efforts to limit roads and derail the Backus plan.[19] The league's local Arrowhead chapter added its voice, fighting Forest Service road projects and pro-road interests hoping for "A Road to Every Lake." Vast road plans were ultimately defeated in 1926 when the Forest Service set aside three roadless areas. As a local organization, the chapter supported policies preserving fish and game for sport. Managed accordingly, it believed, the region's "woods, waters, and wild life are not only its rarest distinction but promise to become its richest asset." The chapter suggested tourism offered possibilities for residents that other industries did not.[20]

As citizens and organizations advocated conservation and land-use policies aiding recreational development, Forest Service officials increasingly linked tourism and reforestation. During the 1920s, Assistant Forester Leon Kneipp pondered how national forests could best serve a public with increased leisure time. He agreed with Minnesota's Ten Thousand Lakes Association that they should be "free to the public for all legitimate forms of outdoor life and enjoyment" and that charging an entrance fee to Superior National Forest would be poor policy even if such funds were designated solely for recreation. Kneipp also wrote the district forester about preserving the Minnesota (now Chippewa) National Forest's scenic

U.S. Forest Service officials L. F. Kneipp and E. W. Tinker scouted the woods and waterways, canoeing near the large island in Lake Insula on the Kawishiwi–Isabella canoe route in the heart of the boundary waters, 1927. FOREST SERVICE, U.S. DEPARTMENT OF AGRICULTURE, EASTERN REGION PHOTOGRAPH COURTESY OF THE FOREST HISTORY SOCIETY, DURHAM, NORTH CAROLINA, USFS NEGATIVE 218852.

beauty, reminding him that forest recreational use depended on maintaining forest cover. Kneipp's concerns were wide-ranging, including access and fee issues for recreational users and managing timber cuts to preserve scenery. His positions reflected the agency's growing awareness of the forest's ability to provide for vacationers and address competition from the Park Service.[21]

Perhaps the most influential Forest Service voice for recreation remained Arthur Carhart. His Superior National Forest recreational survey conceived of the region's wilderness in terms of scenery and human access. Carhart labeled it "one of the most valuable properties in the whole National Forest system so far as human-use potentials were concerned—the last frontier in which forests of the Lake Country, the canoe trails of the red men and the voyageur, could have sanctuary."[22] After traveling the forest in 1921, Carhart suggested a wilderness management policy prohibiting logging along shorelines and waterways. He did not want to exclude cutting timber but noted that in some locations "the aesthetic qualities shall, where of high merit, take precedence over the commercialization of such timber stands."[23] Well aware of the need to balance forest uses, Carhart offered a compromise between industry and recreation premised on the notion that scenic values were, in certain places, more valuable and must be preserved. Carhart viewed recreational forest use as more democratic than other uses because of its long-term sustainability and capacity to provide health, rest, and rejuvenation for the public. Justifying forest recreation as a land use, he provided an odd comparison, remarking, "Several people can enjoy a whole summer's residence on a piece of forest ground that would not begin to graze one hungry steer and because the health of the nation depends as much on recreation out of doors as it does on steaks indoors it is probable that the human use will remain the preferred one in certain localities."[24] Recognizing forest values beyond economics, he defended them vociferously. His vision was not of a wilderness devoid of all other uses but rather an important recreational outlet in a forest guided by sound conservation principles.

Although he hoped to make recreation an integral part of forest policy, Carhart believed the Forest Service did not take his recommendations seriously, because of its emphasis on timber production. Emphasizing the importance of local and regional actors in spurring policy changes, he remarked in 1928, "I think we all know that the Forest Service was not ready to take a progressive, intelligent attitude toward the Superior and recreation until the people in Minnesota and the Middle West rather

Arthur Carhart with pack and canoe, Superior National Forest, 1920. U.S. FOREST SERVICE PHOTOGRAPH COURTESY OF THE FOREST HISTORY SOCIETY, DURHAM, NORTH CAROLINA, USFS NEGATIVE 153950.

kicked them in the ribs." Carhart believed recreation planning demanded landscape architects, but the Forest Service did not use them, instead "approaching human use problems from the angle of timber and cow feed." Carhart ultimately found himself vindicated by plans for Superior National Forest, which drew on his appreciation of its recreation potential.[25] Despite diverging views, foresters, wilderness advocates, entrepreneurs, local citizens, and members of sportsmen's associations brought new philosophies and a pioneering spirit to land issues that helped establish Minnesota's North Woods. In reconceptualizing the landscape, they could also explore forestry, land use, and tourism activities in neighboring Wisconsin and Michigan.

Zoning Wisconsin

Born in Brooklyn, trained at Yale, and hired by Gifford Pinchot in 1898 to promote national forest reserves, Edward Griffith became Wisconsin's first state forester in 1905. In his decade of service, he developed programs to control forest fires and advocated acquiring land for reserves. He believed forests were essential for a successful tourist industry and backed the creation of a permanent northern forest reserve. One of his contemporaries later reported, "Recreation values of the forest reserve had won some appreciation, but Griffith was the first to envision their full potential."[26] In 1906, Griffith wrote of the proposed reserve, "There are hundreds of lakes within the forest area, and when these are protected, together with the forests, and as hunting and fishing constantly improves, the resort business should increase to a very large figure." In 1912, the proposed reserve area contained ninety-one summer resorts. Operators cared for 13,131 guests and had income of $365,025, while total recreation income in the area, including fees for transportation and rentals, stood at $674,444.[27]

Like Griffith, P. S. Lovejoy believed forestry could accomplish far more than the boosterism in Minnesota's four hundred pages of official agricultural promotion literature, Michigan's boasts that it was "The Land of Plenty," and Wisconsin's marketing its access to markets, desirable climate, and improved transportation to potential settlers. Lovejoy claimed that "the land-selling campaigns fail because they are full of bunk and because farmers know it."[28] He recalled how those concerned about forests destroying the region's agricultural potential stonewalled Griffith's reserve effort. Some residents also met Griffith's stance with derision. George Dawes charged forestry advocates with being "academic people who were trying to make the country a place for wealthy pleasure seekers from the cities to spend their summers." Dawes's words captured the sentiment of those who saw the issue in class terms. Lovejoy believed such attacks resulted from people clutching to the "farm-it-all" idea without realizing forest crops, whether used for timber or to attract vacationers, were better than none at all. According to Lovejoy, a lack of knowledge and the deceptive practices of earlier agricultural promoters led to policies harmful to local residents and the land.[29]

The state supreme court ultimately scuttled Griffith's reserve plans in 1915 when it decided the state constitution forbade the program. Griffith left Wisconsin and forestry, but his plans for northern forests ultimately bore fruit when a 1924 state constitutional amendment allowed for a reserve. At a 1933 meeting of Vilas County residents, resort owner Ole Rismon recalled a missed opportunity two decades earlier:

> We have just adopted a land use ordinance; we have our county forest, the first state forest has developed, and the plantation at Star Lake has become an attraction; we have industry forests owned by paper companies, and our recreation resources draw thousands, not only in summer. We have done everything Mr. Griffith advocated. He should have had our support.[30]

Once vilified for his forest plan, Griffith was now praised as a visionary. Others joined Rismon in supporting tourism, including one resident who offered his unabashed solution to northern Wisconsin's land-use problems by urging people to capitalize on lakefront lands, commenting, "I had one little 80 a few years ago and my taxes ran around $18 to $20 on it; today that is bringing in over a hundred because I have sold a few cottages to Chicago people—and they are paying for it."[31] Local resident and resort owner Angus McDonald added that Griffith provided sage advice, "but we laughed at him and threw him out of office, now we are finding Griffith was right, he was far-sighted enough to see just what was going to happen to us."[32] By the mid-1920s, resort owners generally backed state conservation initiatives because they aided tourism. One operator noted that resort owners invested in property and drew visitors. He also urged coordinating conservation policies across states, commenting, "Michigan, Minnesota, and Wisconsin should have uniform game laws and restrictions on out-door life—as we have the only natural playground of the world. We want our money spent in that direction."[33] As operators competed for tourists, conservation and land-planning efforts developed across the North Woods with the most prominent of these—rural zoning—first emerging in Wisconsin.

University of Wisconsin faculty joined residents in continuing Griffith's efforts to transform northern lands. Walter Rowlands, a professor and supervisor of northern Wisconsin county agricultural agents, helped develop the nation's first rural zoning ordinance for Oneida County in 1933. Vilas County adopted a similar ordinance and followed with a recreation plan addressing tourist development. Nicknamed Pyrotol Pete for his work using surplus war explosives to clear northern Wisconsin stump land during the 1920s, Rowlands shifted his attention to pressing regional land-use issues in the 1930s and built support for a zoning ordinance that restricted settlement and set aside land for recreational use. He persuaded residents that new initiatives were necessary, approaching the task differently than Griffith, who mainly looked for support from state officials. To convince residents of the land's recreational value, Rowlands drew on John Bordner's Wisconsin land economic inventory, a collaborative project involving the state's Department of Agriculture, University of Wisconsin's College of Agriculture, and the Wisconsin Geological and Natural History Survey, which surveyed land cover and included information on improvements such as summer homes and hotels along northern lakes. Like Leopold and Olson, Rowlands claimed outdoor recreation and tourism offered spiritual, emotional, and financial benefits and deemed it vital that northern Wisconsin remain "less of Coney Island and more of the calmness and quietness that goes with forest environment and forest atmosphere."[34] By designating specific areas for recreational, commercial, or residential use and by closing certain areas to further settlement, zoning aided the growing tourist industry.

Rowlands's land economist colleague George Wehrwein produced several studies on zoning for tourism and outdoor recreation, highlighting the economic benefits of classifying Vilas and Oneida Counties' waterfront lands for recreational use. In Oneida County in 1929, only 8.5 percent of the land was classified as recreational, but it contributed 37.2 percent of the real estate base, while in Vilas County recreational land comprised 15.7 percent of land and contributed 63.1 percent of the real estate base. Wehrwein believed recreational land could help solve the idle land problem because it remained relatively free from delinquency and provided funds for local services by returning land to the tax rolls. Emphasizing tourism's ability to revive northern Wisconsin, Wehrwein wrote, "Wisconsin has in her forests, streams, lakes and farms unsurpassed natural beauty, quietness and calmness which appeals to the city dweller who is looking for a spot to build a summer home where he can rest and recreate himself. Let us add to these natural attractions a genuine hospitality." Remaining farmers stood to benefit from neighboring recreational land because it contributed to county tax rolls and visitors purchased farm products. Wehrwein believed well-crafted zoning ordinances could foster the most productive use of northern lands for both agriculture and tourism.[35]

Recreational use brought diversification, providing new opportunities for residents and vacationers while also increasing government regulation. Rowlands and Wehrwein worked with residents on tourism and recreation initiatives, coordinating land use for maximum economic and social utility. No longer would a Stevens Point electrician seeking to escape the Depression purchase a tract in remote Oneida County, four miles from a public road and without access to schooling for his children. Rural zoning initiatives were a response to such situations and established forest and recreation districts closed to new settlement. They spread across twenty-seven counties in northern and central Wisconsin. Michigan and Minnesota adopted rural zoning in 1935 and 1939, respectively, reflecting regional consensus on both land-use issues and tourism's potential.[36] A solution to the problem of large swathes of tax-delinquent land from logging or agricultural abandonment, rural zoning allowed states to "regulate, restrict, and determine the areas within which agriculture, forestry, and recreation may be conducted." Wehrwein supported appointing a regional planning director in the highway department to oversee scenic development along roads and believed that "zoning and other land use controls are needed to protect those who have come into the forests for quiet, rest, and true *re*-creation."[37] Along with removing settlers and establishing county and state forests, zoning helped create a new economy of trees and tourists that brought government into people's daily lives through land-use policies.

Preserving a Pleasant Peninsula

As in Wisconsin, foresters and land-use professionals at the University of Michigan, including Filibert Roth and Parrish Lovejoy, contributed ideas for a North Woods recreation landscape. Trained in Germany like many of his contemporaries, Roth wrote about North Woods forest conditions and completed a report on Wisconsin in 1898. From 1903 to 1923, he served as a forestry professor at Michigan, educating the first generation of American-trained foresters. Writing to author James Curwood, who spearheaded a campaign to reform Michigan's conservation affairs in the early 1920s, Roth remarked on the region's plight, "Our North Counties, once filled with poor settlers, ruled by pauper farming, will be as barren of animal wild-life as of trees, it will be pauper country with all the lawlessness that poverty calls forth and defends."[38] To counteract such devastation, Roth called for state intervention and reforestation programs to revive these lands.

Born in Princeton, Illinois, in 1884, Parrish Lovejoy's granduncle was Elijah Parish Lovejoy, the antislavery advocate and *Alton Observer* publisher murdered by a mob in 1837. Lovejoy served under Roth at the University of Michigan and spent years documenting land-use problems, ultimately organizing Michigan's land survey in 1922. In 1920, he left the university to write for Curtis publications, producing a series on the Upper Peninsula. Advocating sound land management, he urged classifying land according to its best use: farming, grazing, recreation, or timber. Upon his death in 1942, the *Ann Arbor News* reported on his efforts to reshape northern lands:

> When the tourists stream into northern Michigan they are likely to think of Indians and lumberjacks, the men who lived in the forest before the white men came and the men who tore the forests down to build the cities of America. Yet the wilderness that now delights the tourist and the hunter stands in large part as a monument to the frail-looking man who loved the forests. He was not alone in restoring trees and game to Michigan but he was one of the greatest and most influential of those who saw the vision and found the way to re-create Michigan's forest wealth.[39]

While tourists and hunters might not consider Lovejoy's work as a writer, forester, and land planner when encountering scenic vistas or a waiting deer, he proved instrumental in reshaping Michigan's landscape. His survey coincided with state efforts designating public lands to address increased recreational demand.

In 1926, Lee R. Schoenmann assumed the Michigan land survey directorship from Lovejoy and worked with sportsmen, landowners, tourist boosters, and local governments to improve land management. Writing to Schoenmann regarding the relationship between recreation and conservation, Lovejoy pointed out that the region's location, including its proximity to population centers, influenced tourist development. He believed research was essential for determining new land uses, posing the question, "If we assume that the bulk of our northern 'wild' land has a principal future in connection with recreation—rather than in agriculture, grazing, commercial forestry . . . and that we should so manage it as to increase its attractiveness to residents of urban and prairies districts how should we proceed?" Lovejoy emphasized the need to inventory resources, calculate demand, measure competition, and develop a plan for each territory based on such information. He also wanted to "engineer our recreational industry development, instead of merely gambling with natural formations," believing reliable information aided planning. In response, Michigan's land survey involved sound research and considered recreation and tourism worthy uses.[40]

The commitment to research brought others into the discussion. Michigan's Conservation Department had enlisted Edward Prophet to survey tourism's economic impact, but in 1934 another Michigan State professor, Wilbur Hedrick, envisioned northern Michigan's vacation possibilities. "The cut-over lands," Hedrick reported, "enjoy a great advantage in the fact that visitors so quickly may be taken from a city's heat, dust and noise to the midst of a resorting region of a wilderness or semi-wilderness nature." Hedrick's "semi-wilderness" stood in opposition to the city in summer. In 1929, two Forest Service observers drew attention to the tourist potential of Michigan's northern lands and emphasized natural features along with growing numbers of commercial enterprises servicing visitors. The authors, though, remained unconvinced that a forest dedicated solely to recreation was the solution. Arguing that the nation needed timber, they saw recreational use as one aspect of a diversified approach to regional land-use policy.[41]

Journalists increasingly appealed to the state to preserve natural spaces for visitors, with Jack Van Coevering of the *Detroit Free Press*, Ben East of the *Grand Rapids Press* and later of *Outdoor Life*, and Albert "Pete" Stoll Jr. of the *Detroit News* contributing to Michigan's conservation and tourism efforts. Van Coevering covered Michigan's outdoors in his "Woods and Waters" columns, serving as a *Free Press* writer from 1931 to 1965. Supporting calls by the Izaak Walton League and other Michigan conservation groups to use hunting and fishing license fees for acquiring and maintaining public access areas, he urged the state to ensure the public's right to fish its waters and hunt in its forests. Sportsmen's organizations increasingly worked with state agencies to promote and protect lands and waters for such activities. Stoll used his *News* post to advocate designating Isle Royale a national park and was joined in the cause by Van Coevering and East.[42]

A more unified North Woods vision emerged as citizens appealed to the state to protect forests and lakes for recreation. Michigan Forestry

Association president Frederick Wheeler called for policies "perpetuating green forests on the millions of acres now covered with stumps and sweet fern or scrubby and nearly worthless tree growth." Agriculture had proven a failure on most northern lands, leading Wheeler to demand that the state establish forests. Wheeler believed this would strengthen the economy by increasing the land's recreational value, allowing for future timber harvests, and protecting against wildfires. He called on the state to safeguard its forest resources and plan effectively. "There need be no conflict between recreational use and intensive utilization for timber production," wrote Wheeler, "Thousands of acres of such pine can be growing and will be steadily enhancing Michigan's pecuniary and recreational resources and scenic values."[43] Through reforestation, he urged development of the state's recreational and industrial potential. Many landowners had given up, including one who reported, "Owning cut-over lands under present conditions, no matter where the land is located, is no longer an asset but it is a liability, and the sooner one gets rid of such land, the better off they will be, even if they have to give it away."[44] Given such dire circumstances, Wheeler argued for state assistance in revitalizing these lands.

Charles Garfield helped establish Michigan's Public Domain Commission in 1909 to manage the state's fish and game, public lands, and forest reserves. As president of the Michigan Forestry Commission, he urged legislation linking reforestation and tourism as part of a rehabilitation policy for Michigan's northern lands that included enforcing game laws, issuing hunting and fishing licenses, and protecting public lands. Garfield wrote, "The State has finally become awake to the importance of rehabilitating its surface in the interest of its great future and contributing to its desirability as a place for beautiful and happy homes and friendly visitation by those who are attracted by the attributes registered in the legend upon the escutcheon of the state." That motto, appearing on the state flag along with the shield, told visitors, *Si quaeris peninsulam amoenam, circum spice* (If you seek a pleasant peninsula, look about you). While not a sportsman, Garfield believed a sound conservation program would preserve that "pleasant peninsula" for Michigan citizens and vacationers. Recognizing the forest had been cut over without considering consequences, the Forestry Commission viewed reforestation programs as key to the tourist industry.[45] Through their service as presidents of organizations and as early proponents of connecting reforestation and recreation, Wheeler and Garfield voiced citizen concerns over Michigan's conservation affairs and supported forest conservation policies that fostered tourist possibilities.

As prolific authors and later as Michigan Conservation Commission members, Harold Titus and James Curwood joined Wheeler and Garfield in linking conservation and tourism. Titus's *Timber*, published in 1922, crystallized the discontent of those who criticized policies that let cutover timberlands lie idle and forest fires spread and who witnessed people hopelessly trying to farm these lands. Titus felt forests would help attract tourists, and his tales concerned preserving and restoring the outdoors. The book drew attention to northern land problems, and as outdoor writer Ben East suggested, Titus "began 'selling' the idea of preserving and restoring the out-of-doors through his stories long before conservation was a major issue in Michigan."[46]

From 1921 until his unexpected death in 1927, Curwood proved a vehement critic of Michigan's conservation affairs. A charter member and active participant in the Izaak Walton League, he advocated policies tackling water pollution, forest fires, sport fisheries, and wildlife protection. Curwood rallied against corruption in Michigan's Conservation Department, which he believed doled out appointments as political favors and laxly enforced and disregarded game laws. In a 1921 letter to Conservation Commission member Tom Marston, he outlined the economic and spiritual benefits of sound conservation policies:

> I have spent a large part of my life next to nature, and possibly that is why I can see and appreciate the vast natural resources of Michigan, and their enormous value to us in health and beauty as well as in dollars and cents more than some others. I am sure the greatest work that can be done in Michigan today, a work which will eventually add fifty million dollars a year to the wealth of the state, is in the conservation and propagation of our forests and wild life.[47]

Frustrated with Michigan's inability to move forward effectively along these lines, he turned to Minnesota's Superior National Forest and hoped for better results, suggesting, "Let us have at least one place left in the Middle West, even though it is not in Michigan, where fathers may take their sons, their wives and daughters into a real wilderness." Worried that timber interests would use roads to harvest resources and destroy the wilderness landscape, his vision stressed spiritual benefits and vacationing outdoors with family.[48]

While patronage still existed in Michigan's Conservation Department a decade after Curwood's passing, citizens continued asserting their voices in conservation affairs. In 1937, sportsmen's clubs formed the Michigan United Conservation Clubs (MUCC) to urge fish and game protection and professional appointments to the department. Behind its leader, Harry Gaines, MUCC supported programs for forests, lakes, and streams that created an improved environment for tourists.[49] Unlike the broad-based MUCC, the Minnesota Emergency Conservation Committee (MECC) operated as the two-man operation of Charles Horn and Olin Kaupanger. As president of Federal Cartridge Corporation, a munitions firm that funded MECC, Horn wanted to preserve hunting along border lakes. Kaupanger lobbied legislators while Horn issued newsletters to conservationists and editors. MECC wanted hunting and fishing license funds directed to wildlife management and attacked Minnesota's conservation commissioner for his management style and fiscal irresponsibility.[50] Despite MECC's limited membership, both MECC and MUCC demonstrate how sportsmen's efforts to influence conservation policy could aid North Woods tourism. Responding to citizen concerns, Michigan conservation official Walter Hastings promoted tourism and conservation. Vacationer Bob Engels thanked Hastings for providing information and remarked, "I am so sold on the way you people live, your surroundings and everything, that I have made up my mind that I am going to cut loose of everything down here, as soon as I can get out, then move up to Gods country." Hastings's films, lectures, and photographs convinced Engels to vacation in Michigan and led him to consider leaving the industrial landscape of Gary, Indiana, to settle in the Upper Peninsula.[51]

State conservation departments bore increasing responsibility for developing recreational resources, particularly as many once private lands moved into public ownership. From 1900 to 1930, twelve states established park systems, including Michigan, Wisconsin, and Minnesota. Increased state park development encouraged tourism and led National Park Service Chief Stephen Mather to convene the National Conference on State Parks. While the Depression rocked people's lives in many ways, it was a boon to state parks, which offered affordable escapes to tourists like Engels and others looking for a brief escape from difficult times. When P. J. Hoffmaster assumed leadership of the Conservation Department in 1934, Michigan's seventy-two state parks attracted nine million visitors annually.[52] Addressing the Upper Peninsula Development Bureau in 1938, Hoffmaster stated, "Build a permanent recreational industry? Yes, in my opinion it is entirely feasible, possible and practicable." On the eve of World War II, the state's tourist industry brought in nearly $400 million annually and employed forty thousand people.[53] Michigan's conservation program, which included scenic highways, fish and game management, state parks, reforestation, education, and publicity, contributed to its development as a vacation destination.

Tourists and Trees

As officials examined regional land-use questions, North Woods residents increasingly contributed to the conservation and tourism dialogue. As noted earlier, some, like George Dawes, disagreed with attracting tourists, while others, like Ole Rismon in Wisconsin and Ocha Potter in the UP, supported tourism. Some northern Wisconsin residents complained that state fish and game regulations and expanded licensing programs catered to tourists over local users. Northern Wisconsin vacationers and resort owners suggested the opposite, blaming the Conservation Department when fishing was poor, accusing it of not planting fish, taking spawn out of lakes, permitting ice fishing, and favoring local residents. But with tourism providing work, residents increasingly cast aside a notion of progress dependent on farming and resource extraction for one relying on tourism. They moved toward Rismon's position and supported advertising, construction, reforestation, and zoning programs benefiting residents and vacationers. While many local residents cast their lot, as George Wehrwein suggested, with the "prosperity, the level of incomes and recreational habits of people living in distant cities," they helped determine the region's future by taking positions on land-use and tourism issues.[54]

North Woods residents enjoyed access to wildlife in woods and waterways and used it to supplement their income and kitchens. Despite growing local support for tourism, conservation regulations and public land ownership heightened concerns over external control of natural resources. Fears of deforestation and the rise of professional forestry contributed to the establishment of the Minnesota (now Chippewa) National Forest in 1908 and the Superior National Forest in 1909. The UP's Ottawa and Hiawatha National Forests and Wisconsin's Chequamegon and Nicolet National Forests followed in subsequent decades, expanding federal land ownership in the region. Combined with increased road construction and automobile travel, these forests offered an environment where the public increasingly experienced leisure in nature. While many residents supported tourism and saw benefits in conservation, government involvement had the potential to create, according to one historian, "landscapes managed by professional bureaucrats in the interests of visiting tourists and national economic power."[55]

Local fears about losing control over access to natural resources pervaded conservation affairs in northern Minnesota. They took root in diverse situations—against industrialist Edward Backus's dam projects, over Forest Service management policies in the boundary waters, and among those who opposed proposals establishing a national park. The Arrowhead Sportsmen's Association (ASA), which supported efforts to stop hydropower dams, expressed objections to a potential national park in the Superior National Forest. It called on the Forest Service to recognize the recreational and industrial potential of the area "and the rights of its people to a voice in these matters." Sensing the region's future was being hijacked, the ASA wanted to ensure fishing and hunting remained accessible to its members and feared a national park would bring a designation that the area was off-limits to such activities. It was not alone in urging greater local control. Hanford Cox of the Minnesota Arrowhead Association (MAA) rallied against the President's Quetico-Superior Committee, suggesting it "has never sought the ideas or support of the Arrowhead Association and has not appeared interested in their views." The MAA claimed that as a regional organization it was better qualified to address land-use issues with a program "more in keeping with actual conditions and more satisfactory to the citizens." Even as he advocated local control, Cox hoped for improved cooperation between the MAA and the committee, suggesting compromise was possible on questions of resource use and outdoor recreation.[56]

While the ASA rallied against increased commercial exploitation and the MAA wanted greater influence in land-use decisions, Forest Service officials advanced forest recreation. Arthur Carhart urged residents to advise Congress that recreational funds were as important as those for other forest activities and that "Ely has the opportunity of becoming a tourist town. It remains for the citizens of the community and surrounding communities to decide if that will come to pass or not."[57] He suggested crowds could be handled without destroying recreational, wildlife, and forest values cherished by locals. Many Ely residents heard Carhart's call and established resorts and outfitting services catering to the growing tourist trade. These operators contributed to area conservation and recreation debates since business depended on their clients accessing public lands.[58]

Under the 1916 Term Permit Act, the Forest Service issued leases for summer cottages and resorts on its holdings, while Minnesota's Department of Conservation promoted lakefront sites. In the Minnesota (now Chippewa) National Forest, individuals built cottages on government-leased land. In 1926, Forest Supervisor G. E. Marshall wrote his boss, Assistant District Supervisor E. W. Tinker, about recreation's future in the forest, "I do not feel that there is any danger for many years to come of a congestion that would result in a need for more sites for public use than the Forest provides under the present plan." Marshall believed northern Minnesota could handle 2,334,000 tourists. How he arrived at that number is unclear, but it was far more than Minnesota would need to accommodate for years. He recommended issuing permits for cottages on platted lands, developing campgrounds, resorts, and other public services, and additional cottage construction once these facilities were complete.[59]

While the primary management objective in portions of the forest remained timber, Marshall's 1926 forest recreation plan took a page from Carhart and deemed recreation the forest's highest use along lakeshores and in campsites. The plan also stressed the forest's location and accessibility to population centers. Marshall called for a resource inventory to develop recreation for the greatest number of people.[60] Tinker, though, was not nearly as convinced of the forest's limitless recreational potential, expressing fears about development and the agency's ability to provide additional recreation opportunities. He worried that private cottage leases, despite the larger number of potential permittees, would limit public use. Instead, he visualized the forest offering "a playground for the general public which in time will be an exceedingly valuable asset." In 1933, Tinker labeled it a mistake to have allowed summer homes in places where they destroyed public use and expressed regret over the agency's policy.[61]

Forest Service officials aimed to provide the vacationing public an economical and pleasant experience, while recognizing the need to avoid overcrowding and ensuring public access in the face of private purchase. Escaping to the forest was different than spending Sundays in a city park or picnic grove. Forest camping provided families an affordable vacation, but the increasing desire and possibility of owning a lakefront plot and the rise of resorts on private lands in and adjacent to national forests led to fears about the demise of public access.[62] Fewer summer-home sites were developed upon passage of the 1916 Term Permit Act in Minnesota's Superior National Forest. Unlike the Chippewa, where cabin development proceeded apace, battles continued over preserving the Superior's canoe country in a more rugged state. The President's Quetico-Superior Committee joined the Quetico-Superior Council in calling for the acquisition and demolition of houses, cabins, and other structures. They believed establishing a wilderness demanded eradicating evidence of human use and consolidating lands under Forest Service jurisdiction to prohibit alternative uses.[63]

Established by Franklin Roosevelt in 1934, the President's Quetico-Superior Committee advocated a land and water resource policy along the Canada-Minnesota border that would "substitute protection, restoration, and balanced use for the older, private system of exploitation." Recreational facilities were deemed "a vital necessity," as existing regional public lands were insufficient to meet needs. Much of the Canadian side remained in public hands, but substantial American lands were privately held. Like the Quetico-Superior Council, the committee framed the debate as one between exploitation and protection, suggesting lumber and power interests wanted to use the region's resources for private benefit. While the Shipstead-Nolan Act limited cutting along lakes, curbed development to existing locations, and preserved an undeveloped interior, the committee joined citizens and sportsmen's groups in advocating for additional government action to preserve wilderness recreation.[64]

Despite differing visions on appropriate land use, people across the North Woods emphasized the benefits of recreating on public land. In Michigan, P. S. Lovejoy encouraged legislation to ensure public access for fishing, boating, and bathing, while Charles Garfield claimed government must "protect these beautiful places in which Nature has been so lavish with her riches so that people who do not own lands and houses and who are not able to have summer cottages and lakes of their own can have forever waving to them the privileges of access to these store houses of Nature." The vast majority could not afford a palatial summer home, and many did not have the means to lease a Forest Service cottage. Developing conservation policies that provided public recreation on forests and lakes offered rewards for residents and visitors alike.[65]

While the New Deal expanded government conservation efforts, it built upon earlier work by state conservation departments and the Forest Service to integrate recreation into conservation policy. These efforts continued into the 1930s, when the federal presence in rehabilitating and managing lands and the number of people laboring and playing on them increased. Across the nation, the Civilian Conservation Corps helped construct hundreds of state parks and thousands of miles of hiking trails, furthering earlier state-level work. The federal government's expanded role in America's recreational landscape also drew attention to forestry issues. Bob Marshall, who served as the first director of forestry for the

U.S. Bureau of Indian Affairs, headed the Forest Service's Division of Recreation and Lands, and helped found the Wilderness Society, argued that government needed to manage the nation's forests in the interests of its citizenry. In *The People's Forests*, his call for federal intervention was to protect not merely the forests but also "the land, the workers, the consumers, and the dependent communities." Marshall viewed forests as an essential foundation for society and believed the nation "must discard the unsocial view that our woods are the lumbermen's and substitute the broader ideal that every acre of woodland in the country is rightly a part of the people's forests."[66] While the people's forests provided a destination for vacationers, the Forest Service mandated that its lands provide timber along with recreation. Carhart and Marshall, Forest Service recreational stewards, helped integrate recreation into the agency's land management policies, which contributed to more people enjoying the forests.

The development of cottages, resorts, trails, and boat launches on public lands brought government into the tourist arena. State laws regulated the activities of commercial and recreational fishermen, altering work and leisure practices. Conservation departments also responded to lake and stream stocking needs. In Minnesota, the Ely Commercial Club requested stocking for many border lakes and then promoted the idea of natural abundance to potential vacationers. Local and regional sporting organizations found themselves better served by associating with the Izaak Walton League, ASA, and MUCC. State promotion of abundant fish and game dovetailed with the views of tourist promoters who saw outdoor recreation as a commodity and knew selling retreats to sportsmen depended on having fish to catch and forests filled with wildlife. Such promotion contributed to licensed hunters increasing from four to seven million nationally between 1920 and 1930. Outdoor sports were big business as people escaped to the North Woods with their rod, reel, and gun. Hunting and fishing licenses aided recreational development by providing funds to purchase public access sites, develop stocking programs, and employ game wardens to police poachers.[67] In the late 1930s, the Northern Michigan Sportsmen's Association urged Michigan's legislature to earmark 40 percent of license fees toward procuring public access sites. Outdoor writer Jack Van Coevering commended his state's efforts, remarking, "Michigan was so far ahead than any other state in the country in the number and acreage of fishing access sites they had."[68] Wisconsin resort owners wanted to issue licenses directly to guests and looked to the Conservation Department to ensure good hunting and fishing. On the eve of the war, the

Wall Street Journal reported on increased land sales in northern Michigan, Minnesota, and Wisconsin with an eye toward further developing them as vacation areas.[69]

Along with government policies, modern consumption-oriented visions of nature altered the North Woods. The region's residents were not alone in addressing questions regarding tourism, land use, and the state. Battles in the Superior National Forest shared commonalities with earlier ones in Yellowstone and the Adirondacks, where the state abrogated local use rights and created, according to historian Karl Jacoby, "a scenic vista for visiting tourists, whose arrival had helped solidify the presence of a wage-based service industry in the region." While this assessment is useful for considering transformations in the North Woods, it risks casting residents as pawns in a process directed by outside interests and the state, when in fact many believed tourism offered opportunities no longer available in mining and logging and helped facilitate this transformation. While tourism altered the nature of work, residents were accustomed to industrial wage labor in the region's mines and forests. Rural people, as historian Richard White suggests, traditionally knew nature through labor. This continued in a new form, as many became providers of leisure in the North Woods. Like their urban counterparts, they also enjoyed leisure in nature. In the often heated debates about wilderness, zoning, and access, they battled for control over area recreational use and future tourist development. From the Adirondacks to the North Woods, rural people worked to influence the development of a modern American countryside increasingly regulated by law, market relations, and the state.[70]

Rural residents' adaptability afforded them opportunities to make a living in a changing landscape but also bred conflict. Some embraced the promotion of surrounding land and lakes, seeing economic potential in marketing their home as a scenic escape. Others complained about the changes tourism wrought. As the state increased its control through conservation laws and land ownership, debates ensued about the future of the North Woods. Would it provide productive farmlands, multiple-use forests, or a recreational landscape? North Woods residents were not alone in the wilderness. Their actions and words helped transform these lands and contributed to conservation policies that aided tourist development. Forests, lakes, and streams proved essential to a region increasingly reliant on tourism.

During the interwar years, government agencies, local residents, tourist boosters, sportsmen's organizations, land-use experts, and wilderness advocates viewed the forest in economic terms. Forests were embedded in the market, and their products, including trees, scenery and wildlife, were seen as commodities. In some ways, the story of the region's forests in the twentieth century varied little from that of the late nineteenth. Then, forest products had been used to build cities and serve industry. In the twentieth century these uses continued, although on a different scale, as the redeveloping northern forest served the industrial order as a tourist landscape. Forests had been decimated to help build that order, and now they were revived and protected in order to support it. In creating the North Woods, a range of actors left their imprint on and battled for control over the landscape. That landscape included more than natural resources. Potential vacationers needed lodging and activities when they arrived. The experience of vacationers, resort owners, and tourist workers on the ground during the interwar years adds another chapter to the North Woods story.

CHAPTER 3

No Dull Days at Dunn's: Labor and Leisure in the North Woods

BETWEEN THE WORLD WARS, NORTH WOODS RESORTS, LODGES, HOUSE-keeping cabins, tourist camps, and state parks attracted growing numbers of vacationers seeking respite in natural surroundings. With more Americans receiving time off from work, proprietors and employees helped shape a new regional tourist identity and landscape with help from vacationers. In the 1920s, companies offered paid vacations to increase productivity while decreasing turnover and absenteeism. Such benefits rarely extended to workers in industries like mining and logging, but their urban counterparts fared better. Ascribing to the principles of welfare capitalism, some companies established vacation savings clubs for workers through payroll deductions and encouraged them to enjoy family vacations at company-sponsored recreation clubs, campgrounds, and rest camps.[1] Workers with more than a year of service at S. C. Johnson and Son in Racine, Wisconsin, enjoyed an annual two-week vacation and could head north to relax. Employees at Chicago's International Harvester who worked at least two years with satisfactory attendance received a one-week paid vacation, which increased to two weeks after five years. At Chicago's Armour and Company, male employees with five years of continuous service earned a week's vacation, while females needed only three years to qualify. At another Chicago meatpacker, Swift, males needed four years, and females three before earning a week's paid vacation. By 1934, 7,829 Swift employees received a one-week paid vacation, and 6,911 enjoyed two weeks. Meatpacking workers joined vacationing colleagues from other industries as a growing urban workforce with paid vacations helped transform the North Woods into a destination for the masses.[2]

Employers remained concerned about vacation activities, producing handbooks and publications about the need for "recreation, refreshment, and relaxation" with an eye toward achieving a more industrious worker. Management's efforts to control leisure time by sponsoring activities, providing information, and forming tourist clubs sought to make workers more productive and compliant.[3] Initially considering vacations "a sign of employer benevolence," workers began regarding them as an earned right, taking advantage of rising productivity and pay to construct a more autonomous space in which they made choices about how to spend their leisure time.[4] Unions initially expressed disinterest in vacation plans, arguing for pay rather than time as a reward. But by 1937, the American Federation of Labor (AFL) urged paid vacations as part of a program for shortening work hours and claimed that only longer vacations allowed for a broadened outlook in which a working-class family could "step out of their daily routine into a life full of new interest, mentally stimulating, with a chance to learn something of the world outside the shop and home."[5]

Working- and middle-class vacationers looked to enjoy leisure outdoors, regain health, strengthen family bonds, reinforce group affiliations, and escape from daily work. Aspects of the North Woods tourist experience were sold to them as commodities. Vacation options included auto tours with stops at state parks, cabins, and lodges, extended family stays at a cottage or resort, or hunting and fishing trips. Others came north with particular purposes in mind—returning home to visit relatives, looking for a summer cottage, attending camp, or searching for work in the expanding tourist landscape. Faced with declining mining and lumber industries, some residents discovered work in major midwestern cities. While these individuals did not enter the tourist industry as operators, they often returned as tourists. Working at meatpacking houses, automobile plants, mills, or downtown offices, they served as promotional emissaries by spinning yarns to fellow workers about wonderful North Woods hunting, fishing, and scenery. Others chose to stay home and explore new tourist industry opportunities. The willing participation of many local residents in the making of a tourist economy offers an alternative to the model of corporate colonialism Hal Rothman described in the twentieth-century American West.[6]

North Woods operators and promoters stressed improved health, productivity, and an escape from the city to a supposedly more natural environment. Attracted by advertising inducements and personal recommendations, vacationers looked for places to recreate in nature. Warner's Forest Home Summer Resort and Ross' Teal Lake Lodge were among the many destinations in northern Wisconsin. The Ruttger family and others provided for vacationers in Minnesota's Brainerd Lakes area, where nearly three hundred resorts marked it as "Va-Ka-Shun Land" in 1929.[7] Roy Dunn's resort in Pelican Rapids attracted a range of guests and employees, while the Gunflint Trail and boundary waters catered to those seeking a wilderness environment. Places like Blaney Park, Keweenaw Mountain Lodge, and Phil DeGraff's Birchwood offered relaxation in Michigan's Upper Peninsula. But resorts and lodges were only one element of the lodging landscape. By the 1930s, housekeeping cabin operations like Bert's Cabins and Pine Woods Log Cabins offered travelers simple places to stop for a night or two. If they desired a longer vacation, cabins also provided an economical alternative, where guests cooked and cleaned themselves. Tourist camps, state parks, and state and national forests offered camping at minimal expense.

While vacations offered a release from daily toil, many residents helped craft the North Woods by entering the tourist businesses and promoting the region for others to enjoy their leisure. Labor at resorts, cabins, camps, and on Indian reservations made the North Woods experience possible, and thus spaces of leisure were also sites of labor. Examining the activities and motivations of tourist industry owner-operators, vacationers, and workers and then focusing on their interactions in particular North Woods locations like Wisconsin's Lac du Flambeau Indian Reservation, Michigan's Upper Peninsula and Isle Royale, and Minnesota's Arrowhead, this chapter reveals how such individuals contributed to a new tourist landscape that supplemented and ultimately replaced mining, logging, and agricultural landscapes and livelihoods of earlier years.

Crafting the Lodging Landscape

In the early 1880s Leonard Thomas opened the Lac Vieux Desert Summer Resort on Lac Vieux Desert, and Orrin Sayner followed with his place on Plum Lake a decade later, inaugurating northern Wisconsin's tourist era. Sayner began his business somewhat by chance when, while operating his father's farm in Eau Claire, he answered a Chicago newspaper advertisement seeking a guide to accompany a couple searching for a summer-home location. After working for them for two years, he settled on his own site. Three years later, the railroad located a station near his home, aiding his business, and named the station in honor of Sayner. In 1894, Herbert Warner began as a guide and handyman at Sayner's, and the experience

Automobiles at Ross' Teal Lake Lodge, Hayward, Wisconsin, 1930. COURTESY OF THE WISCONSIN HISTORICAL SOCIETY, WHS IMAGE ID 37953.

led him to establish Warner's Forest Home Resort on Plum Lake. Warner's catered to a professional clientele in its early years, changing its name in the 1920s to Herbert and Bert's Resort to reflect his son's involvement and to avoid vacationers confusing the resort with the Forest Home cemetery outside Chicago.[8] Farther west, Walter Ross established Pike Lake Resort near Fifield in 1915, selling his interest five years later and purchasing the Cornick Resort on Teal Lake about twenty miles east of Hayward in Sawyer County. The resort had a main lodge, three cabins, and an icehouse. Capturing the label that came to define the region, Teal Lake Lodge offered fishermen and families a "real vacation away from the cares of the business world and the rush of city life in an environment that embodies all the charm, rest, and recreation of the North woods."[9]

Aided by promotion, increased accessibility, and new infrastructure, the Highland Lake District around Minocqua and Eagle River in Vilas and Oneida Counties and the area surrounding Hayward in Sawyer and Washburn Counties developed as northern Wisconsin tourism centers. Many Oneida County resorts evolved from fishing camps that capitalized on the region's natural beauty. At the turn of the century, railroads brought vacationers from Milwaukee and Chicago with weekend excursion fares. After disembarking, anglers could visit Charles Bent's camp with a dozen log cabins on Lake Mamie. Others might call on Herman Pope and his wife at High Lake Lodge in Boulder Junction or John Mann's fishing resort in Manitowish Waters. Some who came to work in the lumber industry or in Michigan's and Minnesota's mines sensed an opportunity to enter the burgeoning tourist business. Moving from Canada to guide for another resort owner, John Oxley purchased five acres on Wolf Lake in Vilas County, built several cabins, and opened his resort.[10]

Arriving in northern Minnesota in 1886, Joseph Ruttger began working in the woods. He met his wife, Josephine, and settled on an island in Deer Lake. Hearing reports of good food and fishing at the Ruttgers, railroad travelers increasingly arrived to inspect their veracity. Originally, the Ruttgers pitched tents for people, but the enterprising family moved their four young sons out of the upstairs rooms in order to rent them out in summer. As business grew, the Ruttgers added cottages, where guests paid five dollars a week for bed, board, and boat, while contributing fish to the communal table. Joseph Ruttger had entered the tourist business.[11]

Wilson Dunn came to Minnesota by oxcart from Wisconsin in the 1880s, purchasing 160 acres of land north of Pelican Rapids that included over 2,500 feet of shoreline along Lake Lizzie. Hunters, fishermen, and families from Chicago and Des Moines camped along the lake, even rent-

Dunn's Resort, Lake Lizzie, Minnesota, circa 1940. COURTESY OF THE MINNESOTA HISTORICAL SOCIETY.

ing sleeping space in farm haylofts. In 1908, Wilson's son, Roy, began serving meals in a small cabin to guests staying in the Dunn home. Roy Dunn expanded the resort to include two dozen cabins along the lakeshore and a main lodge, built in 1929. Dunn's water-powered generator added light at night, attracting curious local farm families. Dunn served as postmaster and rose to majority leader in the Minnesota House while running the resort each summer. A 1930 brochure described Dunn's attractions: "A modern Summer hotel . . . the finest and best to be found . . . fishing as good as to be found anywhere in the state . . . good bathing beach with sand bottom . . . fresh produce from our own farm every day." Potential vacationers learned, "There Are No Dull Days At Dunn's!"[12]

Dunn and Ruttger were among the many tourist operators transforming northern Minnesota. Their activities, along with those of their guests, descendants, associates, and community members, helped create the North Woods. At the turn of the twentieth century, Fred Shadduck operated the Shadduck Family Resort, a six-cottage place in Alexandria, Minnesota, about 140 miles northwest of the Twin Cities outside the North Woods. He relied on word of mouth and picture postcards to attract guests. Half the resort's clientele arrived from the Twin Cities, generally staying two weeks. Others came from cities like Omaha, Lincoln, and Kansas City, often remaining for a month. Guests came to fish, paying local resident Cap Allen for information on the best spots. Room and board ran fourteen dollars per week, and guests enjoyed Shadduck's chickens. Early resort owners embraced a multitude of tasks to remain self-sufficient, including farming and raising livestock to feed guests. The Shadducks were no exception. Fred's son, Nobel, killed chickens and planted crops for the dining table. In January 1913, Fred built two cottages and wrote in his diary, "Minnesota's strength lies in its dairy, swine, cattle as beef and poulty [*sic*] products and lakes for summer tourist business." His vision included tourism alongside dairy and cattle farming. After selling the resort, Shadduck reported, "The last of the cottages gone and truly the end of the summer resort business for us after serving the public 20 years faithfully and successfully. The business more promising than ever now."[13] Providing for vacationers emerged as one of many activities residents undertook to make a living. Despite his decision to leave the tourist business, Shadduck believed it held great promise for Minnesota's future.

In Wisconsin, Herbert Warner established his family's homestead and resort on Vilas County's Plum Lake in the early 1900s. Typical of many North Woods resorts in terms of its rustic architecture, Forest Home's log lodge and cottages were situated along the shoreline. By 1917, four hundred resorts were spread across northern Wisconsin. William Adams operated the Sanborn, Lakota, and Adams resorts on Big Twin Lake in Conover, with a half mile of lakefront and a working dairy providing for guests. Daniel Cardinal worked as a guide and assisted his aunt and uncle, who operated Camp Franklin Lodge Resort north of Minocqua, before purchasing Manitowish Lodge in Manitowish Waters in 1916. Like Warner, Cardinal began by guiding and learning the region's lakes and woods. Olof Valley left his position as music chair at Kansas State Agricultural College, settling on Big St. Germain Lake and opening Normandy Court as a resort. Charles Hazen established Long Lake Lodge in Phelps in 1900, and by the early 1920s stayed open in winter for skiing, tobogganing, and snowshoeing. Milwaukee photo engraver Henry Voss opened Birchwood in Manitowish Waters in 1911 after visiting the area while on vacation. Voss was joined by another Milwaukeean, piano tuner Theodore Koerner, who established Spider Lake Lodge in Hayward in 1916.[14] Some Milwaukee investors purchased land on northern Wisconsin's unfortunately named Swamp Lake to build the Pines. W. H. Love moved to Chicago after operating the Peninsula Inn but returned to northern Wisconsin and acquired the Jaud Resort on Lac Vieux Desert after discovering city life was not for

North Woods charms abound on the rustic porch of Warner's Resort, Sayner, Wisconsin, before 1936. COURTESY OF THE WISCONSIN HISTORICAL SOCIETY, WHS IMAGE ID 37961.

him. Resort owners were an eclectic bunch drawn to the region not merely because of natural beauty but also by tourism and employment opportunities. Several organizations, including the Fish and Game Protective Association of Northern Wisconsin and the Resort Owners Association of the North Wisconsin Lake Region, assisted in putting northern Wisconsin on the tourist map and gathered this diverse array of operators who sought to earn a living through tourism. As landowners shifted from lumbering and farming to sustaining forests and building tourist accommodations, they brought a new order to the landscape.[15]

While the North Woods appealed to tourists before World War I, accessibility was limited and costly. Rail provided cities iron from Minnesota's Mesabi and Vermilion ranges, copper from Michigan's western UP, and lumber from Wisconsin's northern forests. But rail, and later roads, also offered tourist entrepreneurs connections to an urban market and helped Nelson Ross, Herbert Warner, the Ruttgers, and others establish operations. As Vernon Carstensen suggested of Wisconsin, in words that captured tourism's growing regional importance and connection to modern urban industrial life:

> From the beginning of the century, men concerned with the welfare of northern Wisconsin had been aware of the rising importance of vacationers, hunters, and fishermen in the economy of that lake strewn region. Railroad agents, hotel keepers, owners of boat liveries, and a host of others had cultivated the unabashed proclivity of Americans to seek recreation in such simple things as hunting, fishing, boating, and hiking, away from the cities they slaved to create.[16]

In 1923, seven hundred thousand tourists visited Wisconsin's resorts, auto camps, and vacation homes. Five years later, 180 resorts existed in Vilas County. In 1930, tourists spent $1,876,000 in the county. Despite the Depression, two hundred resorts, four thousand summer homes, and seventy-three camps or clubs in Vilas and Oneida Counties existed by 1932.[17] Resorts, lodges, and tourist camps provided jobs for local residents, and commercial centers developed to serve residents and tourists. Together, they transformed the region into a place where people worked and played outdoors.

As consumers, tourists ventured north to enjoy fishing, hunting, swimming, and a change of scene. One measure of those interested in the North Woods exists in *Chicago Tribune* and *Chicago Daily News* travel and resort bureau bulletins listing people who inquired about Wisconsin vacations. In the early 1920s, growing numbers asked about lakefront resorts and land for summer homes or investment. Others, like E. F. Samuelson of Chicago, wanted a cottage in the wilderness. The Hoplas family from Minneapolis previously rented a cottage in Minnesota and hoped to find similar affordable accommodations in Wisconsin. No longer merely focused on the well-to-do hunter or angler, northern Wisconsin operators catered to a growing clientele of middle-class families and others seeking respite in nature.[18]

Warner's Resort originally catered to those who could afford time off from work, but increasingly attracted families. In the early years, trains made a brief escape from the city possible, while others opted to spend the summer. J. C. Harding arrived on the fishermen's special, while his family came a week later for the season. After hearing about Warner's from a friend, Chicago's H. Ware Caldwell wanted "a quiet home like place on some lake in the woods of northern Wisconsin" for himself and his wife. Assuming a full resort, Caldwell hoped to pitch a tent on the Warner's land and take meals in the lodge. The Warners gladly agreed to this request. They also tended to people's cottages and provided services when owners rented to friends and associates. In return, many local cottage owners enjoyed meals at the resort.[19]

The nature-themed lobby at Warner's Resort before 1936. COURTESY OF THE WISCONSIN HISTORICAL SOCIETY, WHS IMAGE ID 37962.

Automobile access, lodging improvements, and the desire to escape cities during summer contributed to the rising number of North Woods vacationers. During the 1920s, improved roads and affordable vehicles made travel easier, creating a need for formal camping areas to prevent indiscriminate roadside camping. Motor camping evolved in stages, from squatting on private land to free municipal camps and finally to pay camps operated by individuals and municipalities offering a place for the night. Wisconsin's Conservation Commission assured tourists that no matter one's budget, a range of lodging options existed.[20] With over three hundred thousand tourists visiting Minnesota in 1921, the *St. Paul Pioneer Press* reported on an expected "Record Tourist Influx" for 1922, while the Ten Thousand Lakes of Minnesota Association claimed, "Even the smallest hamlet has realized the extent of the tourist business and has provided suitable camping grounds."[21] Resort operators expressed delight with increased traffic and the potential for attracting a broad vacationing public. Minnesota's Camp Van Vac reported 1,015 guests in 1929, a 23 percent increase from 1928, and appealed to the "great middle class who want good accommodations at reasonable prices."[22]

On the Gunflint Trail, the Gapen family at Gateway Lodge welcomed eighteen hundred guests and claimed, "This part of the Arrowhead is in its infancy, so far as the tourist trade is concerned, and with the proper treatment, this country will probably develop into the greatest recreation spot in the Middle West." Despite the Depression, the Gapens and other Gunflint operators built new cabins and increased promotion to compete with other destinations.[23] Resort owners believed their presence at Chicago's outdoor shows helped garner business from Illinois, citing figures that 65 percent of the region's fish shipments went there. Tourist cabins and camps were also busier. Englin's Comfort Cove Cozy Cottages attracted hundreds more patrons in 1930 than the previous year. At Burley Park in Ely, fewer people visited, but the business earned more due to lengthier stays. At Ely's tourist camp, 70 percent of 1933 registrations came from Minnesota. By 1937, in-state registrations comprised only 55 percent of the total.[24]

Many North Woods visitors, including those at Dunn's Resort, articulated their vacation expectations. Helen Beebe of Minneapolis, who worked for Dayton's department store for fifteen years, wrote Roy Dunn that she was "in need of real rest" and wanted to escape to the outdoors, explaining, "I am cooped up in a room the year round and when I am on vacation I want a change." Other guests had different motives, including

Municipal tourist camps offered vacationers reasonable accommodations during the 1930s. These children enjoy the tourist park in Ely, Minnesota, circa 1935. COURTESY OF THE MINNESOTA HISTORICAL SOCIETY.

college fraternities using Dunn's for social functions and fishermen looking to catch walleye. Still others viewed the resort as a place for family vacations. Philip Haser of Chicago reported that he and his family enjoyed a wonderful vacation, commending "the 'home-like' atmosphere that Mr. and Mrs. Roy Dunn and daughter Virginia and the rest of you good people created for us." Rev. Hugo J. Bredehoeft from southern Illinois followed a friend's advice to visit, and Norma Brown, whose temperance movement work brought her to the area, vacationed at Dunn's. Leslie Setzer, an employee at St. Paul's West Publishing Co., inquired about accommodations and a ride from the Detroit Lakes train station for her and a friend. While Dunn's clearly attracted people able to afford the twenty-eight dollars per week for the inclusive American plan in 1938, guests came as individuals, families, and groups seeking refreshment and entertainment among Minnesota's northern lakes and woods.[25]

Farther north, vacationers arrived in the "Playground of the Nation" to canoe in the Superior National Forest. Burntside Lake offered a "Camper's Paradise," where people discovered campsites "away from the cares and worries of business, and the congested centers of city and town." The Ely Commercial Club recommended outfitters and guides for canoe trips, while resorts on Lake Vermilion provided a map showing their location. But who were commercial clubs and resort owners trying to attract? One type of client was clear: "the tired business man who must periodically get away from the rush and noise of the city and build up a run down and worn out body."[26] Sure, the tired businessman was a potential client. But as guest lists, letter writers, tourist bulletins, and registers suggest, so were sportsmen, single women, families, and college students.

Resorts explored many avenues to reach these vacationers. Like many operators, Roy Dunn contracted with the nation's largest producer of view postcards, Chicago's Curt Teich and Co., to create ten different cards for his resort. Dunn also worked with state officials, sending the tourist commissioner folders to distribute to potential vacationers. Dunn hoped his position in the legislature would help attract government business, writing state printer George Etzell, "We are very anxious to increase our patronage among those who are in the service of the state."[27] Newspapers provided another means to reach new guests. Ed Shave of the *Minneapolis Star-Journal and Tribune* and former head of the Minnesota Tourist Bureau asked the Pelican Rapids Commercial Club for "a little more fishing news from your territory." When he told the club to "please grab that telephone about twice a week—call a few of the resorts—and send the data, so that I can use it in my daily column," the club quickly passed word on to local resort owners.[28] Shave's columns drew on this information to help lure people north. While city papers requested brochures for their tourist information booths, small-town publishers and editors wrote about exchanging a vacation stay for advertising. *Cedar Rapids Tribune*'s publisher tried to work such a deal with Dunn. When Dunn refused, the publisher claimed his plans changed and he could not visit. *Westmoreland (Kansas) Recorder*'s publisher wanted to exchange an ad for a week's cabin rental, to which Dunn responded he would accept half in cash and half in advertising, and would only provide the cabin in June or September. Dunn recognized advertising's importance but was unwilling to exchange a free stay unless he felt the piece would attract more guests from a particular area.[29]

While resorts and lodges offered opportunities for entrepreneurs and places for tourists to stay, some people reshaped communities and increased the tax base by purchasing summer cottages after vacationing in the region. During the 1910s, the U.S. Forest Service platted Minnesota's Star Island in the Chippewa National Forest and opened it to private development, attracting lakeside cottage owners hoping to escape summer heat elsewhere. Star Island's summer residents adopted a recreational vision free from regular work obligations. Winworth Williams, a Minneapolis high school teacher who purchased a fishing cottage, commented on the island's social divisions reflected in a landscape where "plutocrats lived on the south shore, the intelligentsia on the east shore, and the common folks on the west shore." The south shore with its concrete sidewalk along the beach had a resort-like atmosphere, attracting business people from the northern Plains. The west shore was more rustic, with no beach and swimmers diving off docks, while the east shore attracted professors and doctors. Summer residents brought with them the social markers of their place in urban society, creating a hierarchical structure in this vacation community. But residents also cooperated, establishing the Star Island Protective League in 1916 to encourage the government to establish ranger, telephone, and dock service for better fire protection. Two decades later they began publishing the *Loon*, a newsletter that helped connect the community. Despite constructing cottages on the island, which ultimately limited wider public use, residents claimed national forests were public playgrounds and worked with the Forest Service to limit timber harvests and preserve Star Island's forest.[30]

Star Island summer visitors also developed relationships with local residents who capitalized on the tourist trade by establishing the Cass Lake Commercial Club in 1910. Resident Mathias Koll's Minnesota Scenic Highway Association promoted tourism, and other residents found work in the new industry. Des Moines attorney A. J. Starr worked with a local concern, Lydick Mercantile, to build a summer cottage on Star Island. Far from luxurious, it was a haven in the woods for this professional man and his family. Between 1909 and 1918, Cass Lake residents helped build Star Island cottages, increasing the number from four to thirty-six, and annual leases from the Forest Service rose from five to fifteen dollars. The

The U.S. Forest Service permitted cottage development on certain lands. This is the Conklin family summer home on Star Island, Chippewa National Forest, 1932. FOREST SERVICE, U.S. DEPARTMENT OF AGRICULTURE, EASTERN REGION PHOTOGRAPH COURTESY OF THE FOREST HISTORY SOCIETY, DURHAM, NORTH CAROLINA, USFS NEGATIVE 264323.

island also had one summer resort by 1926. With assistance from local residents and government, Star Island cottagers established a vacation community.[31] In 1932, the Cass Lake Commercial Club promoted twenty-four area resorts in the "Permanent Home of the Pine." By 1941, Cass Lake advertised itself as the center of the forest, suggesting that "Cass Lake and the Chippewa National Forest is the region where summer living is best." Visitors could stay in developed forest campgrounds or choose among 360 area resorts. The Forest Service continued issuing permits for summer homes, resorts, and camps. Agency recreation initiatives increased local work opportunities by generating expenditures on food, lodging, souvenirs, boat rentals, and other services.[32]

Summer cottage construction also spread beyond the Star Island–Cass Lake area. Resorts were sometimes converted into summer homes, as happened to Wisconsin's Birches, which Philip Goelz sold to W. P. Saug of Chicago.[33] In 1925, *Land of Lakes Magazine* reported on growing demand for summer-home property in Wisconsin's Vilas, Oneida, and Sawyer Counties, and state land inventories reported extensive summer-home and hotel development along northern lakes during the 1920s and 1930s. In Sawyer County near Hayward, local realtor Wise Brothers found little success selling farmland and began specializing in lakefront lots, transforming the landscape by developing property for cottage owners. After the opening of a Chicago office in the mid-1920s, sales boomed. Recreational development also created opportunities for lumber and paper companies marketing land to summer-home owners and resort operators.[34]

Technology influenced social practices. In particular, transportation contributed to the development of new lodging options and experiences. Resorts initially counted on trains to deliver guests. Three weekly trains serviced Sayner, Wisconsin, in 1919. For railroads, this was the end of the line, as cars transformed the lodging landscape. In the 1920s, guests increasingly inquired about parking cars during their stay. Tourists could also easily visit multiple locations, creating opportunities for housekeeping cabin businesses where guests cooked their own meals and traveled to lakes to fish. Better roads and public access made it easier for cabin businesses to succeed away from water. Housekeeping cabin operations developed under diverse circumstances, but all benefited from the automobile's proliferation. After fire destroyed Cleo and Ernie Luedtke's resort in 1923, they built cabins for automobile vacationers searching for affordable accommodations. Others saw similar opportunity. Clifford Keith opened Keith's Cliff in 1920, and Harold Weaver erected cabins in the early 1920s on Pelican Lake land owned by his parents. Unlike many resorts that included room, board, and daily cleaning service, housekeeping cabins rented for a weekly or daily rate, and only covered lodging. Responding to growing competition and a desire for affordable accommodations, some former American plan resorts began offering cottages where visitors could cook for themselves.[35]

Like many who participated in constructing the tourist landscape, Bert Pfeifer entered the housekeeping cabin business when he found himself living in an area drawing tourists. Born in North Dakota in 1915, Pfeifer came to work and stay with his great-uncle, who owned a store near Minnesota's Itasca State Park. After marrying in 1939, Pfeifer purchased housekeeping cabins, recalling, "No reservations. Most of them just come off the road and were just touring and looking for a place to stay." Cabin owners valued highway over lake access to attract visitors. Unlike at lodges and resorts, Pfeifer's guests usually stayed a night or two and included farmers looking to fish and enjoy the state park, as well as midwestern folks who "had a little bit . . . so that they could travel some." Pfeifer added new cabins with running water and electricity and advertised through the local resort association in Park Rapids. To make ends meet during slack times, he worked other jobs while his wife operated the cabins.[36]

Gunflint Trail entrance sign, May 11, 1939. LOCAL IDENTIFIER USFS NEGATIVE 380086, RECORDS OF THE FOREST SERVICE, RECORD GROUP 95, THE NATIONAL ARCHIVES AT CHICAGO.

While Pfeifer entered the tourist business after witnessing visitors in the area, others came north during the interwar years with clear intentions, including Jack Stedman's parents, who operated Pine Woods Overnite Log Cabins near Brainerd. Stedman lived in Rochester, Minnesota, through ninth grade with his nurse mother and mechanic father. The family traveled to Brainerd after a friend mentioned a cabin business was for sale, finalizing a deal for forty acres with twelve cabins and a store "in the Heart of the Lake Resort Region." To provide a safety net if things went sour, the Stedmans rented their home in Rochester. Pine Woods had electricity when they bought it in 1938, and they added indoor bathrooms in the 1940s, making it truly "modern." Pine Woods advertised through the local chamber of commerce and posted road signs. One of few cabin businesses in the Brainerd area before the war, it offered privacy and reasonable rates. A single cabin at Pine Woods originally rented for $2.50 per night, and a double for $3.50. Clientele included families, salespeople, and university students. Most business was short-term, but the Stedmans encouraged longer stays by offering the last night free if people stayed a week, hoping to lessen their work attracting new customers and cleaning cabins. While location and facilities often differed from those of resorts, sometimes activities did too. Cabin businesses occasionally served as dens of iniquity for the "hot pillow trade." In other North Woods locations, some visitors were even more notorious. J. Edgar Hoover suggested cabin businesses offered hiding places for criminals, drawing on his efforts tracking members of the Chicago underworld, including Al Capone and John Dillinger, to their vacation hideaways in northern Wisconsin. In addition to regular vacationers, the North Woods also offered FBI public enemies a place of comfort, relaxation, and escape from the long arm of the law.[37]

Places like Pine Woods received repeat business but at a far lower rate than larger resorts. One school supply saleswoman made the cabin her home for several years. Other long-term residents included people building cottages and resorts on lakes who needed a place to stay during construction. Cabins often filled up on weekends and also attracted salespeople early in the week. Stedman recalled, "We had the 'No vacancy' sign, you know. We were always thrilled when we could put that out, because that meant good money tonight." It allowed for a quiet evening and less worry about renting out that last cabin. While the Stedmans attracted many vacationers, they also relied on business travelers to boost occupancy. With gasoline rationing limiting travel during the war, Stedman's parents worked in Brainerd but did not close the cabins. Since money was tight, the family handled all upkeep. While resorts were generally located on lakes, Pine Woods' inland forest location appealed to those who sought cooler temperatures and cheaper lodging.[38] Unlike resorts where guests often communicated with the owner beforehand about their stay, people

Tourists at Sawbill Lake Campground, Superior National Forest, July 14, 1936. LOCAL IDENTIFIER USFS NEGATIVE 326799, RECORDS OF THE FOREST SERVICE, RECORD GROUP 95, THE NATIONAL ARCHIVES AT CHICAGO.

regularly stopped in at cabins unannounced. As vacation and business travel via automobile increased, housekeeping cabins offered visitors flexibility. Along with campgrounds, resorts, lodges, and summer homes, they emerged as an important part of the North Woods' built environment.

Toiling for Leisure

While new accommodations altered the built landscape and vacation experience, tourism also changed employment and trade through hiring, purchasing, and people entering the industry. Many resorts, including Shadduck's and Warner's, had farms providing foodstuffs and relied on local businesses for supplies but turned to larger cities for items unavailable locally. Building on these connections, the Warners contracted with a Milwaukee labor agent to find a baker and looked to the state's employment bureau for a cook. Individuals contacted private businesses and public agencies to find work at destinations needing caretakers, housekeepers, servers, cooks, guides, handymen, and gardeners.[39]

Dunn's Resort provided employment for residents seeking summer work. Those with previous experience at Dunn's received favorable consideration for open positions. Many employees were local women, and teachers, principals, and students inquired as well. Women generally cleaned, cooked, and waited tables, while men served as guides and handymen. In 1937, sisters Ida and Ada Mellum of nearby Pelican Rapids wanted dining room work. Potential employees portrayed themselves as responsible adults. Dunn was impressed with local resident Virginia Korteum because of her food service experience. Inquiries also arrived from those wishing to spend summers in the area. The Spinners of Grand Forks, North Dakota, sought bartending and server work. School principal Albert Farnham inquired about summer employment for him and his wife and planned to bring their children. Others, like Margo Cairns of Minneapolis, were told to inquire at larger resorts, like Ruttger's Bay Lake or Pine Beach Lodge. Dunn turned away many applications, writing one job seeker in 1938, "The season has been such a disappointment from the financial angle that we have found it necessary to reduce our help to a minimum." Resort owners could not always find qualified candidates, leading Dunn to turn to the U.S. Department of Labor employment referral service for someone with gardening and landscaping skills. By 1945, with war forcing resort closures, potential employees turned to the State Tourist Bureau to see if resorts were hiring. Teacher Alice Gerold wrote Dunn after receiv-

Guiding provided work for many local residents, including Marie Sarkipate, an eighteen-year-old guide in Ely, Minnesota, circa 1938. PHOTOGRAPH BY AUBIN PHOTO SERVICE. COURTESY OF THE MINNESOTA HISTORICAL SOCIETY.

ing no response from the state. But Dunn, unsure about business after closing for two summers during the war, believed only a few employees would be necessary when reopening.[40]

Some tourist workers found employment by chance, while others expressed a desire to work at northern resorts and experience natural surroundings. Born in 1920, Ruby Treloar and her family farmed in neighboring Aitkin County just five miles from Ruttger's Bay Lake Lodge. She recalled that when she was a young girl, the "Ruttger's name was always something real high-class and over and above all us farm people." This did not stop local residents from working summers at the resort given the pay and opportunity to meet new people. Initially, Treloar had little intention of working there. She wed in 1939, spent a year in Hinckley, Minnesota, and another in New York City before returning home in 1941. When Alec Ruttger went looking for local help, he persuaded Treloar to work for his family. She first worked at his brother Max's Pine Beach Lodge, but the following year returned to Bay Lake Lodge to lead the dining room staff and remained there for over fifty summers.[41]

Across the North Woods, local entrepreneurs also aided recruitment. D. C. Menefee, editor of the *Vilas County News*, printer, and resort promoter through his Ask Mr. Menefee Bureau, wrote the Warners with a list of people who applied for employment. George Vrooman of Toledo, Ohio, and Gaither Herring of Evanston, Illinois, expressed their desire to work outdoors for health reasons. Some expressed displeasure with work at other area resorts and hoped for a better position at Warner's. Looking for a new labor source in a growing industry, W. J. Minch of Minocqua's Birchwood Pines Resort wrote the Warners about hiring boys from an orphanage and suggested they were industrious workers.[42]

At Teal Lake Lodge, many job seekers were turned away because positions were filled or unnecessary. Others, like Paul Quayle, caretaker for Teal Lake's previous owners, worked and lived at the resort much of their life. Walter Ross also looked to his son, Nelson, who managed a Madison radio station in the late 1930s and 1940s, to recruit employees and guests. Nelson promoted the resort in Madison and Chicago, opening the door to hiring students for summers. While vacationing in Chicago in 1937, Nelson encouraged his parents to advertise family vacations and food along with wonderful fishing, writing, "We *have* to start building up a vacation business and not a fishing camp with other attractions." Ultimately, he rejoined his family at Teal Lake after the war and helped run the resort.[43]

Resort owners hired people to handle many aspects of resort opera-

Ruttger's Resort on Bay Lake near Deerwood, Minnesota, circa 1911. COURTESY OF THE MINNESOTA HISTORICAL SOCIETY.

tion but spent much of their time working to please vacationing guests and to build the business. While the Warner and Ross families worked in Wisconsin's tourist industry before World War I, many others, including William Drewry and the Blaesing family, joined them after the war. Purchasing land from the Thunder Lake Lumber Company in 1928, Drewry built cabins for Drewry Lane Cottages with material found on-site. His experience is typical in that lumber companies often sold land to potential resort owners, and many operators, often with assistance from residents, undertook the manual labor to build their facilities. For Drewry, building the resort meant physically constructing the place and subsequently providing for guests.[44] Originally drawn to northern Wisconsin by agricultural opportunities, George and Hazel Blaesing purchased land intending to farm it. George quickly realized the land's unsuitability for agriculture and built a resort, Shorewood Vista, in 1926. The resort's lodge, four rooms, and one two-bedroom cottage served guests, who were supplied a chamber pot, pitcher, washbowl, linens, and towels. With Hazel managing the kitchen and George tending to other resort operations, they made $635 in their first year. Shorewood Vista's first guests came from Milwaukee, St. Louis, and Chicago, and many stayed for a month, suggesting their employment or financial status afforded them extended vacation time. The Blaesings' first brochure boasted of the lodge's amenities, including a fireplace, dining hall, and Sunday chicken dinners. Guests were reminded, "Virgin pines, birch, and oak trees surround the place in abundance, making it a place of health and haven for hay fever and asthma suffers. For a real thrill in fishing, Lake George holds in its waters, the terror-fighting Muskellunge, Wall-Eyed Pike, Pickerel and Black Bass." At Shorewood Vista, the Blaesings and their employees provided guests a North Woods experience.[45]

Many who lived and worked in the region recognized tourist opportunities while engaged in other enterprises. Norman Johnson turned his trading post at Laona, Wisconsin, into a resort during the summer, capitalizing on increased tourist traffic. Johnson recalled how city residents "could come up there and stay with me for $2.00 a day for their board and they couldn't live for that down in the cities." In 1923, Jennie Neubauer and her husband arrived in northern Wisconsin intending to relax at their recently completed cabin. They realized a business opportunity, establishing a food stand and building cabins to create Oxbo Resort. Guests arrived from across Wisconsin and Chicago, paying fifteen dollars for four days.[46]

Most North Woods resorts operated as family businesses, and some, like the Warners, Rosses, and Ruttgers, continued their enterprises across generations. At Lac Vieux Desert Summer Resort, Louis Thomas assumed operations from his father, Leonard, and enhanced capacity for the upcoming 1920 season to house growing numbers heading north on vacation.[47]

Lodging operators provided the physical location for building a community around a North Woods promotional dialogue that focused on scenery, nature, health, comfort, affordability, congeniality, and family. In the process, they took on a variety of tasks to aid visitors, employees, and residents. *Teal Lake Tidings*, the resort newsletter first published by the Rosses in 1930, provides a window into the life of proprietors and guests. It helped the Rosses create a sense of community. Family and fishing emerged as key themes, reinforced by reports on fish catches and reminders of pleasant times up north. Newsletters sparked memories of past summers and allowed people to stay abreast of new activities. For instance, the Rosses used the publication to encourage fall visits, when fishing was better and autumn colors aglow. Expanding the vacation season was important eco-

Fishing was a major lure for North Woods resorts and lodges. Virginia Hess poses with a muskellunge near the fish scale at Ross' Teal Lake Lodge, circa 1950. COURTESY OF THE WISCONSIN HISTORICAL SOCIETY, WHS IMAGE ID 37957.

nomically, and the newsletter portrayed autumn as a beautiful time at Teal Lake. In the early 1930s, the Rosses added modern cabins, bathrooms, and tennis courts, and Walter Ross promoted the lodge at Chicago outdoor shows during the off-season. When the 1933 Century of Progress Exposition threatened to draw people away from Teal Lake, *Tidings* reminded them that you could not catch muskies in Chicago.[48]

For the Rosses, the purpose of *Teal Lake Tidings* was not formal advertising but instead "to keep our friends informed of what is going on up here in the woods." *Tidings* invited people to become part of the lodge community through shared stories and events. Imagine receiving it in January while toiling away in a Chicago or Twin Cities winter. Not only did it bring back memories, but it also served as a reminder to plan your summer vacation. With the slogan "To Recall Memories of Happy Vacation Days," *Tidings* contributed to a sense of camaraderie among guests by providing information about the resort, allowing guests to reminisce about good times, and encouraging repeat visitors.[49]

Tidings also captured the difficulties of operating a resort during wartime, when the Rosses faced food, gas, and tire rationing along with labor scarcity. Their experience operating Pike Lake Lodge in Fifield during World War I prepared them well. Pointing to the advantages of a wartime Teal Lake vacation, they stressed rail access as a way to deal with rationing. Wartime also heightened the need for people to recharge; as the Rosses suggested, "Vacations are necessary to build morale and to put you in trim for the long tough battle ahead. It is patriotic to go fishing and get your health ready for the job ahead." There might be a shortage of guides during the war, but a restorative leisure experience could still be had at Teal Lake Lodge.[50] The Rosses were not alone in promoting vacations as patriotic. The Boulder Junction Chamber of Commerce suggested vacations kept people fit for wartime service and encouraged them to "Buy Bonds First then Vacation in Boulder Junction." Minnesota's State Tourist Bureau director stressed to the state's twenty-five hundred resort owners that "vacations were important to the morale and physical fitness of all Americans."[51] In their first postwar newsletter, the Rosses expressed gratitude to those who came despite limits on service, food, and labor. While wartime was not easy for Teal Lake Lodge, the work the Rosses put into developing the resort and attracting a regular clientele paid off handsomely when postwar patronage increased. Their efforts, along with those in places like Wisconsin's Lac du Flambeau Reservation, the Upper Peninsula's Copper Country and Isle Royale, and Minnesota's

Arrowhead, reflect the varied yet connected experiences of North Woods tourist operators, workers, and vacationers during the interwar years.[52]

Remaking the Reservation

Waiting at the Chicago and Northwestern Railroad terminus at Lac du Flambeau, Benedict Gauthier stood among the crowd of early-twentieth-century tourist operators ready to transport visitors to their resorts, lodges, and fishing camps. Opened in 1891, Hotel Gauthier was the first lodging establishment on the Lac du Flambeau Reservation. Many of Gauthier's initial guests arrived on logging industry business. When the local sawmill closed in 1913, Gauthier converted the hotel into a resort with nineteen rooms and ten cottages catering to vacationers. Room and board ran fourteen dollars per week, rowboat rentals were fifty cents a day, guides cost five dollars, while a quarter purchased a ride to and from the resort along with the boxing and icing of one's catch. Visitors could pick up items at the resort's general store. The Gauthiers had clearly entered the tourist business. Bureau of Indian Affairs (BIA) officials remarked of Benedict and his wife, "Their resort brings many tourists here, thereby making work for guides. They keep all of their property in good shape and are a credit to Lac du Flambeau."[53]

The Gauthiers were not the only people on the reservation with tourist interests. During the interwar years, Ojibwe participated in an expanding consumer society by operating resorts and shops, guiding, hosting powwows, producing handicrafts, and selling lakefront lots. Visitors also stayed at lodges and resorts, such as Yeschek's Crawling Stone Lodge, operated by people who purchased land on the reservation. Many Lac du Flambeau Ojibwe had worked in the logging industry, but by the early 1900s, much of the timber was harvested. Poor soils and short seasons made agriculture problematic, so many looked to tourism, and BIA policies eventually encouraged such activities. Tourism did not employ as many people as lumbering in its heyday, but it did mix traditional and modern subsistence practices and fit within a regional tradition of seasonal work. At Lac du Flambeau, lakes and waterways offered bounty for fishing tourists and wage work for male Indian guides, while women produced beadwork, moccasins, and handicrafts to sell to tourists.[54]

Lac du Flambeau tourist development occurred within the context of political, environmental, and economic transformations following the decline of lumber that saw tribal members, BIA officials, private organizations, and state agencies debate land use, forestry, and labor initiatives. Tourism ran counter to national BIA efforts to transform Indians into farmers. Like many across the region, BIA officials initially looked to agriculture after the closing of Lac du Flambeau's mill but realized it offered only limited possibilities. In 1909, the BIA superintendent reported on land covered with brush, decayed logs, and stumps, making the area "an uninviting field for agricultural pursuits." Instead, forest regeneration, fisheries management, and Indian culture would serve as a basis for developing tourism on the reservation.[55]

Lac du Flambeau's forests were among the last to be cut in northern Wisconsin, but once the process started, it moved relatively swiftly. Reservation lands were opened to logging companies in 1886, but logging stopped between 1888 and 1892, restarting after an amendment to the Dawes Act allowed leasing and contract logging by non-Indians.[56] When the sawmill closed in 1913, the BIA superintendent feared Ojibwe would leave the reservation, and "those remaining will then have to depend more upon their farming operations, and such harvest of shekels as may be obtained from the summer tourist." Although an interesting choice of words on his part, the statement was reflective of an initially skeptical BIA view of tourism. The superintendent referred to tourists as a new crop that provided "the chief source of revenue of surrounding communities" and suggested policy aimed "to encourage the tourist business for benefit of the Indians." This included developing resorts, summer homes, and children's camps as well as building a fish hatchery. With logging all but gone, BIA officials hoped tourism would provide additional markets for produce, raise land values, and increase employment, growing beyond the "harvest of shekels" it had generated thus far.[57]

BIA officials at Lac du Flambeau encountered Ojibwe already involved in the tourist industry. In the early twentieth century, men often split time between logging camps, the mill, and guiding for Chicago and Milwaukee visitors who arrived on trains. The BIA viewed the reservation as rich in natural assets appealing to tourists—particularly lakes for fishing—and saw that permits offered an additional revenue source. The BIA also encouraged land sales and leases to parties interested in developing summer homes and resorts. While the BIA wanted tourists to visit the reservation, it did not promote vacations directly and instead relied on the work of local resort owner organizations.[58]

As resorts and organizations established facilities at Lac du Flambeau, employment opportunities increased. Ojibwa Lodge, a sportsmen's club on

Fence Lake, opened in 1914, and several Ojibwe guided and worked in the kitchen and laundry. Paul Geidel visited Lac du Flambeau with his wife in 1918 and purchased frontage on Flambeau Lake to build a summer home. With friends arriving nonstop from Chicago, the Geidels decided to make a business out of it, opening Kimrock Lodge. One guest even brought guide Charlie Poupart a motor to add to his collection of seven boats. Poupart's wife crafted moccasins and beadwork to sell to tourists, and his son Benjamin worked as a guide and at the fish hatchery.[59] Chicagoans Bill and Elsie Yeschek journeyed north in 1922, purchasing shoreline on Big Crawling Stone Lake and adding holdings throughout the decade. The Yeschecks subdivided some of the land, keeping a portion to build a twenty-two-room guest lodge and eleven cottages, which employed over thirty people as guides, maids, and kitchen staff. Guests drank, danced, and gambled into the evening and watched powwows on the lodge's lawn. Many also paid for the services of guide Jack St. Germain. Bill Yeschek was also involved in local politics, serving as Flambeau town chairman during the 1930s, lobbying for New Deal public works projects, and helping organize the Flambeau Taxpayer's Association, a lakeshore property owners group committed to tourism.[60]

Among those joining Yeschek in the 1922 purchase of reservation lands was a group of wealthy families from Winnetka, Illinois, who acquired ninety acres for a summer retreat. They spent their first summer at Ben Gauthier's resort while the camp was built, drafting a cooperative ownership agreement and naming the place Camp Wipigaki, Ojibwe for Red at the Leaf. Within three years, additional land purchases increased the camp to five hundred acres. Families stayed in cabins and met for meals in the dining hall. Children enjoyed listening to stories about monster-sized muskies from Harry St. Germain and playing nickel slots at the Dew Drop Inn.[61]

These places illustrate tourism's increasing importance at Lac du Flambeau and the role residents and outsiders played in expanding the trade. Many Ojibwe made fishing with a guide central to the vacation experience. Visitors associated Indian guides with a certain mystique and intimate knowledge of the lakes. For guides, the experience offered pay for something they had done much of their life. As Michael Goc explains, "In the years between World Wars I and II, nearly every male Ojibwe at Flambeau did some guiding. The work started at 8:00 AM and included gathering and preparing tackle and bait, rowing and/or motoring the boat, preparing the shore lunch and cleaning the catch." A guide had to get along with his guests and show them a good time. Guide Nelson Sheppo remarked, "You had to be cordial, you had to be sensitive, you really had to understand people."[62] The opportunity to mix guiding with other labor attracted many Lac du Flambeau men. World War I veteran Joe St. Germain became a successful guide after the war. William Chapman worked as a handyman and guide for a summer resident on Pokegama Lake. Entire families also explored tourism opportunities. Joe Martin was a guide, musician, and resort laborer, while his wife worked winters in Chicago and summers at a local resort. Robert Chapman guided and Edward Christenson worked at Arbutus Lodge, and their wives cleaned laundry for tourists.[63]

Others entered the burgeoning tourist industry in different ways. Henry Guyette and his wife, Nettie Fellows, purchased the old post office and established a store, rented rooms, provided meals, and sold handicrafts, leading the BIA to suggest they were a "very enterprising couple." Sisters Bessie and Sarah Stone rented their home to summer tourists from Milwaukee. Fred LaCass guided and labored at Freyburg's Resort. At their house on Crooked Lake, LaCass and his wife had three acres of potatoes that could be sold to neighboring resorts. Through his work and land cultivation, LaCass found himself enmeshed in the tourist trade.[64]

While many on the reservation continued guiding and working in the tourist industry during the Depression, the Indian Emergency Conservation Work (IECW) program brought federal relief work to Lac du Flambeau and aided tourism. Project workers completed bridges, trails, and a new fish hatchery.[65] Elder Ben Chosa recalled how guiding helped the community fare better than others and claimed that while times were difficult, "I don't remember missing a meal." Chosa's comments reflect how mixing traditional subsistence practices with modern business enterprise helped Lac du Flambeau Ojibwe weather the Depression's storm. Even during lean years, vacationers arrived ready to hire a guide's services. Guides generally could make more than the twenty-one dollars per month plus room and board offered in the CCC–Indian Division camp.[66]

Women also discovered new opportunities in the tourist industry. Tourists attended powwows, where Indians performed and sold handicrafts, offering opportunities for individuals like Wanda Brown Hunt. She and her sister worked as ticket takers. Others entertained children at local summer camps. Agnes Archdale's and Liza Brown's parents were lodge caretakers, and the girls looked after visiting children and cooked at the lodge. Georgian Kinstedt cleaned cottages and worked in resort kitch-

An Ojibwe man in a boxing ring dances for spectators, circa 1938. COURTESY OF THE WISCONSIN HISTORICAL SOCIETY, WHS IMAGE ID 73335.

ens during summers, while Delia Smith and Grace Artishon cooked for a summer family.[67] Tourism offered a variety of opportunities for residents of Lac du Flambeau, leading Ben Guthrie, William Yeschek, and Tribal Council president George Brown to call for making the reservation "the greatest recreational center of our state."[68]

Much had been done during the interwar years to move in this direction. In the 1920s, a new BIA superintendent remarked that this "is not what you would call an agricultural country," describing the cutover lands and small garden plots where Indians raised vegetables and extension specialists worked to improve paltry yields. Many residents also gathered wild berries, which they ate and sold to tourists. It was in this context that the BIA undertook a survey of Indian industry at Lac du Flambeau in 1922, revealing tourism's growing impact on people's daily lives and the landscape.[69] The BIA incorporated domestic agriculture and tourist work into its evaluation of "industriousness." John Patterson Jr. received commendation for being "one of the best farmers on the Reservation," having cleared forty acres and raised two dozen chickens. Joseph Corn cleared thirteen acres and spent time farming, trapping, hunting, and fishing, while his wife produced handicrafts and snowshoes. Rising Sun cleared six acres for planting. His wife did laundry at a local resort and picked and canned wild berries. Through these and other cases, the survey reflected how BIA officials viewed the mixing of traditional and modern practices among Lac du Flambeau Ojibwe, revealing people's ability to work the land and serve tourists while assuming other tasks to support the family, including women's efforts gathering foods and keeping the home.[70]

In April 1922, the BIA superintendent reported that tourists paid guides seven dollars per day and purchased native handiwork, making it "doubly hard to interest our Indians in agricultural pursuits," especially given a short growing season.[71] Fishing permit funds, which amounted to $1,400 in 1921, maintained the fish hatchery. Many Indian men worked as guides, while others built summer homes for tourists and improved roads. Women and men found work at area resorts. Although tourism brought in money, the BIA felt there was room to improve conditions for vacationers. When a woman approached the BIA to establish a campsite at a beach, officials hoped such efforts would encourage more Ojibwe to make conditions "more sanitary and agreeable for tourists."[72]

Non-Indians also increasingly developed tourist lodging on reservation lands. The 1922 survey coincided with substantial land sales on the reservation, which saw Ojibwe like Charles Gauthier join government officials in preparing land assessments. These assessments, along with the log of allotment land sales, reflect the economic and political realities as well as the individual lives involved in transforming a barren landscape into one attracting tourists. Because of their tourist development prospects, lakefront lands held greater value than other locations. Willie Burgess Jr.'s sixty-six acres of sandy soil with a lakefront was typical. Valued at $1,320 because it provided a prime summer resort location, the land was purchased by the Yeschecks for $1,802 in November 1922, and they built Crawling Stone Lodge there. Some sales were Indian-to-Indian exchanges, but many brought outsiders interested in summer homes and resorts. By 1934, much of the reservation's lake frontage had been acquired by non-Indians. BIA land policies and individual Indian decisions to sell land clearly changed Lac du Flambeau.[73]

While tourism provided profits for some residents, such benefits often hid the broader impact it had on the people and land of Lac du Flambeau.

During the interwar years, Lac du Flambeau's forests and lakes became embedded in a consumer society in which their products—trees, fish, and scenery—became marketable commodities to those seeking leisure. Tourists discovered a destination where they could stay at a rustic lodge, explore woods and over 260 lakes with an Indian guide, and return with a substantial catch on waters stocked by the BIA and the state. It was also a time in which the checkerboard pattern of land ownership on the reservation became reality. Tourism provided opportunities for Lac du Flambeau residents, but like many opportunities across the North Woods, they came with a particular price.[74]

Touring the Pleasant Peninsula

A bit farther from population centers than northern Wisconsin's Lac du Flambeau, Michigan's Upper Peninsula operators targeted vacationers interested in a unique experience and landscape. In 1912, the Chicago and Northwestern Railroad promoted the UP's vacation possibilities, suggesting its hotels and camps served sportsmen and proved "equally pleasant for those who merely seek rest and quiet." Michigan's Copper Country purportedly offered a "land of health and pure air; haven for the sick and weary, well and lazy; Mecca for the hay fever and asthma victim; and rendezvous for the best of those who enjoy the great outdoors."[75] Local residents and organizations worked to improve roads and accommodations to provide tourists a pleasant peninsula. As Michigan's first modern lumber town, Blaney helped rebuild Chicago after the 1871 fire by supplying white pine and provided lumber for other cities. Stewart Earle's Wisconsin Land and Lumber Company operated Blaney. With timber in decline, Earle briefly attempted cattle ranching before turning the property into a resort in 1926, offering family vacations in cabins scattered along wooded lakes. Activities included swimming, golf, tennis, and fishing, and the resort also had a game refuge and bird sanctuary. Blaney Park Resort reflected how tourism transformed the workforce and landscape, underscoring the relationship between tourism and earlier industry as well as the connections between UP industry and midwestern cities.[76]

Other residents joined Earle in responding to tourist demand in the wake of declining logging and mining. Phil DeGraff managed Marquette's Hotel Northland and opened his resort, Birchwood, at Trout Lake, attracting families and hunters while its farm provided food for meals. DeGraff informed potential vacationers, "Birchwood gives the exclusiveness of an expensive private club without the attendant high rates. You will find rates here are suited to the purse of the 'average man.'" The "average man" was lured north by the resort's rusticity and casual atmosphere. Formality was cast aside as guests used nicknames while conversing and eating together. Like many UP destinations, Birchwood attracted middle-class tourists searching for a home away from home.[77] On the Keweenaw Peninsula, Alice Mitchell converted an old mining company supply warehouse into Eagle Harbor's Lake Breeze Hotel. Increasing automobile traffic aided business. Chicagoan Austin Raley eventually assumed ownership, and by 1929 he reported vast increases in visitors. Guests enjoyed reasonable prices and cordial service along with fishing, Lake Superior views, and homemade meals. One telegrammed a friend about the "comfortable modern cabin," "cool bracing weather," excellent food, golf, and scenery. Vacationers discovered similar courtesy at tourist homes, housekeeping cabins, and state park campgrounds.[78] The *Development Bureau News* reported, "The day of the civic and private free campsite—entirely aside from the great public county and state parks—will soon pass forever. Our tourists demand more and better camping conveniences and accommodations and are willing to pay for them." By 1930, the UP welcomed nearly five hundred thousand summer visitors, who stayed at places like Blaney Park, Birchwood, and Lake Breeze.[79]

Lake Breeze Hotel, Eagle Harbor, Michigan, late 1920s. COURTESY OF THE MICHIGAN TECHNOLOGICAL UNIVERSITY ARCHIVES AND COPPER COUNTRY HISTORICAL COLLECTIONS.

Vacationers and tourist operators realized the UP differed from Wisconsin and Minnesota given their greater concentration of resorts and cottages. Chicagoan John Ogden proclaimed the Copper Country's Brockway Mountain Drive among the nation's most scenic but suggested surfacing improvements. Others came to fish Lake Superior's deep waters, including one visitor from Belleville, Illinois, whose catch was publicized in the local paper.[80] By 1938, visitors to Eagle Harbor could stay at a hotel, tourist homes, or housekeeping cabins. Driving between Eagle Harbor and Copper Harbor, they encountered scenic vistas, shipwrecks, and lighthouses while learning about the region's immigrant and mining heritage. The Copper Country drew on its industrial past in its tourist pitch. At the end of U.S. Highway 41 in Copper Harbor, vacationers discovered modern amenities and cheaper accommodations "in this as yet unspoiled historic landing place of early copper miners."[81] Tourists remained mobile, staying for a night or two and then moving to another location. To encourage longer stays once they reached Copper Harbor and the Keweenaw Mountain Lodge, one advocate urged developing six-bedroom cabins at the Keweenaw golf course, pointing to their success at Blaney Park and in northern Wisconsin. This suggestion responded to Depression-era realities that saw people split larger cottages among several families to reduce costs.[82]

By the mid-1930s, those initially doubtful of the Copper Country's tourist potential became convinced of its future. Much of this was due to the tireless efforts of Ocha Potter, who spent the 1930s working on tourist development as president of the Copper Country Vacationist League (CCVL), a group of merchants, resort owners, and mining company representatives, and as a superintendent with the Calumet and Hecla Mining Company. Potter assured the "average man" that a Copper Country vacation was possible and emphasized attracting vacationers interested in scenery and history as well as sportsmen.[83] Calumet and Hecla supported the CCVL and allowed some cottage construction on its lands at minimal cost during the interwar years. Employees and local residents purchased cottages, but outsiders also jumped at the offer.[84] One former UP resident, Adolph Isaacson, needed little to assure him of the region's tourist potential. After seeing a UP booth at the Chicago Outdoor Life show, he volunteered to promote the UP among Chicagoans. Houghton's Fred Nichols also wanted to expand people's knowledge and understanding of the Copper Country, remarking, "It is true that our copper mines are a great tourist attraction. But the world little knows what we have up here in the way of fine scenery."[85]

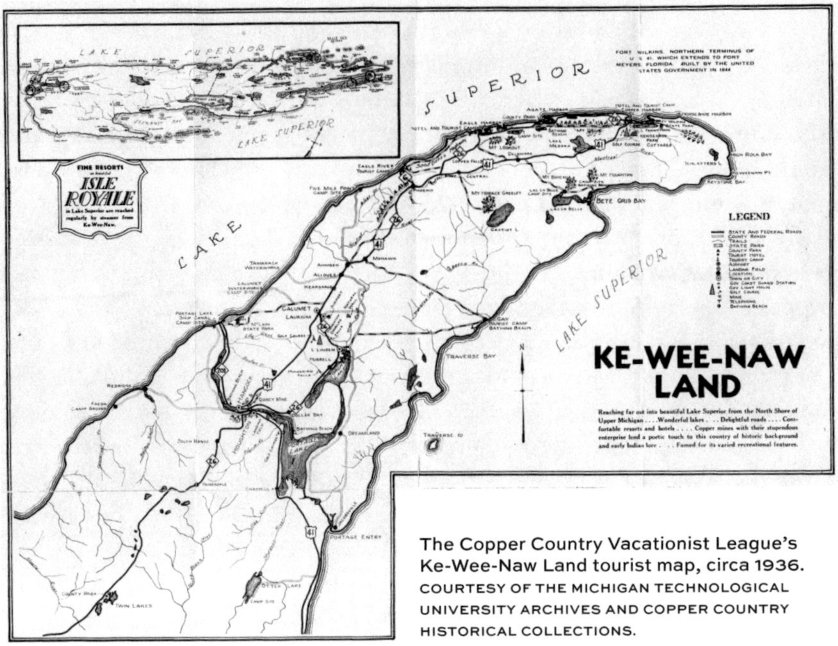

The Copper Country Vacationist League's Ke-Wee-Naw Land tourist map, circa 1936. COURTESY OF THE MICHIGAN TECHNOLOGICAL UNIVERSITY ARCHIVES AND COPPER COUNTRY HISTORICAL COLLECTIONS.

The CCVL also supported efforts to designate Lake Superior's Isle Royale a national park in the 1930s, hoping visitors would travel through the Copper Country before catching the ferry. They were encouraged to visit Eagle Harbor's Lake Breeze Hotel, an easy half-hour drive from Copper Harbor. When departing for Isle Royale on Kauppi's Cabin Cruiser, they could leave their car at the Pontiac Hotel or Keweenaw Cottages. The CCVL advertised a direct route from Chicago to be called the Isle Royale National Park Highway and responded to tourist demand for better lodging by promoting cabins at the Keweenaw golf course.[86] Speakers at the 1935 Upper Peninsula Development Bureau (UPDB) annual meeting, including outdoor writers Ben East and Arthur Stace, believed Isle Royale as a national park would benefit the entire North Woods. The following year, attendees discussed the need for better roads to draw visitors to what would be Michigan's only national park. According to the UPDB, vacationers would find Isle Royale an "island paradise, detached from all stresses and strains of city living" where "one gets complete relaxation, a new viewpoint and renewed zest." Much like the rest of the UP, Isle Royale purportedly offered a remote place detached from urban concerns.[87]

Isle Royale resorts had attracted guests for years and continued promoting a unique experience at an isolated Lake Superior outpost. At

Keweenaw tourism flyer, including sites from Houghton, Keweenaw, Ontonagon, and Baraga Counties, 1935. COURTESY OF THE MICHIGAN TECHNOLOGICAL UNIVERSITY ARCHIVES AND COPPER COUNTRY HISTORICAL COLLECTIONS.

Fred Schofield's Belle Isle Resort, vacationers could golf, fish, hike, scout moose, and hunt for stones. In 1936, Schofield wrote former guests regarding delays in publishing a new brochure. Hoping for new boat service to help increase patronage, he remarked, "We have made preparations to take care of a capacity crowd this year for we feel that the depression is practically over and there will be a general return of vacation travel." A bastion of contentment on rugged Isle Royale, Rock Harbor Lodge had "every comfort at moderate cost, and a very happy combination of living facilities combined with nature's most picturesque and primitive aspects." Managed by Bertha Farmer, who spent winters in Madison, Wisconsin, the lodge informed potential vacationers, "You Need a Rock Harbor Vacation This Year."[88]

Word of the Copper Country's efforts also spread across the UP. Escanaba's leaders viewed tourism as a replacement for lost jobs, claiming, "We can more profitably develop our community through the medium of the promotion of the tourist and travel industry than in the old orthodox factory-grabbing method."[89] Both Eagle Harbor and Copper Harbor, once shipping points for copper, transformed themselves into tourist destinations. WPA writers captured tourism's influence, discussing how residents converted mining structures into cottages and tourist sites, while remarking, "But for its rediscovery by tourists, Copper Harbor may have been today a mere fishing outpost or even a ghost village. The resort is open throughout the year, as winter sports also are an attraction for visitors." By World War II, three hundred vacationing families could be housed north of Calumet, suggesting a substantial increase in the number and quality of accommodations in the northern Keweenaw Peninsula.[90]

Regional interests and the state continued to grapple with tourist issues during the war, particularly over the western UP's Porcupine Mountains. Conservation director P. J. Hoffmaster commented on the region's proximity to forty million potential vacationers and its forested landscape, believing that "with its choicest timber intact, it should bring millions of tourist dollars into the Upper Peninsula mining towns whose future is uncertain because of declining ore reserves."[91] While UP tourist boosters remarked on declining travel during wartime, they believed a conservative advertising campaign would help keep places like the Porcupine Mountains in people's minds. Others, including one UP newspaperman, remained disheartened by the state's lack of progress building an Ironwood tourist information lodge after a promise from the highway commissioner in the 1930s. During wartime, the Highway Department suggested that until the state's existing facilities reopened, it remained difficult to justify building more tourist information centers.[92]

Potential resort owners also turned to the state for assistance. Mrs. Lloyd Taylor of Grand Rapids, who hoped to operate a resort with her husband after the war, wrote the governor about being discouraged after spending six months trying to finance a UP resort purchase.[93] The Taylors were not alone in looking to capitalize on the UP's tourist potential. The Coast Guard's Charles Stetter wanted to enter the tourist business upon returning from wartime service. Stetter believed lumber barons left many communities impoverished but saw tourism as one way to prevent residents from fleeing and leaving behind ghost towns, suggesting, "I have seen the Copper Country pass from the crest of a mining boom to the trough of economic depression, and for years only feeble attempts were made to stimulate the interest of outside capital in this region." Stetter thought the answer involved citizens developing the UP tourist industry with a diverse array of facilities for vacationers, including more municipal campgrounds and state parks "to attract tourists who don't like to spend money at hotels."[94] One such citizen owned Copper Harbor's Minne-tonka Resort and found friends asking him, "Why would a man give up a good executive position to operate a group of cabins in Michigan's remote Copper Country?" He responded that the climate improved his family's health and he enjoyed meeting interesting people while providing comfortable lodging.[95] For many, catering to tourists offered reward beyond the pocketbook. While fewer facilities existed across the UP compared to Wisconsin and Minnesota, vacationers and operators discovered a place filled with enjoyment and opportunity on a pleasant peninsula.

Arrowhead Resorts and Their Offspring

While conversing with their guests at northern Wisconsin's Light House Lodge, Dora Blankenburg and her son, Russell, discovered some were heading to Minnesota's Arrowhead to enjoy Lake Superior's North Shore and canoe in the boundary waters. Others explored mining history on Minnesota's Iron Ranges, and boosters promoted purported curative properties of pine-scented air. Whether one sought health, adventure, relaxation, or a sense of history, northern Minnesota offered opportunities for vacationers and potential resort operators. Sparked by curiosity, Russell visited Minnesota and urged his mother to buy land and establish a resort on Gunflint Lake. They did, opening Gunflint Lodge in 1925.

After operating both places for several years, they sold Gunflint Lodge to the Spunners, friends of Dora's from Illinois, who advised them on their Wisconsin resort purchase. Mae Spunner brought her daughter, Justine, to negotiate terms. Gunflint had three guest cabins without electricity or indoor plumbing, a small lodge, a dining room, and a store. Justine made immediate improvements, enlarging the dining room and adding a lounge. These additions faced the road rather than the lake, underscoring the lodge's orientation toward welcoming auto tourists on the Gunflint Trail. During the Spunners first season in 1930, Mae acted as hostess, planning meals and supervising staff, while Justine handled administration and repaired equipment. Many Indian neighbors shopped at the store and worked as guides, housekeepers, and servers.[96]

In 1933, the Spunners sold their Illinois home and moved to the Gunflint permanently. That summer, Bill Kerfoot arrived on the trail, camping on Gunflint Lake's west end, and was eager for a job. Justine hired him in exchange for room and board. The following year, Bill and Justine married and began operating the lodge together. Their newsletter, *Gunflint Gossips*, reported on lodge activities and, like *Teal Lake Tidings*, created a sense of family among guests. The lodge attracted a large Illinois contingent, including 90 percent of August 1937 guests. Charter membership in the Gunflint Trail Association also helped bring new visitors. Originally, male hunters and anglers came in spring, early summer, and fall. Gradually, more women and families visited. The Kerfoots also attracted outing clubs, like Chicago's Prairie Club, which occupied the resort for a week of canoeing, swimming, and hiking.[97]

While it was somewhat unusual for women to run resorts independently, Justine and her mother were among several who entered the business. Jean Healy, Nyda McClure, and Marion Hall Burton regularly visited Camp Van Vac, established near Ely in 1917 when Van Vacton Harris, a railroad and timber man whose wife taught English to Finnish immigrants and Indian children, began building cabins. Developing their friendship over summers at Camp Van Vac, they decided to purchase forty-seven forested acres on Burntside Lake and established Camp du Nord in 1933. As teachers, they had summers free to operate the resort and hired some of their students to serve Twin Cities, Chicago, and Wisconsin guests. Profits were invested in new facilities for the expanding guest list. A 1940s Camp du Nord brochure captured women canoeing and offered the chance for adventure, relaxation, and sport. Another highlighted the pleasant atmosphere and remoteness, while assuring guests that the camp radio connected them to the outside world. Camp du Nord originally operated on

Four women canoe near an island on Burntside Lake, Minnesota, August 4, 1940. *Left to right*: Betty Shields, Toni Toenberg, Betty Bricker, and Betty Lou Geiger, all of Minneapolis. LOCAL IDENTIFIER USFS NEGATIVE 400537, RECORDS OF THE FOREST SERVICE, RECORD GROUP 95, THE NATIONAL ARCHIVES AT CHICAGO.

the American plan but responded to changing demand by converting to housekeeping cabins where guests cooked for themselves.[98]

Gunflint Lodge and Camp du Nord joined the growing array of accommodations across northeastern Minnesota. By 1926, Lake Vermilion's shores had nineteen resorts valued at over $600,000 and lodging for over nine hundred people. With over four hundred summer cottages, daily boat and mail service, and lakeshore property values up 1,500 percent since 1911, the lake had arrived on the tourist scene. Originally attracting Iowans, the area drew more Chicago guests by the mid-1920s. The mayor of Tower, Minnesota, stressed tourism's contribution to the local economy, remarking, "The very nature of the business makes it highly desirable, the tourist being a liberal buyer and pays cash." Tourism advocates also suggested they were helping create a better citizenry through providing access to the outdoors.[99]

Closer to Ely, tourist operators developed businesses along Burntside and Basswood Lakes. Built by local craftsmen in 1914 using native materials, Burntside Lodge emerged as one of the area's first resorts. In 1911, the site operated as the Brownell Outing Company, renting tents and supplies to campers and hunters plying lakes and woods around Ely. Phineas Brownell arrived in Ely in the late 1880s via railroad. Brownell capitalized on the growing number of auto travelers after a road to town was completed in 1901, erecting a garage and adding a lodge to cater to tourists until his death in 1920. In the early 1930s, Burntside stayed open through winter, as plowed roads made it easier to reach the lodge. In 1941, Ray and Nancy LaMontagne moved from vacationers to owners. Ray had worked summers at the lodge, and after honeymooning there four years earlier, he and Nancy purchased the property with its forty-four cabins and fourteen lodge rooms.[100]

Others also entered the tourist business after vacationing in the North Woods. Ed and Kay Gilman moved from Illinois to Fifty Lakes, Minnesota, to raise their family and run Gilman's Resort. Ed retained fond memories of fishing in northern Minnesota as a youth. After leaving the army and working for nine months, he and Kay came north on vacation and purchased an existing resort. For the first two winters, Ed returned to Chicago and his work at Western Electric. Guests arrived from across the Midwest, including families friendly with the previous owners. Like other operators, the Gilmans depended on guests spreading the word, but they also belonged to the local resort association and advertised in the Twin Cities newspapers. Operating a resort entailed a great deal of toil. Ed cut grass, hauled wood and ice to cabins, handled requests, and took guests fishing, while Kay emphasized hospitality toward all. Catering to children also made visitors feel at home and attracted returning families.[101] Carol Crawford Ryan's family was among those guests, visiting Gilman's starting in 1932, when it was owned by another family. Carol's father, an Iowa City postal worker, heard about the resort from a local gas station owner. The resort attracted a middle-class clientele, including civil servants and farmers. Carol spent vacations in the water playing with other children, while the men fished. Guests stayed at the resort for meals and often ate the fish they caught. Carol's experience led her, like many young North Woods visitors, to return as an adult, and she ultimately bought a summer place.[102]

The development of northern Minnesota's vacation landscape would be incomplete without the Ruttgers. Tourism was their business. All four of Joe and Josephine Ruttger's sons became resort owners at different locations—Alec at Bay Lake Lodge in Deerwood, established in 1898; Max at Pine Beach; Ed at Ruttger's Sherwood Forest on Gull Lake; and Bill at

Ellis Crawford and family at Mitchell Lake, Gilman's Resort, Minnesota, circa 1946. COURTESY OF THE MINNESOTA HISTORICAL SOCIETY.

Ruttger's Shady Point on White Fish Lake. Joe's oldest son, Alec, took over Bay Lake Lodge after returning from World War I, promoting the resort at outdoor shows armed with Oscar the Muskie—a mounted northern pike sporting a steel-wool beard. As Bay Lake Lodge evolved into a family-oriented resort, the Ruttgers attended fewer sports shows. One innovation that spurred this shift came when Zig Ziegler, a Kansas man with a cabin on the Ruttger property, started the resort's golfing tradition in 1925. After returning from California's golf courses, Ziegler persuaded Alec to construct a course, and the leisurely pursuit became a dominant activity at Bay Lake Lodge.[103]

When Alec ran the resort in the 1920s, guests arrived from the Twin Cities, but according to Alec's son, Jack, nearly 80 percent of business came from out of state. Interestingly, Jack compared operating a resort to farming, reporting, "You don't grow crops, but you still try and exist and raise your family and you work off the land." While Bay Lake Lodge attracted vacationers looking to enjoy its amenities and landscape, it was not the only place on the lake. F. I. Boone, who visited in the early 1900s and stayed at Bay Lake Lodge, bought land, built on it, and then

The Ruttger family. *Left to right*: William, Edward, Josephine, Joseph, Alec, and Max Ruttger, circa 1922. COURTESY OF THE MINNESOTA HISTORICAL SOCIETY.

sold parcels to friends in Junction City, Kansas, turning the north shore of Bay Lake into "Kansas Colony." For many of these settlers, fishing was important, but escaping from summer heat offered an even better reason to make northern Minnesota their vacation home.[104]

Like the Rosses and Kerfoots, the Ruttgers distributed newsletters during the off-season, including one reporting on Alec's purported adventures: "I've just been out walking the woods and I discovered eight new lakes that nobody ever knew existed." Alec established Bay Lake Lodge as a destination, and when Jack assumed operations, the resort had thirty-six cottages. Alec stayed involved with the Minnesota Arrowhead and Minnesota Resort Associations, which promoted the area and held programs for operators to improve their facilities and services. Like many resort owners, the Ruttgers worked with the state, including a cooperative project with the Department of Conservation and Arrowhead Association to improve fishing.[105]

In 1927, the Ruttgers established Ruttger Brothers Incorporated, which included the Bay Lake Lodge, Bay Lake Store, and a Deerwood store. Max made his brothers Bill and Ed, who had worked in the mines and farmed, store overseers. His brothers bought him out after a few years, giving Max the $2,500 needed to establish his resort. Traveling with his brother and parents in 1930, Max found a prime resort site. Construction began in 1931, and with help from local workers, by autumn the Ruttgers built the main Pine Beach lodge, twenty-five cottages, and employee housing. During winter and spring, they added electricity and plumbing. The lodge added a new lobby and recreation room in 1935 followed by six new cottages the next year. Max believed people were more likely to return if they befriended fellow guests, so the architecture and layout were designed to create a communal atmosphere. Cottages lacked sitting rooms, so guests socialized near the main lodge's fireplace, playing cards, bingo, and other games.[106]

Pooling their resources, the Ruttgers often placed large tourist advertisements in Sunday papers, and cooperation included Alec sending overflow guests from Bay Lake to Max at Pine Beach. Pine Beach guests generally vacationed for at least one week, and a few families stayed the entire summer. One group from Aurora, Illinois, came regularly, and others arrived from Kansas City, St. Louis, and Oklahoma City. Iowa farmers arrived in July after planting corn. Rates were $35 per week the first summer, and when bookings slowed the next summer, they dropped to $29.75. Given its location a bit off the highway, the resort rarely attracted guests for a single night. Bay Lake and Pine Beach offered the same rate to avoid guests choosing one because of a cheaper rate. By 1935, rates included golf, three daily meals, and water-skiing, and guests could visit other Ruttger resorts for meals and activities. From Pine Beach's inception, Saturday night music and dancing attracted locals and resort guests, helping endear the resort to the community because it provided both work and leisure. Food also attracted vacationers to Pine Beach, and when Max hired a Minneapolis restaurant chef in the late 1930s, he received acclaim from Twin Cities' guests. In the mid-1930s, Bay Lake Lodge developed a children's program, and Pine Beach followed suit. At Pine Beach, guests paddled the lake in rowboats and wooden canoes before the resort added sailboats in 1935 and a ski boat in 1937. Guests golfed at a course owned by a local real estate company, but Max never entered the golf business, feeling it was better to "run one business and run it well." While Pine Beach opened in the midst of the Depression, business continued to flourish.[107]

As more vacationers chose the North Woods, other enterprises joined lodging operations in marking tourism's growth. Summer camps shaped

Interior of Ruttger Bros. General Store at time of sale, Deerwood, 1935. COURTESY OF THE MINNESOTA HISTORICAL SOCIETY.

NE BARGAINS
SELLING OUT
BEST IN FOODS
SELLING OUT
Mops
10¢
10¢
19¢

Guests at Ruttger's Sherwood Forest Lodge, Gull Lake, circa 1940. COURTESY OF THE MINNESOTA HISTORICAL SOCIETY.

children's perception of nature, leading many to return later in life on vacation. While camps catered to a different clientele than resorts, they both emphasized family and the outdoors. John Sprague, physical director at Chicago's Latin School, operated both a camp and resort, Camp Minocqua and Pottawattomie Lodge, in northern Wisconsin. The YMCA's Camp Manito-Wish aimed "to develop square manhood in boys." By 1929, Wisconsin had more camps than any other state west of the Appalachians. North Woods summer camps introduced urban children to the region's outdoors, brought parents north to vacation, contributed to the rustic atmosphere, and provided employment.[108]

Tourist facilities also fostered local business opportunities. For example, printer W. A. Fisher produced publicity materials for resorts. After briefly losing the Ruttger account, Fisher turned to color printing, and the Ruttgers reestablished the account. Bishop's department store in Park Rapids served the local community but also benefited from tourists visiting neighboring Itasca State Park by selling clothes to those unprepared for northern Minnesota's weather. With the state park at its doorstep, Park Rapids attracted many tourists. While some area resorts expressed displeasure with having to compete with the park, it ultimately boosted business at local establishments like Bishop's. Others made a living providing entertainment. Carl Warmington and his orchestra performed at

Breezy Point Resort, and Tom Madden operated slot machines at various establishments. Tom's nephew, Jack, who later opened his own resort, stayed at Ruttger's Pine Beach during its first summer to oversee his uncle's business in the area. The Madden family also ran a golf course, selling tickets for resort owners to distribute to guests and guaranteeing the golf course a certain return.[109]

The 1949 *Tour Guide to Minnesota* reported on tourist industry growth since 1900, capturing the enormous investment of time, money, and labor involved in building a major Minnesota industry:

> The first resorts were built at the turn of the century along the shores of the state's many lakes. Cabins could be rented by families or individuals by the day or the week. Fishing, swimming, canoeing, hiking, and stargazing were among the favorite activities. As transportation systems modernized, vacationers came from all over the Midwest from Iowa, the Dakotas, Illinois, and Kansas to stay at Minnesota resorts. . . . As customers demanded more services, many resorts expanded to provide them.[110]

Lodging owners provided vacationers not only a place to stay but an experience that depended on a new workforce, landscape, and promotional language. While the appeal of lakes and woods attracted people to their northern outposts, resort owners like the Warner, Ross, Ruttger, Dunn, and Earle families created a dialogue and provided places where employees helped ensure people received benefits from a North Woods vacation. By 1940, Minnesota had 2,063 resorts, hotels, and tourist camps, Wisconsin had 2,460, and Michigan's smaller Upper Peninsula had 262.[111]

Tourists, proprietors, and employees were enmeshed in a web of commerce and travel connecting city and country during the interwar years. In the North Woods, work remained connected to the land, but it often meant moving from mining iron and copper or milling lumber to cultivating and caring for a new tourist crop. Herbert and Bert's Resort, Ross' Teal Lake Lodge, Ruttger's, Dunn's, Blaney Park, Bert's Cabins, and Pine Woods Cabins, along with many other North Woods enterprises, catered to people's desire to escape daily life and vacation amid natural beauty and rustic surroundings. They also attracted employees looking for outdoor work and enjoyment, emerging as central to a North Woods vacation culture and landscape that followed lumber and mining in terms of creating jobs and altering the region. Except this time, instead of felling trees or mining ore and shipping goods to cities, people came to consume the region's forests and lakes, which had been cultivated for recreation.

CHAPTER 4

Tell the World about Your Charms: The Promotional Appeal

Welcome TOURISTS to Cloverland,
Brave Hiawatha's home,
Our wishes are for your good luck
Wherever you may roam,
Both day and night you'll find delight
In this enchanted land,
The honest smile will greet you while
You tour Cloverland.
—C. F. Whiteshield, "Tourists," *Cloverland Echoes*

WHETHER RECITING POEMS ON THE UPPER PENINSULA, PULLING OUT a map while driving and looking for directions to Minnesota's Arrowhead, or sitting at home reading about northern Wisconsin's lakes, vacationers encountered an array of promotional materials designed to lure them north during the interwar years. This literature linked urban and rural worlds, offering an image of the region as a rejuvenating and rustic escape from daily life filled with scenic beauty and recreational opportunities. Potential vacationers inquired of resort owners and tourist associations after reading about outdoor splendor in regional and state publications like the UP's *Lure Book*, Minnesota's *Recreation Days*, and Wisconsin's *Heart O' Lakes*, as well as in resort brochures and newspaper travel sections. Information requests also arrived at chambers of commerce, newspapers, and booster organizations, and promoters responded, suggesting the UP's "wild atmosphere and setting" provided for "a genuine, outdoor vacation." Others requested information on summer cottages after seeing advertisements selling land. One Ohio resident informed the Upper Penin-

—Foley in the Minneapolis Daily Star

Promoting Minnesota's natural features, friendly people, and modern infrastructure helped draw tourists in the 1920s. FROM THE *MINNEAPOLIS DAILY STAR*.

sula Development Bureau (UPDB) that its materials enticed him to vacation in the UP.[1] A 1920s *Minneapolis Daily Star* cartoon portrayed tourists as quintessential consumers, choosing particular goods and experiences and expressing a willingness to pay. Pointing to the economic impact of tourist expenditures with the expression, "I'll take $100,000,000 worth of that!" the cartoon also aimed to convince residents that in-state vacations offered enjoyment at reasonable prices.[2]

Public agencies and private promoters portrayed the North Woods as a natural vacation retreat. Like counterparts in other destinations, they packaged and sold climate, scenery, and recreation as commodities.[3] Promotion highlighting scenery, leisure, and pleasure by organizations like the UPDB, Wisconsin Heart O'Lakes Association, and Minnesota Arrowhead Association changed perceptions of the North Woods. As participants in modern consumer culture, tourists came to understand the North Woods through the literature they read and ultimately followed its messages to vacation there.

North Woods vacations functioned as part of a personal search for pleasure through material satisfaction. While tourists sought out and crafted unique experiences, literature promoting self-fulfillment through mind and body refreshment influenced their decisions. As consumers of leisure, tourists made decisions about how, when, and where to vacation. But their choices were also constrained by a consumer culture in which advertising framed such decisions. Before World War I, advertisers focused on selling the product. After the war, they emphasized the benefits and experiences provided by such goods.[4] North Woods tourist literature shared common themes like hay fever relief, avoiding urban congestion, outdoor recreation, adventure, accessibility, and scenic beauty. It presented vacations as an escape from routine, capitalizing on the degradation of work that led many to seek satisfaction through leisure. As such, the experience became a vital element in an expanding consumer culture, even though not everyone shared equally in the ability to vacation. By reading promotional materials produced by government, regional tourist organizations, and individual resorts as well as communicating with boosters, potential tourists encountered a region of splendid scenery and ruggedness, adventure and tranquility, access and escape where promoters guaranteed an enjoyable vacation. Such discoveries led many to follow the promise presented in North Woods promotional literature and plan vacations in Michigan's Upper Peninsula, Minnesota's Arrowhead, and northern Wisconsin.

Lured by the Call of Hiawatha

In 1917, UPDB promotional materials emphasized work sites as tourist destinations, noting that copper and iron mining offered "unusual and spectacular scenes to tourists." Roadbeds built for mining and lumbering provided infrastructure for automobile vacationers venturing to campgrounds and parks. While better roads brought more vacationers, the UPDB assured them of an outdoor experience with little hassle and few crowds.[5] In its 1920 *Cloverland* guide, the UPDB noted tourist industry growth and competition with other areas, marking the UP as having arrived on the tourist scene. This "tourist's paradise," according to the guide, witnessed a "rapidly increasing stream of tourist visitors out of the hot sweltering centers of middle-western industry." It also distinguished between the resorter and the outdoor enthusiast, suggesting the UP held greater appeal for the latter. The UPDB hoped to tap into a niche by promoting outdoor vacations. It described the UP as a place imbued with strenuous life ideals offering outdoor challenges, in contrast to decadent and crowded eastern resorts. But modern technology and tourist planning increasingly encroached on this sense of adventure. Keweenaw Peninsula visitors interested in exploring its natural beauty and copper industry could stay at state parks with free campsites. People continued to enjoy the area's natural environment but discovered an experience increasingly planned and mediated by promoters, tourist developers, and the state.[6]

During the 1920s, the UPDB expanded its promotional efforts, publicizing accessibility and compactness and suggesting that the UP offered a "vest-pocket edition of almost every resort region on the globe."[7] In 1925, the UPDB distributed eighteen thousand tourist booklets at Chicago's Outdoor Life Exposition. The following year, it printed thirty thousand booklets, distributing many to outdoor show visitors, automobile clubs, resort bureaus, and newspapers.[8] Proximity and thrift remained important factors in choosing vacation destinations; as the UPDB claimed, "The poor man and the man of moderate means must take their vacations in summer. Not everyone can afford to go to Florida or California."[9] Tourists responded by discussing their vacation experiences. One Indiana vacationer commented, "I like the Copper Country best. It is an ideal summering place to loaf and dream in. But why doesn't the Development Bureau or some other agency put on an all-around Hiawatha Land summer tour from Chicago or Detroit?" Responding to such concerns, the UPDB produced twenty-five thousand copies of a lake and stream map promoting Hiawatha Land "by the Shining Big Sea Water" in 1930 and 1931.[10] While the UP was the "end of the trail," it was the beginning of adventure with abundant opportunities among "sparkling inland lakes" and "rapid-flowing streams." Despite upscale retreats like Mackinac, Grand, and Les Chenaux Islands, much of the UP remained geared to outdoor enthusiasts. Promoters cultivated an image of the place that attracted "the camper, the hiker, the Izaak Walton, the Daniel Boone, the swimmer, the canoe-

The Elks of Hancock, Michigan, entered a Cloverland float in the 1926 Elks National Convention parade in Chicago, highlighting one of the early Keweenaw Peninsula tourist promotion efforts. COURTESY OF THE MICHIGAN TECHNOLOGICAL UNIVERSITY ARCHIVES AND COPPER COUNTRY HISTORICAL COLLECTIONS.

hound," rather than the leisurely resorter looking for the comforts of home.[11]

Promotion from other private and public organizations supplemented UPDB efforts to have tourism replace lost mining and timber activities. *Upper Michigan Ahoy Vacationist* informed vacationers that the "Charmed Land of Hiawatha Beckons," profiling much of the eastern UP for travelers ferrying across the Straits of Mackinac. Automobile Club of Michigan booklets credited the state with encouraging tourism, highlighting easy access to scenery, historic sites, and recreational facilities. Those reading such items discovered a "spreading panorama of scenic splendor and nerve-healing calm that beckons the nature-lover to recreation and play" in the UP. Tourists could fish from a canoe, visit Tahquamenon Falls, or experience Isle Royale. While the club hoped out-of-state residents would visit the UP, Michigan motorists were also encouraged to make the UP their vacation destination.[12] The Ontonagon County Board of Supervisors marketed the UP as a place to regain one's strength, where streams and lakes provided ample opportunities for fishermen. Visitors to Iron River were asked, "What can compare with a day, a week-end, a fortnight, or a season in the cool, clean, refreshing atmosphere of the vast north woods?" The answer was that the UP had no peer in terms of its natural surroundings.[13] The Copper Country Vacationist League (CCVL) promised visitors rest, health, and a carefree experience and informed them that "when mid-summer cares begin to pile up," nothing would provide greater benefit than "an overnight escape to the cool, pine-scented air of Michigan's Copper Country." *Ke-wee-naw Land in Lake Superior* highlighted new roads and the Keweenaw golf course. Throughout the 1930s, the CCVL advertised accessibility and escape in the beautiful and affordable Keweenaw Peninsula.[14]

Vacationers discovered adventure awaited them in Michigan's Copper Country. Filled with photographs, the CCVL's *Copper Country of Michigan* suggested, "A change of scene, relaxation, diversion—in other words, a VACATION—should be a sound investment." As an emotional and financial investment, vacations offered tourists rejuvenation and provided a regional economic boost.[15] At Lake Breeze Hotel, guests enjoyed reasonable prices and cordial service along with fishing, Lake Superior views, fish dinners, and homemade pie. One guest helped promote the place by writing a friend back home about the "fine clear cool bracing weather—very comfortable modern cabin—food excellent—sporty golf course—finest scenery in Michigan—no dress clothes required—some warm sports clothes sufficient—better come up here." Vacationers also found courtesy at new housekeeping cabins.[16] The CCVL claimed that no matter one's vacation proclivity, the Copper Country offered an ideal place. Many vacationers heeded this call—over ten thousand visited the organization's Ahmeek information booth in 1937. Artists and photographers found welcome diversions and inspiration, while sportsmen fished Lake Superior. The Copper Country offered "every accommodation to fit every purse," and promoters claimed people would discover that "a few days or weeks of your life spent here will be among such people and scenes as will enrich your future."[17] Reasonable prices aimed to attract vacationers who spent locally and would supposedly return home in a better frame of mind and with a little more in their pocket.

Promotional literature cast tourism alongside other industries to sell its benefits to potential providers. In one piece, the head of the UP Agricultural Experiment Station commented on tourism's ability to improve economic conditions and provide work, claiming the UP could satisfy various vacation desires by being "the most charming summer resort for the tenderfoot" and "the most delightful winter resort to the red blooded young and old."[18] Another publication informed residents that given mining's bleak future in the Copper Country, tourism offered substantial promise. Regularly discussing tourism in economic terms, advocates hoped it would provide work and revenues would "flow into the coffers of those who have staked their faith on the future of the Keweenaw Peninsula."[19]

Extending CCVL efforts, the UPDB's *Lure Book* and *Land of Hiawatha* tempted potential vacationers with Indian lore, good roads, scenery, and rejuvenation, while highlighting state involvement, democratic access, wartime sacrifice, and the freedom associated with vacation travel. Promoters drew on these themes to fashion a North Woods image that helped convince people to vacation amid natural beauty and a working landscape.[20] Materials described Indians' engagement with modernity while transforming them into spectacle for the tourist gaze through imagery, language, and slogans. *Land of Hiawatha* covers depicted an Indian nestled among woods as a canoe party traveled along the river catching fish. "Hiawatha Land" welcomed visitors with images of an Indian playing golf and cruising in a car. The UP shifted its moniker from Cloverland to Land of Hiawatha, but it was not alone in using Indian imagery, as northeast Minnesota adopted the Arrowhead appellation, and northwest Wisconsin embraced the Indianhead label. Promotion also emphasized how Indians' knowledge of fishing and hunting spots proved advantageous to tourists hiring them as guides.[21]

Promotional materials quoted tourists praising the UP's scenic, well-maintained roads and reasonable drive from the region's cities. They frequently mentioned repeat visitors, remarking that it was the "real test of a region's attractiveness, after all—to weave such a magic spell as to fairly compel one's return." The UPDB believed high return rates and five hundred thousand summer visitors in 1930 reflected successful promotion. It also encouraged tourists to provide suggestions and inform friends about the area.[22] By 1938, the UPDB claimed on its *Lure Book* cover, "World Travelers Choose Michigan's Upper Peninsula," marking the UP as a worthy destination. Although the statement was perhaps an exaggeration, the fact was that the UP had arrived on the tourist scene even if foreign tourists remained small in number.[23] Far more likely were visitors from Lower Michigan and Ohio, who embarked on state ferries across the Mackinac Straits. Potential vacationers were reminded that the UP was "just one day's or night's ride from the crowds and the hot weary places, away out

Cover of Upper Peninsula Development Bureau's tourist booklet *Lured by the Land of Hiawatha*, 1938. COURTESY OF THE MICHIGAN TECHNOLOGICAL UNIVERSITY ARCHIVES AND COPPER COUNTRY HISTORICAL COLLECTIONS.

in the heart of Lake Superior."[24] Such travel benefited from Michigan's Highway Department incorporating tourist service into its program by building information lodges at strategic roadside points and operating the ferry service. Reflecting the need to balance attracting tourists with maintaining outdoor recreation opportunities and scenery, the UPDB claimed that as automobile tourism expanded, it worked "to avoid disfigurement of the natural beauty of Keweenaw-Land." Vacationers grew accustomed to reading about state support for tourism, and *Land of Hiawatha* informed readers about the natural beauty of the UP's state parks.[25]

Literature informed potential tourists that the UP offered all-season vacations among a "land of infinite variety" in the "roof garden of the United States." While traveling through the Copper Country, they could visit mines, fish in Lake Superior, ferry to Isle Royale, or encounter ghost towns.[26] Given its higher elevation and more consistent snow, the UP promoted and developed winter sports more easily than neighboring regions. Houghton and Hancock received well over two hundred inches of snow annually. In winter, vacationers and residents stored their fishing rod along with their tent and boat and brought out skis, snowshoes, and toboggans for outdoor adventure. Whether looking to attract visitors in summer or winter, physical and mental rejuvenation emerged as essential aspects of promotional dialogue.[27]

Promoters also cloaked vacations in patriotism during wartime, warning, "If you must take a vacation from your duties this year, take one that will do you the greatest good. Come to Michigan's unspoiled Upper Peninsula. . . . the rugged U.P. will send you back to your important job better fitted."[28] Although rationing limited travel, promoters informed potential vacationers and employers that furloughs for war workers could restore mental and physical vigor needed for victory. One brochure quoted the Surgeon General, "To promote health and morale, a nation at war needs healthful relaxation and recreation," and advised that "the ideal vacation land must be located in a safe sector close enough to our centers of population with all types of transportation facilities."[29] Greyhound Bus Lines promoted "Victory Vacations," and the UPDB's George Bishop informed potential tourists, "When victory comes, plan that super vacation that you have been dreaming of in terms of Michigan." Bishop knew people sacrificed vacations during wartime and would be rewarded when hostilities ended.[30] Promoters also connected conservation and recreation by suggesting that those on the home front should guarantee that returning GIs could vacation in nature. In the process, they redefined the UP as a vacation destination during the interwar years. Promotional literature helped tourists discover that the UP offered a place to forget about daily cares among scenic beauty and rich history.

Marvelous Minnesota

Allusions to escapes also appeared in northern Minnesota promotional literature. One piece, for example, suggested the "tired business man" could relax in nature and "build up a run down and worn out body." He would not be alone, as adventurers and families flocked to experience the place and altered the landscape. The Superior National Forest encouraged visitors to explore the area through canoe trips and provided information locally about routes. Motorists could see large open-pit iron mines, while enjoying good roads and accommodations in Minnesota's Arrowhead. Portrayed as both the "Sportland of the North" and a working landscape, the Arrowhead capitalized on its multifaceted identity. *Farming for Profit in Minnesota Arrowhead Country* added another possibility, encouraging local farmers to support tourism because visitors provided a market for crops.[31]

Arrowhead promotion described how conservation efforts contributed to the outdoor recreation landscape. In its 1919 *A Vacation Land of Lakes and Woods*, the U.S. Forest Service emphasized opportunities on public lands, labeling the Superior National Forest an "ideal recreation ground for the camper, the fisherman, and the canoeist." Appealing to the rugged individualist, it discussed how a canoe trip transformed the tourist into an early voyageur among the forest's rivers and streams. It claimed in language evoked to entice visitors that canoeists would see country supposedly little changed since fur company brigades plied these waters. The Forest Service also acknowledged potential economic benefits for Cook, Lake, and St. Louis Counties, offering summer-home sites for annual lease and recognizing the need for improved automobile access.[32]

Echoing Forest Service promotion, railroads and local organizations touted beauty, health, outdoor activities, and the industrial landscape. As early as 1914, the Duluth and Iron Range Railroad promoted travel along its lines, including rental cottages on Lake Vermilion. In 1921, the Chicago Great Western Railroad advertised Minnesota's lakes as "The Land of Sky Blue Water" for those interested in scenery, and "The Home of Muskallonge" for anglers, while suggesting northern Minnesota offered a rejuvenating climate with activities for everyone.[33] In the 1920s, rail still provided a convenient and hassle-free means of vacation travel, especially

The U.S. Forest Service encouraged rugged vacations in national forests, suggesting adventure could be found in places like the Superior National Forest. COVER FROM U.S. DEPARTMENT OF AGRICULTURE, FOREST SERVICE, *A VACATION LAND OF LAKES AND WOODS*, 1919.

on fishermen's special trains that left major cities on Friday evening and returned Monday morning. Railroads continued to issue promotional materials, including one booklet that urged visiting Minnesota's lakes via rail and highlighted the Arrowhead's allure.[34] But the automobile increasingly eclipsed railroads. One 1925 publication stressed the ease with which automobile tourists could now enjoy such activities, since "it is only a step from the towns on the Mesaba Range to that ideal outer paradise of rugged scenery, absolute solitude, clear air, and the indefinable lure of the Wilderness." Placing photographs of mines and miners alongside those of pristine lakes and woods, these 1920s materials framed industrial sites as tourist sites and encouraged vacationers to see the mines. In the Arrowhead, "Industry and Recreation Go Hand in Hand," and in towns like Chisholm, vacationers could visit iron mines while traveling along well-maintained roads to Superior National Forest.[35] Real estate and land companies drew on these efforts when advertising summer homes in the 1920s. Gull Lake Shores lots were, according to its Minneapolis-based developers, "just on the edge of civilization" with access to a hunter's and boater's paradise. Another company marketed cottages to those who could "invest $1.00 down and $1.00 a week in health and happiness."[36]

Chambers of commerce and regional organizations helped shift the message toward tourism by promoting their areas as vacation destinations. Ely developed as a Superior National Forest gateway, providing services and supplies to vacationers. In the early 1930s, the Ely Commercial Club labeled the city the "Playground of a Nation," promoting rustic resorts and lodges with capacity for over one thousand people, and opposing initiatives, including Edward Backus's plan to dam portions of Minnesota's boundary waters, that would destroy the surrounding wilderness. Emphasizing the region's wildlife and scenery, the club tempted city dwellers who "swelter among the tall buildings and breathe smoke and gasses, and who never feel the breezes of the open places, breathe the pure air of the pines, nor hear the murmur of the sparkling waves against the rocks—never hear the soft symphony of the wind through the pine tops." Ely portrayed itself as a place where "breezes that fan its streets carry the perfume of the balsam, and its sky line is the jagged whip-saw of the pines in sharp relief against a clear blue." Such descriptions noted that natural environs could overwhelm the senses. Unlike those about other Arrowhead destinations and Michigan's Copper Country, materials promoting Ely said little about surrounding mines despite the fact that they employed fifteen hundred people with a monthly payroll of $200,000. No tourist would have been

Deer hunters eating in Arrowhead Country Deer Camp, 1930s. PHOTOGRAPH BY BRUCE SIFFORD STUDIO. COURTESY OF THE MINNESOTA HISTORICAL SOCIETY.

unaware of their presence. Local promoters emphasized natural beauty and concealed Ely's connection to the smoke-filled industrial city in order to sell the place to vacationers seeking escape. Ely began marketing itself as a wilderness gateway during the interwar years, and although mining still employed residents, promoters constructed an image of the place that excluded it in order to diversify the economic base.[37]

For those planning to explore the Superior National Forest by canoe or foot, Ely was likely their last stop. A canoe voyage allowed travelers to "lose your business cares in the swirl of your paddle, throw away your worries in the strike of a big fish, swap an artificial social existence for the primitive joys of the camp fire—cough the last traces of soot out of your lungs." Promoted as such, it offered far more than merely an escape from daily life. Ely's Commercial Club did little to obscure its economic motives, recommending renting equipment from local businesses to ensure a sound experience. Outfitters and guides provided both gear and local knowledge, valuable for those venturing into the woods by canoe. While the club welcomed canoeists, it also sought resort guests, hay fever sufferers, and summer-home owners. By 1940, substantial promotional literature and the presence of forty resorts and outfitters operating within a twenty-mile radius helped establish Ely's reputation as a wilderness outpost catering to vacationers.[38]

The St. Louis County Club advertised vacations "Amid the Pines and Lakes of Northern Minnesota." Appealing to visitors seeking escape from heat and humidity, the county, which included Ely and Duluth, offered relief from the summer sun "blistering the plains and prairies" and the city's "scorching winds" by inviting vacationers "to the cool delights of innumerable forest edged lakes" where the canoe country offered mental and physical respite.[39] Farther west, the Detroit Lakes Chamber of Commerce expressed less concern with climate and wilderness, promoting "412 Lakes within 25 Miles" along with modern amenities two hundred miles from the Twin Cities. Other places followed suit. The Brainerd Lakes area advertised itself as "Va-Ka-Shun Land" and distributed a map locating the region's nearly three hundred resorts. The Crosby Tourist Boosters Association issued a Crow Wing County map with information on lodging and activities. Such maps became typical for areas promoting vacation options. Not meant for navigation, they served to lure tourists.[40]

Minnesota Arrowhead Association (MAA) promotion emphasized outdoor adventure. In 1928, the MAA recommended tourists enter the region from seven gateways and claimed that visiting all the region's lakes would take one hundred days each summer for thirty years. Possibilities included a trip along the North Shore of Lake Superior to enjoy tiny fishing hamlets, the towns of Two Harbors and Grand Marais, and, as evidence of an expanded commercial roadside, "summer places skirted by refreshment stands and filling stations." Others might venture to the national forests, Vermilion and Mesaba Iron Ranges, or headwaters of the Mississippi River in Itasca State Park.[41] One guide emphasized that vacationers chose the Arrowhead "to enjoy the fresh and invigorating climate, to play and rest in a carefree way." MAA executive secretary Val Saxby reinforced this message by representing the organization at the 1933 Chicago World's Fair, leading auto tours, encouraging operators to adopt a longer season, and producing promotional materials.[42]

The MAA enticed vacationers with the slogan, "Come to the Arrowhead, where the climate is sublime, come in the winter and in the summertime." One option was Lake Vermilion, summer home of former Izaak Walton League president Dr. Preston Bradley, whose endorsement lured others. The MAA emphasized historical lore, telling stories of Indians, trappers, fur traders, missionaries, and lumberjacks. Canoeists venturing into the border lakes could also "hunt with a camera" to capture scenery. If roughing it in a canoe did not suit one's taste, places like Pipestone Falls Lodge, operated by a Chicagoan, offered a cozy respite. Similar options availed vacationers along the Gunflint Trail, where lodges catered to outdoor enthusiasts year-round. The Gunflint Lodge even lured visitors with poetry extolling its virtues, "Upon the Gunflint Trail is perched / A Lodge complete and full of fun / To find its double I have searched / But could not find a single one."[43]

While many who promoted the North Woods lived and worked in the area, urban businesses and organizations also got involved. St. Paul's Schuneman and Evans department store published *Tips on Minnesota Motor Trips* to sell its camping gear, remarking, "It's all great sport—this getting away from civilization and losing yourself in the North Woods—but you can't get along without a few conveniences." Before leaving on a trip, the retailer urged stopping by for equipment. The Minneapolis Civic and Commerce Association issued guidebooks profiling towns across the state.

Star Harbor Resort cabins along the North Shore of Lake Superior near Two Harbors, Minnesota, circa 1920. COURTESY OF THE MINNESOTA HISTORICAL SOCIETY.

Schuneman and Evans Department Store, Sixth and Wabasha, St. Paul, circa 1890. COURTESY OF THE MINNESOTA HISTORICAL SOCIETY.

Its 1925 edition included a welcome message from the governor commenting on growing numbers arriving in the north for rest and recreation.[44]

State agencies joined private operators and regional organizations in promoting tourism. The Ten Thousand Lakes of Minnesota Association viewed Minnesota's outdoors as a product to sell vacationers. It publicized Minnesota's advantages and encouraged visitors to bring friends and unwind in the outdoors.[45] Catering to growing numbers of automobile travelers, it publicized the state's road system and told visitors to "Drive north to the land where Ten Thousand Lakes are linked by motor highways organized and maintained for your pleasure and convenience. Come to the piney woods for your motor journey."[46] Despite roads opening up northern Minnesota, the association suggested the boundary waters remained "the Venice of the North," where waterways offered travel routes, and assured potential visitors that "it is a real wilderness—make no mistake about that." Canoeists would find serenity on a trip through these supposedly untouched waters.[47] Far from the city's pollution, vacationers could instead "Breathe the Ozone of the Pine Woods" in a place marked as distant from urban life and were asked, "How are you going to spend those wonderful days snatched from the sultry city and the stifling cares of the office?" Vacationers looking for escape and adventure discovered plentiful options in the promotional literature produced by the state with ten thousand lakes.[48]

During the interwar years, state-level organizational changes also influenced promotion. After Minnesota disbanded its Department of Immigration in 1927, the Ten Thousand Lakes Association merged with the Greater Minnesota Association. By combining promotional efforts in one organization, the state hoped to attract tourists and new residents. Initially, it looked to parlay its successful tourist promotion into the agricultural realm, issuing *Come to Minnesota: You'll Do BETTER on a Minnesota Farm*. Tourists provided a growing market for remaining farmers, and the 1930 edition of *Come to Minnesota* stressed that over 1.5 million Minnesota tourists "consume the produce of nearby farms and thus constitute a ready source of income." But the joint state promotional effort was short-lived, and efforts to attract agricultural settlers disappeared as a theme in state promotional literature.[49]

Minnesota increasingly valued tourists for their ability to spend money on vacations rather than for their potential settlement. Adopting this vision, the state's *Recreation Days* and *Minnesota Book* promoted Minnesota as the "Land of Pleasure, Land of Treasure" in the late 1920s and early 1930s, only briefly mentioning agricultural and industrial advantages. Governor Floyd Olson hoped visitors experienced Minnesota as an "ideal vacation-land" with the working landscape as part of the tourist experience. Tourists contributed to work opportunities for residents, but tourist promotion went beyond economics. Minneapolis public schools endorsed vacations as an opportunity for students to learn science, geography, and history. For schoolchildren and others, the state suggested a Minnesota family vacation was fun and educational.[50]

The state tourist bureau filled its *Marvelous Minnesota* publication with photographs of outdoor scenes and a message to "make these pictures come true—vacation this year in marvelous Minnesota." Receiving cooperation from the state, *Fisher's Marvelous Minnesota Manual* suggested in 1937, "Although the tourist industry is the third largest in Minnesota, exceeded only by agriculture and mining, there has been, up to now, no comprehensive tourist guide of the state." Somewhat disingenuous considering the wealth of tourist literature produced over the previous two decades, the claim does exemplify growing cooperation among state agencies. The idea was to promote the entire state, rather than merely a portion, as a vacation destination. Debunking the notion that northern Minnesota resorts captured all the tourist business, the tourist bureau discovered the north was more tourist-conscious because of its dependence on the industry, while southern Minnesota counted on a more diverse economy with tourism in the mix.[51]

During the interwar years, the Ten Thousand Lakes Association spearheaded statewide promotional efforts, while the MAA emphasized northeastern Minnesota. Public and private officials shifted their goal toward capturing tourist expenditures rather than using tourism to attract industry and settlers. In 1940, the state assured potential vacationers that "Minnesota Has Everything" and its natural beauty and friendly people guaranteed a memorable experience. After reading such material and hearing about people's experiences, tourists embarked on vacations in "Marvelous Minnesota."[52]

Wisconsin's Wonderful Waters

With northern Wisconsin experiencing increased visitation and summer-home investment in the 1920s, *Wisconsin Land of Lakes Magazine* aimed "to stimulate interest in the development of this state as a great recreational playground, and to commend and exploit every genuine effort toward conservation of Wisconsin's natural resources." Editor and publisher Burt Williams claimed tourism would create more wealth than agriculture or manufacturing, called on the state to adequately fund promotion and conservation programs, and encouraged public-private cooperation to compete with neighboring states. The Land O' Lakes Association joined Williams's appeal for state funds and publicized the thirty-three thousand inquiries received at its Chicago office.[53] Such efforts linked tourism to the state's natural and scenic resources, as Wisconsin promoters joined Michigan and Minnesota in creating a North Woods image that included outdoor recreation, scenic beauty, health benefits, and adventure.

Like MAA and UPDB publications promoting the Arrowhead and Land of Hiawatha, Wisconsin Indian Head Country's *Call O' the Lakes* invoked Indian lore. The organization's moniker drew on northwest Wisconsin's appearance on the map, encouraging people to "Build with the Indian Head" while advocating conservation programs and legislation aiding tourism. Signage, advertisements, outdoor shows, and promotional tours embedded the name in the public's mind. Others aided in the process, including the Chicago and North Western Railway, which promoted Wisconsin vacations for families. A Chicago real estate firm joined others planning to subdivide and sell northern land for recreational use. The Lake Katherine Improvement Company promoted its attempts to transform the abandoned sawmill town of Hazelhurst into a recreational center. Chicago and Milwaukee residents bought into these efforts, investing in summer homes and providing work for locals, like John Habrich, who served as development manager.[54]

Despite success attracting vacationers in the 1920s, by 1930 both the *Wisconsin Magazine* and *Vilas County News* expressed alarm about regional economic decline and tourists choosing other states due to better advertising, claiming, "The resort business, the tourist camp business and many other allied interests do not have to suffer the same fate. Wake up, Wisconsin, and tell the world about your charms."[55] Adoption of the nation's first rural zoning ordinance in 1933, which permitted designating recreation as a viable use for forested and tax delinquent lands, suggested Wisconsin partially heeded the wake-up call. Lacking state promotional funds, Wisconsin's private tourist interests increased their promotional commitment and realized that protecting natural and scenic resources remained vital for future success.

One of those citizens was Joseph Mercedes, who led Wisconsin's tourist promotion efforts through his Wisconsin Heart O'Lakes Association. Mercedes eventually changed the name to the Wisconsin Tourist Bureau, providing a more official ring but also creating trouble with the state. A former vaudevillian with a flair for showmanship, Mercedes started the association in 1932 at the behest of northern Wisconsin resort owners seeking coordinated promotion. He traveled in a log cabin trailer to promote northern Wisconsin vacations and established a promotional office on Chicago's Michigan Avenue.[56] Mercedes pledged that Wisconsin provided "full vacation money's worth to every visitor," claiming the state had been "hiding its light under a bushel" and needed his promotional services. On the first day of Chicago's 1933 World's Fair, his Heart O'Lakes Association received 5,570 registrations.[57] Mercedes advertised northern Wisconsin as the "Most Concentrated Lake Region in the World," and suggested that its woods, lakes, and streams meant "Nature Runs Riot in the Heart O' The Lakes." With fifteen hundred lakes within a twenty-five mile radius, Minocqua offered a useful tourist base, and Eagle River meant summer adventure along with winter activities like skiing, tobog-

Joe Mercedes with brochures promoting Wisconsin. Mercedes began his tourist promotion activities in the 1930s. COURTESY OF THE WISCONSIN HISTORICAL SOCIETY, WHS IMAGE ID 37925.

ganing, snowshoeing, and sleigh rides. Resorts, developers, and real estate companies selling summer cottage lands provided organizational funding. One sponsor, the Minocqua Lumber Company, encouraged people to "own your own summer cabin in the Heart O' The Lakes." Merrill's Heineman Lumber Company advertised lakefront land for clubs and resorts.[58]

Mercedes operated tourist information offices in Chicago and several Wisconsin towns, appealing to a range of vacationers with literature suggesting Wisconsin offered "the social gayety of a smart hotel, the peaceful and homey comfort of a small resort, the rugged thrills of a fishing lodge, the restful seclusion of a private cottage, or the good fellowship of tourist camps." Potential tourists could choose among these options, guaranteeing something for everyone. Mercedes claimed he protected against disingenuous advertising and investigated all members. Among the resorts meeting these standards were family operations promoting home cooking in rustic yet comfortable surroundings, including Coon's Franklin Lodge, Cardinal's Manitowish Lodge, Ed Gabe's Lost Lake Resort, and Blaesing's Shorewood Vista.[59]

Although private interests led Wisconsin tourist promotion, they also depended on the state to develop and maintain parks, improve roads, and stock lakes. Resorts promoted abundant fish and game along with an invigorating climate. Mercedes and other northern Wisconsin boosters easily attracted Chicago vacationers but looked to draw visitors from the Twin Cities and Milwaukee as well as nearby smaller cities. In 1930, they voiced concerns that Minnesota's improved roads would attract potential Wisconsin vacationers. Mercedes did not believe state promotional funds offered a solution and instead urged the state to focus on improving infrastructure. Otherwise, he claimed, the tourist industry, and subsequently the state, would suffer.[60]

Mercedes fought against state funding to promote tourism, sensing it would damage his business, and remained the voice and face of northern Wisconsin promotion for two decades. While some northern newspapers spoke of promotional expenditures in line with Michigan and Minnesota, Mercedes suggested state promotion was an unnecessary burden and private industry could handle the work. With a prominent Chicago promotional office and wide literature distribution, Mercedes helped convince tourists to vacation in the state. Despite his protests, the state established a recreational publicity department in 1936. Governor Phil La Follette recognized that state efforts to preserve and promote natural resources aided the tourist industry and Mercedes's cause. Wisconsin also claimed its hotels, resorts, camps, housekeeping cabins, and private cottages were "where the nation finds recreation."[61] Increased lodging demands along with higher gas tax and nonresident fishing license receipts indicated growing interest in Wisconsin vacations. A fishing tournament between Wisconsin, Minnesota, and Michigan governors, a Madison tourist information booth, and two Chicago rail station exhibits headlined Wisconsin's 1937 promotional efforts, leading the state's recreational publicity department to comment, "These 'samples of outdoor Wisconsin in Chicago' will serve throughout every day of the year to emphasize the state's vacation appeal and extend the state's vacation invitation to the traveling thousands of the metropolis." The department also distributed stories to transportation organizations and tourist bureaus promoting northern Wisconsin.[62]

While World War II slowed tourism, the department encouraged promoters and operators to "keep the name and fame of Wisconsin's Vacationland fresh in the mind of postwar travelers" through newspaper advertisements, mailings, and promoting future vacation travel.[63] With private promotional efforts initially sparking people's interest in Wisconsin vacations, the state increased its activities and hoped for further postwar cooperation. Unlike Minnesota and Michigan, where regional tourist associations received state support, Wisconsin's efforts remained privatized longer. As a result, Mercedes's Heart O'Lakes Association initially shaped Wisconsin's message, promoting a restorative outdoor experience. It was a message that individual tourist enterprises across the North Woods also sought to capture in their literature.

Promoting the Region "Where Lakes are Legion"

While organizations and state governments promoted tourism, North Woods resorts and lodges helped connect image and experience by marketing themselves as rustic outposts. Guests at Minnesota's Basswood Lake Lodge were drawn by its inaccessibility, boarding twice-daily boat service, which the lodge suggested, "keeps you in touch with civilization, from which you are as far removed as though you were hundreds of miles in the interior regions." While the idea of escaping modern life appeared regularly in promotional materials, the lodge guaranteed comfort. Guests could eat and stay in the lodge or opt for a cabin and cook for themselves. The lodge distributed information at Minneapolis and Chicago tourist offices and attended outdoor shows to expand clientele.[64] Firmly immersed in modern consumer culture, these establishments issued promotional literature and enlisted newspapers to help attract tourists looking for adventure, relaxation, and a change of scene.

Ranging from rustic to modern, North Woods lodging options catered to vacationer desires. While Basswood Lodge emphasized limited access,

Lake Vermilion resort operators promoted the area's egalitarian nature, suggesting, "We have no fashionable and high price hostelries where the 'upper four hundred' like to spend a short time amid surroundings very little removed from city life." Lake Vermilion offered an ideal place for nature lovers, campers, tourists, anglers, and hunters. A journey down the Vermilion River supposedly landed the visitor in a "country seldom visited by white man." Boosters conveyed a sense of mystery by shrouding the region in Indian lore and comparing tourist canoe trips to the travels of those who traversed the waters for centuries. In reality, the experiences were dramatically different. Indians made canoe trips for survival and as a way of life; voyageurs, for trade; and tourists, for pleasure; but promoters linked them to cultivate a sense of adventure.[65]

Other area resorts, including G. A. Crawford's lodge thirty-six miles from Ely, offered cleanliness and cool breezes in a comfortable atmosphere. Guests vacationed among "beauty unspoiled by the hands of Man," and unlike at Basswood, no mention was made of staying in touch with civilization. Jameson's Wilderness Retreat Lodge provided its Depression-era visitors a rustic lodge and twenty-one cabins. Catering to wilderness enthusiasts, it also attracted visitors because of its modest rates and remote location thirty-five miles to the closest restaurant, forty miles to the nearest town, and 126 miles to the railroad station. Jameson's guests were warned to "check your pocketbook upon arrival" because additional funds were unnecessary while vacationing there.[66]

Despite promoting rusticity, Minnesota lodging operations often offered modern conveniences in places of picturesque beauty. Cascade Lodge marketed itself as "Minnesota's Finest Rustic Resort on the Great North Shore of Lake Superior," where visitors enjoyed rest in a "wilderness resort of luxury and good comradeship." While Cascade offered a serene setting along Lake Superior's shores, it was also accessible from the highway and within Cascade State Park. Cabins had electric lights, running water, and amenities found in private homes. Fawcett's Breezy Point on Big Pelican Lake promoted luxury accommodations with a beauty parlor, barbershop, billiards, bowling, and grocery. The Minneapolis couple that owned Clef Camp in Grand Rapids joined other resort owners in promoting their regular Minnesota Board of Health inspections, since some potential visitors were interested in places guaranteeing clean and modern facilities as well as activities.[67]

Many establishments began their existence serving tourists, while others promoted their transformation into resorts, lodges, and cabins by

Breezy Point Resort, Minnesota, circa 1930. COURTESY OF THE MINNESOTA HISTORICAL SOCIETY.

residents deciding to cater to vacationers. In Wisconsin, Eagle River's Balsams on Big Bass Lake was one of the latter, originally built for private use but converted into a main lodge and cabins for thirty-six guests. Iven Johnson informed potential guests about how he developed his Weblake Resort near Spooner. His parents moved to the region during his youth. Iven left and then returned to operate the general store, marrying a local teacher and caring for visiting sportsmen. One visitor, an editor at *Outdoor Life and Recreation*, suggested he build cabins and provide fishermen supplies. Armed with this advice, Johnson entered the tourist industry somewhat unwittingly, expanding his business to provide for guests from Chicago, the Twin Cities, and St. Louis.[68]

Bent's Camp near Land O' Lakes, Wisconsin, originally catered to fishermen and later emphasized the natural environment and casual atmosphere to make guests feel at home. Bent's was for those "who love the sparkle of the sunshine on rippling waters, the song of birds in the forest, the beauty of the setting sun as it sinks to rest in the tree tops, the serene splendor of the moonlight on the surface of a northern lake."[69] On the other hand, Mason Lake Resort told vacationers from what they needed to escape. Hugh Boyd and his sons welcomed those who sought to recoup their physical and mental health. Guests could put behind "all the smoke and dust and grime and smells of the big town and slip away to some lake or stream in the great North Woods where the waters glint and sparkle all day long."[70] While Bent's Camp and Mason Lake Resort offered a North Woods experience, the former promoted nature's splendor, while the latter emphasized escaping urban stresses.

Northern Wisconsin resorts also marketed the health benefits of vacationing amid nature. The Lakota near Conover provided relief for hay fever and asthma sufferers, and the Planets boasted that 95 percent of land in the surrounding area remained in its natural state. At Birchwood Lodge, guests could spend a day in the "crisp, pure air and tonic sunshine" and then relax over a home-cooked meal.[71] The cooler climate and pollen-free air made the North Woods an appealing destination that visitors interpreted as unmarred by industrial pollution and urban noise. At Lost Lake Resort, the owner's personal touch was evident. With a lifetime in the resort business, he remained convinced that a vacation at his resort "removes gloom, sweeps away unhappiness and initiates every newcomer into the Ed Gabe's Lost Lake Resort club of good fellowship and good cheer." Guests received "service with a smile" at a place where "experienced workers guard your comfort, sunny dispositions prevail, and no 'crabs' or 'grouches' are wanted." Such messages said little about whether workers received any health benefits from toiling in the North Woods.[72]

Resort literature also discussed activities to lure vacationers. At Wisconsin's Manitowish Lodge on Trout Lake, John Mann guaranteed guests good fishing and a healthy family vacation. Local guides could take them to the best spots. Others spent time purchasing Indian handicrafts and foodstuffs at Lac du Flambeau. At Oxbo Resort, guests embarked on Flambeau River canoe trips, where they discovered "a real sportsman's paradise, in the uncrowded country filled with myriads of clear, cool lakes and rivers as nature made them." While the Flambeau supposedly offered a natural escape, in reality resort guests paddled a river that humans controlled by harnessing it for power and maintaining a regulated flow.[73]

Lodging operators issued their own promotional literature but also cooperated through local resort associations to promote the North Woods, including one group that encouraged vacationers to "Follow the Big Fish Auto Route" to northern Wisconsin. Resort owners associations worked with private and public partners to promote the benefits of a North Woods vacation. The Chicago, Milwaukee, and St. Paul Railroad provided maps to customers listing resorts and their locations, while the Chicago and North

Western Railway promoted Wisconsin's northern lakes as "The Land of Hearts Desire" for outdoorsmen.[74] Eagle River's information bureau assisted visitors with inquiries and pushed the health benefits of vacationing at nearby resorts. The local organization sponsoring the bureau suggested, "When city streets are sizzling with breathless heat, when parks and beaches, with their seething throngs, offer no relief, the vacationist may come to our lake region secure in the knowledge that he will find refreshing pine-laden breezes and cool, restful nights."[75] The Three Lakes Resort Association claimed doctors prescribed a Three Lakes vacation as a remedy for "those who have lost their zest for living, those who are nervous and high strung, pale children who don't want to eat and those who are suffering from the pressure of business or social demands."[76] The Manitowish Waters Association also emphasized health and a place free of hay fever, hoping to attract summer homeowners by promising them a solid investment and gracious welcome. The Minocqua District Resort Association's *Wisconsin for Muskies* advertised fishing and listed rates, services, and proprietors for member resorts. Both individually and cooperatively, lodging operators used literature to delineate the benefits of vacationing "where lakes are legion."[77]

Resorts, lodges, regional organizations, and the state also worked with urban newspapers to promote the North Woods through articles, advertisements, booklets, and special sections. After reading such material, potential tourists could turn to a newspaper travel bureau or request additional literature from advertisers. In 1916, the *Minneapolis Tribune* published a Minnesota and Wisconsin resort guide, and the *St. Paul Dispatch* and *St. Paul Pioneer Press* Outing Department appealed to those seeking "summer and autumn pleasures."[78] Beginning in 1918, the *Minneapolis Journal* Travel and Resort Bureau published *Vacation Days*, promoting Minnesota and Wisconsin trips as part of the bureau's free travel service. In 1922, the *Pioneer Press* began publishing a special section informing readers about northern Minnesota and Wisconsin vacations and encouraging them to "play where you live." Wisconsin's Conservation Department used the section to publicize summer cottage construction, telling readers, "Wisconsin can make the dream come true. Come up and move in."[79]

Newspapers reached a vast market of potential vacationers through their travel bureaus and in print. In 1920, *Milwaukee Journal* reporter William W. "Brownie" Rowland organized the *Milwaukee Journal* Tour Club, which provided maps and travel information to subscribers. Rowland dispensed much of the advice, authoring *Journal* articles about touring the state. By 1932, the Tour Club received 125,000 requests annually and boasted 45,000 members. In its *Vacation Travel and Wisconsin Resort Guide*, the *Journal* advertised Wisconsin as the "Playground of the Middle West."[80] The *Cleveland Plain Dealer*'s 1924 summer vacation guide described how new technology and promotion contributed to the rise of auto touring. In its *Michigan Resort Directory*, the *Detroit Free Press* looked to help those thinking about a Michigan vacation. During the summer, the *Chicago Daily News* issued a weekly travel directory and later expanded to include more listings. By the early 1930s, the paper and its Resort and Travel Bureau proved essential for vacation planning.[81]

Urban newspapers regaled readers with descriptions of the region's climate and benefits. For instance, the UP offered "a land of cool nights and glorious summer days" with iron and copper mines as attractions.[82] Detroit residents were encouraged to "Spend Your Vacation This Year in Michigan: The State Where Lakes Abound," and *Free Press* readers discovered they could have the paper sent to them while vacationing in Michigan.[83] Vacationers to northern Wisconsin, where promoters suggested the air was "more exhilarating than champagne," could read Chicago papers during the tourist season. Chicagoans also heard about northern Minnesota's "rushing streams and virgin wilderness" and could choose between resorts or the solitude of a tent in the woods.[84] Advertisements highlighting canoeing, fishing, hunting, or relaxing and reading piqued the interest of those looking to "travel into the great out-of-doors where they can forget the cares and worries of everyday life and reside temporarily in a cozy log cabin somewhere amidst the pine-clad, lake-dotted northwoods."[85] No matter the day or the city, opening a newspaper led readers to vacation information. Newspapers also reported on vacationers pitching tents on northern lakes at little cost. Promoters used anything and everything to attract guests, including President Calvin Coolidge's vacation on Wisconsin's Brule River in 1928, which the *Milwaukee Journal* declared helped cement Wisconsin as a vacation state.[86]

Newspapers helped businesses, regional organizations, and state agencies connect with potential vacationers. Cleveland residents learned that Hiawatha Land was "a land of cool nights and glorious summer days" where one could visit copper and iron mines. Potential Milwaukee anglers were lured to the UP with the promise, "Catch Your Limit Everyday in Hiawathaland," while the Ten Thousand Lakes of Minnesota Association promoted affordable vacations in Chicago newspapers. Chicagoans discovered that several northern Wisconsin towns offered the "Lake Geneva of the north," comparing the region to a well-known southern Wisconsin resort area.[87] With more automobiles on the road, railroads used newspapers to advertise fishing at northern Wisconsin resorts and the Arrowhead as the "last remaining wilderness in the middle west." The Ten Thousand Lakes of Minnesota Association emphasized cooler summer weather. Not only were activities plentiful and the environment pleasant, vacations were packaged and available for purchase—Minnesota provided "the kind of vacation you want at the price you can afford to pay."[88] Lakelands, Inc., used the newspaper to promote summer-home development "deep in the heart of the cool north woods" between Eagle River and Minocqua.[89] Clevelanders opened their newspapers in 1937 to discover tourism in Michigan had joined automobile manufacturing as a leading state industry. The Automobile Club of Michigan estimated that 82 percent of Michigan's tourist traffic originated in the Midwest, with forty million people within a day's drive. Visitors sought out the state's extensive shoreline, inland lakes, and health benefits, everything one would want on a vacation except "salt water at a seaside resort."[90]

North Woods papers also helped promote tourism. The 1931 *Menominee Herald Leader* vacation guide emphasized proximity to forty million people and asserted that state and county parks offered something for everyone. Given its position at the UP's southern tip, Menominee was "Cloverland's Gateway," and located along Lake Superior's shore, Munising offered the "Naples of America." The newspaper praised people for telling others about the UP, suggesting this helped increase UP tourists from twelve thousand in 1919 to five hundred thousand in 1930.[91] Wisconsin's *Vilas County News* covered resort activities, publicized tourism's possibilities, and encouraged residents to develop the industry. By reporting on resort guests in the 1920s and claiming on its masthead that it was "The Advertisers Best Medium, Giving Full Coverage of a Famous Resort County with a Real Future," the *News* remained an important voice for tourism. It issued an annual section highlighting both older resorts and new ones.[92]

For its part, the press proved helpful in creating an image of the North Woods, but local newspapers occasionally criticized policies that left some regions swimming upstream to attract tourists. Wisconsin's *Vilas County News* reprinted articles and advertisements from metropolitan dailies to make residents aware of promotion campaigns. As early as 1922, it also expressed concerns about Wisconsin's ability to compete with neighboring destinations, noting that "Wisconsin has been invaded by advertisements emphasizing the natural attractions of Michigan and other advertisements which portray Minnesota as a region of 10,000 Lakes."[93] The *News* also looked to expand the tourist season to improve local prospects, sponsoring a winter sports carnival to spark interest in Wisconsin as "The Year Round Playground." In a 1931 editorial, the paper feared Michigan and Minnesota would garner more tourists unless Wisconsin designated advertising funds. Emphasizing tourism's importance for regional prosperity, the editor claimed, "If this plan does not receive the complete support of the business men of the state then resorts and hotels everywhere might just as well be closed up and Wisconsin might just as well go out of the tourist business."[94] Despite a state advertising appropriation in 1936, the editor continued to point to deficiencies given that Michigan's tourist appropriation remained five times that of Wisconsin's. He proposed that northern Wisconsin secede and become part of the UP or Minnesota to stress that other state's tourism efforts were better advertised and funded, whereas, "In Wisconsin, a $210,000,000 recreational industry, the second largest in the state, is ham-strung, abused, kicked around and knocked askew by any crackpot."[95]

Tourist advocates recognized the power newspaper writers and editors had in framing vacation options. In 1937, Michigan's regional tourist bureau joined the Automobile Club of Michigan, Michigan Hotel Association, and Detroit Convention and Tourist Bureau in sponsoring a writers' tour. Highlighting "Michigan's 1,624 miles of shore line" and "her ten thousand inland lakes and streams," the tour also suggested vacationers could view work in mines and fisheries. Newspapermen returned home to write about Michigan vacations, convincing readers to fish its waters and see its industrial might.[96] Arthur Stace's articles on Michigan vacations appeared in newspapers across the state during the interwar years. As new scenic highways made travel easier, he turned his attention to the UP, where tourists could visit old mining towns. Crystal Falls had one of the first modern hotels in the UP, and Ottawa National Forest and its surrounding lakes offered paradise for sportsmen. The decline of mining and lumbering, according to Stace, left "vast domains of lakes and wilderness in which King Recreation holds full sway."[97]

Stace's articles provided advice for those planning UP vacations and also allowed those unable to physically travel north to journey imaginatively to the UP. He compared the UP's shoreline to Maine's rocky coast, presented the Porcupine Mountains as among the highest peaks in the Midwest, and described the beauty of Copper Harbor and Lake Superior.

Recognizing outdoor recreation had replaced resource extraction in the Copper Country, Stace wrote, "Once mining held chief interest for visitors. Now with the opening of shore roads, scenic grandeur has gone far ahead in tourist appeal. No other part of Michigan is more spectacular in its beauty and fascination." Tourists could travel along the new Brockway Mountain Drive or the Lake Superior shoreline. According to Stace, road construction aided tourist development by providing access and helping visitors forge pleasant memories of vacations along Lake Superior. Brockway was built for tourist use, and the town at the end of the road, Copper Harbor, turned to tourism as a potential savior. Ocha Potter's golf course and cabins continued to attract visitors. Like Potter, Stace believed tourism offered a solution to regional economic problems and the chance for "a new life, a more hopeful life, possibly a far longer life."[98]

Newspaper writers found their services in demand from tourism advocates. In a 1938 brochure, *The Long Bow Country of Minnesota*, journalist and Minnesota Tourist Bureau director Ed Shave wrote an article in the form of a letter to a Tulsa tourist interested in a Minnesota vacation. The "Long Bow" region, according to Shave, was a place for the explorer, voyageur, fisherman, and hunter. The moniker both suggested the general shape of the region and demonstrated how slogans were used to promote native lore and frontier history. Shave wrote, "Once the chosen home of the Ojibway Indian, this land of bewildering loveliness has retained the natural magnificence of a forest empire, replete with sapphire lakes, even while the comfort-loving White Man has claimed it for his own and dotted its lake shores with modern lodges." Tourists discovered the Cuyuna Iron Range in Deerwood and Crosby and encountered citizens festooned with long beards for the Paul Bunyan summer carnival in Brainerd, with its 362 resorts and 500 lakes. Heading north to Nisswa, visitors found 75 resorts where vacations were enjoyable and affordable. Shave told the story of one family who rented a summer cottage for less than the cost of remaining in the city. Farther north, at Leech Lake and Walker, tourists entered the Chippewa National Forest with its Indian burial grounds and fishing. Looping back to Itasca State Park near Bemidji, vacationers could see the Mississippi River headwaters and watch a pageant performed by CCC workers and Chippewa Indians. Trying to build excitement for such a journey, Shave told the potential tourist, "Here's hoping you've enjoyed the trip—but when you make it in reality you'll enjoy it ten thousand times more." Like Stace's articles on the UP, Shave's portrayal helped encourage tourists to visit Minnesota's "Long Bow Country."[99]

Maps provided another vehicle to reach tourists, guiding them through the landscape and offering a medium to advertise attractions. On official state maps, Michigan's highway commissioner commented on wonderful roads and encouraged tourists to traverse them. The MAA and Ten Thousand Lakes–Greater Minnesota Association issued maps listing hotels, resorts, camps, and fish and game laws. Tourists were told to "Follow the Arrows to the Arrowhead," where they would discover a "climactic delight" and a "land of romance." Northern Minnesota printer W. A. Fisher published a canoe wilderness map for those planning a trip. Other promoters offered maps with their guides, including the Ask Benn Wagner Service of Crow Wing County, which listed 267 resorts in the area. Minnesota's Cook County claimed the region as "nature's gift to the Arrowhead Country" and located all resorts along the Gunflint Trail for visitors.[100] By 1938, the Gunflint Trail Association and Grand Marais Chamber of Commerce did the same, listing 59 summer resorts on Lake Superior's North Shore Drive and the Gunflint Trail. The *St. Paul Pioneer Press* printed a state highway map in its 1934 vacation section. Chicago's Motor Club issued a *Map of Northern Wisconsin Lakes Region*, and the *Milwaukee Journal* Tour Club provided northern Wisconsin road and resort maps to its members. The Chicago and North Western Railway also included a large map with resort locations in its *Summer Outings: Wisconsin and Michigan*.[101] Resorts also used maps to guide guests, and the UPDB's *Lure Book* included maps featuring colorful cartoon figures informing potential vacationers about the region's history, activities, and people. Like photographs, they painted an image of the region. A diverse set of tourist advocates, ranging from the state with its official highway maps to local chambers of commerce, incorporated maps into the lexicon and helped tourists visualize and navigate the North Woods.

North Woods maps were part of a larger set of cartographic materials that sold highway travel to Americans. This included Rand McNally's "Blazed Trails" program, which linked highways with services travelers found along the road. Merchants, state highway departments, tourist bureaus, and motor clubs issued free maps to attract visitors.[102] Such demand created additional business not only for Rand McNally but also for local mapmakers and publishers, who contributed to publications like the UPDB's *Lure Book* and resort literature. Road maps helped transform the highway adventurer into a highway consumer. Maps told people where to go, how to get there, and where to stop as they moved through space. They surely helped tourists find their destination, but by charting resort and state park locations along with other elements of the tourist landscape, maps also established a level of conformity that contributed to limiting people's ability to negotiate new paths through the North Woods.

Potential vacationers initially understood and encountered the North Woods through a range of promotional literature that placed the outdoors at center. People received recommendations from friends and family who vacationed there, but suggestions were infused with allusions to the pervasive promotional discourse. Given its wide dissemination and the information it contained, promotional literature helped potential tourists discover the North Woods. Farm and industrial interests selling goods, home builders constructing summer homes, timber and real estate interests marketing land, and a range of tourist operators and organizations employed literature to capture the vacation dollar. Guidebooks, maps, brochures, booklets, postcards, pamphlets, and even stickers and games were part of the package luring tourists. This wealth of material helped fashion a common North Woods image in people's minds. But tourist development demanded more than promotion. It depended on transforming the landscape, working diligently, conserving resources for the purposes of enjoying them, and creating a new conception of the North Woods. The developments of the interwar years, in which the North Woods became a supplier of outdoor recreation to urban and rural vacationers as well as local residents, continued to have profound implications for the region as tourism's growth continued after World War II. While tourism remained the crop to cultivate, residents and tourists encountered both new opportunities and problems as they ventured down this path together.

CHAPTER 5

You've Earned It—Now Enjoy It: Playing in the Postwar Era

Born in Ely, Minnesota, in 1917, Bill Rom was the youngest of nine children of Slovenian immigrants. After graduating from high school in 1935, he attended Ely Junior College before enrolling at the University of Minnesota and majoring in wildlife management. Rom secured a summer position with the U.S. Forest Service through Sigurd Olson, who served as dean of Ely Junior College and found jobs for students in Minnesota's boundary waters. The $22 weekly salary provided Rom college funds, while the experience and relationships developed during summers in the forest fostered an intimate knowledge of the canoe country.[1]

After graduating from Minnesota, Rom considered graduate work at Oklahoma, tested to become a navy officer, and worked in Idaho and Montana mines. Planning to drive a tour bus in Yellowstone, he received a call from the navy to work intelligence in Seattle during the war. While there, he developed the idea for operating an outfitting business back in Ely. He and his wife, who married in 1944, initially considered a summer camp, but increasing demand for outfitting services, along with the realization that it was easier to send tourists out with gear, food, and instructions, led them to establish Canoe Country Outfitters. In 1946, Rom returned to Ely and began outfitting and guiding groups through the wilderness country. He promoted canoe trips with a canoe country film and conversed with people at sports shows during the first winter. By year three Rom was focusing almost exclusively on outfitting, posing a canoe trip as a possibility for all. He appealed to people with little experience, suggesting, "Any neophyte can make a completely successful canoe trip without a guide through our expert outfitting and mapping of the trail." To enjoy the canoe country, one only needed to prepare a meal and follow a compass and map. Nor was the region solely the province of men; one promotional piece declared, "A good number of parties contain women and children and many girl groups venture out alone."[2]

Some of Rom's parties hired guides instead of venturing unaccompanied into the canoe country. Guiding was hard work, and having a guide provided customers a more leisurely experience. Rom's guides worked long days, rising early, making breakfast, paddling, setting up camp, and cooking supper while guests relaxed around the fire. Rom generally remained in town running the business, while his guides took to the woods with clients. Each summer he and his wife embarked on a canoe trip, often bringing their children, who later worked as guides. Running the business presented challenges, but Rom relished meeting people interested in canoeing the region he adored. Canoe Country Outfitters' high return rate suggested solid service, and Rom emerged as the "Canoe King of Ely."[3]

Like his colleagues in the resort business, Rom created a sense of community among his clientele. Newsletters provided trip information, told stories of canoe adventures, and urged people to oppose exploitation of Minnesota's canoe country. While some area resorts demanded road access, Rom believed it would be a mistake, telling customers, "Our bodies and minds need a week or two away from the strains and stresses of everyday life every year—and where can you get so completely away from yakking people, blaring traffic and the weariness of our daily toil." Wilderness offered a mental escape where the sights and sounds of the city disappeared. Affordability also mattered, and Rom appealed to people's desire for rejuvenation at reasonable cost. "For a completely relaxing vacation in 1958," he proposed, "Plan another canoe trip into this last remaining wilderness. Recession or no, a canoe trip hardly costs more than staying at home—and you owe your bodies and your minds a change after weeks of steady routine." He encouraged customers to help preserve the canoe country by joining organizations like Friends of the Wilderness. Rom feared a multiple-use forest would destroy the area, making it no different from the rest of Minnesota, Wisconsin, or Michigan, where he saw unrestrained development threatening one's ability to escape into nature.[4] Rom's view of the land and cultivation of new vacation opportunities highlight how local residents increasingly shaped people's experiences in and perceptions of the North Woods after World War II.

The use of survey data to guide development, year-round activities, increased cottage construction, new business entrants, and policy debates continued to transform the North Woods. Rising tourist demand corresponded with a growing emphasis on consumption as a measure of prosperity in which vacations served as a marker. State policies, including the disbursement of promotional funds, contributed to varied development across the region. As this chapter demonstrates, despite competition and occasional conflict, public and private organizations from Minnesota's Arrowhead to Michigan's Copper Country discovered ways to cooperate across physical, political, and economic boundaries to fashion the postwar North Woods.

Competing and Cooperating for Tourists

Before World War II, Michigan tourism generated nearly $400 million in annual revenue. With wartime restrictions reducing this figure, the state's Michigan Tourist Council (MTC) looked to the future, claiming, "The enormous urge for travel, pent up during the war and considerably curbed during the adjustment year of 1946 will be answered fully as peacetime production moves automobiles and travel equipment out of the factories and tourists again take to the vacation roads." In 1946, the MTC's Chicago, Cleveland, Detroit, and Lansing information offices serviced over sixty-two thousand inquiries, and its "Vacation in Michigan" campaign urged residents to plan an in-state vacation to limit travel time and enjoy more of their vacation. Officials met potential tourists at outdoor shows, and MTC advertising described opportunities for different tastes and budgets. It also collaborated with state universities to publish informational papers and offer seminars for interested operators and communities. MTC initiatives were among a multitude of efforts marking the transition to a peacetime economy in which public and private entities mobilized for a postwar travel boom.[5] Minnesota's Tourist Bureau, Wisconsin's Conservation Department, Ontario's Ministry of Travel and Publicity, and the Northern Great Lakes Area Council (NORGLAC) brought together officials interested in connecting tourism with regional development and conservation. Private organizations both old and new, including Wisconsin's Hayward Lakes Resort Association, Minnesota's Gunflint Trail Association, and Michigan's Copper Country Vacationist League (CCVL), worked to promote and develop destinations. Commercial advertising also highlighted the region. Hamm's Beer, for example, promoted the Land of Sky Blue Waters and reminded operators it was "the only beer telling all America about the wonderful vacationland which is yours."[6]

North Woods promoters encouraged Americans to travel after supporting the war effort. Emphasizing a consumer's ability to purchase health, happiness, and an escape, materials included patriotic appeals to enjoy a "Victory Vacation Year," since "You've Earned It—Now Enjoy It." Guidebooks offered assistance in choosing destinations. The Upper Peninsula Development Bureau's (UPDB) *Lure Book* suggested the UP "was designed by Nature for your happier vacation," and the 1947 edition informed visitors that

> health and happiness are the greatest assets of life. Millions of dollars are spent annually to achieve them and yet many times the money might be better spent on vacation trips that take us away from the artificialities of life, away from the grind of everyday living, affording us an opportunity to get acquainted again with our families, at some restful spot out in God's great out-of-doors.

Subsequent *Lure Books* continued to stress escape and family togetherness. Regardless of one's budget, UP vacations supposedly offered an antidote to modern pressures by allowing visitors to enjoy nature at one of over twelve hundred lodging operations. Published in 1958, the final *Lure Book* urged a sound land and water resource program to aid the tourist industry and suggested the completed Mackinac Bridge would help draw more visitors by providing a direct link to the Midwest's bustling cities.[7]

Growing postwar demand increased regional competition, contributing to new tourist efforts. Michigan's expanded travel campaigns led the Minnesota Arrowhead Association (MAA) to sponsor a contest for veterans to win a free vacation at the 1946 *Chicago Daily News* Travel Show, and MAA member organizations encouraged winter vacations, attended sports shows, and contracted with local enterprises to produce promotional materials.[8] Ontario officials denied a Minnesota request to issue Canadian fishing licenses but worked with U.S. officials to facilitate travel to Canada. Building on wartime friendship between the nations, provincial promoters highlighted reasonable rates for families and encouraged vacationing where one could purchase "A Cabin of Your Own."[9]

Believing tourism made Michigan more prosperous, the MTC urged resorts to create their own literature and advocated summer cottage investment. It produced and distributed photographs, conducted surveys, coordinated regional association efforts, and developed an advertising program to "make Michigan nationally recognized as a delightful vacation state." Growing numbers of people clearly felt so, as vacation expenditures in Michigan increased 22 percent from 1947 to 1952. By 1952, the MTC claimed 85 percent of union workers had vacation clauses in their contracts, providing a growing market.[10] Recognizing the lure of other

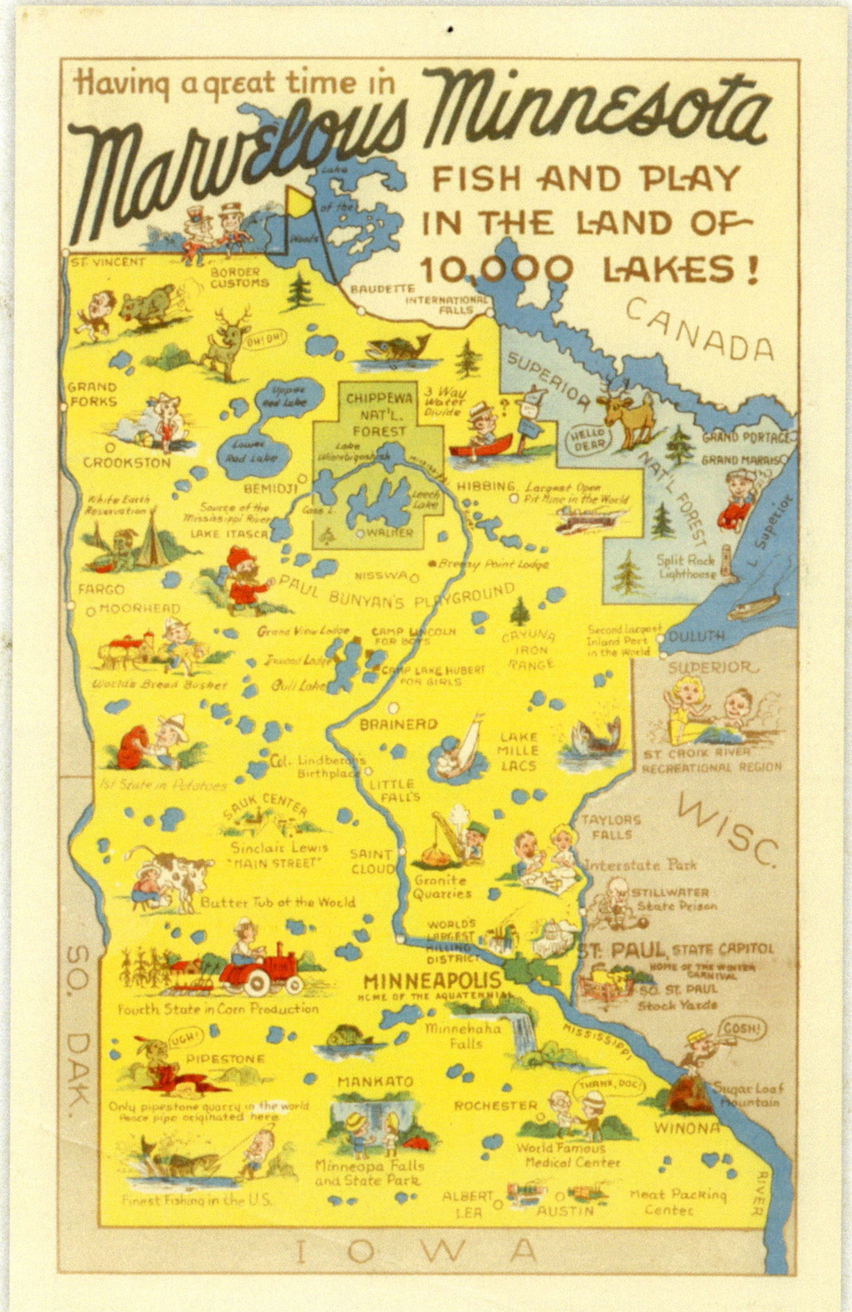

Colorful maps located opportunities available to vacationers, including this pictorial map of Minnesota, circa 1935. COURTESY OF THE MINNESOTA HISTORICAL SOCIETY.

Postcard of Keweenaw Land of Michigan's Copper Country, 1943. COURTESY OF THE MICHIGAN TECHNOLOGICAL UNIVERSITY ARCHIVES AND COPPER COUNTRY HISTORICAL COLLECTIONS.

In 1928, President Calvin Coolidge spent the summer fishing on the Brule River, using a high school in Superior, Wisconsin, as the vacation White House. This stamp was likely issued by the Outdoor Club of Wisconsin to promote northern Wisconsin tourism. COURTESY OF THE WISCONSIN HISTORICAL SOCIETY, WHS IMAGE ID 44768.

Postwar Keweenaw promotional materials highlighted scenery and industry, including these images of the Club House Gardens at Keweenaw Park Resort and the Ahmeek 3 and 4 shaft-rockhouse. COURTESY OF THE MICHIGAN TECHNOLOGICAL UNIVERSITY ARCHIVES AND COPPER COUNTRY HISTORICAL COLLECTIONS.

Postcards promoted a sense of adventure on North Woods canoe trips, circa 1942. COURTESY OF THE MINNESOTA HISTORICAL SOCIETY.

Bill Rom's Canoe Country Outfitters, 629 East Sheridan Street, Ely, circa 1958. COURTESY OF THE MINNESOTA HISTORICAL SOCIETY.

This cover from a 1932 Wisconsin tourist pamphlet captures a typical North Woods scene.
COURTESY OF THE WISCONSIN HISTORICAL SOCIETY, WHS IMAGE ID 37918.

Postwar roadside sign erected by the Copper Country Vacationist League promoting the area's health benefits. COURTESY OF THE MICHIGAN TECHNOLOGICAL UNIVERSITY ARCHIVES AND COPPER COUNTRY HISTORICAL COLLECTIONS.

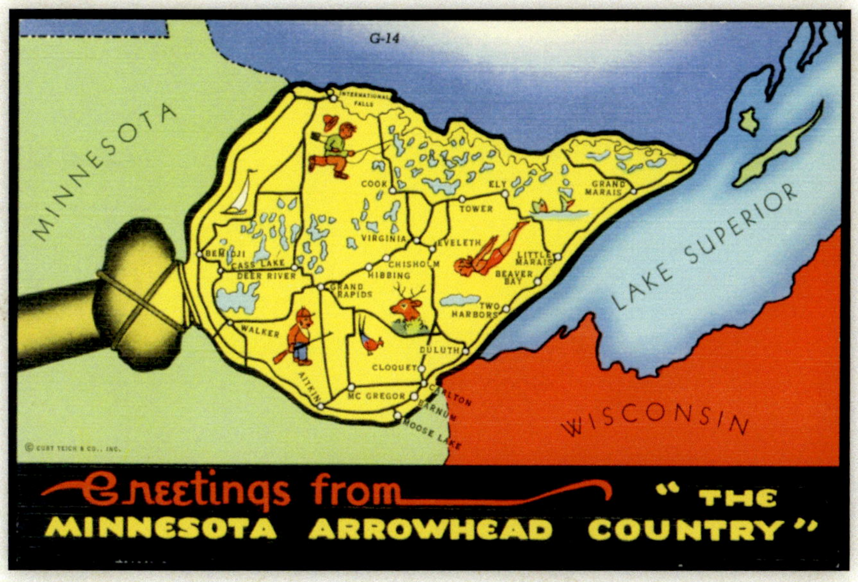

Colorful promotional materials reinforced regional nicknames, as in this piece from 1940. COURTESY OF THE MINNESOTA HISTORICAL SOCIETY.

Vacationers increasingly looked for affordable and accessible options among woods and waters. Here visitors pitch their tents at a tourist camp on Shagawa Lake near Ely, Minnesota, circa 1930. PHOTOGRAPH BY THE FOREST ART COMPANY. COURTESY OF THE MINNESOTA HISTORICAL SOCIETY.

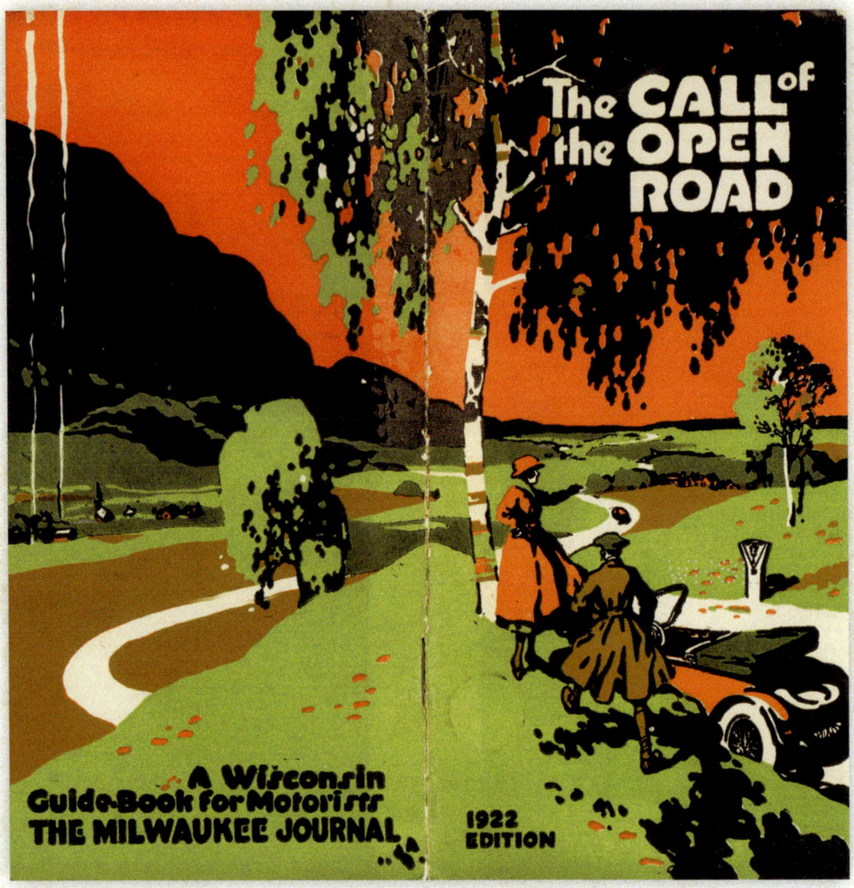

Front and back covers of *The Call of the Open Road* (1922), an annual publication of the *Milwaukee Journal* Tour Department. The publication and the travel services of the *Milwaukee Journal* were addressed not only to Wisconsin motorists but especially to out-of-state tourists; the automobile and the state's highways made northern Wisconsin more accessible to them. COURTESY OF THE WISCONSIN HISTORICAL SOCIETY, WHS IMAGE ID 41273.

destinations, the MTC aimed to set a Michigan vacation apart. "Things to See in Michigan" highlighted natural and historic sites, while "Water and Sun Vacations in Michigan" and "The Magic of Michigan" claimed the state had more beach than along the coast from Maine to Florida and encouraged tourists to "Make a Memory in Michigan."[11] Citing a drop in inquiries at its Chicago office from 1949 to 1956 even as Michigan's tourist business doubled, the MTC closed its Chicago, Detroit, and Cleveland offices and initiated a program backed by the state's regional associations where "vacation salesmen" carried Michigan's tourist message directly to business and industry by having personnel offices distribute literature to workers. In the first quarter of 1957, the program contacted over one hundred organizations.[12]

Despite these successes, the MTC faced challenges to ensure Michigan remained a premier vacation destination. The UPDB's George Bishop expressed concerns about the MTC shirking its responsibility to citizens who invested in tourist enterprises, claiming other states designated more promotional funds. Operators urged more travel show participation. Resort owner Joe Bachunas warned Governor G. Mennen Williams, "If we don't look out, Michigan's second industry will no longer be its second industry and the state economy will suffer for it."[13] Fearing the Copper Country moniker invoked bleak mining areas and would dissuade tourists, MTC chair Robert Furlong advised reconsidering the name, but his recommendation went nowhere. The MTC and Michigan's regional promotion associations also came under attack in the early 1950s from a proposal to make the MTC purely advisory and stripping the four regional associations of matching funds and merging them into one central agency. Opponents of the proposal rallied and won, stressing the existing program's productivity and the need to preserve the public-private partnership.[14]

Increased competition also led states to broaden their tourist appeal. Materials depicted North Woods destinations as a vacation paradise for families, sportsmen, and outdoor enthusiasts. Hunting and fishing magazine readers placed Michigan among top vacation spots. A 1949 Gallup Poll asked respondents to choose a summer vacation destination anywhere in the country with cost not a factor, and they ranked Michigan fifth, Wisconsin thirteenth, and Minnesota fourteenth. Promoting year-round vacations with the slogan "Every Season Has a Reason" and summer homes with "For the REST of your life, Plan a home in the Minnesota Arrowhead Country," the MAA's twelve thousand members benefited from the growing tourist influx. By 1956, nine hundred thousand vacationers spent $55 million in the Arrowhead.[15] State publications portrayed a family vacationland where one could "relax jagged nerves and rebuild muscles tired from work and worry." Minnesota purportedly had "a lake for every vacation mood," along with abundant natural resources and vacation opportunities. The state also offered courses on tourist advertising and provided operators quantitative information about the industry.[16]

Local newspapers continued to assist state tourism efforts. Wisconsin's *Vilas County News* printed materials for resorts and featured resort owner profiles. The paper's vacation section encouraged operators to offer everyone a friendly reception and recognize common interests, suggesting, "If a vacation group contacts you for accommodations and your operation is a little too expensive for him, do you have to drive him off to Minnesota or the Upper Peninsula?"[17] Minocqua's *Lakeland Times* told readers it was "Dedicated to the Development of Northern Wisconsin's Lake Land as the Great Summer and Winter Playground of the Middle West." The paper commented on area resorts and conservation issues. Appearing little concerned with tourism's impact on natural resources, the *Times* reported that the tourist industry was "largely pure profit because we trade almost none of our natural resources for all that cash; what our visitors take home with them is mostly relaxation and health." It supported public funds for conservation mainly because they aided tourism, claiming, "We are playing a million dollar game on a penny-ante basis." Resort owners wanting more fish for their guests, business owners hoping for additional vacationers and advertising, and residents urging expanded public hunting and fishing grounds joined in such calls.[18]

Operators also cooperated through organizations to promote and develop the North Woods. The UPDB urged members to improve service and make the UP a year-round destination, distributing bulletins that included vacationer inquiries as well as information on potential employees, summer-home owners, and resort operators. Chicagoan W. C. Dallman wanted to purchase a resort or build one. Others expressed interest in constructing cabins or, like Virgil Long of Gary, Indiana, sought property for a summer home. Bulletins also marketed services. Former *Chicago Tribune* travel editor Sam Wallace operated Chicago's Michigan Vacation Bureau, which charged resort owners a fee for booking guests. Wallace advertised in UPDB bulletins, appealing to operators to list with him. Claiming to promote all of Michigan, Wallace worked for resorts that paid him and struggled to convince officials that his operation benefited the entire state. Bulletins also aired vacationer complaints. One Ann Arbor resident bemoaned the UP's accommodations while offering Canada accolades, stressing how her trips there left her impressed by the place, people, and promotional literature.[19]

After thirty-five years at the UPDB's helm, George Bishop, whom outdoors writer Jack Van Coevering labeled "a corpulent man with a voice like a fog horn," and Escanaba journalist Jean Worth identified as the "architect of the Upper Peninsula's first great era of growth in recreation business," resigned in 1957. To address financial concerns, the UPDB proposed a membership program for nonresidents that would nominally give them a square foot of land in exchange for their contribution. The program never commenced, and a year later, unable to pay for its *Lure Books*, the organization folded. One resident charged the UPDB with profligate administrative spending at the expense of reaching tourists. He supported a new organization and joined others in believing a program focused on hunting, fishing, and winter sports would aid resident's pocketbooks and offer tax relief.[20] Formed in 1959, the Upper Michigan Tourist Association, which was renamed the Upper Peninsula Travel and Recreation Association, developed such a program under secretary-manager Ken Dorman, who became interested in seasonal sales variations while operating a Marquette advertising agency. Lodging operators also recognized division in their ranks; one large resort owner claimed the small operator "does not understand that by contributing to this organization they can be helped in gaining more visitors to their operations."[21] To allay such concerns and bring businesses on board, the new organization distributed a film in which Dorman explained the services it provided members and compared the UP to a supermarket with activities and attractions to sell to visitors. As Michigan's second largest industry, tourism generated $650 million annually. After qualifying for state matching funds in 1960, the organization advertised and sent representatives to travel shows in Chicago, Milwaukee, and Indianapolis.[22]

Tourism and conservation issues increasingly coalesced as growing numbers sought outdoor adventure. In northeastern Minnesota, the 1948 Thye-Blatnik Act provided funds for acquiring private land in the Superior National Forest. This legislation built upon earlier efforts, including Arthur Carhart's forest recreational plan, the 1926 U.S. Forest Service roadless area designation, the Quetico-Superior Council's efforts to halt dam projects, and the Shipstead-Newton-Nolan Act to protect shorelines.[23] Increased resort development and tourist traffic along Minnesota's Gunflint Trail led the Cook County Tour-Travel Council to claim,

"The day of the rustic fisherman going up the Trail seems to have passed." While Cook County and the Gunflint Trail offered wilderness adventure, the area increasingly saw families enjoying nature in rustic, yet comfortable, environs. Gunflint Lodge's Justine Kerfoot believed the area offered vacationers more than the towns of Ely and Tower.[24] The Gunflint Trail Association's twenty-one members studied problems facing operators, advertised attractions, and responded to requests. Typical were the inquiries of one Chicagoan who wanted to fish and stay in a cabin while taking meals at the lodge. Another mentioned that his family visited Ely for four years and was interested in the Gunflint Trail for a change.[25]

In Wisconsin, several organizations viewed tourism as a community development tool. The Land O' Lakes Chamber of Commerce advertised in UPDB *Lure Books* to attract UP visitors and sent materials to companies encouraging workers to vacation in Land O' Lakes. Its brochures often appealed to women as consumers making choices about family vacations. For example, one asked, "Are there mothers who think a vacationland is a place where the men have all the fun? Not so at Land O' Lakes." To coordinate activities, the Land O' Lakes Chamber of Commerce joined the Vilas County Chamber of Commerce, which represented thirteen local chambers with over one thousand members.[26] Based in Land O' Lakes, Joseph Handlos's Highway 45 Association continued to cooperate with the UPDB by calling for improved highways and labeling tourism the region's principal resource.[27] The Four County Development Group, representing Ashland, Bayfield, Iron, and Price Counties, supported Handlos and advocated including recreation in planning proposals. Reinforcing the interdependence of tourism and conservation for regional prosperity, it claimed recreation depended on Wisconsin's natural resources and "these four counties have more than their share." Planning aimed to improve recreational facilities and public access while encouraging operator involvement in the process.[28]

Northwestern Wisconsin's Hayward Lakes Resort Association brought together operators to promote the "Musky Capital of the World" in the 1950s by attending sports shows and organizing Hayward's Musky Festival. Members received inquiries from outdoor show attendees and lists from organizations like Wisconsin's Indian Head Country.[29] Resort operators also collaborated to solve problems. In 1955, the Hayward Lakes Resort Association hired John and Connie Keehner as tourist booth attendants. They visited members to rate establishments and opened the booth in mid-May. After the first season, some members complained the

Keehners used the booth to rent out their personal cabin. Association leadership confronted them, cleared up the problem, and reappointed them for another summer. But complaints continued as members worried about the Keehners "lack of diplomacy and tact" and expressed concerns that they sent tourists to particular areas, leading to their replacement in 1959.[30]

Responding to activities across the border, Ontario redoubled its efforts to attract American tourists and supported NORGLAC to bridge boundaries. Provincial programs aided local organizations in a system that was more top-down than that of its American neighbors. Ontario's Ministry of Travel and Publicity courted expected postwar tourist throngs by hosting U.S. newspaper editor tours and responding to inquiries from Americans.[31] Of the 57,013 mail inquiries received by the ministry's information branch in 1948, 74 percent came from the United States. As in Michigan, the branch broke requests down by state and distributed regional lists to local chambers.[32] Officials emphasized tourists as key to provincial and national prosperity since they used Canadian products and paid for services. The ministry produced promotional films, distributed booklets, operated reception centers, inspected and licensed tourist camps, participated in outdoor travel shows, and advised those entering the tourist business. It also encouraged residents to promote family vacations and support community tourist organizations.[33]

Ontario officials built upon the efforts of their American counterparts, initially issuing one hundred thousand copies of a vacation book and publishing it in escalating quantity in subsequent years. Potential visitors could view one of seventy-one films emphasizing Ontario's vacation opportunities at the Canadian Travel Film Library in Chicago. Films also circulated to schools, public libraries, sportsmen's groups, and travel clubs. Provincial officials conducted tours for American newspaper editors and measured success by the quantity and size of articles they generated.[34] The ministry even placed advertisements in publications it would have preferred to avoid; the department's deputy minister Tom McCall called the *Chicago Tribune*, "a lousy, stinking rag whose only virtue is its vast circulation, which we need in *our* business."[35] Officials also differentiated southern and eastern Ontario from northern and western Ontario, the latter attracting visitors interested in North Woods experiences. While the department's tours traditionally attracted small-town editors, it initiated northwest Ontario hunting and fishing tours for writers and editors from large American papers.[36] Officials also highlighted the province as a middle-class destination, elaborating, "We are not after the luxury trade, and practically all of our resorts are geared for people of modest means." While traveling to Ontario might cost more, upon arrival Americans would discover it was cheaper than home. In 1956, Ontario ran its first American television spots promoting vacations. The following year, it posted billboards in American cities and added a winter promotional program in 1960. Taken together, these efforts helped mark Ontario as a worthwhile vacation destination for Americans.[37]

Across the North Woods, local and regional organizations discovered a range of government support for tourism. Responding to roadsides plastered with signage, Michigan's highway department developed design standards.[38] Minnesota lodging operators regularly requested assistance and information on vacationer requests from the Department of Economic Development. One operator wanted the state to construct a roadside marker for his lake. Others wrote for suggestions or to provide information about new services and activities.[39] State government also helped people find work in the tourist industry. Minnesota's Department of Employment Security interviewed students and teachers for summer jobs and referred them to resort owners. Operators discovered a one-stop shop for seasonal workers at Wisconsin's Employment Office, which made 780 tourism-related job placements in 1952. Since tourism provided jobs, Minnesota Governor Luther Youngdahl urged facilities "for both the millionaire who can afford the best and the family man of modest means." To aid in this task, operators could call on state extension agents, who now focused on more than agriculture.[40]

Government served as both a target and remedy when disputes arose over measures affecting the tourist industry. In 1950, former Minnesota Tourist Bureau chair Ed Shave claimed the state lost tourists because its promotional appropriations trailed others. A decade later, the funding problem remained, leading the state conservation commissioner to comment that residents must demand government "stop playing tiddledywinks with an ante of a few dollars when asked to provide means to really promote tourist-travel in the North Star State."[41] In northern Wisconsin, resort operators expressed outrage over having to close bars an hour earlier than Milwaukee taverns and appealed to the state for equal footing, claiming guests needed entertainment. Later hours would help business and remedy a policy that favored one region over another. State legislator and resort operator Marvin Dillman supported the measure and also introduced a bill to benefit tourist interests by celebrating holidays on Friday or Monday. Some Wisconsin resort owners claimed they suffered because of the state's small promotional budget, finding a voice in the *Vilas County News*, which suggested Wisconsin offered substantial attractions but unorganized publicity left the state "lagging far behind in bidding for this business." Local organizations produced and distributed vacation booklets, but many tourist proponents continued to scoff at Wisconsin's promotional appropriation of $50,000 compared to Minnesota's $175,000, Michigan's $250,000, and Ontario's $500,000.[42]

While promoters debated the level and merits of increased state involvement, Joe Mercedes continued to operate his Wisconsin Tourist Bureau in Chicago and advertised in the *Vilas County News* for new clients. Unlike the newspaper, Mercedes campaigned against state involvement and cited his success attracting tourists. With seventy-five thousand people visiting his Chicago office annually, he claimed, "It is a service unique in recreational promotion, and made possible only through the cooperation of resort owners and alert communities that have learned that what benefits all the state, benefits all in the state."[43] Wisconsin resort owners generally expressed satisfaction with Mercedes's efforts. In 1949, he staged a "Why I Would Like a Vacation in Wisconsin" contest on Chicago's WGN radio where contestants could win a vacation by writing about why they wanted one.[44] The following year he embarked on a ten-state automobile tour with a Wisconsin map and "Where the Nation Finds Recreation" slogan emblazoned on the side of his vehicle. Despite Mercedes's protests against state promotional funding, the governor supported his efforts to showcase Wisconsin and claimed few citizens did "more for a single industry than you have done for Wisconsin resorts." Several Wisconsin companies also claimed Mercedes's work helped open up the Chicago market.[45]

As the ultimate salesman, Mercedes eventually attracted controversy when Wisconsin's attorney general asked his Wisconsin Tourist Bureau to change its name because people believed it was a state agency. Mercedes argued that his organization never passed itself off as such. Outraged by the charge, he claimed his organization's work helped bring millions into the state and did "what neither the state nor any other agency can or does do—promote individual communities and individual resorts—in such a fashion as to bring direct benefit to these sponsors who, in promoting their own commercial interests, promote the welfare of the entire state as well." Remarking on a community's billboard that informed tourists not to patronize its neighbor, Mercedes claimed, "It is precisely this sort of regionalism and short-sighted pettifogging that the Wisconsin Tourist

The Chicago office of the Wisconsin Tourist Bureau at 209 North Michigan Avenue, established in the 1930s. COURTESY OF THE WISCONSIN HISTORICAL SOCIETY, WHS IMAGE ID 37936.

Bureau has religiously discouraged." The attorney general was willing to work with Mercedes but wanted to ensure that he did not speak on behalf of state government. Mercedes's words and actions suggest he had no such desire. Rather, he saw himself as the voice of Wisconsin tourist interests, especially the members of his organization, and aimed to convince officials that his work served the state.[46]

The naming issue was one of several battles Mercedes had with officials. In 1955, he fought against increasing state advertising funds, calling for an investigation into those pushing for additional appropriations. Arguing that Wisconsin's tourist trade did not need a subsidy, he labeled the state's promotional efforts "foolish and idiotic" and received support from Joseph Handlos's Highway 45 Association in opposing a state tourist bureau office in Chicago that would compete with his operation.[47] Despite Mercedes's protests, the state opened a Chicago office in April 1956 providing, in what seemed a shot at Mercedes, "free impartial information on all parts of the state to satisfy any travel interest." Conservation Department publicity director Jim Alexander managed the office, and in its second year, the state hired permanent employees rather than assigning personnel on leave from regular duties. In 1958, the office received more than forty thousand inquiries, leading many, including the state chamber of commerce, to advocate for additional funding.[48]

Despite the success of Wisconsin's promotional office, Mercedes dismissed a resort owner's request to advocate for additional state funding. He maintained it was ludicrous to rely on government to advertise one's product and emphasized that resort owners never received information on tourist inquiries made to the state. Mercedes believed further state involvement would actually decrease funds spent on promotion because resort owners would assume the state would handle the work. He felt the state mishandled the existing appropriation and limited the ability of private promoters to do their job, claiming, "I endorse a program in which the state uses tax money wisely to encourage private industry—like the resorts and communities affiliated with the Wisconsin Tourist Bureau—to get to work and do a concrete job of merchandising." Mercedes downplayed the impact of the state's Chicago tourist office, suggesting that its few visitors made it a taxpayer's boondoggle.[49]

Although Wisconsin saw its share of battles, private and public officials also worked together. The MTC coordinated Michigan's regional association efforts and worked with NORGLAC to promote North Woods tourism. Formed in 1945, NORGLAC aimed to "conserve and develop the tourist and recreational resources of the States of Michigan, Minnesota,

Wisconsin and the Province of Ontario for the economic benefits which will accrue to its citizens." It provided information to those entering the tourist industry and inaugurated an advertising program in 1947. Officials met semiannually and recognized common interests in promoting tourism and protecting resources. The three states and Ontario each contributed $5,000 to the organization.[50] George Bishop, who served as a NORGLAC official while also leading the UPDB, claimed cooperation would guarantee that the "wilderness appeals of the entire area be preserved and made more accessible and the recreational appeal of this great area effectively sold on a vacation market." Ontario Premier Leslie Frost joined in supporting NORGLAC's efforts.[51]

NORGLAC fostered public-private cooperation on tourism and conservation issues, allowing officials to test new ideas. Ontario Deputy Tourist Minister Tom McCall corresponded with American colleagues. American officials also looked to Canada. For example, MTC chair Robert Furlong requested Ontario's annual advertising figures to support a state budget request.[52] These relationships served officials well when problems arose. In one instance, McCall wrote the MAA's Hubert Dear regarding a Duluth sign advising people of Ontario's poor roads and warning them to travel there with caution. Outraged at this accusation and approach to keeping tourists in Minnesota, McCall expressed concerns about future cooperation. He relayed to Dear, "As you know, our relations with our neighboring States—particularly Minnesota—have been extremely cordial and an incident of this kind hardly comes under the heading of good neighborliness." Such events could impact the MAA's cooperation with Canadian promoters, which included producing tourist brochures and keeping the Pigeon River Bridge crossing open at all hours.[53] While such incidents show the potential for conflict, relationships developed through NORGLAC helped soothe tensions. Even as they competed for tourists, officials often found common ground to resolve difficulties across the North Woods.

A Tourist-Friendly Land

One such contentious place occupied a small sliver of land in the northwest corner of Michigan's Upper Peninsula where mining interests, citizens, and the state battled over the future of the Porcupine Mountains, or Porkies. Mining companies wanted to tap potential copper resources. Conservationists urged protecting the area, emphasizing wilderness tourism and recreation. Residents considered these options within the context of future economic development as well as the region's past. Such debates dated back to 1925, when state park superintendent P. J. Hoffmaster studied a potential Porkies state park. Eighteen years later, the state unveiled a program to acquire forty-six thousand acres, preserving a wilderness "kept apart from the 'civilization' of the motor-jammed highway, the billboard, and the hotdog stand" and stopping logging companies from "nibbling at the fringes." By establishing a park at one of the Midwest's highest elevations, the state hoped "to preserve forever, as a forest museum, the last large stand of mixed hardwoods and of hemlock still existing in Michigan." Advocates of a Porkies park, including the UPDB, suggested it would complement Isle Royale by serving the public and protecting natural resources.[54] The governor believed the Porkies offered a unique recreation area, but not everyone supported the state park initiative. Connor Land and Lumber Company claimed the area included salable timber, informing the governor, "We challenge the statement of the Department of Conservation that the timber is being exploited and the scenic beauty destroyed. We claim the timber is being HARVESTED. The trees are ripe for cutting." Connor stressed forestry's importance to the regional economy, noting the twelve hundred employees at its UP and Wisconsin plants.[55]

Despite such protests, the state appropriated $1 million for a state park to preserve the forest and provide primitive tourist facilities, reinforcing the UPDB's George Bishop's vision of the Porkies as "the Yellowstone of the Middle West." Knowing a park would draw people, Hoffmaster feared advertising it before having infrastructure to support visitors and prevent despoliation.[56] In 1945, writer Harold Titus of the Conservation Commission spent three days in the western UP and reported to Hoffmaster, "I encountered no fixed ideas. No one in the vicinity wants the wilderness flavor spoiled. All, however, are impatient for us to get something started." Well aware of local fears of a state tourist monopoly, Hoffmaster urged residents to establish accommodations and services near the park. Many did, and by 1957, the Porkies attracted 225,000 visitors, up from 73,350 in 1946.[57]

While Porkies tourists sought wilderness experiences, mining companies scouted for minerals in the 1950s. Samuel Dana, dean of the University of Michigan's School of Natural Resources from 1927 to 1951, questioned the motives behind Porkies mine proposals and expressed outrage over compromising the park's wilderness qualities. While a mine might employ one thousand people, he asked, "Can commercial resource development on lands acquired at public expense to preserve natural values be justified on the basis of either private profit potential or local economic need?"[58]

Controversy erupted over a possible mine lease in the park in 1958, pitting those hoping for broad development against others urging preservation and wilderness tourism. The Ironwood Chamber of Commerce looked for a way to bridge viewpoints, claiming the mine could become a tourist attraction like the Soo Locks. One resident suggested, "We want only 930 acres of cut-over, rock-infested land for a mine. Revenues would pay the entire cost of the park every year."[59] Another discussed the emotional benefits of a wilderness area but supported the mining site, claiming it would remain invisible from tourists viewing Lake of the Clouds and that an access road would generate more tourists for nearby towns. Suggesting that granting the mine request was "conservation at its best," the writer portrayed the mine and tourism as mutually beneficial.[60]

Others saw the issue differently. A Parks Division observer feared the mine lease would set a "precedent for all kinds of commercial exploitation of the State Parks."[61] *Detroit Free Press* outdoor writer Jack Van Coevering favored a Porkies wilderness. Claiming that past dependence on mines had led to current economic troubles, he argued that by preserving the

Lake of the Clouds in the Upper Peninsula's Porcupine Mountains, 1941. LOCAL IDENTIFIER USFS NEGATIVE 413997, RECORDS OF THE FOREST SERVICE, RECORD GROUP 95, THE NATIONAL ARCHIVES AT CHICAGO.

region's wilderness for posterity, tourists could help provide prosperity. The Michigan Natural Areas Council followed Van Coevering's thinking, suggesting the region depended too much on exploitation of exhaustible resources. It viewed tourism, unlike mining, as renewable.[62]

Newspapers pointed out the need to not assume all UP residents supported mining. The *Milwaukee Journal* commented on the growing desire for a balanced approach to the issue, suggesting the UP "would like to have both tourist traffic and a new mine, if possible." The *Lansing State Journal* claimed residents wanted more than merely a seasonal playground for outsiders, while the *Ironwood Daily Globe* supported a lease for mining exploration with regulations to protect the public interest. Despite its name, the *Marquette Mining Journal* argued that surveying could take place but mining should not be permitted until copper was needed for national security.[63] Conservation Director Gerald Eddy ultimately denied the mining application, deciding that a mining operation was incompatible with the wilderness concept, provided only limited employment, and would not substantially aid tourism despite interest in copper mining history. Instead, state policies and activities supported recreational use of the Porkies.[64]

While mining leases caused a stir, questions also arose over what constituted a wilderness park. Some conservationists supported building tourist cabins overlooking the Lake of the Clouds, while others opposed it as commercialization, claiming, "This is the last and only chance for the average wage earner to make contact with a primitive area in this region."[65] Many feared cabins, even if only available for rental, would damage wilderness character. One study noted the inadequacy of applying economic value to a Porkies wilderness and emphasized the "unmeasurable satisfaction in just knowing that this great area of unmatched mountains, forests, rivers and lakes exists in Michigan for the perpetual enjoyment of the public." Nonetheless, the study still captured the economics of wilderness tourism and Michigan's natural resources by examining the impact of park attendance on local purchases.[66]

Given the UP's vast shoreline, promoters portrayed the area as wild and looked to promote places beyond the Porkies. In 1959, the National Park Service's *Our Fourth Shore* emphasized preserving Great Lakes shoreline for scenic, natural, and recreational values, recommending establishment of Pictured Rocks National Lakeshore along Lake Superior's shore. A national lakeshore would attract tourists to the sandstone cliffs and help offset lost commercial fishing revenue.[67] The western UP's

Sylvania Tract, purchased by U.S. Steel officials in the early 1900s for a hunting and fishing club, passed through multiple ownership hands before the federal government purchased the land for $5.7 million in 1966 and designated a wilderness area in the Ottawa National Forest.[68]

Public and private tourism efforts depended on maintaining a forested landscape that could be sold to consumers of leisure. Tourism's emergence as a primary land use during the interwar years contributed to debates over how to manage the region's natural resources to sustain a healthy postwar economy and environment. By 1949, Michigan United Conservation Clubs (MUCC) claimed a membership of two hundred clubs, and its monthly newsletter reached sixty thousand people. Declaring it was "for more sport, for better sportsmen, for a better state," the group rallied against commercial activities and automobile access, instead urging the preservation of places for sport. The MUCC defended the public's right to Michigan's natural resources and valued public-private cooperation to meet such ends. Its efforts reinforced a tradition of sportsmen advocating for conservation initiatives, although the connection to tourism developed fully during the interwar and postwar years. In organizing sportsmen to advocate for wild areas, MUCC helped transform northern lands.[69]

The development of state-supported scenic roadsides and other amenities also linked conservation and tourism. Appealing to tourists looking for comfort and scenery, Wisconsin promoters claimed, "Nature has been lavish in this state, and needs only a little encouragement to make visitors select Wisconsin for their motor trips."[70] Vilas County's 1941 recreation plan called for developing trails, canoe routes, parkways, picnic areas, and parks, and the state's rural zoning policies transformed northern lands from 1930s depression to 1950s prosperity with recreation as a major land use.[71] In 1953, Wisconsin outdoors writer Lyle Kingston urged financing conservation programs with general state funds rather than relying solely on license fees. According to Kingston, vacationers not only spent money on their travels but also appreciated conservation efforts and "take nothing home with them (we hope)." Both promoters and conservation advocates surely hoped that they took wonderful memories of relaxing times and that anglers left with a good catch. Highlighting tourism's benefits garnered attention for improving conservation programs and funding.[72]

Kingston's remarks reflected an era in which growing demand on recreational resources coincided with increased government attention to balancing preservation and access. From 1945 to 1955, Wisconsin hunting and fishing licenses increased from 700,000 to 1.7 million. Conservation Department officials became more involved in recreation issues, restructuring the department to focus on promotion, encouraging private sector tourism investment, and funding projects. In his campaign for governor in 1958, Gaylord Nelson appealed for support from tourism and recreation advocates by promising an increase in state advertising funding and the formation of a tourist council similar to Michigan's. Upon assuming office, he reorganized the Conservation Department to better meet needs. As Thomas Huffman explains in his study of Wisconsin's environmental movement, Nelson backed the "pet project of northerners to survey Wisconsin's tourist industry; conclusions from the research would support increased recreational development in the north country." Such state support led University of Wisconsin faculty to explore tourism's social and economic impact.[73]

Nelson's policies and programs also spurred new land uses in rural areas, particularly in the north. By the 1960s, members of northern business organizations and resort associations set aside concerns over public-private tourist competition, and state representative Paul Alfonsi of Minocqua pushed legislation for improving outdoor recreation. Nelson's 1961 Outdoor Recreation Act Plan (ORAP) created a ten-year, $50 million program funded through a one-cent cigarette tax to purchase privately owned lands and preserve scenic, wildlife, and recreation areas. As the first initiative of its kind in the nation, ORAP connected outdoor recreation to environmental planning. Nelson's goal, according to one observer, was to elevate outdoor recreation's status from its position as the "stepchild of the state conservation system," believing it would contribute to a more egalitarian society. ORAP provided Wisconsin the largest state recreation-conservation program in the country, with expenditures of $12.50 per citizen. The act provided a new direction for natural resource planning, leading Nelson to comment, "Our vastly expanded conservation efforts in northern Wisconsin will benefit not only the economy of the north, but all the people in southern Wisconsin who depend on the north for outdoor recreation." Nelson emphasized natural resources and recreation in his 1962 U.S. Senate campaign, highlighting tourism and public forestry in Vilas County along with the recreational potential of the Apostle Islands. Nelson's innovative ideas made him a popular figure in northern Wisconsin, and his efforts were also felt in Minnesota, which adopted a measure similar to Wisconsin's ORAP in 1963.[74] Nelson backed programs regulating resource use, expanding lake access, preserving scenic beauty, and limiting billboards. He also questioned the prohibition against using state funds to advertise within the state, recognizing it was better to have Wisconsin residents vacation in state than elsewhere. By regulating hunting and fishing, building highways, adding public parks and rest areas, and promoting conservation and outdoor recreation, government policies and programs provided citizens spaces of leisure and helped transform North Woods lands, waters, and communities.[75]

Measuring Tourism

State initiatives extended to gathering tourist industry data to better manage promotion and development. Capturing the typical postwar North Woods vacationer with a single example remains problematic, but beginning in 1947 the MTC conducted surveys on demographics, expenditures, and vacation choices to better understand tourists. Between 1947 and 1952, per party vacation expenditures increased $50, and the state generated over $500 million in annual tourist revenue. Surveys also enumerated the state's natural resources, which included 11,037 lakes, 36,000 miles of streams, and 3,121 miles of Great Lakes shoreline. Such information led Governor G. Mennen Williams to remark, "Vacationing in Michigan is a recreational pursuit enjoyed by hundreds of thousands each year. But it is also a business, a major source of revenue. We must protect it. We must insure its future." Industry and state officials relied on surveys to target potential customers as well as to understand economic impact and vacation desires. While data described the "average" vacationer, surveys said far less about the sense of connection to people and place that drew visitors to the North Woods.[76]

A 1949 Wisconsin survey provided operators information about tourists and their choices. Thirty percent stayed in cottages, 23 percent in resorts, 16 percent in hotels and motels, and 13 percent with friends and relatives. Growing numbers vacationed for several summers and then purchased lakeshore property for summer homes, generating income for local builders and suppliers. Over half of Wisconsin's out-of-state vacationers hailed from Illinois, and 75 percent of those visitors came from the Chicago area. The survey recorded criticism about embellished advertising, while personal recommendations received special mention for their trustworthiness. Providing a folksy and informal portrayal of resort life, newsletters also reinforced themes of comfort and familiarity. Tourists complained about diminishing fish stocks and inadequate conservation. One visiting fisherman wanted motor trolling like Michigan and Minnesota. Another suggested, "Resort owners create ill will by over-rating the fishing—a good fisherman competing against nature *knows* his chances and doesn't like the milarkey [*sic*] resort owners hand out." Unregulated development also raised concerns. One respondent commented, "Wisconsin is not doing enough to preserve wild life . . . I hope and pray something can be done to help keep northern Wisconsin the north woods of our country." Another remarked on commercialization and recommended more effective zoning to avoid having the North Woods "change to neon." Others were more forgiving, highlighting the importance of familiarity and suggesting, "Wisconsin has all the things I want in a vacation—land, trees, scenery, lovely lakes, swimming, fishing, boating, plenty of cozy little bars and other Chicagoans." Although tourists registered complaints, the survey indicated general satisfaction with northern Wisconsin's offerings.[77]

Surveys also revealed tourism's benefits and supported calls for additional promotion. While seventeen cents of every tourist dollar went to operators, the remainder helped sustain other businesses. The owner of Wisconsin's Hiawatha Inn suggested tourist expenditures aided everyone, claiming, "This vast, floating population could well mean the difference between solvency and bankruptcy in our state." He wanted the state to increase its advertising appropriation and felt others who benefited should help attract tourists. Some operators emphasized noneconomic benefits to garner public support, including one who suggested tourism "brings into the state people who have new ideas, different conceptions of life, and these they share with local residents."[78] Tourism could open communication lines, establish a foundation for future business connections, and provide vacationers and residents a broader view of the world. In a word, boosters used survey data to claim tourism made society better.

While information on tourism's benefits proved useful, operators also required better guidance. Former Michigan highway commissioner Grover Dillman believed the UP lacked adequate recreational facilities and requested a manual to help operators select sites, construct cabins, purchase equipment, and generate capital. Industry experts responded by producing handbooks.[79] A 1955 UP study commented that fish, game, and scenery were attracting vacationers, who now enjoyed better roads and lodging. These improvements contributed to attendance at Tahquamenon Falls State Park rising nearly tenfold from 1947 to 1953. The number of vehicles crossing the Straits of Mackinac almost doubled in the same period. By 1948, UP tourist revenues stood at $50 million, doubling since 1941. Efforts to upgrade lodging and develop year-round attractions relied on the continued promotion, development, and analysis advocated by Dillman.[80]

Along these lines, the MTC's 1957 Michigan tourist survey contributed to a new promotional approach. Michigan residents comprised 32 percent of vacationers, and another 40 percent came from Ohio, Indiana, Illinois, and Wisconsin. Slightly more tourists spent their vacation in one place than on the move, and the vast majority were repeat family visitors. Providing diverse facilities remained essential, but middle-class tourists generated the most income for operators given their increased numbers and expenditures. Before the survey, a large portion of the MTC's $300,000 advertising budget was spent on national media. With data suggesting most Michigan vacationers came from nearby, the MTC focused on Great Lakes states in future campaigns. By 1964, 4.7 million people visited the UP, the western UP drawing from Minneapolis, Milwaukee, and Chicago, and the east from Ohio, Indiana, and southern Michigan. Nearly 72 percent of visitors lived and worked in or near major cities. Such information allowed UP promoters to target vacationers, and annual Michigan tourist expenditures increased from $400 million to $960 million between 1945 and 1965.[81]

Minnesota operators also benefited from survey data, including the Minneapolis Federal Reserve branch's monthly reports on resort income and visitor preferences. One report analyzed regional tourist competition, concluding that Minnesota's promotion was better than Wisconsin's but worse than Michigan's.[82] The 1958 MAA *Vacation Travel Survey* examined tourism in nineteen northern Minnesota counties and determined the northeastern Arrowhead offered a more rustic vacation than southern Arrowhead counties. Over 92 percent of travelers to the Arrowhead were urban residents, and nearly 90 percent were repeat visitors. The region appealed to young and moderate-income vacationing families. Tourists spent $32 million in the summer, producing income that the survey suggested equaled eighty plants employing one hundred workers at $4,000 each. Cosponsored by the Iron Range Resources and Rehabilitation Board (IRRRB), a state economic development agency, the survey marked tourism's importance for local livelihoods. It also signaled a new era for the IRRRB, which now viewed tourism as a means to recovery. Established in 1941, the IRRRB did not initially include tourism as part of its program, even though Governor Harold Stassen recognized its potential along the Iron Range. As an MAA-IRRRB project, the survey brought together private and public regional organizations. Surveyors collected data, visited businesses, and conducted interviews with tourists and summer-home owners, who named relaxation, fishing, and sightseeing as reasons for visiting the Arrowhead. By 1961, the Arrowhead contained 89 percent of the state's resort facilities with eighty-five hundred employees.[83]

Other agencies gathered information on the relationship between tourism and conservation. The Wisconsin Conservation Department studied visitors to state parks and forests, and the National Park Service conducted its Great Lakes shoreline survey, which helped establish national lakeshores. The U.S. Forest Service analyzed recreation on the area's national forests and discovered that some summer-home lessees felt they should have exclusive access to waterfront abutting their property. Surveys documented growing demand for lakefront land, noting the many lakes sporting the private cottages of urban visitors. By the late 1950s, one estimate placed the number of vacation homes in Wisconsin at fifty-five thousand. In 1960, Wisconsin's tourism industry generated $440 million annually, of which half came from Wisconsin residents. That same year, northern Wisconsin's Vilas County had 671 housekeeping resorts, 78 American plan resorts, 32 children's camps, 39 motels, and 3,099 summer homes.[84] Numbers tell only part of the story, but in the postwar era private citizens and public officials increasingly relied on survey data to measure tourism's economic impact and direct its future.

Vacationing for All Seasons

Although surveys provided concrete numbers on visitors, revenue, and accommodations, they also functioned in the abstract, measuring the typical tourist but offering little on how tourist operators and the state crafted postwar North Woods vacation experiences. While building portages in the forest surrounding Ely in the 1930s, Bill Rom rarely saw people. After the war, growing numbers arrived in the boundary waters looking for adventure. Some flew from Chicago, landed in the backcountry, and left without reporting the number of fish they caught. Although a pilot himself, Rom believed flights marred wilderness experience. His positions often made him the center of local controversy as residents fought over measures they felt infringed on their ability to enjoy the forest. For Rom, the canoe country was essential for business, and he urged others to recognize that "Ely's salvation is preserving this wilderness, because it'll be here forever."[85] Many resort owners joined Rom in urging protection, believing the area's uniqueness aided business. They expressed concerns about building roads in addition to the two roads traversing the area's perimeter, worried they would contribute to overcrowding and destruction. In 1961, traffic often exceeded twelve hundred vehicles per day on the Fernberg Road, which served nineteen resorts, fifty-eight residences, three canoe outfitters, five boat landings, two campgrounds, and loggers. From her lodge on the Gunflint Trail, Justine Kerfoot commented on the boundary waters' uniqueness, "If it was all opened up and developed, heck, it would be like the middle of Wisconsin."[86]

Rom's work in the Superior during college followed by operating an outfitting business after World War II underscores how residents adapted to shifting desires and helped shape new regulations guiding tourist development. His operation took advantage of northern Minnesota's wilderness character and, like North Woods resorts, targeted a changing postwar vacationing public by catering to families and fostering connections among guests. The Ruttgers advertised their operations as "A Family Resort Operated by a Family," while the Kerfoots broadcast Gunflint Lodge's friendly atmosphere at outdoor shows and distributed *Gunflint Gossips* to inform current and former guests about lodge happenings. Northern Minnesota's Camp du Nord switched to housekeeping cabins in the 1950s, and in 1960, the St. Paul YMCA purchased it to operate as a family camp. In 1952, Roy Dunn's resort switched from American plan with meals to the European plan. By offering guests cabins where they could cook, Camp du Nord and Dunn's expanded their clientele to include economizing families.[87]

Ross' Teal Lake Lodge continued to attract families to northern Wisconsin. In 1948, the Ross family's twenty-eighth season at Teal Lake, Walter Ross's son, Nelson, joined his parents in managing the lodge. As many resorts changed ownership during and after the war, the Rosses were among the longest-serving resort operators in the Hayward area. As members of a local property and resort owner association, they worked to ensure the area remained a destination. Guests at Teal Lake Lodge enjoyed the leisurely pace, delicious meals, modern cabins, and lakefront. Nelson Ross expanded operations by adding a motor lodge near Mt. Telemark for winter skiers. The Rosses also looked to expand their season, promoting autumn's vibrant colors and spring's excellent fishing opportunities. First published in 1930, *Teal Lake Tidings* continued to provide vacationers a sense of community and familiarity. The spring 1949 edition informed them, "After a winter's rest, all the Teal Lake Lodge 'family' looks forward to the letters saying we'll be up, reserve a cabin." *Tidings* kept guests informed about lodge and area activities, including father-son fishing weekends, river trips, tube fishing, and the Hayward Musky Festival. Fishing weekends, according to Nelson Ross, helped business during normally slack times of year while encouraging father-son bonding. In 1955, the resort offered its sixth such weekend, placed advertisements in metropolitan newspapers, promoted free golf at a local course, and produced a cookbook containing lodge recipes. The following year the lodge extended its season until Thanksgiving. The family who opened a small fishing camp on Teal Lake four decades earlier regularly entertained sixty-five guests in seventeen cabins. While the lodge's natural setting remained important, the Rosses, like the Ruttgers in Minnesota, expanded offerings to cater to the entire family.[88]

Operating a resort in the postwar years involved far more than catering to guests' desires. The Rosses recruited and trained staff to lead activities and make guests comfortable. They developed relationships with local businesses to promote the resort and helped filter tourist dollars through the regional economy by purchasing supplies at area merchants, banking locally, and working with local laundry operations. The Rosses also subscribed to state and local organizations supporting tourism, including the Wisconsin Hotel Association, Wisconsin Indianhead, and Hayward Lakes Resort Association. The lodge paid Wisconsin's State Board of Health for a hotel permit, the Town of Spider Lake for a cigarette license, the state conservation department for fish licenses, and a local printer for *Teal Lake Tidings*.[89]

While resort owners like the Rosses continued operations after World War II, the postwar era also attracted newcomers who pursued opportunities in the North Woods tourist industry. Born on Chicago's South Side, William Flagg worked as a Chicago police officer until 1968, first visiting Minnesota on a 1950 fishing trip and returning every May for vacation. In 1961, Flagg and his wife, Virginia, purchased a resort in Emily, Minnesota, and renamed it Flagg's Lake Mary Resort, becoming one of few African American resort owners in Minnesota. When possible, William took leaves of absence from the police force during summer to help run the resort, and he and his wife returned to Chicago each fall, where William resumed police duties. Flagg's guests included many vacationing police colleagues. Former Minnesota schoolteacher Ted Leagjeld joined the Flaggs as a new operator, buying Fuller White Fish Lake Lodge in 1959 and renaming it Driftwood Resort. After examining over thirty different resorts with his wife, who grew up in the family business at Fair Hills Resort, he bought Fuller's and turned it into a family resort. Leagjeld benefited from the advice and cooperation of older resort owners involved in the Minnesota Resort Association.[90]

Born in Lutsen, Minnesota, in 1927, John Lyght built on his regional roots and resort experience. His parents arrived in Minnesota from Alabama via western Pennsylvania during the 1910s. Lyght's father bought

Walter and Virginia Ross relaxing by the fireplace at Ross' Teal Lake Lodge, circa 1948. COURTESY OF THE WISCONSIN HISTORICAL SOCIETY, WHS IMAGE ID 37958.

land on Caribou Lake and started the Northern Lights Resort in 1925, which closed after 1941 when wartime gas rationing made business difficult. Despite limited transportation in Cook County, the resort and its seven cabins attracted vacationers from Chicago and the Twin Cities. Word of mouth brought families back annually. For John, growing up at the resort involved work as well as pleasure. John and his siblings cleaned cabins and served as guides, learning to mingle with people. After World War II, he briefly entered the trucking business, but his resort roots pulled him back. In 1950, he left to manage a private resort along Lake Superior's North Shore for Indiana's Foster Forbes Glass Company, hiring his sister to cook, and continuing in this position until 1972. Salesmen, distributors, and other clients came north to relax and conduct business. During the off-season, Lyght drove a school bus. From 1968 to 1972, he served as a part-time sheriff's deputy and was appointed sheriff in 1972. In 1974, he was elected to the position and served for another twenty years as the state's first and only African American elected sheriff. Born into the resort business, Lyght worked at his father's place as a youth and managed another resort in his adulthood before leaving the resort field for law enforcement.[91]

One postwar tourist entrepreneur looked in a different direction than many others by establishing a winter destination in northern Wisconsin. Born in Hayward, Tony Wise returned after serving in the army and earning a Harvard business degree. Wartime experience in Europe and time spent in New England convinced him winter sports could aid his home region, so he undertook market research before opening Mt. Telemark in December 1947. Wise exclaimed, "We plan to go into partnership with Old Man Winter and see if we can create a 'second' tourist season during that period." Over the subsequent decades, Wise became one of northern Wisconsin's premier tourist entrepreneurs, starting Hayward's Historyland in 1954. Built on a former logging site, Wise relocated local historic buildings and hired Lac Courte Oreilles Ojibwe to staff a reconstructed Ojibwe village for tourists. He also founded the Lumberjack World Championship in 1960 and the Birkebeiner cross-country ski race in 1973. The former allowed Wise to expand efforts into summer, while the latter boosted winter business.[92]

Despite lower elevations, Wise believed northern Wisconsin ski resorts could attract vacationers from nearby cities. He studied existing Midwest ski operations, examined weather patterns, and determined that over forty thousand people would take winter vacations in northern

Wisconsin. Wausau's Rib Mountain faced uncertain snow conditions, and winter playgrounds in Michigan's UP, including Blaney Park, Houghton-Hancock, and Iron Mountain were farther from major population centers. Minnesota's Resources Commission director informed him that Minnesota had not surveyed winter sports areas and that Wisconsin was more invested in winter activities. Wise also sought advice from Wisconsin's State Planning Board, which recommended locating near rail lines, given uncertain winter road conditions.[93]

Like other destinations, Wise's Telemark attracted local residents looking for entertainment and employment. To sell community members on his winter destination ideas and encourage further development, Wise claimed that Telemark's $2,500 tax payment on land previously considered worthless improved the area, while its thirty-seven employees spent money in Cable and Hayward, adding to the regional economy. Urging town board funding for improving the road to Telemark, Wise demonstrated how winter tourism spurred the local economy during a traditionally slow time and helped increase interest among potential vacationers and providers. Many Cable and Hayward lodging operators who previously closed during winter responded to Wise's call and opened for skiers, providing lodging during Telemark's first season. Scheer's Ghost Lake Lodge anticipated winter guests and joined Wise in encouraging the Soo Line railroad to promote skiing and increase winter ridership. During the 1950s, Wise distributed snow reports to businesses, ski clubs, and universities. After a season with little snow, Wise secured a Small Business Association loan in 1961 for snowmaking equipment, allowing Telemark to guarantee skiing.[94]

Increased state involvement, new operators, and technological innovation helped winter tourism emerge as part of the North Woods experience. Despite a history of Michiganders enjoying winter activities, Michigan's winter tourist program developed slowly. Organizations like the UPDB encouraged investment, publishing its first winter *Lure Book* in 1949. The MTC, UPDB, and Michigan College of Mining and Technology cooperated on a ski survey that determined the UP had a more rugged and greater snow-covered area than Lower Michigan, but distance and weather conditions could limit use. Local papers like the *Iron Mountain News* encouraged additional funds for winter promotion, while experts provided advice on activities and site selection. In 1953, Michigan also sponsored the first Governor's Winter Sports Conference. Growing state involvement also occasionally drew operator ire. Tony Wise supported state promotion but complained about competing with state-operated ski areas like Michigan's Porcupine Mountains and Wisconsin's Rib Mountain that charged lower rates.[95] New technologies also made winter sports more accessible. In Sayner, Wisconsin, Carl Eliason developed a motor toboggan in 1924. Thirty-two years later, Polaris Industries of Roseau, Minnesota, began manufacturing the first modern snowmobiles, and tourists ventured north to experience snow and ice in these new machines. Eagle River, Wisconsin, held the first World Championship Snowmobile Derby in 1964 to promote this activity.[96] Firmly established by the mid-1960s after decades of efforts by public and private interests, winter tourism made the North Woods an all-season vacationland.

"Air Conditioned by the Cool Breezes of Lake Superior"

Activities in Michigan's Copper Country underscore how a variety of actors and policies helped foster this year-round vacationland after World War II. Sharing similarities to other North Woods destinations regarding conservation, land use, business expansion, and promotion, the place where tourists found themselves "Air Conditioned by the Cool Breezes of Lake Superior" was also different in some ways.[97] While MTC chair Robert Furlong once suggested the Copper Country consider a name change, the region chose instead to capitalize on its mining heritage in its pitch to vacationers. Dating back to the interwar years, tourists joined with the UPDB and CCVL to forge a vacation landscape that included historic mining sites, the Porkies, Brockway Mountain Drive, Fort Wilkins State Park, and Isle Royale. But who came on vacation, how did they decide where to go, what did they experience, and how did their actions alter this place? Surveys, recreation plans, land-use debates, promotional literature, and site development help explain the Copper Country's postwar transformation.

The 1958 *Summer Tourist Survey of the Michigan Copper Country* described vacationers' backgrounds, experiences, and desires. Promotion remained essential for attracting tourists, who were categorized as "vacation shoppers" requiring information about their options. As "vacation shoppers," tourists were, as Lizabeth Cohen's work on postwar consumer society suggests, purchaser citizens "who simultaneously fulfilled personal desire and civic obligation by consuming."[98] North Woods promoters informed tourists that they could improve the economy, help the nation, and satisfy escapist dreams. Copper Country tourists were older and more prosperous and spent more than most Michigan vacationers. Farther from urban centers and lacking the plentiful resorts found in other parts of the North Woods, the region hosted fewer families with children. The majority of visitors came from Michigan, while the largest number of out-of-state guests arrived from Illinois and Wisconsin. Copper Country visitors had a higher median annual income compared to all Michigan tourists. Given the greater number of older visitors, it is not surprising that more than half had incomes in excess of $7,500, compared to only 27 percent statewide. With nearly four hundred thousand visitors, Copper Country tourist expenditures totaled $14,300,000 annually.[99]

Tourists were lured to the Copper Country by personal recommendations, articles and advertisements, and the UPDB's *Lure Book*. Limited lodging options and the desire to explore the entire UP contributed to tourists not making long visits. Seventy percent of guests stayed five days or less, while the rest were classified as "resorters," who spent a week or two at one place, like the Keweenaw Mountain Lodge. Visitors indicated general satisfaction with the area, especially its reasonable prices, but complained restaurants and lodging focused on the transient tourist and did not pay enough attention to the region's forests and lakes. Others clamored for additional lodging but found existing facilities generally met needs. Over 50 percent of tourists stayed in motels; other options were housekeeping cottages, hotels, resorts, and camping. The most serious criticism was a lack of information identifying historic sites, abandoned mines, and ghost towns. Tourists made suggestions such as "have roadside story-type signs" and "better directions and publicity on historic sites" to "more historic background information" and "keep information stands open in late evening." Tourists claimed, "You have done little to promote your area from the standpoint of this rich, historic tradition, or to inform the visitor of your romantic past." Such interest in regional history contributed to the development of mining sites as destinations.[100]

While the Copper Country survey provides a glimpse into visitors and opportunities in the late 1950s, it says little about the work of those who promoted and developed the tourist infrastructure. Built by William Raley as a warehouse in 1858, the Lake Breeze Hotel in Eagle Harbor emerged as one of the Copper Country's first tourist facilities. Nearly a century later, the Raley family continued to welcome guests, including one who commented, "This New England-like hotel—informal, modestly priced—has been our headquarters for several summers and is the annual meeting place for many vacation 'repeaters.'" At Ontonagon's Twin Lakes Resort

Postwar rustic resort directory signs by the side of the road, Copper Harbor, Michigan. COURTESY OF THE MICHIGAN TECHNOLOGICAL UNIVERSITY ARCHIVES AND COPPER COUNTRY HISTORICAL COLLECTIONS.

and Hokan's Motel, guests stayed in cabins while venturing to waterfalls, mines, and ghost towns. Twin Lakes promoted itself as a family resort for photographers, rock hunters, and nature lovers. Promotional literature also helped transform mining sites into tourist destinations, disconnecting them from the industrial world of which they were a part. The Lake Linden Chamber of Commerce promoted *The Shoreline Scenic Route to Keweenawland*, a tour highlighting industry and recreation at Ripley's Arcadian Mine, the Quincy Mining Company plant at Mason, and the Calumet and Hecla plant at Hubbell. Traveling farther, tourists discovered inns, fishing, lakeside cottages, and scenic beauty.[101]

Vacations in the scenic and rugged Copper Country benefited more than just those taking them, since tourism provided business, work, and outdoor opportunities for residents. Promoters portrayed the region as "a tourists' playground, a sportsman's paradise, a land of opportunity to its businessmen and God's country to its hardy and completely dedicated natives." As a healthy and economical vacationland with distinctive foods and landscapes, the Copper Country catered to all budgets and was only a day's drive from most midwestern cities.[102] Road signage welcomed tourists, and the CCVL's *Copper Country Holidays* promoted a cool climate,

Lake Superior breezes, and hay fever relief in "America's Most Healthful Vacationland." For amateur geologists and botanists, the Copper Country's rock formations and wildflowers were unmatched.[103] While summer was busiest, autumn vacations provided "A Pageantry of Flaming Color." Forests and lakes invited automobile tourists to a "land of unspoiled enchantment" where local residents provided tourist services.[104]

Postwar UPDB *Lure Books* broadcast a Copper Country studded with hills and shores, waves and coves, scenic highways and blue waters, hardy and hospitable people, and modern lodging. The UPDB marketed vacations as fulfilling personal desire and civic obligation, benefiting the individual and nation by returning people to their daily lives refreshed. Promoters told people what they would encounter and from what they needed to escape. One *Lure Book*, for example, recommended, "If you are tired of a musical fare of blaring horns, jangling telephones, strident voices, industrial hums, and the incessant percussion tones of the industrial world, come north this summer and fall to sleep with the wind whirling through the pines and trembling aspens."[105]

Landscape imagery offered potential visitors a sense of the area's industry and people. Harold and Beatrice Putnam's guidebook *North to Adventure* sold fifty-five thousand copies and enticed many with its stunning pictures. The Putnams first visited the Copper Country in the early 1950s, staying at the Lake Breeze Hotel. They met Alex Nelson, a restaurant owner and promoter who became CCVL's manager. The Putnams produced *We Fell in Love with Keweenaw Land* for the CCVL in 1955 and 1956, comparing the landscape to other destinations: "It seems like a section of the Maine coast, transported intact to the Midwest; like a piece of Colorado, misplaced to the East. Certainly, it doesn't belong in the flat-chested Middle West. But here it is—a spectacular remnant of nature at her rawest."[106] While the Putnams broadcast a new conception of the region, infrastructure and lodging improvements also helped attract vacationers. James Wescoat recalled limited options in the 1930s in Copper Harbor, when his father ran the only hotel in town, "When the hotel got full, we'd put up wall tents, then we'd put up bed frames, springs, mattresses, and hang up a kerosene lamp. We'd rent the beds for $2 a night." After the war, if people arrived to discover Fort Wilkins State Park and Copper Harbor lodging full, they often turned around, never to return. Since tourists contributed to the local economy, Wescoat argued for more facilities to ensure they stayed.[107]

As the UP's most prominent mining concern and one of its largest landholders, Calumet and Hecla (C&H) advocated for tourism, hoping to increase profits while stressing tourist contributions to local businesses. C&H promoted vacations, subscribed to the CCVL, and purchased *Lure Book* ads outlining its new recreational lands policy. While C&H's cottage-leasing program generated $8,800 in 1946 and $11,022 in 1949, the company sought greater returns with a recreation plan that included resorts, cottages, and a ski area. C&H informed potential purchasers, "You Are Invited to Consider a Vast Recreational Area to the North." With 250,000 acres, including fifty miles of Lake Superior frontage that it compared to the Pacific Coast, C&H looked to spearhead the region's tourist future by developing lots on Lake Superior.[108]

With northern Wisconsin offering over twelve hundred resorts, Wisconsin's Lake Superior shore providing a similar atmosphere, and the UP's Huron Mountains to the east attracting vacationers, Copper Country tourist advocates recognized regional competition. Emphasizing its uniqueness, the Copper Country offered a scenic drive to the end of U.S. Highway 41 and the lure of copper mining history. With an average snowfall of 136 inches, it also provided winter activities. The *Daily Mining Gazette* and CCVL pointed out tourism's importance and forecast its bright

Pontiac Resort, Copper Harbor, Michigan (formerly the Mariner Inn North, owned by Jim Wescoat's parents), late 1930s or early 1940s. COURTESY OF THE MICHIGAN TECHNOLOGICAL UNIVERSITY ARCHIVES AND COPPER COUNTRY HISTORICAL COLLECTIONS.

future. Many people agreed with this assessment, including a local developer promoting the Copper Harbor Club to attract vacationers, and urged expanding winter activities following publication of the UPDB's winter lure book.[109]

Tourist development was not confined to the Copper Country mainland. Isle Royale attracted interest, but unlike at other national parks in the postwar era, limited transportation to and from the island and inadequate trail development curbed visitation. While the National Park Service improved guest and employee lodging, it hoped a private carrier would transport passengers. State governments also raised access concerns. Michigan established an Isle Royale Development Commission, and Wisconsin governor Walter Kohler wrote counterpart Mennen Williams that he was "more than a little interested in your appraisal of its potentialities as a tourist attraction" and "happy to discuss the problem of adequate transportation to the Isle."[110] Noting the expansion of paid vacations, Williams joined residents in believing Isle Royale could lure the adventurous vacationer. Given government expenditures on western park roads, one county road commissioner asked, "Would it not seem reasonable therefore that the Government should provide adequate transportation across the Lake in lieu of an access road."[111] Others joined the effort, including one resident who labeled the existing Isle Royale Queen an uncomfortable, unpleasant, and inadequate craft, and called on government to "provide a 'good road' to Isle Royale," by which he meant a larger, safer, and more dependable boat.[112] A Chicago-area vacationer also grumbled about access, accusing the National Park Service of "the worst in advertising when it calls that 'boat service' and lures the sweating city dweller north with the thoughts of a pleasant five-hour Lake Superior boat ride." Fielding complaints from residents and visitors and believing government expenditures to acquire Isle Royale were wasted if it did not provide a means to travel there, tourist advocates proposed transportation solutions. One suggestion included bringing a Mackinac ferry to Isle Royale.[113]

Complaints also emerged that Isle Royale received attention at the expense of other UP areas and programs. Recognizing the island as "a great treasure in our recreational chest," the *Escanaba Daily Press* claimed a forest recreation program for the UP's federal forests would actually benefit more people, given their accessibility. Such criticism was familiar to Bert Stoll, the father of the 1920s Isle Royale park campaign, who answered those claiming the island was a "God forsaken place" where "the average tourist could neither afford to go there nor be attracted by scenery

Isle Royale National Park sign erected by the Keweenaw County Road Commission, 1971. COURTESY OF THE MICHIGAN TECHNOLOGICAL UNIVERSITY ARCHIVES AND COPPER COUNTRY HISTORICAL COLLECTIONS.

only."[114] By urging government boat service and trail development, Isle Royale tourist proponents countered such arguments and sought to make it accessible to the masses.

Other tourism promoters clamored for state government to restore, preserve, and tell the story of Michigan's copper mining history to attract tourists. The executive secretary of the Michigan Historical Commission recommended converting the Ahmeek shaft house and steam hoist into a tourist site where people could learn about the region's industrial history. He supported state acquisition and preservation for economic and educational purposes, pointing to the private Arcadian mine, where tourists entered the mine, learned about its operation, and became familiar with mining terms. The MTC supported the plan but suggested that given inadequate state funds, perhaps C&H or other local organizations might operate it.[115] Backing also came from the Department of Conservation and a mining professor who saw it as an educational and business opportunity. With the Keweenaw suffering from copper's decline, he commended efforts to grow tourism. Preserving the history of copper mining through museums and state parks would "commemorate the part played by the industry in Michigan's economic growth" and "help attract tourists to this lovely region." Decades before formal recognition of the Keweenaw National Historical Park, calls emerged for preserving and interpreting the Copper Country's mining's history and landscape for visitors.[116]

The WPA's 1941 guide to the Wolverine State labeled the Keweenaw the "treasure chest of Michigan." Despite the image of riches, the Depression left 85 percent of the county on relief. Economic conditions brightened as the tourist trade, facilitated by state government programs, the WPA guide, and other federal relief projects, slowly turned places like Copper Harbor into small summer resorts and ensured communities they would not become ghost towns. Copper Country residents increasingly relied on tourism and looked to the state and private interests to capitalize on the growing trade. Ocha Potter claimed that early opposition to tourism disappeared as summer homes sprang up on Lake Superior and new resorts opened after the war. Towns saw new groceries, bars, shops, pasty and hot dog stands, and cabins. Copper Harbor had nearly fifty fishing boats for tourists, and the modernization of Fort Wilkins created a popular state park.[117]

Increased affluence along with improved access expanded Copper Country tourism and generated local employment. State government continued to do its part by improving efforts to attract tourists, operating tourist sites, and funding surveys. Despite these changes, debates over tourism continued as residents saw possibilities to continue to transform the region. In 1936, the UPDB portrayed the UP as the "most picturesque, beautiful and interesting outdoor playground in America."[118] Other North Woods destinations advertised vacations in equally glowing terms in the postwar years, and similar language is still used to lure tourists north. But such terminology also hid conflict in the North Woods. From Michigan's Copper Country to Minnesota's boundary waters and across the nation, tensions between preservation and use as well as work and leisure continued to play out on the landscape after World War II.

CHAPTER 6

The Not So Quiet Crisis: Tourism, Wilderness, and Regional Development

In 1962, one year after the Outdoor Recreation Resources Review Commission's (ORRRC) *A Progress Report to the President and to the Congress* claimed, "As our open spaces are bulldozed or paved and our accessible lakes and streams deteriorate from pollution, there is that much less for outdoor recreation," President John F. Kennedy received a letter from a seven-year-old boy concerned about no longer having a place to play because the woods surrounding his home had vanished for new subdivisions. The scope of the outdoor recreation crisis had clearly expanded since 1924, when President Calvin Coolidge informed the National Conference on Outdoor Recreation (NCOR) that people "need an opportunity for outdoor life and recreation no less than they need opportunity of employment" and the 1930s, when the President's Research Committee on Social Trends studied the nation's outdoor recreation needs.[1] In the North Woods, the President's Quetico-Superior Committee brought federal attention to land-use issues beginning in 1934, but the postwar era saw new concerns emerge. The ORRRC emphasized maintaining the nation's woods and waters for outdoor recreation, addressing growing demand that left "picnic grounds and campsites crowded to overflowing, the lakes jammed with boats, the beaches crowded with people," and raised alarm about "a tidal wave from inland" arriving on the nation's seashores and lakeshores.[2]

Diverse voices emerged during 1957 congressional hearings establishing the ORRRC, but they shared an interest in surveying national outdoor recreation resources and determining future needs to address this crisis. Oregon Senator Wayne Morse advocated for "preserving certain areas of our primeval outdoors unspoiled," while the Izaak Walton League highlighted rehabilitative and economic benefits.[3] The Sierra Club appealed for a scenic resources review to postpone development in certain areas, and the Wilderness Society urged wilderness preservation as part of land-use programs. Both saw wilderness as essential to a healthy and productive citizenry and urged the ORRRC to include it in its outdoor recreation survey.[4] The Outboard Boating Company of America (OBCA) supported a survey but wanted to ensure motorized access. It objected to Senator Hubert Humphrey's proposed wilderness legislation and used Minnesota's boundary waters to emphasize people's desire for a less arduous recreation experience, stating:

> Because the Indians were compelled by force of circumstances to convey themselves by canoe seems little reason to require modern-day Americans to adopt this exact type of behavior. . . . If we are to encourage the use and enjoyment of wilderness areas by greater numbers of Americans, we ought where possible to permit them to more readily traverse the wilderness in other than 17 [*sic*] century style.

OBCA claimed it was feasible to limit commercialization and allow more Americans to access wild areas, suggesting motorboats did not destroy flora and fauna and were harmless conveniences that did not automatically lead to "a bevy of filling stations, hotdog stands, and billboards."[5]

Chaired by conservationist Laurance Rockefeller, the ORRRC documented the nation's outdoor recreation needs and examined threats to open space and natural resources hindering recreational opportunities. Its final report, *Outdoor Recreation for America*, advised Congress to establish a funding source to safeguard natural areas and recommended federal government assistance to state and local officials to help provide outdoor recreation for all Americans. Recreation was both "the activity which uses leisure time for relaxation and enjoyment" and "the refreshment of body and spirit (the re-creation) which results from that activity." Since outdoor recreation could improve individual and national health, the ORRRC proposed a Bureau of Outdoor Recreation to coordinate federal programs and urged states to develop outdoor recreation plans, acquire areas, and preserve natural sites.[6] *Outdoor Recreation for America* also invoked a tradition of reverence for nature in American thought and culture, claiming, "The outdoors is a *right* of Americans—not only something to be enjoyed but vital to our spirit."[7] Interior Secretary Stewart Udall posited, "When an American looks for the meaning of the past, he seeks it not in ancient ruins but more likely in mountains and forests, by a river, or at the edge of the sea." According to Udall, who explored environmental concerns in his 1963 *The Quiet Crisis*, the ORRRC's recommendations would "assure all Americans permanent access to their outdoor heritage."[8]

While state governments provided the cornerstone for addressing planning and acquisition concerns, the ORRRC also emphasized effective public-private cooperation to preserve America's outdoor recreation landscape and meet future national needs.[9] Such a recommendation resonated in the North Woods, where cooperative efforts had helped construct a tourist landscape during the interwar years. In the postwar years, new policies and activities related to public lands, summer cottages, and wilderness contributed to a contested North Woods landscape where debates were far from quiet.

Federal Lands and Vacation Cabins

Nearly a decade before the ORRRC's final report, the Quetico-Superior Committee invited President Dwight Eisenhower to vacation in Minnesota's boundary waters. Preferring comfort over adventure and suggesting the First Lady would rather relax on a porch and play canasta, the president declined, remarking, "I don't want to do any of that packing on those portages."[10] While a wilderness vacation did not tempt the president, many Americans sought such journeys, and government action increasingly helped them do so. With the North Woods offering wilderness close to population centers, debates exploded over the area's future. The Quetico-Superior Committee claimed Minnesota's boundary waters were crucial to the region's economic and cultural life and, despite some exploitation, offered "the most famous recreational region in mid-continent" with the "finest wilderness waters in America."[11] Other federal lands in the North Woods offered visitors and residents places to recreate. By the early 1970s, people vacationed at Apostle Islands and Pictured Rocks National Lakeshores, Isle Royale and Voyageurs National Parks, numerous national forests, and Indian reservations with a federal presence. At these and other locations, individuals and the state continued to transform a region formerly reliant on forestry and mining into a place where wilderness, scenic, and historic sites drew vacationers.[12]

One such place was in the Upper Peninsula's Alger County on Lake Superior's shores. Proposed by Senator Philip Hart, Pictured Rocks became the nation's first national lakeshore in 1966. It was a scenic attraction long before Alger County officials began promoting it to tourists in the 1920s. While Interior Secretary Harold Ickes supported lakeshore preservation for public recreational use in the 1930s, the National Park Service's 1959 *Our Fourth Shore* and the ORRRC's work contributed to the creation of Pictured Rocks and Apostle Islands National Lakeshores under National Park Service management.[13]

The Bureau of Indian Affairs (BIA) noted Ojibwe involvement in tourism-related activities dating back to the 1910s. After the ORRRC issued its final report in 1962, the BIA commissioned tourist and recreational resource studies for northern Minnesota and Wisconsin reservations. These reports used a system developed by ORRRC to review and classify recreational lands as one of four types: general outdoor recreation areas, historic and cultural sites, natural environment areas, and unique natural areas. Wisconsin's Lac du Flambeau and Lac Courte Oreilles reservations earned praise for their "well-developed tourist industry," the former providing fishing lakes and pine forests, and the latter offering historical and cultural sites in the "Muskie Capital of the World." Despite these positive comments, reports also underscored problems.[14]

A checkerboard pattern marked land ownership on North Woods reservations. At Lac du Flambeau, tribal members owned only 35 percent of reservation land. Of Lac Courte Oreilles' original 69,000 acres, a meager 4.5 percent, or 3,080 acres, remained in tribal hands. Recognizing the recreational land shortage on reservations, the BIA looked to tourism to address ORRRC concerns and assist Ojibwe economically. The Lac du Flambeau study made recommendations based on ORRRC land classifications. A 100-acre site on the northeast shore of Crawling Stone Lake could host one hundred summer homes while maintaining the area's large pines. It recommended seventy-five campsites at a 40-acre site on Fence Lake and encouraged day-use areas for visitors in other locations. Opportunities also existed for canoeing, guide services, and handicraft production, which had declined due to an aging population and cheap imports. The study suggested, "The loss of this colorful link with the ancient Indian culture, which could be the reservation's truly unique tourist attraction, is most unfortunate." To address this concern, it proposed a craft guild similar to one suggested for Minnesota's Red Lake Reservation to "revive interest in arts and crafts, set uniform charges, train new workers, and determine the products to be prepared."[15]

At Lac Courte Oreilles, New Post and Reserve Indian villages offered potential destinations for those interested in Ojibwe history and culture. With only one historical marker on the reservation, the study suggested developing interpretive material for vacationers, including a map showing historical and natural points of interest with the slogan "Vacation with the Chippewas." Minnesota's Red Lake Reservation developed a guide-training program to engage the public in learning about Ojibwe history and culture, which was presented as a model for others. Public interest in visiting reservations and learning about Ojibwe history and culture remained high despite obstacles. Existing promotional literature rarely mentioned reservations and did little to convince potential vacationers to visit. A 1962 *Chicago Sun Times* contest asking readers to respond to the question, "Why I would like to visit an Indian reservation on my vacation?" helped slightly, garnering 135 letters from children. To boost tourism, tribal governments and the BIA connected with local and regional organizations and state planning initiatives. Public-private cooperation could help shape tourism on Indian reservations, and the ORRRC report offered a framework for assessing resources and recommending uses.[16]

The expansion of cottage ownership also contributed to transforming the landscape, as inland lakes and streams offered scenic vistas, recreation, and summer-home sites for an expanding middle class traveling to cottages on new roads. Cottage development generated conflict as well as consensus. As one observer of summer cottage culture noted, vacationers chose environments that "stir age-old conflicts between farmers and sportsmen, land developers and lovers of wilderness, those who live for social interaction and those who guard their privacy."[17] Another characterized the cottage as a symbol of the good life in Wisconsin. If that was the case, as early as 1931 three thousand families enjoyed that privilege within forty miles of Minocqua, and the number expanded after World War II. Cottage ownership also had an economic impact, inducing long-term investment and expanding the local customer base. A 1949 Minnesota survey determined cottage owners spent $173 during vacation and added to the tax base by purchasing property.[18]

By buying into appeals stressing health and relaxation in nature, North Woods cottage owners contributed to new approaches to managing the land. Unplanned development had consequences, leading Wisconsin Senator Gaylord Nelson to claim in 1965, "The new enemies of conservation are not timber barons but the innocent cottage owner who needlessly cuts down trees along the lake front and plants his septic tank so it will drain into the lake." Nelson believed effective planning and education could help solve land-use issues. He recognized people wanted to enjoy northern Wisconsin's lakes and suggested developing cottage clusters to preserve natural conditions along lakefronts and provide access for all.[19]

Improving public access: camping in the Superior National Forest near Ely, Minnesota, June 1964. U.S. FOREST SERVICE PHOTOGRAPH COURTESY OF THE FOREST HISTORY SOCIETY, DURHAM, NORTH CAROLINA, FHS2868.

While much cottage construction took place on private land in the North Woods, cottages on federal lands increased government's presence in managing the tourist landscape. In the early 1940s, the U.S. Forest Service issued 150 summer home permits and others for resorts, docks, and camps in Minnesota's Chippewa National Forest.[20] People continued building cottages on land leased from the government, raising questions about public versus private forest use. By 1955, 280 summer cabins existed in the Chippewa with annual fees ranging from \$25 to \$45 in addition to county property tax. Given ORRRC recommendations to expand public access, the agency determined private lakefront summer homes were inconsistent with the forest's mission and should yield to a greater public good. Thus in 1963, the Forest Service changed its cottage permit program in the Chippewa, informing some lessees that their permits would terminate in a decade. The agency added, in terms many found offensive, "We hope that you and members of your family and your friends may fully enjoy your summer home pending the time it must give way to other general public service facilities which permit use by great numbers of people without discrimination."[21]

Cottage owners often displayed antipathy toward regulations that impinged on their ability to enjoy the forest, but their complaints also reinforced ORRRC concerns about overcrowding. Before mobilizing to protest lease terminations, owners clashed with campers and the Forest Service by lodging concerns about traffic, people speeding down access roads, and waterfront access. A seventy-year-old retired minister who served as president of a local permit holders association in the Norway Beach section of the Chippewa National Forest wrote the Agriculture Department, "We cannot afford the financial loss involved in the loss of our rights here."[22] Cottagers expressed displeasure with the government demolition program, but precedent existed on the Superior National Forest, where the government purchased forty-two resorts with a total value over $2 million, and ninety-seven summer cabins valued over $1 million in the forest's roadless area by 1964. With few exceptions, summer cabins in the Superior roadless area no longer existed. The primary goal of the Chippewa program, unlike the Superior's, was to improve public access rather than establish a wilderness. Responding to increased demand captured in the ORRRC report, the Forest Service maintained that its efforts would better meet the nation's recreational needs.[23]

Increased summer cottage construction on private land along with the removal of cottages on federal lands altered the tourist landscape. Government purchases, both outright and through eminent domain, often uprooted families who had vacationed in the North Woods for generations. James R. Bailey, who spent summers at a Grand Sable Lake cabin that became part of Michigan's Pictured Rocks National Lakeshore recalled:

> It seemed that my whole life was consumed with my next visit to the Cabin. I found security in the fact that the Cabin was there, no matter what happened in my life I knew that the Cabin existed, in all its beauty, in the harsh Grand Marais winters, the grizzly Canadian winds and the unpredictable spring rains. It was there alive, not only in my memory but in reality. I didn't have to actually be there, just knowing it was there added to the comfort level of my state of being.

Bailey's cabin was eventually purchased through the Park Service's land acquisition program in 1985. For Bailey and others, a North Woods cabin offered mental and spiritual rewards. In purchasing private lands for public use, the government believed establishing spaces for recreation and contemplation could help guarantee that the feelings Bailey expressed could be enjoyed by all.[24]

Historian Ted Karamanski suggests Pictured Rocks area residents relinquished control in exchange for economic development, claiming, "Just as the region's old extractive economy had been managed from outside the Upper Peninsula, so would the tourist industry give the people of Detroit, Chicago, and Milwaukee a large voice over development issues." Urban tourists voiced opinions, and their actions surely helped shape the region. But North Woods residents and cottage owners were far from quiet, whether on Indian reservations, the Chippewa National Forest, or near new national lakeshores. As they did during the interwar years, they fought for control over the region's future, and they made sure this future included tourism.[25]

Where Wilderness Begins: Minnesota's Boundary Waters

In 1960, author and environmentalist Wallace Stegner wrote the ORRRC about the need for wilderness preservation, rallying against commercialization and urging acceptance of humanity's place in the natural world. Referring to both the vanishing prairie of his youth and the Great Lakes forests, Stegner opined, "We simply need that wild country available to us, even if we never do more than drive to its edge and look in. For it can be a means of reassuring ourselves of our sanity as creatures, a part of the geography of hope."[26] Stegner's "geography of hope" could include wilderness recreation. In the North Woods, one person's wilderness might be Minnesota's boundary waters; another's, the Pictured Rocks; a third's, a northern Wisconsin retreat. In the postwar years, northern Minnesota's "watery wilderness" witnessed Forest Service officials, local entrepreneurs, and vacationers promoting and experiencing the area's unique qualities. The boundary waters were a "watery wilderness" for some, but also a highly contested space managed, packaged, and sold to consumers, where people fought over what tourism should look like in a wilderness landscape. The "watery wilderness" was surely a physical place, but it was also one in which the very definition of wilderness tourism was often as slippery as the region's lakes in winter. In the post–World War II years, Minnesota's boundary waters emerged as a battleground in environmental debates about tourism's place in conservation, wilderness, and public land management.[27]

Minnesota's boundary waters offered a paradise of islands and lakes for canoeists. This photograph shows the Lac La Croix Islands in the upper west half of Lac La Croix, looking west with Canada in the right background, 1940. LOCAL IDENTIFIER USFS NEGATIVE 400686, RECORDS OF THE FOREST SERVICE, RECORD GROUP 95, THE NATIONAL ARCHIVES AT CHICAGO.

With thirty-two million people enjoying recreation on the national forests in 1930, northern Minnesota residents and the U.S. Forest Service recognized Americans' growing desire to experience the outdoors. Resorts in the Superior National Forest increased from sixteen to sixty-five between 1936 and 1950, and the first two fly-in resorts in the boundary waters appeared on Crooked Lake in 1940.[28] While residents capitalized on tourism, attempts to please multiple interests also led to conflict. By 1945, disagreements over access and land-use issues in the forest boiled over because of a federal proposal to purchase resorts in the Superior roadless areas, deeming them incompatible with wilderness. Minnesota's Conservation Commissioner Chester Wilson wrote Ely's mayor to express surprise over local opposition, "since the completion of the roadless area program will unquestionably be a very great benefit to the people of Ely and vicinity."[29] Like Arthur Carhart a generation earlier, Wilson envisioned the area as a place with resorts "located at the gateways to the wilderness areas" rather than "scattered all through those areas." He believed Ely residents should support a unique wilderness rather than pursue developments common to other vacation destinations.[30]

While Ely resident and wilderness proponent Sigurd Olson promoted canoe country fishing and an airplane ban over the area, the Ely Chamber of Commerce's Ted Wynn penned columns in the *Ely Miner* blaming wilderness preservation for Ely's financial problems. Since the paper's editor refused to publish pro-wilderness letters, the Quetico-Superior Committee produced *Wilderness Canoe Country*, a film script penned by Olson with support from seventy-five northeastern Minnesota organizations favoring the airplane ban.[31] Olson recognized the economic impact of the boundary waters on the surrounding area—$10 million was pumped into local economies in 1947. Preserving wilderness served Olson's vision for the area, and he claimed Ely's residents stood to benefit.[32] The *Minneapolis Star* also supported the air ban, claiming, "Nobody's real rights are being hurt" since "resort owners have had 25 years' notice that it is U.S. Forest Service policy to keep out commercialization." But attracting canoe tourists to Minnesota's watery wilderness clearly involved commerce.[33]

Wilderness advocates like Olson and Ernest Oberholtzer opposed airplane access and additional road construction into the boundary waters, claiming planes disturbed campers looking to experience "the primeval character of one of the last remaining fragments of original America."[34] Among this group was Superior National Forest ranger J. W. Trygg, who believed flights should only occur to protect and administer the area. Trygg maintained that uncontrolled flying resulted in planes from Chicago bypassing resorts and outfitters and returning the same day to the detriment of local businesses. Arguing that the air ban benefited local tourist interests, he worked to build support for the measure but found tough sledding among local fly-in resort operators, who saw it as a threat to their operations.[35]

Conservation Commissioner Wilson justified the air ban by suggest-

Two forest officers (Bill Trygg, *far right*, and Merle Moltrup, *center*) visit three vacationists at a canoe camp site on Birch Point on the south arm of Knife Lake. On a thirty-day canoe trip in the wilderness area, these campers discuss their itinerary with the forest officers, who refer to a map of the area to route an interesting return trip for them, 1940. LOCAL IDENTIFIER USFS NEGATIVE 400506, RECORDS OF THE FOREST SERVICE, RECORD GROUP 95, THE NATIONAL ARCHIVES AT CHICAGO.

ing that planes delivering visitors to fly-in resorts cast enormous shadows, both literally and figuratively, over the wilderness. Supporting government land purchases, except for thirty-three accessible resorts that were "so well established and of such value that the U.S. Forest Service does not contemplate attempting to force them to sell out," he agreed with the Forest Service that the air ban would increase rather than reduce tourist visits. Wilson urged purchase and elimination of eight isolated resorts on canoe routes that were "truly a thorn in the flesh of the wilderness" and hoped to accomplish this through the voluntary agreement of owners, which proved difficult in several cases. William Zupancich refused a federal government offer of $75,000 for his Curtain Falls Resort, whose main lodge and thirteen cabins slept fifty with additional space for twenty-five employees and family. Other places on the government's list included Martin Skala's Lac La Croix Lodge and Joseph Perko's Crooked Lake Fishing Camp.[36]

Local fly-in resort owners claimed they provided a necessary service

Lac La Croix, Boundary Waters Canoe Area, July 15, 1960. LOCAL IDENTIFIER USFS NEGATIVE 494941, RECORDS OF THE FOREST SERVICE, RECORD GROUP 95, THE NATIONAL ARCHIVES AT CHICAGO.

and argued the air ban violated their property rights and ability to earn a living. Several operators responded to President Harry S. Truman's institution of the air ban by defying it, eventually forcing the government to pay more for properties and expanding Forest Service enforcement. Zupancich complained about the cost of restricting access to his lodge, saying, "I worked nine years to get this place going. . . . I've got something to take care of me the rest of my life. If I sold out or traded I'd have to start all over again. If the Government wants me out of here they will have to pay me. I've got three kids to think about." He did not give up without a fight. Skala claimed flights fostered democratic access to wilderness because seaplanes helped his older guests reach the backcountry.[37] Perko intended to reside summers on Crooked Lake after purchasing property before the war. But when pilots started dropping off fishing parties, he sensed an opportunity, remarking, "If it is going to be like this, I might as well build a couple more cabins and rent them out and commence a little resort."[38] Facing acquisition, Perko alleged the government wanted to acquire his property without due process and that the Forest Service and wealthy people used outdoor organizations as fronts to institute the air ban. He suggested the Forest Service had "a fixed price and a rope around my neck." That price was $79,500. Not content with the offer, Perko initially provided guests a four-and-a-half-hour boat shuttle to his lodge. Realizing the lengthy trip was deterring visitors, Perko sold his property to the government in 1956 and retained personal use of one cabin.[39]

While fly-in resort owners fought to maintain their operations, local and regional wilderness advocates founded Friends of the Wilderness (FOW) in 1949 to support the air ban proposal and federal land acquisition in the Superior roadless areas. FOW studied area resorts for purchase and used newsletters and the press to campaign against commercial activities in the forest. Born in Duluth, FOW's executive secretary William Magie attended college on the East Coast, returning to work for a mining company before leading FOW. In supporting the air ban, Magie emphasized the inequity of having a few people exploit public land for private gain, remarking, "I hope and pray that many of the conflicting ideas and motives can be settled in the near future and that the Quetico-Superior will become safe from all those clutching hands that are trying to reap a profit through its destruction by commercialization."[40] While Magie expressed a hopeful tone, controversy continued as people and organizations presented different visions of wilderness tourism in the boundary waters.

FOW had little sympathy for operators unwilling to accept government purchase offers, claiming they knew their land was in the roadless area when they established operations. But such an argument neglected to note that flying restrictions emerged later. To combat the air ban proposal, Zupancich and other fly-in resort owners financed the pamphlet "Isolate and Exploit," which was published in local papers and distributed regionally. It argued that the air ban hid activities of power and lumber interests planning to gut the canoe country and suggested flights provided an eye in the sky for citizens to maintain control. Fly-in operators distrusted the government and, in language oddly similar to that of wilderness proponents who opposed the Backus dam proposal during the interwar years, portrayed themselves as fighting rapacious industrialists who would ruin the wilderness if their activities were not scrutinized.[41] Zupancich described the ban as detrimental not only to his business but to Ely as a whole, citing his conversations with local business people about a declining summer trade. He labeled the ban "unjustified, inhuman and undemocratic," adding "it was unthinkable in a free nation to deprive the owner of a resort of the right to reach his property by any form of transportation he desired."[42]

During the early 1950s, resort owners advocating unfettered tourist development found support within the Ely Chamber of Commerce.[43] The Chamber's Stan Pechaver defended Zupancich, declaring, "We in Ely are not racketeers and people who want to break down the wilderness area. Our goal is to provide means of transportation to the resorts as it means a great deal to the economic future of Ely."[44] One resort owner's attorney claimed the airspace reservation and other restrictive legislation cost the local economy $665,000, but the Minnesota Arrowhead Association (MAA) argued that business improved.[45] The Chamber alleged the ban placed unnecessary restrictions on businesses, while FOW countered that it affected only three of the region's two hundred resorts and suggested the Chamber exaggerated its impact for political purposes.[46]

While the Chamber spoke for some Ely interests, it did not represent the range of opinions in Ely and across the state that emerged in this occasionally vituperative debate. The Izaak Walton League joined Conservation Commissioner Wilson in opposing increased access via automobile and aircraft. The president of the league's Minnesota division, Karl Danielson, called on "the thoughtful people of Ely to openly disown these individuals, and do their utmost to prevent further exploitation of the Roadless Area by such local residents." Unlike Wilson, Danielson accused roadless area resort owners of being concerned only with profit. Arguing that this was a national as well as local issue and that Ely had garnered a reputation as a wilderness destination, he called on residents to serve as "local guardians."[47] Danielson criticized the Chamber for supporting air travel to roadless area resorts and declared, "We deeply regret that the City of Ely, which has always advertised itself as the 'Gateway to the Wilderness' should now take this fatal step to exploit and finally destroy that wilderness." He urged Ely residents to disavow the Chamber's actions, which he felt protected the interests of a few resort owners at the larger community's expense. Behind the scenes, the Chamber remained divided. One local resort owner informed Olson that a majority of members backed the roadless area and air ban, but the minority who opposed it controlled the organization. Opposition to the air ban ultimately reached the U.S. Supreme Court, which upheld the ban. In 1954, Canada instituted a similar ban.[48]

Debates over wilderness tourism in the boundary waters reverberated beyond Ely. A 1948 *New Yorker* cover portrayed a party emerging from a portage with canoe and gear in tow heading to a wilderness campsite only to confront two women on beach chairs enjoying cocktails at a new fly-in resort.[49] A Minneapolis resident criticized fly-in operators and their guests, remarking, "Let's continue to preserve this small area of wilderness for the enjoyment of those of our citizens who enjoy the peace and quiet of a purely wilderness area. The airplane sportsmen have a much larger area to fly into than the wilderness area comprises."[50] Magie's comments about a Gunflint Trail resort owner highlighted growing antipathy among wilderness advocates toward those operators who saw only dollar signs: "They come up here to Minnesota to make an easy million sitting on their big fat fannies. Well they found out different that running a resort is hard work and not as easy as they thought and not the money maker either that it seemed to be before buying." Perhaps such hostility emerged because the individual joined other resort owners in opposing the ban despite having a resort outside the designated area.[51] Northern Minnesota resort owners were certainly not unified behind a single position. FOW gathered support from those outside the air ban area, including Jean and Dick Raiken of Tofte's Sawbill Lodge, who informed FOW that they supported tourist development but "always with the best conservation principles and fighting any encroachment of the roadless area." Looking to retire to other property in the area, the Raikens positioned themselves as tourist industry advocates and land stewards by telling the FOW that their purchase would help reduce commercial development and "guard against the possibility of an undesirable tenant procuring it."[52]

While FOW generated substantial local and regional support, several roadless area resort owners and Ely Chamber of Commerce members formed Outdoor America United (OAU) to fight the air ban and potential restrictions on motorized use. OAU also advocated cleaning up portages and campsites, discontinuing state land sales and transfers to the federal government, and increasing reforestation funds. Positioning itself as an organization of common people, it condemned "the practice of miss-use [*sic*] of public funds by the Federal Forest Service through the use of personnel and equipment such as guides, boats, cabins and planes in the entertainment of Very Important People." OAU argued that it protected land, while government officials countered that OAU was promoting the interests of select resort owners rather than offering a reasonable conservation program. Asserting that the air ban was undemocratic, OAU said that they believed the local economy would suffer with the elimination of six seaplane operators and two hundred jobs and that tourists who did not canoe would be unable to enjoy the wilderness. According to OAU, the air ban was a "perversion of public policy in behalf of the few at the expense of the many." OAU posed flights as a public safety and oversight measure, claiming they provided rescue services for canoeists in trouble.[53]

While some residents sided with OAU, others fought to preserve a wilderness canoe country. Local outfitter Bill Rom worried about the area being overrun with tourist facilities and losing its uniqueness. He even questioned whether the Quetico-Superior Committee was capitulating to the Forest Service in developing a less restrictive land-use policy. Forest Service multiple-use policies, according to Rom, were "destroying the recreational value of the wilderness Canoe Country"; he suggested that "you cannot log a wilderness and still have a wilderness." While he backed agency efforts to purchase and remove roadless area resorts, Rom suggested the Park Service might be better suited to the task given its emphasis on aesthetic values.[54] FOW and Quetico-Superior Committee member Frank Hubachek assured Rom that the priority remained acquiring private property in the roadless areas and placing it under public ownership. Rom continued to express frustration with the Forest Service and advocated for forest protection, since his business depended on preserving such places.[55]

Prior to the 1964 Wilderness Act, other national forests designated wilderness areas under Forest Service regulations, and Rom believed this approach was appropriate for the boundary waters. Rom also registered discontent with fly-in resort owners, commenting that if FOW bought out Perko and Zupancich, the others would sell. FOW's Bill Magie told Rom that incursions by loggers and resort interests spelled "the death knell of you and other Canoe Outfitters." To limit further encroachment, FOW urged the Forest Service to purchase properties as they became available rather than holding out for high-priority sites.[56] Rom knew his public positions supporting the air ban and wilderness designation put him at odds with some in Ely, but he worked to forge alliances. Rom believed policies preserving and enlarging the wilderness would aid the cause so that those "who would like to see the Canoe Country exploited and destroyed as a wilderness will have notice of a united front and that they are bucking a stone wall." Despite these conflicts, the number of visitors arriving to explore the boundary waters via canoe increased tenfold from 1947 to 1959, aiding Rom's business. His employees and customers also spent money locally, generating awareness of wilderness tourism's economic benefits.[57]

The Ely Chamber claimed it recognized the canoe country's importance, while aiming to ensure everyone's happiness with a range of options. Rom believed the Chamber was "awakening slightly" to the canoe country's ability to attract visitors to Ely but believed Chamber leaders still did not understand the importance of keeping the area "inviolate—no roads, no logging, no planes, no resorts, in short just kept as a protected unspoiled wilderness for today and generations to come."[58] Rom's steadfastness even led to criticism from those who supported wilderness designation. Rom lashed out at one advocate after hearing comments suggesting the need for access roads "to keep Bill Rom from having a monopoly." Citing his hard work and dedication, Rom responded:

> How silly can one get? This is a country of free enterprise and anybody can buy a bunch of canoes and equipment and if he's willing to put in a sixteen hour day seven days a week, pour everything back into the business for years, fight sometimes dirty competition, make as many as five sports shows while staying in YMCAs, spend more money on advertising than all the other outfitters put together, and withstand a lot of criticism by living right here in Ely in the midst of all the opposition to the wilderness, I think one's entitled to a little success.[59]

Like resort owners fighting against the air ban, Rom argued that his entrepreneurial spirit and efforts to earn a living should not be restricted. While his rhetoric shared similarities with that of fly-in resort owners and the Ely Chamber of Commerce, he adopted a dramatically different approach to preserving wilderness because his business depended on a roadless area without flights.

Competing and multifaceted wilderness visions involving land use, tourism, and economic development long divided the community and intensified in postwar battles between FOW and the Ely Chamber of Commerce. FOW questioned the Chamber's motives, believing it was sacrificing the area "for a little more private enrichment of a few selfish tradesmen who demand their pound of flesh from the irreplaceable public lands . . . for a few more paltry dollars in these entrepreneurs already fat bank accounts."[60] The Chamber responded that it was not opposed to the wilderness area but rather the manner in which it developed and the harm it believed it inflicted on Ely's economy, asking, "Do you know that the acquisition program and the flying ban have resulted in the loss of more than a score of resorts with some 900 accommodations for tourists?" Both organizations saw tourism as crucial to the region's future, but their views on the place of wilderness within it differed. The Chamber supported Forest Service multiple-use policy but not what it labeled the "non-use" policy of FOW, which it claimed crippled the economy. Lambasting FOW for being "utterly retrogressive," the Chamber continued, "You are not creating jobs for Labor. You are not creating trade for Small Business. You are neither conservationist nor altruist."[61] One resident lashed out at FOW and other wilderness supporters, believing citizens north of Duluth deserved modern roads and recreation and claiming, "If visitors from Chicago don't like it, I suggest they stay at home and do their canoeing on Lake Michigan."[62]

On the other hand, FOW believed breaching the wilderness meant losing tourists. In 1945, Ely had two motels, four outfitters, and thirty-five resorts within a twenty-mile radius. Ten years later, it boasted eleven motels, eight outfitters, and ninety resorts. FOW used the Chamber's own marketing of Ely to argue that as long as the town maintained wilderness at its doorstep, the scarcity of similar areas elsewhere meant more visitors for Ely. FOW referred to the canoe country as "the goose that lays the Golden Eggs" and claimed it would "continue to lay them if Ely can continue to live up to its boast—Where Wilderness Begins." FOW's position echoed Senator Humphrey's rebuke of the *Ely Miner*'s editor for attacking the wilderness bill he proposed in 1957, which included designating Superior roadless areas federal wilderness. Rather than causing injury to Ely, Humphrey opined, "It should aid Ely commercially by attracting new lovers of wilderness."[63] To support this effort, FOW urged land purchases to limit development, including its own bid for Canadian land being considered for a Boy Scout camp. FOW also hoped the federal government would purchase eleven resorts along with fifty-six cabins and fifty-eight unimproved properties in the Superior roadless area to solidify the wilderness.[64]

In addition to battling FOW, Chamber leadership also clashed with the Forest Service. The Chamber's Ted Wynn penned an open letter to Representative John Blatnik opposing further federal acquisition of private lands. While Chamber letterhead read "the friendly city," Wynn's tone was heated, "We do not quarrel with the principles of primitive areas but we cannot reconcile our thoughts—or our economy—to the feverish rapidity of the metamorphosis from private enterprise to federal government ownership with its consequent destruction of our community's economy."[65] According to Wynn, Ely had become an island surrounded by federal lands. Echoing Senator Humphrey, Forest Service chief Richard McArdle portrayed agency policy as benefiting Ely's interests and believed efforts to consolidate ownership would create "an extremely attractive and unique region which will attract an ever-increasing number of recreationists." Claiming private ownership was incompatible with managing and preserving a wilderness area, the Forest Service suggested residents capitalize on wilderness tourism. After the Multiple Use-Sustained Yield Act of 1960, recreation emerged as one of many uses for which the agency managed national forests. Like the FOW and the Chamber, the Forest Service and the Chamber held competing visions of wilderness on the tourist landscape.[66]

In the postwar years, the Superior National Forest's boundary waters emerged as the only national forest area with an air-space reservation and a program to purchase private properties. Its unique recreational potential attracted ORRRC attention, but the ORRRC viewed the canoe country debate in somewhat simplistic terms. It determined that "attention to the area has tended to involve a local point of view—which admits of many

Map of the Superior National Forest in the Voyageur Visitor Center lobby, July 1965. LOCAL IDENTIFIER USFS NEGATIVE 512342, RECORDS OF THE FOREST SERVICE, RECORD GROUP 95, THE NATIONAL ARCHIVES AT CHICAGO.

legitimate recreational uses of land and water—rather than aggressive attention to the special values of this area in a national perspective, which may require that some local views be subordinated." The story was more complicated than the ORRRC presented, since support for the "national" approach came from vacationers who expressed desires to experience such a place as well as residents like Rom and local FOW members who supported wilderness travel as key to the area's future. One vacationer reported, "I like to be someplace where it hasn't been taken over by a maze of tourists and others, spreading their garbage, etc. The more remote it is, the more likely it will be in its original state," while another added that it was vital "to get back where you can be yourself without automobiles and a lot of noise from other people." Still others focused on the physical and mental challenges of outdoor adventure.[67]

Such vacationer comments would have interested Arthur Carhart. Four decades after serving as the Forest Service's first landscape architect, Carhart positioned himself as a moderate on Superior National Forest recreational use. He was well aware of wilderness advocates battling those who "would have laced the Superior country with roads and had, in the words of one person bent on 'improvement' of the forest, a double row of cottages around every lake in the forest and the greatest 'resort area' in the world."[68] Unlike Wallace Stegner, who saw wilderness possibilities in land scarred by mining, Carhart believed mining's presence made wilderness designation difficult. He also felt making portions of the boundary waters a national park would not protect it from automobile travel, commenting, "Just the name national park triggers the thundering herd type of use." Operating between Chamber and FOW positions, Carhart sought compromise between a wilderness that might limit human use and a national park geared to extensive tourist use.[69]

In the early 1960s, the Forest Service looked for effective ways to manage both this unique wilderness recreation resource and the debates that swirled over its future. On February 13, 1963, the agency approved the acquisition of sixty-eight properties in the Boundary Waters Canoe Area (BWCA), explaining government attempts to negotiate mutually acceptable purchase prices in all cases. Sixty-three properties reached agreements, and five would be acquired through condemnation. With passage of the Wilderness Act and formal establishment of the BWCA Wilderness in 1964, Minnesota Conservation Commissioner George Selke led hearings as chair of the Boundary Waters Area Review Committee, which raised local havoc over recommendations for extending the no-cut area, banning snowmobiles, and regulating motorized use. Unlike the earlier ORRRC report, the committee's report recognized that while some residents preferred unrestricted resort development, most "realize that such development would seriously impair the very qualities that bring people to the region and, in the long run, would adversely affect local business and payrolls and the local tax base." Increased interest in BWCA vacations necessitated a new management approach. To limit overcrowding, in 1965 visitors had to obtain Forest Service permits to enter the BWCA.[70]

The creation of the BWCA helped solidify a particular vision of the area as a wilderness landscape, although some individuals presented alternatives within this context. John Smrekar, who led OAU in the 1950s and the MAA in the 1960s, proposed a multiple-use recreational approach. With canoe travel possible only during certain seasons, Smrekar and the MAA supported winter snowmobile access and promoted "every season has a reason." Sharing the stage with Smrekar at a 1964 event, FOW's William Magie backed canoe-only use. Claiming motor use would make the area indistinguishable from others, FOW joined local outfitters to argue that preserving a nonmotorized area offered greater economic and spiritual benefits for local residents and the nation.[71] One observer suggested that while the BWCA "provides a refuge from mechanized recreation but permits some logging and other uses," its main use remained recreational "with inspirational overtones." Such use shared similarities with Carhart's initial recreation proposal for the Superior four decades earlier.[72]

In 1973, resident John Chelesnik expressed support for wilderness preservation while raising economic concerns. Reflecting on early resorts, the air ban, mine closings, the Wilderness Act, and BWCA establishment, he remarked, "Some of these changes, I must admit, were for the good of the area, however, regulations instituted during the past five years worry me." He reserved antipathy for canoeists who "arrive in Ely on a Sunday night, sleep in a car or camper at a government campsite and disembark on their bold journeys Monday morning leaving a trash can full of garbage and little or no income with the merchants of Ely." If wilderness tourists did not contribute to the local economy, Chelesnik questioned whether it was worth attracting them.[73] In 1978, Congress passed the Boundary Waters Canoe Area Wilderness Act, which effectively eliminated logging and snowmobiling, restricted mining, and allowed motors on only a limited number of lakes in the BWCA. Controversies regarding management policies did not fade, but by the late 1970s wilderness tourism emerged as the area's dominant use.[74]

The Current and Future Tourist Landscape

Wilderness tourism debates extended beyond Minnesota. Ontario's tourist minister Bryan Cathcart addressed the wilderness and development dichotomy ubiquitous throughout the province's tourist industry. Northwestern Ontario outfitters, according to Cathcart, needed "to accept the fact that as industrial and other development move north and northwest, they must not expect to keep a wilderness condition in existence for their own commercial reasons." In order to survive, the government suggested some outfitters transform their operations into family resorts rather than merely attracting sportsmen looking for wilderness. Provincial officials viewed this as a way to engage the wilderness enthusiast while also attracting families who vacationed in Michigan, Minnesota, and Wisconsin.[75]

In Michigan's Upper Peninsula, Porcupine Mountains State Park again attracted attention after a 1971 state management plan proposed setting aside thirty-five thousand acres as permanent wilderness. Margery Fahrenbach, daughter of former state parks superintendent and conservation director P. J. Hoffmaster, recalled her father's efforts to protect the Porkies. At a hearing on the measure, she exclaimed, "My father fought long and hard to help acquire this area for the people of Michigan. He loved those mountains with their wild and unspoiled beauty, and I believe he envisioned them as a 'preservation,' a bit of country that should and can be preserved as God made it." Gordon Connor, who previously sought to log in the area, was the only person at the hearing to speak against the designation. The state once again rejected his entreaty, and the park became Porcupine Mountains Wilderness State Park.[76]

In 2004, President George W. Bush signed legislation designating approximately 80 percent of Wisconsin's Apostle Islands National Lakeshore as the Gaylord Nelson Wilderness, honoring the former governor and senator for his environmental accomplishments. The National Park Service encouraged visitors to learn about those who settled the islands as well as the park's rewilding into a wilderness landscape infused with cultural meaning. Rather than seeing human land use as inherently violent and abusive, rewilding aimed to help visitors consider how humans have altered the landscape. In many ways, Stegner foreshadowed this approach when he wrote the ORRRC in 1960, "I am not moved by the argument that those wilderness areas which have already been exposed to grazing or mining are already deflowered, and so might as well be 'harvested.'" Stegner claimed grazing need not "conflict with the wilderness feeling or the validity of the wilderness experience." Rewilding emphasizes the intertwined nature of the Apostle Islands' natural and human history of farming, fur trading, fishing, shipping, logging, quarrying, and touring. As William Cronon has suggested, "To acknowledge past human impacts upon these islands is not to call into question their wildness; it is rather to celebrate, along with the human past, the robust ability of wild nature to sustain itself when people give it the freedom it needs to flourish in their midst."[77] In North Woods destinations like the BWCA and the Apostle Islands, wilderness tourism certainly has a human history.

Since the 1960s tourism has continued to shape the North Woods, reflecting competing visions of the region's resources as well as the changing relationship between human action and environmental change in modern America. When the 1983 *Voigt* decision affirmed the treaty rights of Lake Superior Ojibwe to harvest off-reservation natural resources, conflict erupted over members of the Lac du Flambeau band spearing walleye in off-reservation lakes. Non-Indian tourist and sporting interests feared spearfishing would deplete the resource and leave little for tourists. This contributed to protests in which signs sporting statements like "Save a Walleye, Spear an Indian" appeared as tribal members entered lakes at night. Local news coverage fanned the flames. For example, the *Lakeland Times* emphasized supposed dangers to tourism by printing letters from Illinois residents critical of spearfishing. Wisconsin's Department of Natural Resources went so far as to suggest tourism and spearfishing could not coexist. Today, the climate has cooled from the heated days of the 1980s. Tourists fish northern Wisconsin's bountiful lakes, and members of the Lac du Flambeau Ojibwe exercise their off-reservation rights, working through the Great Lakes Indian Fish and Wildlife Commission, a consortium of tribal governments from the three states, and Wisconsin's Department of Natural Resources. The state fish hatchery at Lac du Flambeau produces over thirty million walleye fry annually, much of them eventually ending up in reservation lakes to be consumed by residents and tourists.[78]

State tourism agencies continue to promote and research the tourist industry, telling people to Travel Michigan, Explore Minnesota, or Travel Wisconsin. Today's northeastern Minnesota vacationer encounters a plethora of options amid wilderness lakes and lush forests, home to abundant wildlife. Tourists can learn about the history of Ojibwe, voyageurs, miners, lumbermen, and lighthouse keepers. Continuing an approach from the interwar years, the state tourist agency maintains distinct regions for marketing purposes. In the Arrowhead, tourists can vacation on one of sixteen hundred lakes, visit Duluth, travel the Gunflint Trail

Ruttger's Bay Lake Resort, Bay Lake Township, Crow Wing County, 1981. COURTESY OF THE MINNESOTA HISTORICAL SOCIETY.

to the Boundary Waters Canoe Area Wilderness, explore mining history along the Iron Range, or drive along the scenic North Shore of Lake Superior to Canada. State designated scenic byways like Highway 38, "Edge of the Wilderness Drive," and parts of the Great River Road crisscross the region, allowing travelers to take in the scenery, wildlife, and open-pit mining from the comfort of their car. In Grand Rapids, they can learn about papermaking at Blandin Paper or visit a logging camp reconstruction at the state's Forest History Center. Along the Gunflint Trail, historic lodges continue to attract vacationers and provide opportunities for winter activities among wildlife and snow. On the Iron Range, activities extend beyond the region's mining and immigrant history. The Greyhound Bus Company Museum, which traces the company's origins to a local shuttle service for miners, and the U.S. Hockey Hall of Fame also attract tourists. Visitors can enjoy Voyageurs National Park and the state's sixty-six state parks with 1,260 miles of trails, waterfalls, and beaches. The state's 11,842 lakes provide water-based activities, and golf courses attract business and pleasure travelers. Winter offers skiing, snowmobiling, snowshoeing, and ice fishing.[79]

Travel Wisconsin is the state's tourist promotion, development, and research agency. Since the 1950s, surveys have examined tourism's impact, and today agencies study the industry to a degree unimaginable to early promotional pioneers like George Bishop and Joseph Mercedes. The majority of Wisconsin vacationers arrive from the Chicago area, Minnesota, Iowa, and within Wisconsin. Promoters continue to capitalize on the region's history for tourist purposes. In 2001, the Department of Tourism joined the Wisconsin Historical Society in conducting a survey of visitors to historic sites that determined those interested in heritage tourism spent more and stayed longer than the average tourist. Wisconsin's historic site visitors were generally educated and affluent baby boomers who enjoyed traveling, reading, camping, sightseeing, and hiking. With its inland lakes, rivers, and 650 miles of Great Lakes shoreline, the DNR also promotes recreational boating, reinforcing ORRRC recommendations of fifty years ago.[80]

Like Minnesota, Travel Wisconsin divides the state into regions to entice vacationers looking for particular experiences and landscapes, noting that "the vast pinestral forests of the Northwoods give off an exhilarating scent that spells 'vacation'—an ever-present invitation." In Bayfield, travelers encounter a charming town with modern amenities where in summer its Lake Superior harbor is filled with sailboats, kayaks, and fishing vessels. Visitors can enjoy the Lake Superior Big Top Chautauqua or venture to the Apostle Islands National Lakeshore, whose twenty-two islands house lighthouses, sea caves, and hiking trails. The Lakeland Area of Vilas and Oneida Counties contains over thirty-two hundred lakes, streams, and ponds. Eagle River sits on a chain of twenty-eight lakes that offer a boon to anglers. During winter, residents and vacationers cross-country ski and snowmobile. Dating back to the days of Tony Wise, Hayward still holds the Lumberjack World Championships each summer, and its National Fresh Water Fishing Hall of Fame attracts visitors. Hayward and Cable also host the Birkebeiner cross-country ski races and

Chequamegon Fat Tire bicycle races. Heritage tourism is also present in the North Woods. Hurley's nineteenth-century county courthouse offers a museum examining the region's mining, logging, and farming heritage, and in Lac du Flambeau, visitors can learn about Ojibwe culture.[81]

Travel Michigan works with regional and state organizations to market the state. As an agency of the Michigan Economic Development Corporation, it also seeks to create and retain tourist industry jobs. In 2004, Governor Jennifer Granholm's "Hidden Treasures Showcase" highlighted unique opportunities for vacationers, encouraging residents to travel in Michigan and promoting economic development tied to tourism. Granholm kayaked at McLain State Park on Lake Superior, rafted the Sturgeon River, biked the Pere Marquette Rail-Trail, watched bald eagles at the Shiawassee National Wildlife Refuge, and enjoyed a performance at Marquette's Lake Superior Theatre. High gas prices have contributed to promotion of staying close to home on vacation: "Don't cancel your travel plans, reroute them to stay in Michigan. Why spend countless hours on a cross country trek, when there are thousands of one-tank trips you can take right in your own backyard?" With Michigan tourism a $15 billion annual industry, the state encourages residents to enjoy and spend money on Michigan vacations throughout the year.[82]

While summer and winter offer distinct vacation seasons, autumn also brings visitors to the North Woods. For many, November's brisk air means deer hunting. Men, women, and children sport fluorescent jackets and camouflage, carrying rifles and roaming the region's woods. A slight chill chaps the skin, but the thrill of the hunt and perhaps a few cocktails mitigate the cold. Leaves on the trees are no more, and snow gently begins to fall, as patches of white cover a brown landscape. Things are serene, yet active, in the woods and taverns. As has occurred for over a century, the autumn ritual attracts thousands seeking adventure and recreation in the North Woods during a time of year when people give thanks, celebrate autumn's passage, and begin preparations for the cold winter ahead.

Transforming the North Woods into a landscape of leisure has involved its share of battles over nature as a source of pleasure and profit. A decade ago, I enjoyed several days at a cottage on Torch Lake in Michigan's Copper Country. It was a pleasant place that allowed me to visit Lake Superior, tour Keweenaw National Historic Park, and conduct research at Michigan Tech before returning to watch the sunset over Torch Lake. While looking out on this landscape, I wondered what the promotional materials neglected to say about this place. For nearly a century, copper mining activities produced tailings that contaminated Torch Lake. To find this information, one must visit the Environmental Protection Agency's Superfund website. Tourist literature simply will not do. Despite the smelter's closure in 1971, this place was still grappling with the transformation from mining to tourism and the environmental problems associated with previous uses. Torch Lake reminds us that landscapes have complicated histories and those that often seem pristine have certainly experienced the imprint of humans' labor and leisure.

In 2009, Michigan Senator Carl Levin hosted an open house celebrating historic preservation efforts at the very Quincy Smelter that contributed to the Torch Lake contamination. He remarked, "I am proud of the work that has been accomplished by the community, the National Park Service and the Environmental Protection Agency to begin preserving this historical treasure, which helped power the nation's industrial revolution." Like so many others across the North Woods, this was also a story of public-private cooperation to transform a landscape of production into one of consumption. Rather than focus on tourists consuming this place, Levin hoped that today's preservation work would help future visitors connect to the history of this place, commenting, "I look forward to the day when everyone will be able to visit the smelter and understand its significance in the copper mining history of this nation and its contribution to the growth of the country's economy."[83] From the Copper Country to the Boundary Waters Canoe Area Wilderness and across the North Woods, work and leisure have proven inseparable from nature. Over the years, promoters have marked the region as an industrial behemoth, a land of agricultural plenty, a natural paradise, a rustic escape, and a vacation utopia. But, as they have for centuries, the humans who inhabit the region and the actions they take toward nature, each other, and the past will continue to determine the future of the North Woods.

Acknowledgments

LIKE MANY IN MY STORY, I HAVE VACATIONED IN THE NORTH WOODS and labored there, spending days and nights traversing roads, rivers, and lakes, hunkering down in archives, hiking and snowshoeing through the forest, and occasionally catching fish. But what made this project so worthwhile were the people who aided my travels, and it is a pleasure to thank them.

Finding records on tourism proved far easier because of the diligent work of several archivists. Erik Nordberg at the Michigan Technological University Archives and Copper Country Historical Collections has been a staunch supporter of my work from an early stage. At the Iron Range Research Center in Chisholm, Minnesota, Steve Harsin provided helpful advice. At the Minnesota Historical Society, Debbie Miller, Jim Fogerty, and Craig Wright gave me access to uncataloged resort materials and offered suggestions. The Minnesota Historical Society dealt with budget cuts that limited hours, reduced staff, and eliminated its grant program, but despite these unfortunate events, its dedicated staff makes it a treasure for researchers. At the Michigan State Archives, Mark Harvey and David Johnson supplied guidance on tourist association records as well as inexpensive photocopies to a poverty-stricken graduate student. I was fortunate to receive an E. Genevieve Gillette Research Travel Fellowship from the Bentley Library; Bill Wallach and his staff helped make my time there immensely productive. Pat Maus at the Northeast Minnesota Historical Center in Duluth extended helpful research advice. Wayne Crocket of the Ontario Provincial Archives readied materials for my time north of the border. The staffs at the Wisconsin Historical Society in Madison and at the Area Research Centers in Ashland and Kenosha went out of their way to aid my research. Cheryl Oakes and Jamie Lewis at the Forest History Society contributed thoughtful advice on the nation's forest history.

I have been fortunate to present my work in a variety of forums, including conferences, symposia, public lectures, and teacher workshops. While space precludes mentioning everyone by name, feedback from colleagues in these and other venues had a profound impact on this project. I also thank Pieter Martin, Kristian Tvedten, and the reviewers for the University of Minnesota Press for critical feedback.

The University of Chicago was a fascinating place to do graduate work and fostered this project in its early days. My advisor, Neil Harris, was steadfast in his support, meticulous in his critiques, and a model of a fully engaged professional. His incredible knowledge on just about every subject is exceeded only by his kindness and honesty. Amy Stanley is perhaps most responsible for guiding me through my first year of graduate school. Her dedication to her students and her directness made me buckle down and improve my writing. She furnished incredible support during particularly difficult circumstances that first year. I was fortunate to tap Kathleen Conzen's wealth of knowledge on midwestern history, and her suggestions made me a better scholar. It was my privilege to serve as Mae Ngai's research assistant for my first three years of graduate school. David Goodwine, Diane Brady, and Joanne Berens made the history office a welcome place to work. My colleagues in the department, particularly Mike Wakeford and Michael Stamm, offered generous friendship. As a Penn undergraduate uncertain of future plans, I had the privilege of participating in a research mentorship program with Walter Licht. The experience introduced me to labor history but proved far more important in showing me how engaged faculty can inspire their students. I found my work challenged, valued, and utilized and aim to accomplish the same with my students. I thank all of my Auburn University, University of Chicago, and Daley College students, Wells and University City High School students, and fourth graders, who inspire me to keep doing what I do. They give me hope that future educational opportunities will be more equitable and lead to a brighter tomorrow.

I first became involved with the Newberry Library while conducting preliminary research for this project. Later, I presented at the Rural History Seminar with Susan Rugh, a session that proved immensely helpful in writing chapter 3 of this book. When I began working at Newberry's Scholl Center, my colleagues Toby Higbie and Jen Koslow provided support along with needed distraction. I am glad that David McLeod, Mary Graham, and the anonymous reviewers for *Michigan Historical Review* decided to publish my essay on Upper Peninsula tourism; their feedback improved not only that article but this manuscript as well. Grants, fellowships, and support from the College of Liberal Arts and Department of History at Auburn University, Mellon Foundation/University of Chicago Social Sciences Division, Bentley Library, Wisconsin Historical Society, Copper Country Historical Collections at Michigan Technological University, University of Chicago History Department, and the University of Chicago Office of Graduate Affairs helped cover expenses.

My years as historian with the U.S. Forest Service were a wonderful experience, and I am especially thankful to all my agency colleagues who daily care for the land and serve people. For their guidance, advice, and support, I am particularly grateful to Dick Paterson, Martha Ketelle, Steve Dunsky, and Dave Steinke. At Auburn University, my colleagues in the history department make it an exciting place to work, and my chair, Charles Israel, offers steadfast encouragement.

My wonderful friends and family outside the academic world were unwavering in support and provided needed distraction at crucial times. You know who you are, and I thank all of you. Bruce Springsteen often provided necessary musical inspiration, and for many years Ellington always presented a friendly face and bark when it was time to go for a walk or, preferably, a run or swim. Today, Satchel does the same, although without the bark and with a bit more resistance to the walk in the South's grueling heat.

I save my final words of gratitude for several special people. My good friend Will Kraft lost a courageous battle with cancer in early 2003. Several months earlier, Will and I attended a Boss show in Boston just days after he had walked 26.2 miles to raise money for cancer research. His devotion to his friends, wry sense of humor in the face of a devastating disease, love of good barbecue and the Windy City, and commitment to making the world a better place remain an inspiration to me. In 2005, I lost my father to a crippling disease. Not an hour passes when I do not think about him. Like my father, my mother is a wonderful parent, dispensing constant support and guidance, a prod when necessary, and good humor always. I thank both of you for raising me, giving me untold opportunities, and instilling in me a sense of curiosity about this world: I am forever grateful. And to Suzi, if we made it this far, we can make it through anything. I look forward to sharing the journey ahead.

Notes

Abbreviations

AO	Archives of Ontario
BHL	Bentley Historical Library
C&H	Calumet and Hecla Mining Companies Collection
CCCC	Cook County Civic Council
CCHC	Copper Country Historical Collections
CCVL	Copper Country Vacationist League
CNF	Chippewa National Forest
EOHP	Minnesota Environmental Issues Oral History Project
FOW	Friends of the Wilderness
HLRA	Hayward Lakes Resort Association
IRP	Detroit News Isle Royale Papers
IRRC	Iron Range Research Center
LDF	Lac du Flambeau Agency Records
MAA	Minnesota Arrowhead Association
MDC	Michigan Department of Conservation
MHS	Minnesota Historical Society
MSU	Michigan State University Archives and Historical Collections
MTC	Michigan Tourist Council
MUCC	Michigan United Conservation Clubs
NARA-GL	The National Archives at Chicago
NR-PORC	Natural Resources Department, Parks Division, Porcupine Mountains
ORRRC	Outdoor Recreation Resources Review Commission
QSC	President's Quetico-Superior Committee
RG75	Department of the Interior, Office of Indian Affairs, Record Group 75
ROHP	Minnesota Resort Industry Oral History Project
SAM	State Archives of Michigan
UPDB	Upper Peninsula Development Bureau
UPTARA	Upper Peninsula Travel and Recreation Association Collection
USFS	U.S. Forest Service
WHS	Wisconsin Historical Society Archives
WHS-ARC	Wisconsin Historical Society, Ashland Area Research Center
WPA	Works Progress Administration; Work Projects Administration after July 1, 1939

Introduction

1. Promotional brochure for Ross' Teal Lake Lodge, folder 3, box 1, and B. A. Claflin, "Blazed Trails for Sportsmen," March 1928, folder 4, box 1, Ross' Teal Lake Lodge Collection, WHS, Madison.
2. On regional history, see Lankton, *Cradle to Grave*; Lankton, *Beyond the Boundaries*; Gough, *Farming the Cutover*; Karamanski, *Deep Woods Frontier*; Searle, *Saving Quetico-Superior*; Backes, *Canoe Country*; Kates, *Planning a Wilderness*. Lankton, *Hollowed Ground*, briefly discusses tourism in the final chapter. Johnson, "Conservation, Subsistence, and Class at the Birth of the Superior National Forest," analyzes local actions and recognizes tourism's growing presence within the context of environmental, wilderness, and land-use issues at the turn of the twentieth century. Summers, *Consuming Nature*, describes modern environmentalism's roots in consumer society in Wisconsin's Fox River valley, which lies south of the North Woods. Summers shows how energy and transportation networks transformed the valley and divorced residents from seeing the connections between their consumption and the natural world. As a result, they increasingly saw the outdoors as a place to recreate rather than work.
3. On the relationship between Chicago and its hinterland and the idea that city and country share a common history, see Cronon, *Nature's Metropolis*.
4. On deindustrialization's social, cultural, environmental, and economic impact as well as connections between industrial decline and environmental disaster, albeit in the post–World War II era, see Cowie and Heathcott, eds., *Beyond the Ruins*; High, *Industrial Sunset*.
5. On interwar environmentalism, see Sutter, *Driven Wild*; Maher, *Nature's New Deal*. On connections between work, leisure, and environmental consciousness, see White, "'Are You an Environmentalist or Do You Work for a Living?'" Chiang, *Shaping the Shoreline*, explores shared histories of work and leisure to highlight connections between extractive industry and tourism.
6. A substantial literature exists on urban working-class leisure spaces, but rural spaces have received less attention. On urban experiences, see Rosenzweig, *Eight Hours for What We Will*; Peiss, *Cheap Amusements*; Nasaw, *Going Out*; Cohen, *Making a New Deal*. On rural experiences, see Higbie, *Indispensable Outcasts*; Fine, "Rights of Men, Rites of Passage"; Montrie, *Making a Living*, 91–112. On economic and social connections between farm, town, and city helping construct regional identity, see Neth, "Seeing the Midwest with Peripheral Vision."
7. Rothman, *Devil's Bargains*. Long neglected by historians, scholarship on the history of tourism in the United States has expanded in recent years. Among others, see Belasco, *Americans on the Road*; Brown, *Inventing New England*; Aron, *Working at Play*; Shaffer, *See America First*; Blackford, *Fragile Paradise*; Cocks, *Doing the Town*; Starnes, ed. *Southern Journeys*; Harrison, *The View from Vermont*; C. Brenden Martin, *Tourism in the Mountain South*; Rugh, *Are We There Yet?*
8. Barron, *Mixed Harvest*. On the automobile's influence, see Flink, *The Automobile Age*; Flink, *The Car Culture*; Rae, *The Road and Car in American Life*; Berger, *The Devil Wagon in God's Country*. On 1920s vacations, see Horowitz, *The Morality of Spending*, 140.
9. On New Deal conservation, see Gregg, *Managing the Mountains*; Maher, *Nature's New Deal*; Phillips, *This Land, This Nation*. Phillips briefly discusses how midwestern state officials applied land economics and created a useful

national model. While the New Deal expanded federal conservation efforts, Maher's suggestion that it brought recreation policy under the conservation umbrella minimizes earlier recreation work of state conservation departments and the U.S. Forest Service.

10. On local engagement with conservation regulations in other areas of the country, see Jacoby, *Crimes against Nature*; Warren, *The Hunter's Game*; Spence, *Dispossessing the Wilderness*; Reiger, *American Sportsmen and the Origins of Conservation*.
11. Gough, *Farming the Cutover*.
12. Robbins, *Landscapes of Promise*, 309–10. On Oregon's postwar land-use controversies, many of which centered on recreational use of natural resources, see Robbins, *Landscapes of Conflict*.

1. A Crop Worth Cultivating

1. The *Minneapolis Daily Star* cartoon appeared on the cover of the Ten Thousand Lakes–Greater Minnesota Association, *Annual Report* (1929). On the emergence of quasi-public agencies producing and selling goods and services, see Radford, "From Municipal Socialism to Public Authorities."
2. Ely and Wehrwein, *Land Economics*; Wehrwein and Johnson, "A Recreation Livelihood Area." Wehrwein and Johnson reported 1938 tourist expenditures of $189,350,000 in Michigan, $129,000,000 in Minnesota, and $125,950,000 in Wisconsin. In 1928, resort owner and state senator Roy Dunn reported tourists spent over $90 million in Minnesota. Dunn to Mathias Koll, 29 March 1929, "Koll, Ten Thousand Lakes of Minnesota Association, 1928–1933," box 10, Koll Papers, MHS. Other growth indicators include out-of-state automobile traffic, ferry crossings, and fishing and hunting licenses issued.
3. UPDB Annual Report, 1919, folder 10, box 10, UPTARA, SAM; Carstensen, *Farms or Forests*; Mark Davis, "An Empire in Waiting"; Bawden, "Reinventing the Frontier."
4. Michigan Public Domain Commission and Michigan Immigration Commission, *Michigan*; Minnesota Board of Immigration, *Northeastern Minnesota*; Minnesota Board of Immigration, *Northwestern Minnesota*.
5. Henry, *Northern Wisconsin*, 23; On the Northern Wisconsin Development Association, see *Vilas County News*, 22 September 1920; Haswell and Alanen, "Colonizing the Cutover."
6. Quote from editor of *Antigo Journal* in *Vilas County News*, 22 September 1920; Angus McDonald quoted in Carstensen, *Farms or Forests*, 77. On Griffith and Wisconsin forestry, see Wilson, *E. M. Griffith and the Early Story of Wisconsin Forestry*; Wilson, "Zoning for Forestry and Recreation." Burlowe, "Changing Land Use Policies in the Lake States."
7. Haswell and Alanen, "Colonizing the Cutover," 176; Gough, *Farming the Cutover*. On Joseph Habrich and the Velebit Croatian settlement near Eagle River, see Espeseth, "Lodestar in the Northland." On Faast, see Clark "Cutover Problems."
8. Bogue, *Fishing the Great Lakes*, demonstrates how seasonal work was ingrained in regional culture. On seasonal work in urban and rural worlds, see Higbie, *Indispensable Outcasts*. On "making do," see Neth, *Preserving the Family Farm*.

9. Gough, "Richard T. Ely and the Development of the Wisconsin Cutover." On one family lured north by Faast's land company, see Groves, *Land of the Tamarack*. Paylin, *Cutover Country*, 6, discusses her father reading magazines aimed at luring settlers to the cutover. Steinberg, *Down to Earth*, 65, captures the cutover's grim reality and the deception speculators used to attract settlers.
10. Michigan Forestry Association Newsletter, 15 March 1927, box 2, Wheeler Papers, BHL; Agnes M. Larson, *The White Pine Industry in Minnesota*, 263–64 and 340–42; Searle, "Minnesota Forestry Comes of Age."
11. UPDB, *Seven Million Fertile Acres in the Upper Peninsula of Michigan; Detroit Free Press*, 24 April 1904, "Clippings," box 1, Roth Papers, BHL; Michigan Public Domain Commission and Michigan Immigration Commission, *Michigan*.
12. Stephenson, *The Story of Cloverland*, 3, 17. The land was in Delta, Marquette, Dickinson, and Menominee Counties. Ontonagon County Board of Supervisors, *Ontonagon County*. For additional promotional literature linking agriculture, settlement, and tourist activities, see UPDB, *Homes and Farms in the Upper Peninsula of Michigan*; Donnelly, ed., *Cloverland, the Upper Peninsula of Michigan*; Stephenson, *Recollections of a Long Life*. Born in 1829, Stephenson was a lumberman and served as U.S. senator from Wisconsin.
13. UPDB, *Homes and Farms in the Upper Peninsula of Michigan*.
14. Andrews's 1910 comments quoted in "Annual Meeting Programs, Silver Anniversary Meeting, June 1936," folder 1, box 2, UPTARA.
15. George Bishop to Herbert A. Hall, 16 March 1940, in "Studies of Development Bureau, ca. 1940," folder 1, box 11, UPTARA.
16. Andrews quoted in Franklin, "Cloverland, My Cloverland," 91.
17. Quote appears in "From the Record" in "Studies of Development Bureau, ca. 1940," folder 1, box 11, UPTARA; "Looking Back over the Years Briefly" in "Development Bureau: Study and Recommendations, 1940," folder 9, box 2, UPTARA. On Cleveland Cliffs' agricultural promotion efforts, see Reynolds, "'Quite an Experiment.'"
18. UPDB, *Cloverland in Clovertime* (1917). Subsequent editions were published with slightly different titles in 1920, 1923, and 1930. On UPDB history, see George Bishop to Herbert Hall, 16 March 1940, in "Studies of Development Bureau, ca. 1940," folder 1, box 11, UPTARA; *Development Bureau News*, 1 November 1925, folder 15, box 8, UPTARA.
19. UPDB, *Cloverland in Clovertime* (1917). For a theoretical analysis of work displays as tourist sites that contextualizes how mines appeal to tourists, see MacCannell, *The Tourist*, 36, 57–59, 62–63.
20. UPDB, *Annual Report*, 1919, folder 10, box 10, UPTARA; Ten Thousand Lakes of Minnesota Association, *Proceedings of the Conference of Northwest Tourist Association Secretaries in Saint Paul, Minnesota, November 20–21, 1919*.
21. John Doelle to Harold Titus, 16 April 1921, "Correspondence, 1921," box 1, Titus Papers, BHL; Doelle to Herman Lunden, 26 June 1928, "Doelle Personal Correspondence, 1928," box 3, Lunden Papers, BHL. Doelle wrote Lunden, a former Michigan conservation commissioner, to ask for his support in a run for lieutenant governor.
22. UPDB, *Annual Report*, 1922, folder 10, box 10, UPTARA; *Development Bureau News*, 1 October 1926, folder 1, box 9, UPTARA. For similar statements, see *Development Bureau News*, 1 February 1930, folder 3, box 5, UPTARA.
23. UPDB, *Annual Report*, 1919, and UPDB, *Annual Report*, 1922, both in folder 10, box 10, UPTARA; *Vilas County News*, 16 August 1922. On car-ferry crossings, see *Development Bureau News*, 1 November 1925, folder 15, box 8, UPTARA. On the Land of Hiawatha slogan and image, see UPDB, *Land of Hiawatha* (1929), and subsequent annual issues of this publication.

24. "Minutes of East Michigan Tourist Association, 1924," folder 3, box 4, East Michigan Tourist Association Papers, SAM; Chester Wells to Margaret Stace, 13 February 1950; Liz Hyman to Margaret Stace, 26 May 1967, "Correspondence 1950," box 1, Stace Papers, BHL.
25. "Northern Lake States Regional Committee, 10 August 1938 and undated," folder 67, box 532, Prophet Papers, 1923–61, University Archives and Historical Collections, MSU, East Lansing. Prophet conducted several tourist and outdoor recreation surveys of 1930s Michigan.
26. Testimonial for Hugh J. Gray Book, folder 1, box 2, Stace Papers, BHL.
27. "Reminiscences," Cragun Papers, 1934–86, MHS.
28. "20,000 More Tourists Attracted to Minnesota's Vacation Playground by 10,000 Lakes Boosters," *St. Paul Pioneer Press*, 28 December 1919.
29. Ten Thousand Lakes of Minnesota Association, *Annual Report* (1919).
30. Ten Thousand Lakes of Minnesota Association, "A Review of the Campaign of Advertising Conducted by the Ten Thousand Lakes of Minnesota Association, 1919–1920," MHS; also see Ten Thousand Lakes of Minnesota Association, *A Report to the Members of the 10,000 Lakes of Minnesota Association* (1919).
31. Ten Thousand Lakes of Minnesota Association, *Annual Report* (1923).
32. Northern Minnesota Development Association Convention-Declaration of Principles, 20–21 June 1919, "NMDA, 1919–22, Minutes, Resolutions, Financial Statements," box 9, Koll Papers, MHS.
33. Responses to M. N. Koll's Minnesota Scenic Highway Questionnaire, 27 March 1917, "Minnesota Scenic Highway Association, March 1917," and "Minnesota Scenic Highway Association, April–July 1917," box 8, Koll Papers, MHS; Responses to M. N. Koll's Minnesota Scenic Highway Questionnaire, February 10, 1920, "Minnesota Scenic Highway Association, Questionnaires (towns) A–Z, 1920," box 8, Koll Papers, MHS. On Cass Lake Commercial Club support for state tourist promotion, see Mathias Koll statement, "Ten Thousand Lakes of Minnesota Association, undated, 1918–19," box 10, Koll Papers, MHS.
34. Minnesota Board of Immigration, *Minnesota*. Also see Minnesota Board of Immigration, *Northeastern Minnesota*; Drache, *Taming the Wilderness*, 267–73.
35. U.S. Forest Service, *A Vacation Land of Lakes and Woods*. On the establishment of Superior National Forest, see Benjamin Johnson, "Conservation, Subsistence, and Class at the Birth of the Superior National Forest." On the Term Permit Act, see Sutter, *Driven Wild*, 60–62.
36. MAA, *1925 Annual Report*, "Minnesota Arrowhead Association Annual Reports," box 7, Koll Papers, MHS. Timothy Brady, "The Road to the Lake," *Minnesota Monthly* (May 1987), box 3, Ruttger Family uncataloged material, MHS. I conducted research in the Ruttger collection before it was accessioned and cataloged. Citations reflect the material as I encountered it. The collection is now cataloged as Ruttger Resorts Records, MHS.
37. "50 Years of Service to the Vacation Travel Industry, Minnesota Arrowhead Association 1924–74," "Minnesota Arrowhead Association, Miscellaneous 1938–76," box 2, Conservation Printed Matter from Minnesota Organizations, 1921–81, MHS. MacCrickart is quoted in Backes, *Canoe Country*, 55; MAA, *President's Report* (1936–38); Writers' Program of the WPA in the State of Minnesota, *The WPA Guide to the Minnesota Arrowhead Country*.
38. Ten Thousand Lakes of Minnesota Association, *Annual Report* (1925, 1926, and 1928), MHS; Roy Dunn to Mathias Koll, 29 March 1929, "Koll, Ten Thousand Lakes of Minnesota Association, 1928–1933," box 10, Koll Papers, MHS.
39. Ten Thousand Lakes–Greater Minnesota Association, *The Minnesota Book* (1931).

40. Minutes of the St. Louis County Club and Farm Bureau Association Annual Meeting, 19 May 1920, box 3, St. Louis County Club and Farm Bureau Association Papers, MHS.
41. Justine Kerfoot Oral History Interviews with Margaret Robertson, November 1986 and March 1987, Interview 58.15, EOHP, 1986–90, MHS; Cash Book 1937–69, Bylaws 1949, Membership Correspondence 1950–81, Fiftieth Anniversary 1986, all in "Gunflint Trail Association, 1937–86," box 2, Kratoska Papers, MHS.
42. "Reminiscences," Cragun Papers, 1934–86, MHS; Paul Bunyan Playground Association, *Come to Paul Bunyan's Playground in Minnesota for a Perfect Vacation* in "Pamphlets Relating to Minnesota Tours and Tour Guides," MHS; "Facts about Your Minnesota Arrowhead Association, What Is the Minnesota Arrowhead Association," and "50 Years of Service to the Vacation Travel Industry, Minnesota Arrowhead Association, 1924–74," "Minnesota Arrowhead Association, Miscellaneous, 1938–76," box 2, Conservation Printed Matter from Minnesota Organizations, 1921–81, MHS.
43. *Vilas County News*, 25 October 1922. Letter from John R. Powell, 8 May 1917; D. C. Menefee to Herbert Warner, 6 June 1917; C. E. Hazen to Herbert Warner, 16 October 1919, all in folder 1, box 1, Warner Papers, WHS-ARC; Jones and McVean, *History of Lincoln, Oneida and Vilas Counties Wisconsin*; Mead and Hunt, "*Land of Silver Lakes and Streams*."
44. *Vilas County News*, 16 August 1922; *Vilas County News*, 25 October 1922; *Vilas County News*, 6 June 1923; *Wisconsin Land of Lakes Magazine* 2 (November-December 1926); Mark Davis, "Northern Choices," Winter 1995–96, 115.
45. *Vilas County News*, 25 August 1926; Mark Davis, "An Empire in Waiting," 314–15; *The Wisconsin Magazine* (December 1927); *Wisconsin Land of Lakes Magazine* 1 (December 1925).
46. *Wisconsin Land of Lakes Magazine* 5 (April 1929); *Vilas County News*, 24 October 1935.
47. Joseph Handlos Autobiography, folder 3, box 1, Handlos Papers, WHS-ARC; *Land O'7000 Lakes Journal: Outdoors Pictorial* 1 (January-March 1927). The publication's masthead read, "This Magazine Is Published Quarterly to Serve in the Up-Building, Development and Conservation of the Great Outdoors of Minnesota, Wisconsin, and Michigan."
48. Minnesota Department of Transportation, *Official Road Map of Minnesota* (1940).
49. Michigan Highway Department, *Official Michigan Highway Map* (1934 and 1936); Wisconsin Conservation Commission, *Biennial Report of the State Conservation Commission of Wisconsin* (1936); Grover Dillman, "Parks and Highway Beautification," 12 November 1929, speech to fifteenth annual meeting of American Association of Highway Officials, "Papers and Addresses of Grover C. Dillman, 1927–31," box 10, Dillman Papers, CCHC, Houghton, Mich.
50. UPDB, *The Lure Book of Michigan's Upper Peninsula* (1939); Grover C. Dillman, "The Post-War Planning Program Applied to the Upper Peninsula of Michigan Presented to Michigan Municipal League, Kingsford, MI, June 24, 1943," "1942–44," box 10, Grover Dillman Papers, CCHC; Barnett, "Paper Trails," 18–23; "Key Dates in Michigan Transportation Map History," http://www.michigan.gov/mdot/ (accessed 28 May 2010); Dempsey, "'The Lady of the Parks.'" On Michigan's roadside parks, see Herbert F. Larson, *Be-wa-bic Country*; "Roadside Park Idea Began with Disrupted Picnic," *Ann Arbor News*, 8 August 1964, "Parks" Vertical File, Michigan Historical Collections, BHL.
51. On Hoffmaster's visit, see *Annual Report*, 1922, folder 10, box 10, UPTARA; MDC, *The Biennial Report of the Department of Conservation of the State of Michigan* (1922); MDC, *Biennial Report* (1924); Dempsey, "'The Lady of the Parks,'" 17.

52. "75th Anniversary Brochure 'Michigan's State Parks . . . a living legacy for generations to come,'" Michigan Tourist Council Vertical File, Michigan Historical Collections, BHL.
53. Pammel quoted in Conard, *Places of Quiet Beauty*, 100.
54. MDC, *Biennial Report* (1922).
55. MDC, *Biennial Report* (1926).
56. MDC, *Biennial Report* (1924).
57. MDC, *Biennial Report* (1930).
58. *Development Bureau News*, 1 March 1927, folder 1, box 9, UPTARA.
59. *Development Bureau News*, 1 March 1929, folder 2, box 9, UPTARA.
60. MDC, *Biennial Report* (1930). Established in 1927, the fourth regional bureau, the Southeastern Michigan Tourist Association, focused on promoting Detroit, while the East Michigan Tourist Association promoted the rest of eastern Michigan. Also see Senate Bill No. 21, 12 January 1937, and "The Upper Peninsula Development Bureau of Michigan: Program, Aims, Accomplishments, Service," in "Studies of Development Bureau, ca. 1940," folder 1, box 11, UPTARA.
61. Minutes of the Twenty-first Annual Meeting of the UPDB, Houghton, Michigan, 12 June 1931 in "Annual Meeting Minutes, 12 June 1931 to 11 August 1933," folder 4, box 1, UPTARA.
62. MDC, *Biennial Report* (1930).
63. "Michigan Recreation, 1932 and undated," folder, 62, box 532; "Northern Lake States Regional Committee, August 10, 1938, and undated," folder 67, box 532; "Recreational Resource, 1939," folder 37, box 531, all in Prophet Papers, 1923–61, MSU; *Development Bureau News*, 1 August 1931, folder 3, box 5, UPTARA. Efforts to quantify tourism's benefits continued during the 1930s. See Arthur Stace to W. L. Austin, Department of Commerce, Bureau of the Census, 21 August 1939, box 1, Stace Papers, BHL. Stace encouraged the census to examine tourism, asserting, "The industry [tourism] is much more important to Michigan economics today than mining or lumbering, and more important on a money-return basis and social basis than mining and lumbering ever were in the days when they were considered as Michigan's leading industries." Austin wrote back indicating it was impossible to collect the data Stace desired. W. L. Austin to Arthur Stace, 31 August 1939, box 1, Stace Papers, BHL. See also George Bishop to Tom Marston, 18 August 1939, box 1, Stace Papers, BHL.
64. Minnesota Conservation Commission, *Biennial Report of the Commission of Conservation* (1932), 55–57; Minnesota Department of Conservation, *Biennial Report* (1934), 194–200. The quote is on p. 194. Minnesota Department of Conservation, *Biennial Report* (1936), 269–80.
65. Minnesota Department of Highways, *1934 Condition Map of Minnesota Trunk Highways*; Minnesota State Planning Board, *Report of the Minnesota State Planning Board* (1938).
66. MAA, *Report on Tourist Business for the 1929 Season*; MAA, *Annual Tourist Report 1930–1931*; MAA, *Publicity Program*; "Reminiscences," Cragun Papers, MHS; "Crow Wing County: Northern Minnesota in Paul Bunyan's Playground," Map Collection, MHS.
67. Wisconsin Conservation Commission, *Biennial Report of the State Conservation Commission of Wisconsin* (1923); Wisconsin State Planning Board and Conservation Commission, *A Park, Parkway and Recreational Area Plan*.
68. *Vilas County News*, 8 May 1930; *Wisconsin Land of Lakes Magazine* 5 (April 1929). On support Lacy received from tourist operators, see *Vilas County News*, 25 April 1929.

69. Wisconsin Hotels and Restaurants Division, Board of Health, "Index to Applications, Inspection Reports, and Fee Payments, 1932–43," WHS. The reports highlight the range of lodging options available and list name, address, and proprietor of each property along with comments and a rating.
70. Wisconsin Conservation Commission, *Biennial Report of the State Conservation Commission of Wisconsin* (1936), 113; *Vilas County News*, 8 May 1930.
71. Wisconsin Conservation Department, Recreational Publicity Division, *Follow the Birds to Vacation Land, Wisconsin*; Image 4265, "Conservation Activities-Recreational Publicity," box 2, Wisconsin Conservation Department, Photographic Record, 1930–42 Series 2375, WHS.
72. Holway, "How a State Publicity Campaign Popularized Conservation." For signage, see Images R4851 and R1839, "Conservation Activities-Recreational Publicity," box 2, Wisconsin Conservation Department, Photographic Record, 1930–42 Series 2375, WHS; Wisconsin State Planning Board, *The Cutover Region of Wisconsin*; Wisconsin State Planning Board, *A Recreational Plan for Vilas County*; 1942 campaign newsletter, folder 1, "Miscellaneous Correspondence and Campaign Materials, 1942–48," Walter S. Fisher Papers, WHS-ARC.
73. *Vilas County News*, 19 May 1926 and 19 April 1926; *Development Bureau News*, 1 November 1926, folder 1, box 9; 1 April 1927, folder 1, box 9; 1 June 1928, folder 2, box 9; 1 May 1930, folder 3, box 5, all in UPTARA; Minnesota Arrowhead Association, *Annual Report* (1931).
74. *Development Bureau News*, 1 November 1927, folder 1, box 9, UPTARA.
75. *Development Bureau News*, 1 February 1933, and *Development Bureau News*, 1 March 1933, both in folder 4, box 5, UPTARA.
76. On the Chicago and branch offices, see *Development Bureau News*, 2 April 1923, folder 15, box 8; 1 July 1929, folder 2, box 9; 1 March 1930, 1 May 1930, 1 November 1930, 1 June 1931, folder 3, box 5; 1 January 1933, folder 4, box 5, all in UPTARA; *Chicago Daily News*, 16 June 1934.
77. "Tourist Inquiry Bulletin No. 3, April 15, 1940," folder 1, box 11, UPTARA; *Development Bureau News*, 2 April 1923, folder 15, box 8, UPTARA.
78. Lee A. White, "A Chronological History of the Isle Royale National Park Movement: A Project of the *Detroit News* from 1921 to 1946," folder 336, box 7, Chynowyth Collection, CCHC.
79. George Bishop to Governor William Comstock, 2 January 1934, "1934," box 4, IRP, BHL.
80. White, "A Chronological History." Vandenberg's quote is from material dated 23 July 1935.
81. Vandenberg proclamation, 6 August 1934, "1934," box 4, IRP, BHL; Arthur Vandenburg to Albert Stoll, "July 16–30, 1935," box 4, IRP, BHL.
82. "Gessner Gives 4-Point Program for Developing U. P. Tourist Industry" in "Annual Meeting Minutes, 12 June 1931–11 August 1933," folder 4, box 1, UPTARA.
83. "The Lure Book Epoch," "The Lure Book," and "Comments on the Lure Book," in "Studies of Development Bureau, ca. 1940," folder 1, box 11, UPTARA.
84. *Vilas County News*, 18 October 1928, 31 October 1929, and 22 October 1931; MDC, *Biennial Reports* (1938, 1940); Jamerson, *Winter Wonderland*. On the park's history, see http://www.hansonhills.org. On the history of skiing and its relationship to changing understandings of culture, place, identity, and consumption, see Coleman, *Ski Style*.
85. MDC, *Biennial Reports* (1938, 1940); Jamerson, *Winter Wonderland*; Tri-State Winter Sports Conference, 20 February 1939, "UPDB 1936–39 (2)," box 10, Ken Dorman Papers, CCHC; Dempsey, "'The Lady of the Parks.'"

86. Steiner, *Americans at Play*, 60. On the WPA's American Guides, see Bold, *The WPA Guides*. On the CCC, see Maher, *Nature's New Deal*. On the CCC in Minnesota, see Sommer, *Hard Work and a Good Deal*.
87. Writers' Program of the WPA in the State of Minnesota, *The WPA Guide to the Minnesota Arrowhead Country*; WPA in the State of Minnesota, *Minnesota*.
88. Writers' Program of the WPA in the State of Michigan, *Michigan*, 11 and 87.
89. WPA in the State of Wisconsin, *Wisconsin*.
90. MDC, *Biennial Report*, 1938; "The Copper Country and the Tourist" speech is in C&H, box 74, folder 35, CCHC. Additional material on Potter's efforts is in C&H, box 73, folder 88; box 74, folders 35, 71, and 72; box 75, folders 33 and 69, all in CCHC. On the CCVL, see Calumet and Hecla Recreational Lands, C&H, box 77, folder 11, CCHC. "Potter's Folly" recalls the initial indignation over Seward's 1867 purchase of Alaska. John W. Jackson, "Keweenaw Mountain Lodge and Golf Course Story," Clippings Files, "Buildings-Keweenaw Mountain Lodge," CCHC. Ocha Potter to L. M. Nims, Deputy Administrator, WPA, Lansing, 24 September 1936, C&H, box 74, folder 71, CCHC. Steinberg, *Down to Earth*, 242, writes, "During the 1930s, the packaging of the natural world as a recreational resource gained momentum, as the New Deal, through organizations such as the Civilian Conservation Corps, added roads and campgrounds to the country's national parks and forests."
91. Ocha Potter to James McNaughton, 25 July 1924, C&H, box 71, folder 30, CCHC; Ocha Potter, "Keweenaw Highways," Address to Calumet Lions' Club, 17 October 1933, C&H, box 74, folder 35, CCHC.
92. Ocha Potter, "A Copper Country Opportunity," 4 September 1935, C&H, box 74, folder 72, CCHC.
93. Ocha Potter to W. T. King, Chairman of the Keweenaw County Board of Supervisors, 21 September 1937, C&H, box 75, folder 33, CCHC.
94. Ocha Potter, "Sixty Years," Ahmeek, Michigan, May 1939, CCHC. Representative John Leucke of Escanaba viewed Wisconsin, Minnesota, and Michigan as sharing the same problems—declining jobs and a concomitant decline of resources—and argued that only through a coordinated restoration with federal support could the region recover. Preliminary Organization Meeting report, 2–3 June 1938, Madison, Prophet Papers, box 532, folder 65, MSU. For Copper Country tourist promotion examples, see CCVL, *The Copper Country of Michigan*.
95. *Development Bureau News*, 1 April 1927, folder 1, box 9, UPTARA; "Gessner Gives 4-Point Program," in "Annual Meeting Minutes," folder 4, box 1, UPTARA. After Florida and California, Michigan regularly had the highest annual tourist expenditures in the 1920s and 1930s. On Snody, see "Annual Meeting, 5 October 1933, Minutes of the Northeastern Michigan Development Bureau," folder 1, box 1, East Michigan Tourist Association Papers, SAM.
96. *Development Bureau News*, 1 September 1925, folder 15, box 8, UPTARA.
97. Grover C. Dillman, "The Post-War Planning Program Applied to the Upper Peninsula of Michigan," presented to Michigan Municipal League, Kingsford, MI, 24 June 1943," Dillman Papers, CCHC. Dillman mentions the National Automobile Chamber of Commerce and *Lansing State Journal* figures. The 5 June 1938, *Detroit Free Press* pegged 1937 tourist expenditures at $330 million with 6.4 million tourists visiting the state. Grover Dillman, "The Most Urgent Problems Confronting the Upper Peninsula of Michigan," speech delivered 21 August 1945, box 10, Dillman Papers, CCHC.
98. *Detroit Free Press*, 22 May 1938 and 29 May 1938; "Testimony of Aurey Strohpaul, Secretary-Manager of the West Michigan Tourist Association, before Senate Interim Tourist Study Committee at Traverse City, Michigan, 9

November 1961," and "Testimony of James H. Hall, Secretary-Manager of the East Michigan Tourist Association before Michigan State Senate Tourist Industry Relations Committee, 3 March 1964," folder 9, box 7, West Michigan Tourist Association Papers, SAM. For Minnesota looking to Michigan, see MAA, *Annual Reports* (1931, 1941–46). On Wisconsin, see *Wisconsin Land of Lakes Magazine*, May 1927 and April 1929, Mercedes Papers, WHS; *Vilas County News*, 8 May 1930, 1 October 1931, 19 November 1931, 12 July 1945, and 11 October 1945.

2. Tourists Do Not Deplete Our Soil

1. P. S. Lovejoy, "In the Name of Development."
2. Draft of proposed letter to be sent to Governor of Michigan, "1918–24," box 1, Lovejoy Papers, BHL. On Lovejoy's trip, see Kates, *Planning a Wilderness*, 39.
3. J. H. H. Alexander, "Tourist Game Comes of Age," *Vilas County News*, 6 January 1949. Alexander served as the first head of the Wisconsin Department of Conservation's Recreational Publicity Division in the mid-1930s.
4. Minnesota and Wisconsin appointed forest wardens in 1896, and Michigan followed in 1903. Wisconsin established a State Forestry Commission in 1897, which was renamed the State Board of Forestry in 1905. Michigan and Minnesota established forestry boards and commissions in 1899, and Michigan added a Public Domain Commission in 1909. These entities increasingly addressed tourism-related issues. Michigan Department of Natural Resources, *History of Hunting and Trapping License Sales, 1895–1969*; Burlowe, "Changing Land Use Policies in the Lake States."
5. Hays, *Conservation and the Gospel of Efficiency*, remains important over a half century since publication. Recent scholarship explores people's changing conception of nature during the interwar years. Sutter, *Driven Wild*; Kates, *Planning a Wilderness*; Jacoby, *Crimes against Nature*; Judd, *Common Lands, Common People*; Judd, "Reshaping Maine's Landscape"; Stroud, "The Return of the Forest." Sutter shows how wilderness advocates like Aldo Leopold, Robert Marshall, and Benton MacKaye helped Americans forge a recreational relationship with the natural world that rejected automobile accessibility for recreation in nature. Kates examines experts concerned with regenerating the Great Lakes cutover but says little about how people on the ground, both residents and visitors, experienced the place and constructed a recreation landscape. In New England, Judd discovers a common political culture rooted in the land, while Jacoby uncovers how rural people who lived in Yellowstone, the Grand Canyon, and the Adirondacks influenced and contested state conservation measures that often undermined traditional natural resource uses. Stroud uses the concept of "metropolitan nature" to show how urban desire for nature study, recreation, and watershed protection helped reforest the northeastern United States. This concept is important in the North Woods as well, but it should not minimize the role local residents played in creating a recreational landscape.
6. Leopold, "The Wilderness and Its Place in Forest Recreational Policy," 719. Leopold, "Wilderness as a Form of Land Use" [1925], reprinted in *The Great New Wilderness Debate*, ed. Callicott and Nelson, 75–84. On Leopold, see Flader, *Thinking like a Mountain*; Turner, "From Woodcraft to 'Leave No Trace.'"

7. Leopold, "Conservation Esthetic," in *A Sand County Almanac*, 256–69. The quote appears on p. 269. The essay was written in 1938.
8. Olson, "Reflections of a Guide," *Field and Stream*, June 1928, reprinted in *The Meaning of Wilderness*, ed. Backes and Olson, 13.
9. Olson, "We Need Wilderness," *National Parks Magazine*, January-March 1946, reprinted in *The Meaning of Wilderness*, ed. Backes and Olson, 74.
10. Olson, "Why Wilderness?," *American Forests*, 1938, reprinted in *The Meaning of Wilderness*, ed. Backes and Olson, 47.
11. Olson, "The Superior National Forest Must Be Saved," Sigurd Olson website, http://www4.uwm.edu/letsci/research/sigurd_olson/speeches/snfmustb.htm (accessed 3 June 2010).
12. Waugh, *Recreation Uses on the National Forests*; Tweed, *Recreation Site Planning and Improvement in the National Forests, 1891–1942*. On Forest Service recreation policy, see Graves, *A Policy of Forestry for the Nation*; Graves, "A Crisis in National Recreation." Henry Graves was Forest Service chief from 1910 to 1920. On interagency battles, see Rothman, "'A Regular Ding-Dong Fight.'"
13. "An Outline Plan for the Recreational Development of the Superior National Forest," "Carhart-Miscellaneous," box 15, USFS, IRRC, Chisholm, Minn. Carhart's plan led some to decry that preservation of forest in a wilderness state, rather than managing for timber use, was wasteful. On the other hand, motorboat access provisions offered a rallying cry for wilderness proponents, who equated it with automobile access. Leopold, "The Wilderness and Its Place in Forest Recreational Policy," 719.
14. Oberholtzer to William Jardine, 7 November 1927, and Jardine to Oberholtzer, 26 November 1927, both in "Correspondence and Miscellaneous Papers, 1927–39 (1)," box 2, QSC, MHS. On Oberholtzer see, Paddock, *Keeper of the Wild*.
15. Oberholtzer to Joseph Klobucher (Secretary, Arrowhead Sportsmen's Association), 23 February 1933, "Arrowhead Sportsmen's Association, 1933," box 4, Quetico-Superior Council Papers, MHS; Joe Pluth to Oberholtzer, 31 December 1928, folder 2, box 61, Quetico-Superior Council Papers, MHS. Pluth reported he had four thousand people take canoe trips, and at least ten thousand canoeists passed through Ely the previous year.
16. Oberholtzer to Charles Kelly, 6 July 1932, and Oberholtzer to Jardine, 7 November 1927, both in "Correspondence and Miscellaneous Papers, 1927–39 (1)," box 2, QSC, MHS. Also see Edward M. "Ted" Hall Oral History Interviews with Margaret Robertson, 5, 6, and 8 February 1987, Interview 58.8, EOHP, 1986–90, MHS; Oberholtzer to Seth Gordon (Izaak Walton League Conservation Director), "Wilderness Areas-General Correspondence," box 15, CNF, IRRC.
17. Oberholtzer to William Bagley, 21 March 1929, "Wilderness Areas-General Correspondence," box 15, CNF, IRRC. On Oberholtzer's and the Quetico-Superior Council's position, see articles he published in *American Forests and Forest Life* in 1929: "A Lakeland Archipelago," "The Ancient Game of Grab," and "A University of the Wilderness." Also see Oral History Interviews with Ernest Oberholtzer by Lucile Kane and Russell Fridley, 21–22 October and 6 December 1963, OH 81, MHS.
18. Frank Hubachek letter to *Ely Miner* editor, 22 August 1949, folder 2, box 6, QSC, MHS. Hubachek hoped the community would hear his position and looked to counter what he viewed as attacks from the newspaper's editor, Fred Childers.
19. Michael Furtman, "Izaak Walton League of America: 75 Years of Canoe Country Advocacy," http://www.breckenridgeikes.org/canoe_country_furtman.

html (accessed 4 June 2010). Furtman quotes the April 1923 edition of *Izaak Walton League Monthly*, which was renamed *Outdoor America* in 1924.

20. Arrowhead Division of the Izaak Walton League of America, "The Issue of Conservation," in "Quetico-Superior Politics, 1927–34," box 4, QSC, MHS. The W. J. McCabe chapter of the Izaak Walton League of America website, http://www.duluthikes.org/ (accessed 4 June 2010), contains information on the league's Superior National Forest and boundary waters efforts.
21. L. F. Kneipp to Ivan Coppe, 2 September 1921, "Recreation Plans," box 7, CNF, IRRC; Kneipp to Allen Peck, 24 April 1922, "Recreation Plans," box 7, CNF, IRRC; Kneipp, "Forest Recreation Comes of Age." On Kneipp, see http://www.foresthistory.org/ASPNET/People/WO_Staffs/Kneipp.aspx, (accessed 4 June 2010).
22. Biographical Information on Arthur Carhart, "Carhart-Miscellaneous," box 15, USFS, IRRC. On Carhart, see Baldwin, *The Quiet Revolution*.
23. Carhart quoted in George A. Selke, Report of 15 December 1964, "Subject Files, BWCA (2)," box 3, QSC, MHS. Arthur Carhart, "An Outline Plan for the Recreational Development of the Superior National Forest, Preliminary Prospectus," "Carhart-Miscellaneous," box 15, USFS, IRRC.
24. Arthur Carhart, "Recreation in the Forests," 270.
25. Carhart to Ramsdell, 25 February 1928, "Carhart-Miscellaneous," box 15, USFS, IRRC. Also see Carhart to James Gould, 28 January 1928, "Carhart-Miscellaneous," box 15, USFS, IRRC; Backes, "Wilderness Visions."
26. Wilson, *E. M. Griffith and the Early Story of Wisconsin Forestry*, 36.
27. Griffith quoted in East, "Water Power and Forestry in Wisconsin," 70; Wilson, *E. M. Griffith and the Early Story of Wisconsin Forestry*; Wilson, "Zoning for Forestry and Recreation."
28. Land Series (1), box 5, Lovejoy Papers, BHL.
29. Land Series (2), box 5, Lovejoy Papers, BHL. Dawes quoted in Carstensen, *Farms or Forests*, 49. State Land Policy in Michigan, box 4, Lovejoy Papers, BHL.
30. Rismon quoted in Wilson, *E. M. Griffith and the Early Story of Wisconsin Forestry*, 51. On Rismon, see Jones and McVean, *History of Lincoln, Oneida and Vilas Counties Wisconsin*, 696–97.
31. Quoted in Clark, "Cutover Problems," 18.
32. Carstensen, *Farms or Forests*, 77.
33. Henry Hanson quoted in *Vilas County News*, 15 July 1925.
34. Rowlands, "The Great Lakes Cutover Region." Also see Rowlands, "County Zoning for Agriculture, Forestry, and Recreation in Wisconsin"; and Carstensen, *Farms or Forests*, 98–100. Bordner Survey maps are at: http://digicoll.library.wisc.edu/EcoNatRes/subcollections/WILandInvAbout.html. On Bordner, see Koch, "Touching Every Forty."
35. Wehrwein and Parsons, *Recreation as a Land Use*, 7 and 31. On Wehrwein, see the Wisconsin Conservation Hall of Fame profile at http://www.wchf.org/inductees/wehrwein.pdf (accessed 4 June 2010).
36. Wilson, "Zoning for Forestry and Recreation," 104; Stoltenberg, "Rural Zoning in Minnesota."
37. Carstensen, *Farms or Forests*, 1; Wehrwein and Johnson, "A Recreation Livelihood Area," 195. Wehrwein helped develop a rural regional planning program at the University of Wisconsin, traveling in similar circles as Rowlands and Aldo Leopold.
38. Roth to Curwood, 1 October 1921, reel 2, Curwood Papers, BHL; Roth, *On the Forestry Conditions in Wisconsin*. On Roth, see Samuel T. Dana's essay in "Biographical Data," box 1, Roth Papers, BHL.

39. *Ann Arbor News*, 22 January 1942; and Arthur Stace, "Parrish S. Lovejoy Great Force for Conservation" *Ann Arbor News*, 21 January 1942; both in Parrish Lovejoy Files, Biographical Materials, Hazzard Papers, BHL. For Lovejoy's articles and correspondence with the editor of *Country Gentleman*, see box 4, Lovejoy Papers, BHL. On Lovejoy's role in Michigan conservation affairs, see Schmaltz, "P. S. Lovejoy."
40. Lovejoy's Notes on Schoenmann Paper on Relationship between Conservation and Recreation, "1931," box 1, Lovejoy Papers, BHL.
41. Hedrick, *Recreational Use of Northern Michigan Cutover Lands*; Sparhawk and Brush, *Economic Aspects of Forest Destruction in Northern Michigan*, 68.
42. Jack Van Coevering, "A Brief History of Conservation in Michigan," box 20, Van Coevering Papers, BHL. This box also contains background information on many individuals. Filibert Roth suggested Stoll's *Detroit News* helped make state government aware of the conservation situation. Roth to James Curwood, 1 October 1921, reel 2, Curwood Papers, BHL. On conservation in Michigan, see Dempsey, *Ruin and Recovery*.
43. Frederick Wheeler, "The Law and the Forests," in "Forestry, Manuscript," box 1, Wheeler Papers, BHL; also see Frederick Wheeler, "Conservation and Forests," in "Forestry, Manuscript," box 1, Wheeler Papers, BHL.
44. William Bonifas to Joseph Herbert, 10 March 1931, "Correspondence, March 1931," Bonifas Family Papers, BHL.
45. Charles W. Garfield, "A Bit of Forest History," in "Drafts of Speeches or Articles," box 1, Garfield Papers, BHL; Charles W. Garfield, "What the State Should Do to Perpetuate the Forests," in "Drafts of Speeches or Articles," box 1, Garfield Papers, BHL; Insert on Michigan Forest Commission, box 43, Mershon Papers, BHL.
46. Ben East, "Titus Prophet of Conservation for Michigan's Wilds," Newspaper Clippings, box 5, Titus Papers, BHL; on Curwood and Titus, see Kates, *Planning a Wilderness*, 67–88 and 114–30; Titus, *Timber*.
47. Curwood to Marston, 15 July 1921, reel 2, Curwood Papers, BHL.
48. "Conservation Memos," reel 4, Curwood Papers, BHL.
49. On patronage in Michigan's Conservation Department, see Norman Hill to Harold Titus, 24 May 1937, "Correspondence, 1937," box 2, Titus Papers, BHL. On the MUCC, see Paul Herbert Interview with Harry Gaines, Paul A. Herbert Sound Recording, 1969, Herbert Papers, BHL; 9 November 1937 notes, "MUCC, Convention 1937," box 1, and "History, Undated, 1937, 1947, 1949," and "History, 1956–58, 1962–63," box 4, MUCC Records, BHL.
50. Letter to All Conservationists in Minnesota, 21 April 1941, "Newsletters, 1941–44," box 33, Minnesota Emergency Conservation Committee Records, MHS.
51. Edward Ash to Governor Comstock, 18 May 1933, "1929–33," and Bob and Mrs. Engels to Walter Hastings, 13 July 1933, "1929–33," both in Hastings Papers, BHL. Wisconsin distributed films to schools and resorts promoting the state's outdoor opportunities. See *Vilas County News*, 15 July 1937.
52. MDC, *Biennial Report of the Department of Conservation* (1930 and 1932); MDC, *Forty Years of Conservation*; Michigan Department of Natural Resources, *Managing Michigan's Natural Resources*. On the history of state parks, see Conard, *Places of Quiet Beauty*; Korn, *Yesterday through Tomorrow*.
53. Hoffmaster's address appears in the *Escanaba Daily Press*, 21 January 1938, "UPDB 1936–39 (2 of 2)," box 10, Dorman Papers, CCHC. George Bishop to Members of Subcommittee of State Planning Commission, November 3, 1943, "Correspondence June–Dec 1943," and Progress Report of the Tourist and Resort Advisory Committee to Governor Harry F. Kelly, "Correspondence Jan–Aug 1944," both in box 1, Stace Papers, BHL.

54. Wehrwein and Johnson, "A Recreation Livelihood Area," 203. On UP residents' efforts to garner state funds for tourist promotion, see the *Development Bureau News*, 1923–29, folder 15, box 8, and folders 1 and 2, box 9, UPTARA Papers, SAM. On resort owners supporting and enforcing conservation measures, see *Vilas County News*, 16 April 1924. On shifting local sentiment in Wisconsin, see Mark Davis, "Northern Choices," Winter 1995–96, 122. On Minnesota, see Backes, *Canoe Country*, 54–59.
55. Benjamin Johnson, "Conservation, Subsistence, and Class at the Birth of the Superior National Forest," 81.
56. J. J. Boldin (Arrowhead Sportsmen's Association) to F. A. Silcox, 15 June 1934, USFS, IRRC; Statement from Hanford Cox (MAA Conservation Commission Chairman), folder 1, box 1, QSC, MHS.
57. Arthur Carhart, "Ely's Opportunity," *Ely Miner*, 15 July 1921, in "Carhart-Miscellaneous," box 15, USFS, IRRC.
58. Carhart to James Gould, 28 January 1928, in "Carhart-Miscellaneous," box 15, USFS, IRRC; Burntside Lake and Lodge, Clippings File, IRRC. Many northern St. Louis County resorts were built in the 1930s, although some, like Camp Van Vac and Burntside Lodge, date to earlier years. Before World War II, the Ely area contained approximately thirty resorts.
59. Marshall to Tinker, 13 July 1926, in "Recreation Policy," box 7, CNF, IRRC. Summer-home sites were not owned but leased from the government on a long-term basis. This emerged as a major issue in the 1960s, when many sites were deemed detrimental to public use, resulting in the termination of some leases on the Chippewa.
60. G. E. Marshall, Draft of Recreation Plan, 4 March 1926, in "Recreation Policy," box 7, CNF, IRRC; "Recreational Use Policy: Minnesota National Forest (15 June 1926)," in "Recreation, MNF, Recreational Use Policy (1926)," box 7, CNF, IRRC.
61. E. W. Tinker to Forest Supervisor, Minnesota, 30 March 1926, in "Recreation, Minnesota National Forest, Recreational Use Policy (1926)," box 7, CNF, IRRC; Tinker to Forest Supervisor, 29 May 1933, in "Recreation Plans-Forest," box 7, CNF, IRRC. Tinker commented on one area, "Perhaps more careful planning in connection with the development of Norway Beach would have rendered the area even more attractive than it now is, and would have facilitated the accommodation of the public to a greater degree."
62. "Forest Recreational Plan-A Foundation," in "Recreation Plans-Forest," box 7, CNF, IRRC. In 1933, there were 191 such resorts. See U.S. Natural Resources Board, Land Planning Committee, *Supplementary Report of the Land Planning Committee to the National Resources Board*, particularly, "Recreational Use of Land in the United States, Part XI of the Report on Land Planning, 1938."
63. Report on the National Forest Recreation Resource Survey (Region 9), p. 34, box 3, USFS, IRRC; Minutes, 10 October 1934, "Minutes of Meetings and Related Papers, Background Materials, 10 October 1934–5 June 1946," box 1, QSC, MHS.
64. "Report to the President of the United States on the Quetico-Superior Area by the Quetico-Superior Committee, 1938," in "Correspondence and Misc. Papers (1), Undated, 1934–49," box 3, QSC, MHS. Shipstead-Nolan Act, Public Law 539, 71st Cong., 2nd sess. (10 July 1930).
65. "Enjoyment of the Country Roadside," in "Drafts of Speeches or Articles," box 1, Garfield Papers, BHL; Lovejoy's drafts of bills, "1931," box 1, Lovejoy Papers; Whiteley, *A Post War Public Works Program for Conservation and Recreation for the State of Michigan*.
66. Marshall, *The People's Forests*, 119 and 219.

67. On licensing, see state conservation department biennial reports. Michigan Department of Conservation, *Biennial Report of the Department of Conservation*. Pages 34–36 of the 1932 *Biennial Report* contain information on licenses since 1921. Wisconsin Conservation Commission, *Biennial Report* (1922–39); Minnesota Commission of Conservation, *Biennial Report* (1932); Minnesota Department of Conservation, *Biennial Report* (1934–1960). On stocking requests and fishing generally, see Backes, *Canoe Country*, 91–92; and Bogue, *Fishing the Great Lakes*.
68. Resolutions from 20th Annual Convention of Northern Michigan Sportsmen's Association, 28 September 1938, Hunting Vertical File, Michigan Historical Collections, BHL; Ben East interview for "A Brief History of Conservation in Michigan," 28 September 1968, "Collected Background Information, Ben East," box 20, Van Coevering Papers, BHL.
69. Letter from Conservation Commission, 16 April 1928, folder 12, box 2, Warner Papers, WHS-ARC; Wehrwein and Johnson, "A Recreation Livelihood Area," 197; "Tourist Bureau, Vic Johnston, 1942," box 7, Minnesota Department of Conservation Records, MHS; 4 February 1938 letter on Advertising, "Ed Shave, Director Tourist Bureau," box 34, Minnesota Department of Conservation Records, MHS; *Wall Street Journal* mentioned in Bulletin from National Organization of Travel Officials, 17 June 1941, "Tourist Bureau, Vic Johnston, 1942," box 7, Minnesota Department of Conservation Records, MHS.
70. Jacoby, "Class and Environmental History," 336; White, "'Are You an Environmentalist or Do You Work for a Living?'"

3. No Dull Days at Dunn's

1. On paid vacations in the first half of the twentieth century, see Allen, *Fringe Benefits*, 50 and 58; National Industrial Conference Board, *Vacations with Pay for Wage Earners*; "Vacations for Factory Workers"; "Vacations with Pay for Wage Earners"; "Vacations with Pay for Production Workers"; Pugh, "Vacations with Pay." On the development of industrial vacation plans and leisure choices, see Mills, *Vacations for Industrial Workers*; Steiner, *Americans at Play*. Gary Cross suggests 10 percent of American wage earners had paid vacations in 1930, and 85 percent of salaried workers had plans by the end of the 1930s. Elizabeth Blackmar claims that by 1930, 10 to 15 percent of the industrial labor force had paid summer vacations. Cross, *Time and Money*; Blackmar, "Going to the Mountains."
2. Eleanor Davis, *Recent Trends in Vacation Policies for Wage Earners*, 5–9.
3. Allen, *Fringe Benefits*, 82; "Industrial and Labor Conditions: Vacations with Pay for Wage Earners"; Mills, *Vacations for Industrial Workers*.
4. Masse, "Vacations with Pay." European employers generally viewed the vacation as a reward for services rendered, while American employers saw them as a business practice to increase productivity. On workers crafting leisure spaces, see Rosenzweig, *Eight Hours for What We Will*.
5. AFL-CIO, *American Federation of Labor*, 2477.
6. Rothman, *Devil's Bargains*. My conversation with Dave Thomas at the Copper Country Symposium, Houghton, Michigan, 2 July 2004, helped in considering some of these issues. Thomas recalled family members heading south to work in the auto industry but returning to Michigan's Copper Country for vacation.

7. “Visit Va-Ka-Shun Land in 1929,” folder 1, Pamphlets Relating to Description and Travel in Minnesota, MHS.
8. Jones and McVean, *History of Lincoln, Oneida and Vilas Counties Wisconsin*; John McCormick, “History of Sayner and Star Lake,” SC10, WHS-ARC; Collection Guide, Warner Papers, WHS-ARC.
9. “Ross’ Teal Lake Lodge, Hayward, Wisconsin,” folder 3, box 1, Ross’ Teal Lake Lodge Collection, WHS.
10. Doucette et al., *Oneida County*, 102; Jones and McVean, *History of Lincoln, Oneida and Vilas Counties Wisconsin*, 430, 484; Currey Collection, WHS-ARC; Mead and Hunt, “*Land of Silver Lakes and Streams*”; Dunn, *Wisconsin’s Northwoods*; Heritage Research, Ltd., and Wisconsin Historical Society, *Historical/Architectural Resources Survey, Historic Resorts of Vilas County*.
11. Margaret Robertson interview with Jack Ruttger, 11 June 1991, Interview 79.8, ROHP, MHS.
12. Collection Description and Biography, Dunn Papers, MHS; Roger Pinckney, “No Dull Days at Dunn’s,” http://www.pelicanrapidschamber.com/history happenedhere/no_dull_days_at_ dunn.htm (accessed 9 June 2010).
13. Entries from 2 January 1913, 13 January 1913, and 26 February 1920, Fred Shadduck Diary, 1 January 1912–31 March 1921, MHS. Adam Nelson interview with Nobel Shadduck, 16 July 1991, Interview 79.13, ROHP, MHS.
14. For biographies of early resort operators, see Jones and McVean, *History of Lincoln, Oneida and Vilas Counties Wisconsin*. Also see Mead and Hunt, *“Land of Silver Lakes and Streams”; Wisconsin Land of Lakes Magazine*, Madison, 1925–29.
15. On the Pines, see *Vilas County News*, 6 October 1920. On W. H. Love, see *Vilas County News*, 11 May 1921. On organizations, see Bawden, “Reinventing the Frontier,” 213–17.
16. Carstensen, *Farms or Forests*, 103–4.
17. Wisconsin Conservation Commission, *Biennial Report of the Wisconsin Conservation Commission, 1922–23* (1924); Mead and Hunt, “*Land of Silver Lakes and Streams*”; Wisconsin Committee on Land Use and Forestry, *Forest Land Use in Wisconsin*; Carstensen, *Farms or Forests*, 77.
18. “Bulletin #10,” “Bulletin #12,” and “Tribune Company Bureau of Travel and Resorts,” folder 2, box 1, Warner Papers, WHS-ARC.
19. J. C. Harding to Herb Warner, 19 June 1916, folder 8, box 5; H. Ware Caldwell to Herbert Warner, 18 April 1920, folder 1, box 6; Mrs. W. L. Lewis to Warner, 3 July 1917, folder 8, box 5; John Thomas Harding to Bert Warner, 20 July 1927, folder 10, box 5, all in Warner Papers, WHS-ARC.
20. Wisconsin Conservation Commission, *Biennial Report of the Wisconsin Conservation Commission, 1922–23* (1924), 16; Mead and Hunt, “*Land of Silver Lakes and Streams*.” On autocamping and municipal tourist camps, see Belasco, *Americans on the Road*.
21. “Record Tourist Influx to Minnesota Expected during Season of 1922,” *St Paul Pioneer Press*, 18 December 1921, “Clippings,” box 11, Koll Papers, MHS.
22. MAA, *Annual Tourist Report* (1930 and 1931).
23. MAA, Annual Tourist Report, 12 November 1930, “1925–31, Annual Reports and Printed Material,” box 7, Koll Papers, MHS.
24. MAA, *Report on Tourist Business for the 1929 Season*; MAA, *Annual Tourist Report, 1930–1931*; Tourist Camp Register, 1926–41, City of Ely Records, box 56, IRRC.
25. Helen Beebe to Roy Dunn, 29 June 1938 and 12 July 1938, Resort Files, “1938 Dunn’s Lodge, A–C,” box 8; Mr. Kline to Roy Dunn, 6 August 1941, Resort Files, “1940–41 Dunn’s Lodge, Jon–Le,” box 9; Philip Haser to Roy Dunn, 26

September 1941, Resort Files, "1940–41 Dunn's Lodge, Hos–Joh," box 9; letters from Sydney Anderson and Hugo J. Bredehoeft to Roy Dunn, Resort Files, "1937 Dunn's Lodge, A–D" box 8; Miss Leslie Setzer to Roy Dunn, Resort Files, "1937 Dunn's Lodge, N–S," box 8, all in Dunn Papers, MHS.

26. Duluth & Iron Range Railroad Co., *The Playground of a Nation in the Arrowhead Country*; St. Louis County Club, *Sportland of the North*.
27. Roy Dunn to Curt Teich Company, 3 March 1937, and Curt Teich Company to Roy Dunn, 31 March 1937, both in Resort Files, "1937 Dunn's Lodge, A–D," box 8; Roy Dunn to George Bradley, 2 July 1937, Resort Files, "1937 Dunn's Lodge, A–D," box 8; Dunn to George Etzell, 4 June 1941, Resort Files, "1940–41 Dunn's Lodge, E–Har," box 9, all in Dunn Papers, MHS.
28. H. L Larson to Roy Dunn, 23 July 1941, Resort Files, "1940–41 Dunn's Lodge, Jon–Le," box 9, Dunn Papers, MHS. Larson served as Commercial Club secretary and included Shave's request in a form letter to members.
29. M. O. Hill to Roy Dunn, 7 June 1941, and Roy Dunn to M. O. Hill, 11 June 1941, both in Resort Files, "1940–41 Dunn's Lodge, Hos–Joh," box 9, Dunn Papers, MHS.
30. On Williams and other Star Island residents, see Ryan, *Star Island*. Williams's quote appears on both pages 12 and 29. Commercial Club of Cass Lake and Committee representing the Government Tenants on Star Island to the National Bureau of Forestry, 19 August 1918, box 11, Koll Papers, MHS; Star Island Protective League, *The Loon*, MHS.
31. Letter from Lydick Mercantile Co. to A. J. Starr, Esq., "Koll, Correspondence, March 1914," box 3, Koll Papers, MHS; Commercial Club of Cass Lake and Committee representing the Government Tenants on Star Island to the National Bureau of Forestry, 19 August 1918, box 11, Koll Papers, MHS; Recreational Use Policy (1926), "Recreation, Minnesota National Forest," box 7, CNF, IRRC.
32. "Cass Lake, The Permanent Home of the Pine," in "January-May, 1932," box 5, Koll Papers, MHS. "Forest Recreational Plan-A Foundation," in "Recreation Plans-Forest," box 7, CNF, IRRC. This 1933 survey of the Chippewa National Forest found vacationers staying at resorts and campgrounds throughout the forest. "Cass Lake, Minnesota in the Chippewa National Forest (1941)," box 6, Travel Literature Collection, Research Center, Henry Ford Museum, Dearborn, Michigan; U.S. Department of Agriculture, Forest Service, *Chippewa National Forest* (Washington, D.C.: Government Printing Office, 1942), 12, box 3, CNF, IRRC.
33. *Vilas County News*, 30 April 1919, 18 June 1919, 16 July 1919, and 16 September 1919.
34. *Land of Lakes Magazine* 1 (December 1925); *Land of Lakes Magazine* 2 (November-December 1926); Obituary of Scipio Wise, folder 9, box 1, and microfilm reel, Wise Collection, WHS. Wisconsin Land Economic Inventory (Bordner Survey) maps are available online at: http://digicoll.library.wisc.edu/EcoNatRes/subcollections/WILandInvAbout.html. The project surveyed Vilas County in 1931, Sawyer County in 1932, and Oneida County in 1939.
35. Pre-1920 correspondence from guests in the Warner papers regularly requests pickup from the rail station. After 1920, these requests become fewer, and people ask about roads and parking their cars. See Warner Papers, folder 7 and 8, box 5, for pre-1920 correspondence, and folder 9 and 10, box 5, WHS-ARC, for post-1920 correspondence. Mead and Hunt, "*Land of Silver Lakes and Streams*," discusses resort conversions to housekeeping cabins in the 1920s.
36. James Fogerty interview with Bert Pfeifer, 17 November 1999, Interview 79.6, ROHP, MHS.

37. James Fogerty interview with Jack Stedman, 17 October 1995, Interview 79.14, ROHP, MHS. On northern Wisconsin's gangster getaways in Couderay and Land O'Lakes and resorts like Little Bohemia, see Kevin Revolinski, "Where Public Enemies Went for a Little Peace and Quiet," *New York Times*, http://travel.nytimes.com/2009/06/26/travel/escapes/26Gangster.html (accessed 23 May 2011).
38. Fogerty interview with Stedman, ROHP, MHS.
39. Joseph Curley to Herbert Warner, 25 May 1920, folder 7, box 1; G. M. Householder to Herbert Warner, 17 May 1922, folder 7, box 1; F. Dahmen to H. L. Warner, 18 August 1922, folder 7, box 1, all in Warner Papers, WHS-ARC; Davis, "An Empire in Waiting," 279. Dunn, *Wisconsin's Northwoods*, suggests over forty resorts in Vilas and Oneida Counties had small farms or gardens in the 1920s.
40. List of employment inquiries, Resort Files, 1937, "Letters of Application," box 8; List of potential employees and Dunn's remarks, "Resort Files, 1941 Letters of Application," box 9; Dunn to Margo Cairns, 2 May 1941, Resort Files, 1941, "Letters of Application," box 9; Letter from Dunn, 14 July 1938, Resort Files, 1938, "Dunn's Lodge, H–L," box 8; Letter from U.S. Department of Labor, U.S. Employment Service to Dunn, 23 April 1937, Resort Files, 1937 "Dunn's Lodge, A–D," box 9; Dunn to Alice Gerold, 19 March 1945, Resort Files, "1942–49 Dunn's Lodge," box 9, all in Dunn Papers, MHS.
41. Theresa Ruttger interview with Ruby Treloar, 19 August 1997, Interview 79.15, ROHP, MHS.
42. D. C. Menefee to Herb Warner and Son, 30 June 1924, folder 8, box 1; George Vrooman to Bert Warner, 9 June 1930, folder 8, box 1; Gaither Herring to Bert Warner, 28 May 1928, folder 8, box 1; Elmer Andersen to Bert Warner, n.d., folder 7, box 1; W. J. Minch to Bert Warner, 26 May 1924 and 5 June 1924, both in folder 8, box 1, all in Warner Papers, WHS-ARC.
43. Letter from Nelson Ross to Virginia Ross, 22 February 1937, folder 6, box 1, Ross' Teal Lake Lodge Collection, WHS. On Paul Quayle, see Inventory and Guide, Ross' Teal Lake Lodge Collection, WHS.
44. Mead and Hunt, "*Land of Silver Lakes and Streams*."
45. Mead and Hunt, "*Land of Silver Lakes and Streams*"; Shorewood Vista, *Blaesing's Shorewood Vista*; "The History of Holiday Acres," http://www.holidayacres.com/history.html (accessed 11 June 2010).
46. Oral History Interview with Norman Johnson, WHS; Oral History Interview with Jennie Neubauer, 1965, WHS.
47. *Vilas County News*, 29 October 1919.
48. *Teal Lake Tidings*, June 1933 and September 1935, folder 2, box 1, Ross' Teal Lake Lodge Collection, WHS. Other resorts also published newsletters, for example, Gunflint Lodge's *Gunflint Gossips*, MHS.
49. Quote from *Teal Lake Tidings*, April 1934, folder 2, box 1, Ross' Teal Lake Lodge Collection, WHS; *Teal Lake Tidings*, June 1938, folder 2, box 1, Ross' Teal Lake Lodge Collection, WHS.
50. *Teal Lake Tidings*, Spring 1942, folder 2, box 1, Ross' Teal Lake Lodge Collection, WHS.
51. Boulder Junction Chamber of Commerce, *Boulder Junction, World's Greatest Musky Waters*; Victor Johnson, director of State Tourist Bureau quoted in Merrill Cragun, "Why the Minnesota Resort Association?," Cragun Papers, MHS.
52. *Teal Lake Tidings*, Christmas 1945, folder 2, box 1, Ross' Teal Lake Lodge Collection, WHS.
53. Magite Gauthier, Surveys of Indian Industry, 1920–22, LDF, Records of the Bureau of Indian Affairs, 1793–1999, RG75, NARA-GL. The survey is now

available through searches on the National Archives website at http://www.archives.gov/research/arc/index.html. On the Gauthiers, see Goc, *Reflections of Lac du Flambeau*, 92; Jones and McVean, *History of Lincoln, Oneida and Vilas Counties Wisconsin*.

54. Surveys of Indian Industry, LDF, RG75, NARA-GL.
55. "Annual Report, 1909," and "Annual Report, 1910," Annual Reports, 1909–16, LDF, RG75, NARA-GL. Also see Bawden, "Reinventing the Frontier," 209–11.
56. Valliere, "A Brief History of the Waaswaaganing Ojibweg," 21–24.
57. "Annual Report, 1913," and "Annual Report, 1914," Annual Reports, 1909–16, LDF, RG75, NARA-GL.
58. "Annual Report, 1911," and "Annual Report, 1912," Annual Reports, 1909–16, LDF, RG75, NARA-GL.
59. Goc, *Reflections of Lac du Flambeau*, 89. Charles Poupart, Surveys of Indian Industry, LDF, RG75, NARA-GL. On Ojibwa Lodge, see George Peterson, Rising Sun, and Alice Carufel, all in Surveys of Indian Industry, LDF, RG75, NARA-GL.
60. Goc, *Reflections of Lac du Flambeau*, 90; Laabs, "A Collection of Northwoods Nostalgia from the Pages of the Lakeland Times," http://www.caughtintime.com/Wisconsinmag_SigNW7people.html (accessed 11 June 2010). On Yeschek land purchases, see Vol. 177, Land Sales Book; Log of Allotment Land Sales, 1922–29; LDF, RG75, NARA-GL. On the Flambeau Taxpayer's Association, see Nesper, "Simulating Culture."
61. Blatchford and Rice, eds., *Camp Wipigaki*. Land purchases included 45.5 acres from Mrs. George Amour for $3,650.
62. Goc, *Reflections of Lac du Flambeau*, 96–97.
63. Louis Vederneck, Joe St. Germain, Joe Martin, Robert Chapman, Edward Christenson, Louis LaBarge, William Chapman, all in Surveys of Indian Industry, LDF, RG75, NARA-GL.
64. Henry Guyette, Bessie and Sarah Stone, Fred LaCass, all in Surveys of Indian Industry, LDF, RG75, NARA-GL.
65. See CCC–Indian Division correspondence in Great Lakes/Lac du Flambeau Emergency Conservation, 1933, Records Relating to Emergency Conservation Work and the CCC, 1933–42, LDF, RG75, NARA-GL; Goc, *Reflections of Lac du Flambeau*, 122. In 1935, the IECW changed its name to the Civilian Conservation Corps–Indian Division (CCC-ID).
66. Tornes, *Memories of Lac du Flambeau Elders*, 4, 132, 139, 141. The quotation is on p. 141.
67. Ibid., 89, 232, 247, 256, 275.
68. Nesper, "Simulating Culture," 450.
69. J. W. Balmer to Commissioner of Indian Affairs, 3 April 1922 and 15 August 1922, and Charles H. Burke re: Circular No. 1701 Work of Farmers, 21 August 1921, both in Industrial Survey, Correspondence and Instructions, Records Relating to Indigent Indians, 1929–32; LDF, RG75, NARA-GL. The BIA conducted a similar survey at Iowa's Tama reservation with a follow-up several years later, both of which are available in the Tama Agency (Sac and Fox) Records, NARA-GL.
70. Joseph Corn, John Patterson Jr., Rising Sun, William McArthur, Joe Vederneck, James LaBelle, all in Surveys of Indian Industry, LDF, RG75, NARA-GL.
71. J. W. Balmer to Commissioner of Indian Affairs, 3 April 1922, Industrial Survey, Correspondence and Instructions, Records Relating to Indigent Indians, 1929–32; LDF, RG75, NARA-GL
72. Case of Jack Doud Sr., 5 May 1927, Heirship Case Files, 1920–32, LDF, RG75, NARA-GL; Response to Circular 1819, 8 November 1922, and J. W. Balmer to Commissioner of Indian Affairs, 26 June 1922 and 15 August 1922, all in

Industrial Survey, Correspondence and Instructions, Records Relating to Indigent Indians, 1929–32; LDF, RG75, NARA-GL.

73. Charles Gauthier, Surveys of Indian Industry, LDF, RG75, NARA-GL. Gauthier served as government interpreter, chauffeur, and Indian policeman. His wife kept boarders and his son Ben worked at the fish hatchery and had a Sand Lake resort. Case #200: Daniel Burgess, Certificates of Appraisement (Form 5-110a) 1920–21, Records Relating to Indigent Indians, 1929–32, LDF, RG75, NARA-GL. This folder contains appraisals and sales records, including John Bison's selling of 77.5 acres to the YMCA for $4,800, and Oji Chog Bichikins's selling of 22.5 acres for $1,155. Also see Tornes, *Memories of Lac du Flambeau Elders*.

74. The tribe owns 45.4 percent of the land, 21.4 percent is allotted land, and 33.1 percent is alienated land. See Lac du Flambeau Chamber of Commerce, http://www.lacduflambeauchamber.com/community.htm (accessed 24 May 2010).

75. Chicago and North Western Railway Company, *Lakes and Resorts of Northwest; Cloverland in Clovertime* [1915?] in Northern Peninsula, Vacation Guides, folder EA.7, Michigan Historical Collections, BHL.

76. "Blaney Park," in Blaney Park Vertical File, CCHC; "Your Holiday in Michigan's Famous Copper Country," in Copper Country Description and Travel Vertical File, CCHC; Edward Dreier, "The Story of Blaney Park" in Resorts Vertical File, CCHC. Also see Wisconsin Land & Lumber Company, *Blaney Park in Upper Michigan*; *Development Bureau News*, 15 April 1929, folder 2, box 9, UPTARA.

77. Phil DeGraff's Birchwood booklet mailed to F. F. Pray, MD, Jackson, Mich., Library of Michigan Rare Book Collection, Lansing.

78. Eckert, *Buildings of Michigan*, 482; *Development Bureau News*, 1 April 1929 and 1 August 1929, folder 2, box 9, UPTARA. The Lake Breeze quotations appear in CCVL, *The Copper Country of Michigan* (1940).

79. *Development Bureau News*, 1 July 1927, folder 1, box 9, UPTARA.

80. *Daily Mining Gazette*, 15 September 1935, and *Daily Mining Gazette*, 12 August 1938, both in "Tourist Trade (Pre-1969)," Pamphlet and Clippings Collections, CCHC; Edward Prophet, "What Is the Tourist and Resort Industry Worth to Michigan?," 20 February 1940, "UPDB 1939–1941 (folder 1 of 2)," box 10, Dorman Collection, CCHC.

81. CCVL, *The Copper Country of Michigan* (1941).

82. Ocha Potter to James McNaughton, 23 August 1935, folder 72, box 74, C&H, CCHC.

83. Ocha Potter, "The Copper Country and the Tourist," 6 November 1933, folder 35, box 74, C&H, CCHC; John W. Jackson, "Keweenaw Mountain Lodge and Golf Course Story," in "Buildings-Keweenaw Mountain Lodge" Vertical File, CCHC; Ocha Potter to L. M. Nims, Deputy Administrator, WPA, 24 September 1936, folder 71, box 74, C&H, CCHC.

84. Calumet and Hecla Recreation Lands Report, folder 11, box 77, C&H, CCHC; "You Are Invited to Consider a Vast Recreational Area to the North: The Highly Restricted Lands of Calumet and Hecla," and "Recreational Land Program Memo, February 3, 1950," both in folder 11, box 77, C&H, CCHC. Calumet and Hecla was not the only mining company involved in tourism, as companies recognized the need to diversify. Cleveland Cliffs developed Grand Island in Munising Bay into a game preserve and resort. Grand Island became part of the Hiawatha National Forest in 1990. Magnaghi, *An Outline History of Michigan's Upper Peninsula with Bibliography*.

85. *Development Bureau News*, 1 June 1927, folder 1, box 9, UPTARA; *Development Bureau News*, 1 December 1926, folder 1, box 9, UPTARA.

86. "Visit Isle Royale: The New National Park Via Keweenaw-Land," EC Isle Royale (folder 1) Vertical File, Michigan Historical Collections, BHL; Ocha Potter to James McNaughton, 23 August 1935, folder 72, box 74, C&H, CCHC.
87. UPDB Annual Meeting reports, 1935 and 1936, folder 1, box 2, UPTARA; UPDB, *Lure Book of the Upper Peninsula* (1936), 22 and 41.
88. Bertha Farmer to Ben Chynowyth, 8 April 1934, folder 29, box 1, Chynowyth Collection, CCHC; "You Need a Rock Harbor Vacation This Year," folder 343, box 7, Chynowyth Collection, CCHC; Letter from Fred Schofield to Former Guests, 1 July 1936, folder 26, box 1, Chynowyth Collection, CCHC.
89. H. P. Lindsay "What's the Matter with the Tourist Business?," 19 January 1938, "UPDB 1936–39 (1 of 2)," box 10, Dorman Collection, CCHC.
90. "Michigan's Upper Peninsula—Its Places and People: Background Observations for members of the Advanced Training School Field Trip of the Department of Conservation," compiled by workers of the Writers' Program of the Work Projects Administration in the State of Michigan, 1940, CCHC; UPDB, Annual Meeting Reports, 1941, folder 1, box 2, UPTARA.
91. *Detroit News*, 2 July 1944, in folder EA.7 Northern Peninsula Misc. and Genl (Outbox) Vertical File, Michigan Historical Collections, BHL.
92. George Bishop to A. E. Peterman, 11 September 1943, folder 57, box 46, C&H, CCHC; Ralph Swan to Governor Kelly, 8 October 1945, folder 5, box 45, Administrative Records Relating to State Boards and Commissions, RG-42, Records of the Executive Office, Harry Kelly, Governor, SAM.
93. Mrs. Lloyd E. Taylor to Governor Harry Kelly, 30 July 1945, folder 5, box 45 Administrative Records Relating to State Boards and Commissions, RG-42, Records of the Executive Office, Harry Kelly, Governor, SAM.
94. Charles Stetter to George Bishop, 7 November 1944, "Correspondence, Sep–Dec 1944," box 1, Stace Papers, Michigan Historical Collections, BHL.
95. "Minne-tonka Resort," folder 343, box 7, Chynowyth Collection, CCHC.
96. "History of Gunflint and the Kerfoots," http://www.gunflint.com/about_us/about_us.htm (accessed 11 June 2010); *Justine Kerfoot* (Minnetonka, Minn.: Hennepin County Library, 1988), Videotape 274, MHS; Justine Kerfoot Oral History Interviews with Margaret Robertson, November 1986 and March 1987, Interview 58.15, EOHP, 1986–90, MHS; Mark Lowry, *Lady of the Gunflint Trail* (St. Paul: Twin Cities Public Television, 1980), videotape 131, MHS. On Minnesota's mining landscape, see Alanen, *A Field Guide to the Architecture and Landscapes of Northeastern Minnesota*; Francaviglia, *Hard Places*.
97. *Gunflint Gossips*, 8 October 1938, 5 February 1939, and 17 February 1940, MHS; *Justine Kerfoot*, Videotape 274, MHS; Justine Kerfoot Oral History Interviews with Margaret Robertson, November 1986 and March 1987, MHS. Gunflint Trail Association Cash Book, 1937–69, "Gunflint Trail Association, 1937–86," box 2, Kratoska Papers, MHS. Members of the Association in 1938 included Greenwood Lodge, Camp Bearskin, Clearwater Lodge, Gateway Lodge, Swanson's Lodge, Balsam Grove Resort, Northwoods Lodge, Camp Rockwood, Loon Lake Lodge, Gunflint Lodge, Tuscarora Lodge, Sea Gull Lodge, Windigo Point, Wildwood Lodge, Chik-Wauk Lodge, and Saganaga Fishing Camp.
98. Tornquist, Camp du Nord Scrapbook, MHS. Also see Dahlquist, *Then and Now, Camp du Nord*. The YMCA of Greater Saint Paul purchased Camp du Nord in 1960 and continues to operate it as a family camp.
99. G. C. Carlson, "History and Growth of the Tourist Business on Lake Vermilion," 28 October 1926, MHS; Mayor Herman Olson quoted in MAA Brochure (ca. 1930), "MAA, 1925–31, Annual Reports and Printed Material," box 7, Koll Papers, MHS.
100. Burntside Lake and Lodge, National Register Nomination, Clippings File,

IRRC; "Frolic in Winter, Fun in Snow: Burntside Lodge, Ely MN," in "MAA, 1925–31, Annual Reports and Printed Material," box 7, Koll Papers, MHS. On Burntside Lodge, see http://www.burntside.com/history/.

101. James Fogerty interview with Ed and Kay Gilman, 24 June 1993, Interview 79.3, ROHP, MHS.
102. James Fogerty interview with Carol Crawford Ryan, 24 June 1993, Interview 79.12, ROHP, MHS.
103. Margaret Robertson interview with Jack Ruttger, 11 June 1991, ROHP, MHS.
104. Ibid.
105. Ibid.
106. Theresa Ruttger interview with Max "Buzz" Ruttger Jr., 19 August 1997, Interview 79.9, ROHP, MHS. Buzz assumed operations from his father in 1947 and sold the resort in 1969 to another pioneering Minnesota resort family, the Maddens.
107. Ibid.
108. Camp Manito-wish Collection, WHS-ARC; Camp Minocqua Brochures, folders 1 and 2, Camp Minocqua Records, WHS-ARC; Bawden, "Reinventing the Frontier," 242, 287. On summer camps, see Van Slyck, *A Manufactured Wilderness*; Paris, *Children's Nature*.
109. Theresa Ruttger interview with Max "Buzz" Ruttger Jr., ROHP, MHS; James Fogerty interview with Rollis Bishop, 17 November 1999, Interview 79.1, ROHP, MHS; Summary and Description, Warmington Papers, MHS; Photo of musicians at Grand View Lodge, Resorts and Recreational Facilities in St. Louis County, ca. 1925, Album 162, MHS.
110. Commissioner J. W. Clark's quote opening the 1949 guide appears on the project description sheet in Margaret Robinson interview with Ted Leagjeld, 11 June 1991, Interview 79.4, ROHP, MHS; Robert Johnson, *Tour Guide of Minnesota*.
111. *Ely Miner*, 6 June 1940.

4. Tell the World about Your Charms

1. *Development Bureau News*, 2 April 1923, June 1923, and October 1923, all in folder 15, box 8, UPTARA, SAM. *Development Bureau News*, 1 July 1927, folder 1, box 9, UPTARA; Tourist Inquiry Bulletin, 15 April 1940, folder 1, box 11, in "Studies of Development Bureau, ca. 1940," UPTARA.
2. The cartoon was reprinted on the back cover of the Ten Thousand Lakes–Greater Minnesota Association, *Annual Report* (1929).
3. Brosnan, *Uniting Mountain and Plain*, 91–117.
4. Cohen, *A Consumers' Republic*; Marchand, *Advertising the American Dream*; Lears, *No Place of Grace*; Lears, *Fables of Abundance*. Lears highlights the importance of individual fulfillment, arguing that moral, religious, and psychological changes, and not merely a developing national apparatus of marketing and distribution, marked the cultural shift toward a therapeutic ethos of self-realization concerned with psychic and physical health on which advertisers capitalized.
5. UPDB, *Cloverland in Clovertime* (1917).
6. UPDB, *Cloverland* (1920).
7. UPDB, *Cloverland* (1923).

8. *Development Bureau News*, 1 September 1925, folder 15, box 8, UPTARA; *Development Bureau News*, 1 May 1926, and 1 June 1926, both in folder 1, box 9, UPTARA.
9. *Development Bureau News*, 25 December 1928, folder 2, box 9, UPTARA.
10. Alex Magruder quoted in *Development Bureau News*, 1 November 1928, folder 2, box 9, UPTARA; *Special Map of Lakes and Streams in the Upper Peninsula of Michigan*, folder 5, box 9, UPTARA.
11. UPDB, *Cloverland* (1930).
12. *Upper Michigan Ahoy Vacationist!*; Automobile Club of Michigan, *Upper Peninsula of Michigan as Seen by the Old AAA Traveler.*
13. Ontonagon County Board of Supervisors, *Ontonagon County*; Ottawa Tourist Association, *The Vacation Guide.*
14. CCVL, *Ke-Wee-Naw Land in Lake Superior* (1936).
15. CCVL, *The Copper Country of Michigan* (1938).
16. CCVL, *The Copper Country of Michigan* (1940).
17. CCVL, *The Copper Country of Michigan* (1939).
18. Geismar, *Upper Peninsula of Michigan.*
19. Hamilton, *Our Hiawatha Land.*
20. For examples, see "Tourist Inquiry Bulletin No. 3, 15 April 1940," folder 1, box 11, UPTARA; *Development Bureau News*, 2 April 1923, folder 15, box 8, UPTARA. UPDB tourist inquiry bulletins and its *Development Bureau News* (1923–33) provide responses and questions from vacationers and potential vacationers.
21. UPDB, *Land of Hiawatha* (1929 and 1931); UPDB, *Cloverland in Clovertime* (1921–23), folder 5, box 9, UPTARA. On Indians, consumer culture, identity, and authenticity, see Deloria, *Indians in Unexpected Places*, 136–82; Deloria, *Playing Indian*, 95–180; Trachtenberg, *Shades of Hiawatha*; Dilworth, *Imagining Indians in the Southwest*. Dilworth's discussion of the Fred Harvey Company constructing a version of southwestern Indian life that met middle-class desires shares similarities with efforts of North Woods promoters.
22. UPDB, *Land of Hiawatha* (1929 and 1931).
23. UPDB, *Lured by the Land of Hiawatha* (1938).
24. UPDB, *Land of Hiawatha* (1934).
25. UPDB, *The Lure Book of Michigan's Upper Peninsula* (1939).
26. UPDB, *Land of Hiawatha* (1930); UPDB, *The Lure Book of Michigan's Upper Peninsula* (1939).
27. CCVL, *The Copper Country of Michigan* (1940); UPDB, *Cloverland* (1930).
28. UPDB, *The Lure Book of Michigan's Upper Peninsula* (1943).
29. Dr. Thomas Parran quoted in "Michigan for Service and Civilian Wartime Furloughs," "Travel Literature—Brochures-Michigan," box 73, Travel Literature Collection, Research Center, Henry Ford Museum, Dearborn, Michigan; CCVL, *The Copper Country of Michigan* (1942).
30. UPDB, *The Lure Book of Michigan's Upper Peninsula* (1944).
31. St. Louis County Club, *Sportland of the North*; *Farming for Profit in Minnesota Arrowhead Country* is mentioned in "50 Years of Service to the Vacation Travel Industry, MAA, 1924–74," "Minnesota Arrowhead Association, Miscellaneous, 1938–76," box 2, Conservation Printed Matter from Minnesota Organizations, 1921–81, MHS.
32. U.S. Forest Service, *A Vacation Land of Lakes and Woods.*
33. Duluth & Iron Range Railroad Company, *Lakes and Streams of Northern Minnesota*; Chicago Great Western Railroad, *The Minnesota Lakes.*
34. *Minnesota Lakes Reached via Burlington Route*, 1928, item 9:64, box 2, Chicago, Burlington, and Quincy Railroad Company Collection, Newberry Library, Chi-

cago. The piece suggests tourists increased from 22,000 in 1917 to 1,441,000 a decade later.

35. *The Playground of a Nation: The Arrowhead Country of Northern Minnesota*; Duluth & Iron Range Railroad Company, *The Playground of a Nation in the Arrowhead Country*.
36. Dickinson and Gillespie, Inc., *Gull Lake Shores*; Tingdale Bros., *The North Woods Are Calling You*.
37. Ely Commercial Club, *Ely, Minnesota, The Playground of a Nation*. Arthur Carhart, "Ely's Opportunity," *Ely Miner*, 15 July 1921, "Carhart-Miscellaneous," box 15, U.S. Forest Service Collection, IRRC. On Minnesota's Iron Range in the 1930s, see Landis, *Three Iron Mining Towns*.
38. Ely Commercial Club, *Ely*.
39. St. Louis County Club, *The Vacation Land Supreme amid the Pines and Lakes of Northern Minnesota*.
40. Detroit Lakes Civic and Commerce Association, *Detroit Lakes, Minnesota*; *Minnesota's Greatest Lake District*; "Crow Wing County: Northern Minnesota in Paul Bunyan's Playground," folder 1, "Pamphlets Relating to Minnesota Description and Travel," MHS. UPDB *Lure Books* also included cartoon maps.
41. MAA, *Main Highways and Some By-ways Duluth*.
42. Silfverston, *This Minnesota Arrowhead Country*; "50 Years of Service to the Vacation Travel Industry, MAA, 1924–74," "Minnesota Arrowhead Association, Miscellaneous, 1938–76," box 2, Conservation Printed Matter from Minnesota Organizations, 1921–81, MHS.
43. MAA, *Minnesota Arrowhead Country: Hotel and Resort Directory*.
44. *Tips on Minnesota Motor Trips* in "Pamphlets Relating to Tour Guides," MHS; Minneapolis Civic and Commerce Association, Publicity Bureau, *Vacation Days*.
45. *The Land of Ten Thousand Lakes over Jefferson Highway Minnesota* (1920 and 1922); "Making Money for the State"; Coppe, "Minnesota Opens Wide Her Gates."
46. Ten Thousand Lakes of Minnesota Association, *A Report to the Members of the 10,000 Lakes of Minnesota Association*.
47. Ten Thousand Lakes of Minnesota Association, *Minnesota Canoe Trails*.
48. Ten Thousand Lakes of Minnesota Association, *Minnesota*.
49. Ten Thousand Lakes–Greater Minnesota Association, *Come to Minnesota* (1930); Ten Thousand Lakes of Minnesota Association, *Annual Report* (1928).
50. Ten Thousand Lakes of Minnesota Association, *Recreation Days* (1927–28); Ten Thousand Lakes–Greater Minnesota Association, *The Minnesota Book* (1929–32); Minneapolis Public Schools, *A Summer Vacation Guide*.
51. Minnesota Tourist Bureau, *Marvelous Minnesota*; Minnesota Tourist Bureau, *Fisher's Marvelous Minnesota Manual for 1937*. In Wisconsin, the Fox River valley maintained a diverse industrial base, while areas farther north relied more heavily on tourism. See Summers, *Consuming Nature*.
52. Minnesota Tourist Bureau, *Minnesota Has Everything*.
53. *Wisconsin Land of Lakes Magazine* 3 (May 1927); *Wisconsin Magazine* 5 (December 1927). In 1929, Williams's magazine merged with *Wisconsin Magazine* and continued issuing an annual travel guide.
54. Wisconsin Indian Head Country, *Call o' the Lakes*; Wisconsin Indian Head Country, *Wisconsin Indian Head Country*; *Wisconsin Land of Lakes Magazine* 4 (June 1928); *Wisconsin Land of Lakes Magazine* 1 (December 1925); *Wisconsin Land of Lakes Magazine* 2 (November-December 1926); *Wisconsin Land of Lakes Magazine* 5 (January 1929); *Wisconsin Land of Lakes Magazine* 5 (February 1929).

55. The *Wisconsin Magazine* article is reprinted in *Vilas County News*, 6 February 1930.
56. On Mercedes, see Mercedes Papers, folder 1, box 1, WHS. On members and the Chicago office, see 1 April 1936 and 2 February 1939, Heart O'Lakes Trailograms, folder 5, box 1, Mercedes Papers, WHS. On the name issue, see correspondence between Mercedes and the Wisconsin Attorney General, 30 December 1953 and 6 January 1954, folder 3, box 1, Mercedes Papers, WHS. For more on the organization, see *Vilas County News*, 14 April 1938 and 10 April 1947.
57. Wisconsin Heart O' The Lakes Association, *Visit Wisconsin's Beautiful "Heart o' the Lakes." Lakeland Times, The First 100 Years.*
58. *Wisconsin Heart O'Lakes* (1934 and 1935).
59. *Wisconsin Heart O'Lakes* (1937). The organization had branch offices in Eagle River, Merrill, and Antigo.
60. Heart O'Lakes Trailograms, 1 April 1936 and 2 February 1939, folder 5, box 1, Mercedes Papers, WHS. On Minnesota roads, see *Development Bureau News*, 1 May 1930, folder 3, box 5, UPTARA
61. *Wisconsin Heart O'Lakes* (1936 and 1939).
62. Wisconsin Conservation Commission, *Sixteenth Biennial Report, 1937–38*, 88; Wisconsin Conservation Commission, *Fifteenth Biennial Report, 1935–36*, 107–13.
63. Wisconsin Conservation Commission, *Nineteenth Biennial Report, 1943–44*, 84.
64. Wilderness Outfitters, Inc., *Basswood Lake Fishing Lodge Located on the Canadian Border*; The Wilderness Outfitters (Basswood Lake Fishing Lodge) in "Pamphlets Relating to Minnesota Resorts, 1919–," MHS.
65. Vermilion Boat and Outing Co., *Beautiful Lake Vermilion*. Also see G. C. Carlson, "History and Growth of the Tourist Business on Lake Vermilion," 28 October 1926, MHS.
66. Crawford Lodge, *Crawford Lodge on Beautiful Lake GeGoKa*; Jameson's Wilderness Retreat Lodge, 1933 in folder 1, box 1, "Pamphlets Relating to Cook County," MHS; Jameson's Wilderness Retreat Lodge, 1939 in folder 2, box 1, "Pamphlets Relating to Cook County," MHS.
67. Cascade Lodge, *Cascade Lodge, Cascade State Park*; Breezy Point, *Fawcett's Breezy Point*; J. F. Martin, *Clef Camp, Grand Rapids, Minnesota on Lake Pokegama*. Inspections were not limited to Minnesota. Wisconsin inspected lodging beginning in 1932.
68. Balsams, *The Balsams in the Big North Woods*; Iven Johnson, *Johnson's Weblake Resort*.
69. Bent's Camp, *Bent's Camp*.
70. Mason Lake Resort, *Recreation at Mason Lake Resort, Northern Wisconsin*; Mason Lake Resort, *Mason Lake Resort, Incorporated, Fifield, Wis.*
71. Lakota Resort, *Lakota Resort*; Planets, *The Planets, Planets, Wisconsin*; Birchwood Lodge, *Gertrude Doyle's Birchwood Lodge, Rhinelander, Wisconsin*.
72. Lost Lake Resort, *Ed Gabe's Lost Lake Resort*.
73. *The Manitowish Lodge* (1906, 1908, 1909 1911, 1913); Oxbo Resort, *Oxbo, Resort on the Flambeau*. On dams and the wilderness movement, see Harvey, *A Symbol of Wilderness*.
74. Mead and Hunt, Inc. "*Land of Silver Lakes and Streams*"; Chicago, Milwaukee and St. Paul Railway Company, *Northern Wisconsin Lake Region, the Milwaukee Road*; U.S. Railroad Administration, *The Northern Lakes*. The Chicago and North Western advertisement appeared in Wisconsin Heart O' The Lakes Association, *Wisconsin's Heart O' Lakes* (1934).
75. 70–155 Advancement Association Information Bureau, *The Lake Region*.

76. Three Lakes Wisconsin Resort Association, *For Health, For Recreation, For Sports on Land and Water*.
77. Manitowish Waters Association, *Vacation on the Manitowish Waters on U.S. 51*; Manitowish Waters Chamber of Commerce, *Vacation Days Are Happy Days* (1936 and 1938); Minocqua District Resort Association, "*Wisconsin for Muskies*."
78. *Where to Go? A Guide to the Leading Summer Resorts of Minnesota and Wisconsin* in "Pamphlets Relating to Tour Guides," MHS; Dispatch Printing Company Outing Department, *Outing Book* in "Pamphlets Relating to Minnesota Resorts," MHS.
79. *Call of the Open* (1932, 1936, 1939); *Vacation Days* (1918–22).
80. On "Brownie" and the Tour Club, see Heinen, "Hitting the Road for the *Journal*." *Milwaukee Journal*, 15 June 1930.
81. "Auto Touring Takes Big Stride in Last Decade," *Cleveland Plain Dealer*, 15 June 1924; *Detroit Free Press*, 26 June 1938; "Vacation Trips Made Easy by These Experts," *Chicago Daily News*, 18 June 1932.
82. *Cleveland Plain Dealer*, 9 May 1927 and 22 May 1927.
83. *Detroit Free Press*, 28 April 1929, 27 June 1935, and 28 June 1935.
84. *Chicago Daily News*, 17 June 1933. The *Chicago Daily News* began delivering newspapers via airplane to Vilas County in 1928 so Chicagoans could read news from home while on vacation. See *Vilas County News*, 9 August 1928.
85. *Chicago Daily News*, 16 June 1934.
86. *Chicago Daily News*, 10 June 1925; *Milwaukee Journal*, 17 June 1928.
87. *Cleveland Plain Dealer*, 22 May 1927; *Milwaukee Journal*, 28 July 1929; *Chicago Daily News*, 28 May 1924; *Chicago Daily News*, 10 June 1925.
88. *Chicago Daily News*, 28 May 1924; *Milwaukee Journal*, 22 June 1926.
89. *Milwaukee Journal*, 7 July 1926.
90. *Cleveland Plain Dealer*, 13 June 1937, contained a special Travel and Resorts Section; "Michigan Tourist Business Faces Another Record Season," *Detroit Free Press*, 5 June 1938.
91. *Cloverland Tourist's Guide* (1931).
92. *Vilas County News*, 20 April 1920 and 25 May 1921. The longtime editor of the *Vilas County News* sold the paper to Ernst Stewart of Chicago. On the sale, see *Vilas County News*, 11 November 1925. On the paper's calls for increased tourist development, see *Vilas County News*, 6 February 1930. For examples of special sections, see *Vilas County News*, 23 May 1923 and 12 May 1926.
93. *Vilas County News*, 12 April 1922.
94. *Vilas County News*, 20 January 1926, 10 February 1926, 17 February 1926, and 19 November 1931.
95. *Vilas County News*, 12 July 1945.
96. "The Governor's Tour of Michigan," "Guidebooks-Michigan, 1930–37," box 22, Travel Literature Collection, Research Center, Henry Ford Museum, Dearborn, Michigan. These tours were common in Ontario, where the provincial tourist bureau invited American small-town newspaper editors on trips with the expectation they would promote the region upon return.
97. Stace, *Touring the Coasts of Michigan*.
98. Ibid.
99. Northern Minnesota Publishing Company, *The Long Bow Country of Minnesota*.
100. Michigan State Highway Department, *Official Michigan Highway Map* (1934–38); MAA, *Tourist Guide and Map of Minnesota Arrowhead Country*; Ten Thousand Lakes–Greater Minnesota Association, *Minnesota* (1928 and 1931); MAA, *The Minnesota Arrowhead Country*; W. A. Fisher Company, *Ely; Vacationland*

in Northern Minnesota; Toftey, *Cook County, Minnesota* (1920 and 1930); Auto Road Map Company, *Sportsman's and Automobile Map of the Upper Peninsula of Michigan*; Rand McNally and Company, *Rand McNally Official 1924 Auto Trails Map*.

101. Grand Marais Chamber of Commerce, *Come See; Call of the Open* (1934); Chicago Motor Club, *Map of Northern Wisconsin Lakes Region*; *Milwaukee Journal Tour Club Road Map of Wisconsin* (1924 and 1930); Chicago and Northwestern Railroad, *Summer Outings*.
102. Akerman, "Selling Maps, Selling Highways"; Akerman, "Blazing a Well-Worn Path."

5. You've Earned It—Now Enjoy It

1. Interview with William H. Rom, Interview A-96-3650, Ely Oral History Project, IRRC; William Rom Oral History Interview with Margaret Robertson, 2 April 1987, Interview 58.24, EOHP, 1986–90, MHS. The "boundary waters" officially became the Boundary Waters Canoe Area in 1958.
2. Interview with Rom, Ely Oral History Project, IRRC; Rom Interview with Margaret Robertson, 2 April 1987, EOHP, MHS; The Canoe Trip, "Canoe Country Outfitters (Ely, Minn.), 1949–77," box 1, Conservation Printed Matter from Minnesota Organizations, 1921–81, MHS.
3. Interview with Rom, Ely Oral History Project, IRRC; Rom Interview with Margaret Robertson, 2 April 1987, EOHP, MHS.
4. Bill Rom's newsletters offer insight into his operations and appeals to guests. Spring 1955 (first quote), Spring 1957 (second quote), Spring 1958 (third quote), and Rom to Supervisor, Superior National Forest, 11 September 1965, "Canoe Country Outfitters (Ely, Minn.), 1949–77," box 1, Conservation Printed Matter from Minnesota Organizations, 1921–81, MHS. Also see Rom Interview with Margaret Robertson, 2 April 1987, EOHP, MHS.
5. MTC, "Biennial Progress Report 1 July 1945–30 June 1947," folder EA.4b, BHL; 1947 MTC Year End Report, folder 4, box 25, RG 77-96, Department of Commerce-Tourist Bureau, SAM.
6. Odd Moe to Mr. and Mrs. Resort Owner, 1 June 1951, "April-December 1951," box 5, St. Louis County Club and Farm Bureau Association Papers, MHS.
7. UPDB, *The Lure Book of Michigan's Upper Peninsula* (1946–52); UPDB, *The Lure of Michigan's Upper Peninsula* (1953–58). The UPDB changed the title of the *Lure Book* with the 1953 edition. Information comes from the following *Lure Books*: 1946, 1947, 1951, 1952, 1953, 1955, and 1958.
8. MAA, *Annual Report* (1946); George Kratoska to W. A. Fisher Co., 30 January 1958, "CCCC Correspondence, 1957–59," box 1, Kratoska Papers, MHS; for examples, see folder 1, "W. A. Fisher Co, Printed Material," box 5, Kratoska Papers, MHS.
9. Kratoska to Chief of Fish and Wildlife in Ontario, 24 July 1959, "CCCC Correspondence, 1957–59," box 1, Kratoska Papers, MHS; *Ontario: The Heart of the New World, A Neighbour Worth Knowing* (1945), no. 18, box 2, Government Documents: Travel and Publicity, AO; *A Cabin of Your Own* (1943), no. 29, box 3, Government Documents: Travel and Publicity, AO; *Fun in Ontario* (1951), no. 28, and *Northern Ontario for Real Holiday Fun* (1949), no. 26, both in box 2, Government Documents: Travel and Publicity, AO. Additional publications

include *Family Variety Vacation in Ontario*; *Fishing for Fun in Ontario*, no. 31; *With Rod and Gun in Ontario*, no. 32; *The Fisherman's Ontario*, no. 34; *Cruising Ontario's Waters*, no. 35; all in box 3, Government Documents: Travel and Publicity, AO.

10. Minutes of MTC, 25–26 June 1952, folder 4, box 12, UPTARA, SAM.
11. MTC, "Things to See in Michigan," "Water and Sun Vacations in Michigan," and "The Magic of Michigan," all in MTC Vertical File, Michigan Historical Collections, BHL.
12. Aurey Strohpaul to George Bishop, 9 December 1956, and Frederick Tripp to Henrietta Hruby, 30 October 1956, both in "Tourist Council, 1956," box 203, Williams Papers, BHL; Minutes of the UPDB Resort and Travel Committee, 25 October 1956–16 July 1957, folder 13, box 7, UPTARA; 4 March 1958 News Release, folder 4, "News Releases, 1957–58," box 4, RG 68-106, Records of Department of Conservation, Being the Records of the MTC, 1957–61, SAM; 1957 MTC Year End Report, folder 4, "Year End Reports, 1945–1959," box 25, RG 77-96 Department of Commerce-Tourist Bureau, SAM.
13. Letter from George Bishop, 19 June 1951, folder 6, box 2, UPTARA; Joe Bachunas to G. Mennen Williams, 18 March 1952, "Tourist Council-General, 1952," box 89, Williams Papers, BHL.
14. *Grand Rapids Herald*, 5 November 1951, folder 1, box 12, UPTARA; Reactions to Report No. 23 Submitted to the Michigan Joint Legislative Committee on Reorganization of State Government, folder 3, box 12, UPTARA; Robert J. Furlong to Members of the MTC, 12 February 1952, 29 February 1952, and 27 March 1952, all in folder 3, box 12, UPTARA; Frank Davis to Robert Furlong, 8 April 1953, and Chester Wells to George Bishop, 8 April 1953, both in folder 3, box 12, UPTARA; Furlong to Bishop, 19 June 1952, folder 12, box 11, UPTARA.
15. Poll mentioned in *Saturday Evening Post* clipping, 17 September 1949, "Public Relations-Publicity Vacation July 1949–June 1952," box 2, Minnesota Economic Development Department, Tourism Bureau, Public Information Division, Correspondence 1947–54, State Archives, MHS; 1947–1952 Overview of Surveys, folder 8, box 11, UPTARA; *The Story of the Minnesota Arrowhead Association, Inc.* (1956), folder 3, "Pamphlets Relating to the Arrowhead Region of Minnesota," MHS; MAA, *Report on Activities at Annual Meeting and Luncheon*; MAA, *Minnesota Arrowhead Country and Canadian Lakehead Visitor Directory* (1952, 1957, 1958, 1960, and 1961) helped attract tourists to Minnesota and Ontario.
16. *Marvelous Minnesota: Land of 10,000 Lakes* (1949) and *Minnesota: Where There's a Lake for Every Vacation Mood* (1949), both in "Publicity Notebook, Pamphlets, and Press Releases 1947–58," box 3, Correspondence 1947–54, Minnesota Economic Development Department, Tourism Bureau, Public Information Division, MHS.
17. *Vilas County News*, 13 September 1951. Also see *Vilas County News*, 23 September 1948 and 13 July 1950. Special summer issues, "Your Guide to Vacation Fun and Activity," were published from June to September 1953. *Vilas County News*, 19 June 1953, 26 June 1953, and 10 July 1953. On cooperation, see *Vilas County News*, 28 May 1958.
18. *Lakeland Times*, 27 January 1949. On outdoor and travel shows, see *Lakeland Times*, 18 March 1948. Leon Conroyd's regular feature "A Visit with People You Know" discussed vacationers and summer-home owners.
19. UPDB, "Inquiries, Notices, Information, 1949–1952," CCHC. The bulletins are from 22 April 1949 (#8), 28 April 1949 (#9), 3 May 1949 (#10), 4 May 1950 (#10), 20 March 1950 (#1), 14 June 1950 (#16), 21 June 1950 (#17), and 12 July 1950 (#20). Inquiry Bulletin, 13 March 1960, folder 2, box 1, UPTARA.

On Wallace, see Letter from Claire Bullis, 10 July 1951, folder 12, box 11, UPTARA; on complaints regarding Wallace, see Letter from Elizabeth Richards to Editor, *Ann Arbor News* and copies to Dorman and Furlong, 3 August 1961, and Ken Dorman to Elizabeth Richards, 17 August 1961, both in folder 6, box 2, UPTARA.

20. Jack Van Coevering, "A Brief History of Conservation in Michigan," chapter 4, page 4, box 18, Van Coevering Papers, BHL; Jean Worth, "UP General, Editorials, George Bishop undated," box 8, Worth Papers, BHL. On the land program, see Advisory Board Meeting Minutes, 19 March 1958, and 23–24 October 1958, folder 14, box 5, UPTARA. On the Michigan Tech professor challenging the UPDB, see Minutes of Eight Companies meeting, 18 April 1958, folder 4, box 7, UPTARA.
21. Minutes of Five Man Committee, 28 July 1959, folder 4, box 7, UPTARA; Ken Dorman, "A Study of Tax Dividends from Michigan's Travel Industry," box 2, Dorman Papers, CCHC; Minutes Board of Directors Meeting, 3 February 1960, folder 1, box 6, UPTARA. The quote is from John Earle, a member of the family that operated Blaney Park Resort.
22. "Upper Michigan Tourist Association," filmstrip, box 15, UPTARA.
23. Statement from Friends of the Wilderness, 17 July 1964, and Draft of Proposed Presentation on BWCA Mineral Rights Problem, 15 September 1969, both in "Correspondence 1953–69 (2)," box 2, President's Quetico-Superior Committee Collection, MHS.
24. Quote appears in "Observations in Booth during First Month of Operation," 14 July 1955, "CCCC, Information Booth, 1952–65," box 1, Kratoska Papers, MHS; Grand Marais Chamber of Commerce to CCCC, 28 January 1958, "CCCC, Information Booth, 1952–1965," box 1, Kratoska papers, MHS; R. Tom Simmons to Justine Kerfoot, 10 February 1958, "CCCC Correspondence, 1957–59," box 1, Kratoska Papers, MHS.
25. Cash Book of Gunflint Trail Association, 1937–69, "Gunflint Trail Association, 1937–86," box 2, Kratoska Papers, MHS. For inquiries, see Letter from R. E. Snodgrass, 10 February 1952; Letter from Charles Winslow, 9 February 1952; Letter from Mr. P. Dockendorff, 18 January 1952; Letter from W. J. Sztuczko, 18 February 1952; Letter from Henry O. Nelson, n.d., all to Gunflint Trail Association in "GTA, Membership Correspondence, 1950–81," box 2, Kratoska Papers, MHS.
26. Quote appears in "Fun for Everyone the Year Around at Land O' Lakes Wisconsin," folder 2, box 3, Land O' Lakes Chamber of Commerce Records, WHS-ARC); Minutes, 7 May 1947 and 20 March 1948, folder 5, box 1, and Minutes, 6 December 1956, folder 6, box 1, all in Land O' Lakes Chamber of Commerce Records, WHS-ARC.
27. Wisconsin U.S. Highway 45 Association Meeting Announcement, 19 September 1947, folder 1, box 1, Handlos Papers, WHS-ARC; "U.S. 45 Main Highway to the Playground of the North" map and guide, folder 9, box 1, Handlos Papers, WHS-ARC.
28. F. W. Altenburg, President, Four County Development Group to Governor Vernon M. Thompson, 25 November 1957, and Four County Development Group, "Developing Our Recreational Resources," 9 November 1960, both in Four County Development Group Papers, WHS-ARC.
29. HLRA, Minutes, 6 May 1954, 12 May 1954, and 15 March 1955, "Minutes, 1952–56," box 1, HLRA, WHS-ARC; also see HLRA, Minutes, 5 October 1957 and 10 April 1958, "Minutes, 1957–59," box 2, HLRA, WHS-ARC. *Vilas County News*, 21 December 1950, and 12 April 1951.
30. HLRA, Minutes, 15 April 1955, 13 November 1955, 21 November 1955, and 28

November 1956, "Minutes, 1952–56," box 1, HLRA, WHS-ARC. HLRA, Minutes, 22 August 1958, 3 December 1958, 5 January 1959, and 10 February 1959, "Minutes, 1957–59," box 2, HLRA, WHS-ARC.

31. *Report of the Minister of Travel and Publicity, Province of Ontario* (1946–47), AO.
32. *Report of the Minister of Travel and Publicity, Province of Ontario* (1947–48 and 1948–49), AO. The breakdown included 1,702 requests from Illinois, 4,171 from Michigan, 938 from Minnesota, 2,058 from Wisconsin, 4,272 from Pennsylvania, and 6,497 from New York.
33. Arthur Welsh, "Our Welcome Guests," radio address, 3 May 1947, folder 1.3, box 34, RG 5-11, News Releases, Speeches and Broadcasts of the Minister of Tourism and Information, AO; "The Visitor Industry," "Tourist Council-NORGLAC, 1951," box 66, Williams Papers, BHL; 1946 Report of Activities, folder 1.3, "General Correspondence, 29 July 1946–31 December 1946," box 104, RG 5-36, Correspondence of the Director of the Publicity Branch of the Department of Travel and Publicity, AO.
34. *Report of the Minister of Travel and Publicity, Province of Ontario* (1950 and 1951), AO. *Lure Book* copies totaled 315,000 in 1954, 350,000 in 1955, and 400,000 in 1960. Films included *Winter Holiday*, *Vacation Land of Algoma*, *North Superior Shore*, and *Blue Water Holiday* and are in Film Productions, 1950–72, RG 5-2, Ontario Government Tourism Films, AO. Also see Films of U.S. Editors' Goodwill Tours of Ontario, RG 5-3, AO. On U.S. film distribution, see Cecile to Eunice Wishart, 1 April 1949, and 22 June 1949, folder 175, box 2, RG-4, Correspondence of the Minister of Tourism and Information, AO; Summary of Publicity, Editors' Tours 1952–56, folder 3.18, box 106, RG 5-36, Correspondence of the Director of the Publicity Branch of the Department of Travel and Publicity, AO. The 1953 tour led to 6,725 inches of copy and 2,557 inches of pictures for a total of 9,282 inches.
35. McCall comment on Sam Wallace Letter, 7 January 1947, folder 2.2 "Chicago Tribune," box 39, RG 5-15, Correspondence of the Deputy Minister of Travel and Publicity, AO.
36. McCall to Ernie Calvert, 20 April 1949, folder 1.2 "U.S. Editors Tour 1949," box 67, RG 5-29, Deputy Minister of Travel and Publicity's United States Editors' Goodwill Tour of Ontario Correspondence, AO.
37. McCall to Russell Dyche (*Sentinel Echo* of London, Ky.), 12 July 1949, folder 1.6 "U.S. Editors' Tour July 4–12, 1949," box 67, RG 5-29, Deputy Minister of Travel and Publicity's United States Editors' Goodwill Tour of Ontario Correspondence, AO. *Report of the Minister of Travel and Publicity, Province of Ontario* (1956, 1957, 1960), AO. Cities with billboards included Michigan City, South Bend, Des Moines, Port Huron, St. Paul, Akron, Dayton, Toledo, Altoona, Erie, Harrisburg, and Madison.
38. Michigan State Highway Department, "Tourist Guide Signs on Michigan State Trunklines," May 1953, box 3, Dorman Papers, CCHC.
39. Letter from Ida LaVasseur (Tri-Birches on Four Point Lake), 12 September 1956; Correspondence from Hansen's Camp, Deer River, Minnesota, and George Nelson of Lutsen Resort, all in "Vacation and Travel Industry-Facilities Resorts," box 13, Department of Economic Development, Minnesota State Archives, MHS.
40. Letter from State of Minnesota Department of Employment Security, 15 April 1959, "CCCC Correspondence, 1957–59," box 1, Kratoska Papers, MHS; *Lakeland Times*, 16 April 1953; Luther Youngdahl address, 14 August 1949, "Correspondence 1947–54," box 1, Economic Development Department, Tourism Bureau, Public Information Division, State Archives, MHS.

41. Shave, "Why Is Minnesota Losing the Race for Travel and Industry Dollars?"; Rita Sagi to John H. Caldwell, 16 August 1954; Letter to *Look Magazine*, 23 March 1954; John Henricksson to Gus Carlson, 30 December 1953; Letter to *Duluth News-Tribune*, 12 November 1953, all in "Public Relations-Publicity VACATION July '52," box 2, Economic Development Department, Tourism Bureau, Public Information Division, Correspondence 1947–54, State Archives, MHS; George A. Selke, "Potentials of Northern Minnesota," talk given at MAA Annual Meeting, Duluth, 2 October 1964, box 2, Conservation Printed Matter from Minnesota Organizations, 1921–81, MHS.
42. Quote appears in *Vilas County News*, 31 October 1946. Also see *Vilas County News*, 12 July 1945, 11 October 1945, 3 October 1946, and 23 January 1947; *Lakeland Times*, 27 August 1953, 12 August 1954, and 14 February 1957.
43. *Vilas County News*, 10 April 1947.
44. Letter from William's Grindstone Lake Resort to Wisconsin Vacations, Inc., 22 April 1949, Mercedes Papers, folder 3, box 1, WHS; *Lakeland Times*, 14 July 1949, and 25 August 1949.
45. Governor Oscar Rennebohm to Joe Mercedes, 8 March 1950, folder 3, box 1, Mercedes Papers, WHS; *Lakeland Times*, 12 January 1950, and 25 October 1951.
46. Vernon Thomson to Joe Mercedes, 30 December 1953, and 19 March 1954; Mercedes to Thomson, 6 January 1954, all in folder 3, box 1, Mercedes Papers, WHS.
47. *Vilas County News*, 10 March 1955, 17 March 1955, and 7 April 1955; *Lakeland Times*, 14 April 1955. For the debate between Marvin Dillman and Mercedes, see *Lakeland Times*, 24 March 1955, and 31 March 1955.
48. Quote appears in *Vilas County News*, 3 January 1957; also see *Vilas County News*, 19 December 1957, and 30 April 1959; *Lakeland Times*, 23 May 1957.
49. Mercedes to Pat Wilsie (White Birch Lodge, Boulder Junction), 14 May 1957, folder 3, box 1, Mercedes Papers, WHS; Mercedes speech to Joint Finance Committee, 8 March 1955, folder 5, box 1, Mercedes Papers, WHS.
50. 1949 MTC Year End Report, Department of Commerce-Tourist Bureau, folder 4, "Year End Reports, 1945–59," box 25, RG 77-96, SAM; NORGLAC, *Progress Report of a United Tourist Program in the Northern Great Lakes Area of Ontario, Minnesota, Wisconsin, Michigan*; NORGLAC Annual Meeting, 23–24 June 1947, and NORGLAC Annual Meeting, 23–24 February 1954, box 1, NORGLAC, WHS.
51. Bishop to G. Mennen Williams, 18 August 1949, "Tourist Council-NORGLAC, 1949," box 23, Williams Papers, BHL; Secretary's Annual Report, 1 September 1954, box 1, NORGLAC Records, WHS. Leslie Frost to Tom McCall, folder 7.14, "Minneapolis, January 1950," box 41, RG 5-15, Correspondence of the Deputy Minister of Travel and Publicity, AO.
52. Arthur Welsh to S. Valentine Saxby, 11 March 1946, folder 6.18, "NORGLAC 1946–47," box 41, RG 5-15, Correspondence of the Deputy Minister of Travel and Publicity, AO; McCall to William Palmer, 30 April 1945, folder 9.4, "NORGLAC, General-Michigan 1945–52," box 42, RG 5-15, Correspondence of the Deputy Minister of Travel and Publicity, AO. Furlong to McCall, 10 August 1951, folder 1.19, "MTC, 1951–62," box 62, RG 5-22, U.S. Correspondence of the Deputy Minister of Travel and Publicity, AO.
53. McCall to Hubert Dear (MAA), 9 May 1951, folder 1.13, "Inspectors-General Development Branch, 1948–56," box 63, RG 5-24, Department of Travel and Publicity files of the Minister of Tourism, AO. MAA, *Report on Activities at Annual Meeting and Luncheon*; *Minnesota Arrowhead Country and Canadian Lakehead Visitor Directory* (1952, 1957, 1958, 1960, and 1961).

54. Michigan Department of Conservation, *The Porcupine Mountain State Park*. Also see Michigan Department of Conservation, *A Program for the Purchase of a Recreation Area in the Porcupine Mountains*.
55. Governor Kelly to Bert Stoll, 22 December 1944, and M. R. Laird (Connor Land and Lumber) to Governor Harry Kelly, 3 February 1944, both in folder 1, box 72, RG-42, Records of the Executive Office, Harry Kelly, Governor, SAM.
56. George Bishop to A. E. Peterman, 11 September 1943, folder 57, box 46, C&H, CCHC; P. J. Hoffmaster, "The Porcupine Mountains State Park," delivered to UPDB, 9 October 1947, Ontonagon, Mich., "Porcupine Mountains, undated and 1940–77," box 13, Van Coevering Papers, BHL.
57. Harold Titus to P. J. Hoffmaster, 28 May 1945, folder 1, box 21, Records of the Department of Conservation, Executive Section, RG 66-2-A, SAM; P. J. Hoffmaster, "The Porcupine Mountains State Park," delivered to UPDB, 9 October 1947, Ontonagon, Mich., "Porcupine Mountains, undated and 1940–77," box 13, Van Coevering Papers, BHL. On skiing in the Porkies, see Jamerson, *Winter Wonderland*. On visitation, see Len Barnes and Erik Pierce, "Decision in the Porcupines," *AAA Motor News* (October 1958), folder 1, box 13, Van Coevering Papers, BHL.
58. Samuel Dana, "Porcupines and Progress," "Speeches and Articles 1953–1960," box 9, Dana Papers, BHL.
59. *Detroit Free Press*, 5 December 1958, folder 1, box 2, NR-PORC, 1925–74, RG 94-106, SAM.
60. Memo to Board of Directors of MUCC, folder 1, box 2, NR-PORC, SAM.
61. Special Committee Report filed by Stanley Cain, 5 October 1958, folder 1, box 2, NR-PORC, SAM.
62. Jack Schwartz to Jack Van Coevering, 19 September 1958; Van Coevering to Schwartz, 14 October 1958, both in folder 2, box 13, Van Coevering Papers, BHL; Robert O. Belcher, "The Position of the Michigan Natural Areas Council in the Proposed Lease of Mineral Rights in the Porcupine Mountains Park," folder 1, box 2, NR-PORC, SAM.
63. Reprint from *Milwaukee Journal* in *Daily Mining Gazette*, 22 December 1958. *Marquette Mining Journal*, 26 August 1958, and 7 January 1959; *Ironwood Daily Globe*, 19 August 1958; *Lansing State Journal*, 24 August 1958, all in folder 1, box 2, NR-PORC, SAM.
64. Memo from Gerald Eddy, 11 December 1958, folder 1, box 2, NR-PORC, SAM.
65. Materials from 1951 MUCC Convention, "MUCC, Convention 1951," box 1, MUCC Records, BHL.
66. "An Economic Study of the Tourist and Resort Business in the Porcupine Mountains Area, Michigan," 18 August 1958, folder 2, box 2, NR-PORC, SAM.
67. U.S. Department of the Interior, National Park Service, *Our Fourth Shore*; "Pictured Rocks National Lakeshore: A Proposal" (1963), page 23, box 2, Dorman Collection, CCHC.
68. Charles F. Boehler, "Michigan's Resources for Outdoor Recreation," "Outdoor Recreation-General," box 8, Gillette Papers, BHL; *Vilas County News*, 4 August 1966, in folder 15, box 8, Lemmer Collection, BHL.
69. "For More Sport, for Better Sportsmen, for a Better State," "MUCC, Convention 1949," box 1, MUCC Records, BHL; MUCC Histories, "History, Undated, 1937, 1947, 1949," box 4, MUCC Records; Combined Report of Parks and Recreation, Study Committee, "MUCC Parks and Recreation Committee," box 8, Gillette Papers, BHL; Reiger, *American Sportsmen and the Origins of Conservation*.
70. *Vilas County News*, 7 July 1949.
71. Carner, "Rural Land Zoning in Vilas County, Wisconsin, 1933–1954."
72. *Lakeland Times*, 15 January 1953.

73. Huffman, *Protectors of the Land and Water*, 24; Fine and Werner, *The Wisconsin Vacationer*.
74. Huffman, *Protectors of the Land and Water*, 34, 46–48; quotations appear on pages 34 and 46. L. P. Voigt, "ORAP Gets Underway," *Wisconsin Conservation Bulletin* 27 (May-June 1962): 3–6, online facsimile at http://www.wisconsinhistory.org/turningpoints/search.asp?id=1169 (accessed 30 June 2011). The Minnesota measure was known as the Minnesota Natural Resources and Recreation Act.
75. *Vilas County News*, 29 September 1960. Wisconsin Cartographers' Guild, *Wisconsin's Past and Present: A Historical Atlas*.
76. 1952 Michigan Vacationer compared to 1947 Michigan Vacationer, folder 7, box 12, UPTARA; MTC, *A Typical Michigan Vacationer* (1947), folder 12, box 11, UPTARA; *A Typical Michigan Vacationer* (1950), "Tourist Council-General, 1950," box 44, Williams Papers, BHL; *A Typical Michigan Vacationer* (1953), folder 14, box 12, UPTARA; Governor Williams's quote in Memo for MTC meeting, 22 April 1953, "Tourist Council-Meeting, 22 April 1953," box 112, Williams Papers, BHL; MTC, *Survey of Vacationers in Michigan*, January 1948, and *Survey of Effectiveness and Results of Michigan's Tourist Industry Advertising*, both in folder 2, box 23, RG 77-96, Department of Commerce-Tourist Bureau, SAM; Gunn and Luck, *Winter Resorts in Michigan*. In 1950, the average vacation ran 12.3 days with a party of three, and average income was $3,435.
77. Lanning, *The Wisconsin Tourist*, 25, 62, 58, 66, 61; *Lakeland Times*, 4 January 1951.
78. *Lakeland Times*, 12 May 1949.
79. Grover Dillman, "The Most Urgent Problems Confronting the Upper Peninsula of Michigan," 21 August 1945, "1945–47," box 10, Dillman Papers, CCHC. Examples include Duke, *Some Notes on Planning for Tourism in Michigan's Upper Peninsula*; "Signs and Entrances for Attracting Tourists," Circular R-202, Tourist and Resort Series, "Tourist Council, 1955," box 171, Williams Papers, BHL; Gunn, *Planning Better Vacation Accommodations*; Gunn, *A Study of Changes in Buildings for Tourists and Resorters in Michigan*; "Tourist and Resort Services for Michigan"; Robert W. McIntosh, *Financial Returns from Housekeeping Cottages for 1951*, folder 9, box 12, UPTARA.
80. McIntosh, "Wildland Planning Procedures with Emphasis on Recreational Land Use in the Tahquamenon-Pictured Rocks Region, Upper Peninsula of Michigan," 93, in folder 2, box 1, NR-PORC, SAM. Park attendance rose from 22,418 to 222,340, and straits crossings increased from 501,109 to 900,782. Grover Dillman, "The Economic Future of the Upper Peninsula," 30 January 1950, "1948–50," box 10, Dillman Papers, CCHC.
81. *1957 Michigan Tourist Survey*, "Tourist Council, General 1958," box 266, Williams Papers, BHL; Michigan Facts and Figures (Tourist Survey Numbers 1958), "Tourist Council, General, 1959," box 295, Williams Papers, BHL; Uel Blank and Clare A. Gunn, "Guidelines for Tourism-Recreation in Michigan's Upper Peninsula: A Report and Recommendations," 1966, page 19, box 11, Dorman Papers, CCHC; MTC, *Annual Report* (1965), State Library of Michigan, Lansing.
82. Federal Reserve Survey, 1949–50, "Vacation & Travel Industry-Research Federal Reserve Index," box 13, Department of Economic Development, Subject Files—Vacation Travel Industry-Welfare, State Archives, MHS; Report of 10 November 1952, "Correspondence and Misc. Papers, Maps, 1952," box 2, FOW Papers, MHS; Report of 23 October 1953, "Correspondence and Misc. Papers, Sept.–Nov. 1953," box 2, FOW Papers, MHS.
83. MAA, *1958 Vacation Travel Survey*, "Publications," box 15, USFS, IRRC;

Sielaff and Gronseth, *A Look at Employment in Minnesota Resorts for 1961*. Cass, Cook, Lake, and St. Louis Counties had more resorts open in winter than other counties and thus offered greater year-round employment. Also see U.S. Department of Commerce, *Suggestions for the Economic Development of Northeastern Minnesota* (Washington, D.C.: U.S. Department of Commerce, 1960), box 15, USFS, IRRC; "A Survey of the Minnesota Resort Industry" in "Recreation-General, Various Publications," box 13, USFS, IRRC. On the IRRRB, see Dana Miller, *The Iron Range Resources and Rehabilitation Board*; Manuel, "Developing Resources."

84. "Report on the National Forest Recreation Resource Survey (Region 9)," box 3, USFS, IRRC. These included Chequamegon, Chippewa, Nicolet, Ottawa, Hiawatha, and Superior National Forests. *Vilas County News*, 30 August 1956, 8 January 1959, 15 January 1959, 13 August 1959, 9 June 1960, 22 December 1960; Isadore Fine, *Wisconsin Vacation Recreation Papers*; Thompson, *The History of Wisconsin*.
85. "Mailings/Newsletters from Canoe Country Outfitters," "Canoe Country Outfitters (Ely, Minn.), 1949–77," box 1, Conservation Printed Matter from Minnesota Organizations, 1921–81, MHS; Interview with William H. Rom, Ely Oral History Project, IRRC; William Rom Oral History Interview with Margaret Robertson, 2 April 1987, EOHP, MHS. Rom's quote appears on p. 31 of the transcript.
86. Interview with Rom, Ely Oral History Project, IRRC; Rom Interview with Margaret Robertson, 2 April, 1987, EOHP, MHS; June 1961 Memo, "Summer Roads-General," box 13, USFS, IRRC; Justine Kerfoot Oral History Interviews with Margaret Robertson, November 1986 and March 1987, Interview 58.15, EOHP, MHS.
87. Uncataloged Ruttger materials, Resort Volume 2, Early 1950s–1969, MHS; *Gunflint Gossips*, 14 April 1956 and 3 February 1957, MHS; Tornquist, Camp du Nord Scrapbook, MHS; Dunn to Lt. Col. Thomas R. Hannah, 4 July 1950, Resort Files, 1950, "Dunn's Lodge H–K," and Correspondence in Resort Files, "Dunn's Lodge A–E," 1952, both in box 9, Dunn Papers, MHS.
88. *Teal Lake Tidings*, Spring 1948, August 1948, December 1948, Spring 1949, December 1949, Autumn 1951, Spring 1953, Spring 1954, Autumn, 1953, Spring 1955, Spring 1956, Autumn 1956, Spring 1957, Spring 1959, Spring 1960, folder 2, box 1, Ross' Teal Lake Lodge Collection, WHS.
89. Ledger, 1948–58, and Disbursements Journal, 1948–50, both in folder 1, box 2 (Oversize), Ross' Teal Lake Lodge Collection, WHS; Brochure for Ross' Teal Lake Lodge, Hayward, Wis., folder 3, box 1, Ross' Teal Lake Lodge Collection, WHS; 1953 Ledger, folder 7, box 1, Ross' Teal Lake Lodge Collection, WHS; 1955 Ledger, folder 9, box 1, Ross' Teal Lake Lodge Collection, WHS.
90. James Fogerty Interview with William Flagg, 27 June 1994, Interview 79.2, ROHP, MHS. Margaret Robertson Interview with Ted Leagjeld, 11 June 1991, Interview 79.4, ROHP, MHS.
91. Margaret Robertson Interview with John Lyght, 13 March 1992, Interview 79.5, ROHP, MHS.
92. Anthony Wise statement, 31 July 1947, quoted in 33rd Anniversary Grand Opening, folder 38, box 6, Wise Papers, WHS; Biography of Anthony Wise by Rick Pifer, 12 March 1997, Notes to Wise Papers, WHS.
93. Materials in Tourism Analysis, ca. 1945–47, folder 1, box 6, Wise Papers, WHS; Anthony Wise Memo on Winter Tourist Trade in Wisconsin to President, Hayward Chamber of Commerce, and Materials in Planning Notebook, ca. 1945–46, folder 2, box 6, Wise Papers, WHS; J. W. Clark, Director of Minnesota Resources Commission to Wise, 6 December 1946, folder 13, box 7, Wise Papers,

WHS; M. W. Torkelson, Director of Regional Planning, Wisconsin State Planning Board to Wise, 9 January 1947, folder 15, box 7, Wise Papers, WHS.

94. Earlene Roberts to Wise, 14 August 1957, and Wise to Town Board and Town Meeting, Cable, Wis., 5 April 1955, both in folder 4, box 6, Wise Papers, WHS; Scheer's Ghost Lake Lodge to Wise, October 1, 1947, and Wise to T. J. Wall, 22 October 1947, both in folder 15, box 7, Wise Papers, WHS; Soo Release from A. T. Erickson, 25 November 1947, folder 4, box 6, Wise Papers, WHS; Mailing List: 1947–49, folder 14, box 6, Wise Papers, WHS; History Piece on Small Business Administration Loan, folder 24, box 6, Wise Papers, WHS. Organizations in Minneapolis, Milwaukee, Chicago, Duluth, Superior, Eau Claire, Madison, Ashland, Hayward, La Crosse, and Appleton received information.
95. UPDB, *The Winter Lure of Michigan's Upper Peninsula*; Louis S. Drake and the MTC, *Survey of Skiing in the Upper Peninsula of Michigan: A Report of the Industry, Its Facilities and Potentials*, folder 15, box 12, UPTARA; *Iron Mountain News*, 14 October 1954 in folder 6, box 7, UPTARA; Gunn, *Planning Winter Sports Areas*; Bishop to Williams, 21 May 1953, "Tourist Council-Winter Sports, 1953," box 113, Williams Papers, BHL; Wise to Williams, 29 September 1958, "Tourism-Winter Sports," box 411, Williams Papers, BHL.
96. Eliason Snowmobiles, http://www.eliason-snowmobile.com/ (accessed 30 June 2011); Polaris Industries, "History and Heritage," http://www.polaris industries.com/ (accessed 30 June 2011).
97. *Copper Country Holidays* (Houghton: CCVL, n.d.), Copper Country-Description and Travel (1980–89) Vertical File, CCHC. The booklet was filed by acquisition date rather than publication date and dates from the 1950s.
98. *Summer Tourist Survey of the Michigan Copper Country*, April 1959 (cosponsored by the CCVL and the Michigan College of Mining and Technology), box 3, Ken Dorman Papers, CCHC; Cohen, *A Consumer's Republic*, 119.
99. *Summer Tourist Survey of the Michigan Copper Country*, April 1959, box 3, Dorman Papers, CCHC.
100. Ibid.
101. On Lake Breeze, see Eckert, *Buildings of Michigan*, 482. The quote from Harold and Beatrice Putnam appears in Lake Breeze Hotel Brochure, Tourist Trade (Pre-1969) Vertical File, CCHC; Twin Lakes Resort Brochure, Resorts Vertical File, CCHC; Hokan's Motel and Cottages Brochure, Tourist Trade (Pre-1969) Vertical File, CCHC; *The Shoreline Scenic Route to Keweenawland*, Tourist Trade (Pre-1969) Vertical File, CCHC.
102. "Copper Country Contains Wealth of Opportunity," "Your Holiday in Michigan's Famous Copper Country," and "Visit Ke-Wee-Naw Land in Lake Superior," all in Copper Country-Description and Travel (no date) Vertical File, CCHC.
103. CCVL, *We Fell in Love with Keweenawland*; *Copper Country Holidays*, Copper Country-Description and Travel (1980–89) Vertical File, CCHC.
104. "Relax and Play in Michigan's Scenic Wonderland," Copper Country-Description and Travel (no date) Vertical File, CCHC.
105. UPDB, *Lure Book* (1952).
106. CCVL, *We Fell in Love with Keweenaw Land*; "Keweenaw Peninsula" Vertical File, Michigan Historical Collections, BHL; Putnam Collection, box 12, CCHC; Harold Putnam biography file, CCHC; *Daily Mining Gazette*, 15 August 1977. Putnam was a photographer who produced guidebooks with his wife, Beatrice.
107. *Milwaukee Journal*, 16 April 1989, Copper Country-Description and Travel (1980–89) Vertical File, CCHC; Keweenaw Historical Society Collection, folder 559, CCHC. Wescoat chaired the Isle Royale Development Commission in the 1950s and reflected on tourism's acceptance over the past half century.

108. Recreational Land Program Memo, 3 February 1950; Report on Calumet and Hecla Recreation Lands, 1949; "You Are Invited to Consider a Vast Recreational Area to the North: The Highly Restricted Lands of Calumet and Hecla, all in C&H, folder 11, box 77, CCHC; 5 May 1949 article, "1949–51," box 11, Chynowyth Collection, CCHC. One hundred eighty prime lots were leased at $25–$50 per annum, but sixty-three were by company employees, who paid 40 percent less, and twenty-one by fishermen, who paid $100. The company believed its profits from recreational lands could reach $1.5 million.
109. Report on Calumet and Hecla Recreation Lands, 1949, folder 11, box 77, C&H, CCHC; quote appears in *Daily Mining Gazette*, 8 February 1952. On the Copper Harbor Club, see *Daily Mining Gazette*, 27 October 1952. On winter sports, see folder 12, box 6, RG 77-104, Houghton County Road Commission Records, CCHC. On community support for tourist development, see *Daily Mining Gazette*, 10 January 1955.
110. *Motor News* (January 1956), folder 93, box 3, Chynowyth Collection, CCHC; Robert Gibbs to James Wescoat, 22 October 1954, and 20 April 1955, and Kohler to Williams, 27 May 1954, all in folder 2, box 6, Houghton County Road Commission Records, CCHC. Williams also wrote Minnesota's C. Elmer Anderson for support. Williams to Anderson, 21 May 1954, "Isle Royale Park Study Commission, 1954," box 120, Williams Papers, BHL.
111. C. F. Winkler to Sen. Potter, 27 January 1953, folder 2, box 6, RG 77-104, Houghton County Road Commission Records, CCHC; Memo from Governor Williams to James Wescoat, 12 January 1953, and Memo from Isle Royale Development Commission, 15 March 1953, both in folder 391, box 9, Chynowyth Collection, CCHC.
112. Dennis Copper to Vandenburg, 27 April 1950, folder 2, box 6, RG 77-104, Houghton County Road Commission Records, CCHC.
113. Frank Stewart to Douglas McKay (for Fred Seaton, Interior Secretary), 24 July 1957, and Roger Ernst to Frank Stewart, 4 September 1957, both in "Isle Royale Park Study Commission, 1957," box 210, Williams Papers, BHL. On using a Mackinac ferry, see letter from Richard Aro, 17 April 1957, "Isle Royale Park Study Commission, 1957," box 210, Williams Papers, BHL.
114. *Escanaba Daily Press*, 22 March 1958, Keweenaw Historical Society Collection, folder 587, CCHC. Critical claims are characterized in "Isle Royale Is Yours," *Inside Michigan* 5 (February 1955), folder 93, box 3, Chynowyth Collection, CCHC.
115. Lewis Beeson to Sweeney (Administrative Assistant), 13 September 1957, folder 4, box 2, and Robert Furlong to Sweeney, 6 November 1957, folder 3, box 2, both in RG 68-106, Lot 41, Records of the Department of Conservation, Being the Records of the MTC, 1957–61, SAM.
116. C. O. Frush to Williams, 13 October 1957, "Tourist Council, General 1957," box 234, Williams Papers, BHL. The Department of Conservation director agreed, commenting, "I think this is emblematic in the history of the Copper Country and very definitely should be preserved as an historic site and as an attraction to the tourist." See Gerald Eddy to Sweeney, 25 October 1957, folder 3 box 2, RG 68-106, Lot 41, Records of the Department of Conservation, Being the Records of the MTC, 1957–61, SAM. On preservation and memory in the Copper Country, see Hoagland, *Mine Towns*, 217–47; Lankton, *Hollowed Ground*, 304–16. Keweenaw National Historical Park was established in 1992.
117. Writers' Program of the WPA in the State of Michigan, *Michigan*, 581. "Plus Twelve" addendum written in September 1950 in Ocha Potter, "Sixty Years," Ahmeek, Michigan, May 1939, CCHC. Thurner, *Strangers and Sojourners*, 259, argues, "In the Keweenaw private enterprise and federal, state, and local gov-

ernments worked in tandem, literally paving the way for the emerging tourist industry."

118. UPDB, *Lure of the Land of Hiawatha* (1936). On Minnesota mining landscapes as tourist sites, see Goin and Raymond, "Recycled Landscapes." On a mine smelter and Superfund site becoming a golf course, see Curtis, "Greening Anaconda."

6. The Not So Quiet Crisis

1. ORRRC, *A Progress Report to the President and to the Congress*, 12. Scott Turner's letter is quoted in Rome, *The Bulldozer in the Countryside*, 128. Coolidge to NCOR, 22 May 1924, at http://www.calvin-coolidge.org/html/at_the_national_conference_on_.html (accessed 17 July 2010). On NCOR, see Clements, *Hoover, Conservation, and Consumerism*; Krog, "'Organizing the Production of Leisure.'"
2. ORRRC, *A Progress Report to the President and to the Congress*, 1. Howard Zahniser quoted David Brower at Senate committee hearings establishing the ORRRC: "Maybe you would like to ad lib that the highway program may very easily bring to our seashores a tidal wave from inland." Senate Committee, *Outdoor Recreation Resources Commission*, 92.
3. U.S. Congress, Senate Committee, *Outdoor Recreation Resources Commission*, 37 and 98.
4. Ibid., 58, 94.
5. Ibid., 51–52.
6. ORRRC, *Outdoor Recreation for America*; "ORRRC, 1959 (1)," box 6, Dana Papers, BHL; Marked-up copy of Proposed Outline for ORRRC, Chapter 1: Problems, Prospects, Policies, "ORRRC, 1960 (1)," box 6, Dana Papers, BHL. Also see "A Quick History of the Land and Water Conservation Fund Program—1964 and All That," http://www.nps.gov/lwcf/history.html (accessed 17 July 2010). On Rockefeller's conservation initiatives, including his ORRRC leadership, see Winks, *Laurance S. Rockefeller*, 121–39.
7. ORRRC, *Outdoor Recreation for America*, 13. On America's fascination with natural sacred sites, see Sears, *Sacred Places*.
8. U.S. Congress, Senate Committee, *Outdoor Recreation Act of 1962*, 13.
9. ORRRC, *Outdoor Recreation for America*, 23, 49, 79, 137, 189; Sutter, *Driven Wild*, 41–48 and 258–59.
10. Notes of Schulz, Zimmerman, Olson, and Kelly meeting with Eisenhower, 17 December 1953, "Docket Files C3207 EEEE (3), 1953," box 5, QSC, MHS.
11. Memorandum for State Department, 3 February 1948, "Subject Files: U.S. Dept. of State (1), Correspondence and Miscellaneous Papers, 1947–57," box 3, QSC, MHS; Committee to Bernard Gladieux, Ford Foundation, "Docket Files C3207 ZZZ (1), 1949–51," box 5, QSC, MHS.
12. Witzig, *Voyageurs National Park*; Searle, *Saving Quetico-Superior*; Backes, *Canoe Country*; Proescholdt, Rapson, and Heinselman, *Troubled Waters*.
13. U.S. Department of the Interior, National Park Service, *Our Fourth Shore*; "Sculpted Beauty in a Northern Wilderness," *Detroit News*, July 18, 1965, in "Parks" Vertical File, Michigan Historical Collections, BHL; "Pictured Rocks National Lakeshore: A Proposal," 1963, box 2, Dorman Papers, CCHC; Karamanski, *The Pictured Rocks*; Symon, ed., *Alger County*; Kalt, *Sixties Sandstorm*.
14. Gawboy et al., *Tourist and Recreational Resources, Lac du Flambeau Indian Res-*

ervation; Gawboy et al., *Tourist and Recreational Resources, Lac Court Oreilles Indian Reservation*; Gawboy et al., *Tourist and Recreational Resources, Wisconsin Indian Reservations.*

15. Gawboy et al., *Tourist and Recreational Resources, Lac du Flambeau Indian Reservation*, 8; Gawboy et al., *Tourist and Recreational Resources, Lac Court Oreilles Indian Reservation, Wisconsin.*
16. Gawboy et al., *Tourist and Recreational Resources, Lac Court Oreilles Indian Reservation*; Gawboy et al., *Tourist and Recreational Resources, Wisconsin Indian Reservations*, 7.
17. Paul Larson, *A Place at the Lake*, 8.
18. Hart, "Resort Areas in Wisconsin"; Mead and Hunt, "*Land of Silver Lakes and Streams*"; Minnesota Department of Business Research and Development, *Steps to Better Vacations in Minnesota*. On the familial experience of summer home communities, see Schultz, *Shoreline*. On one northern Minnesota summer community, see Ryan, *Star Island*. On Ontario vacation cottages, see DeVisser and Ross, *Summer Cottages*.
19. Remarks by Senator Gaylord Nelson at the Governor's Conference on Natural Beauty in Wisconsin, 21 October 1965, in Gaylord Nelson, Speeches and Other Documents on Environmental Issues, 1962–71 (Gaylord Nelson Papers, MSS 1020, in WHS). Online facsimile at: http://www.wisconsinhistory.org/turning points/search.asp?id=1670 (accessed 30 June 2011).
20. USDA Forest Service, *Chippewa National Forest* (Washington, D.C.: Government Printing Office, 1942), box 3, CNF, IRRC; Hays, "Human Choice in the Great Lakes Wildlands," 300–301; Steiner, *Americans at Play*, suggests that national forests contained 1,201 hotels and 10,770 summer homes in 1930.
21. "1955 Tours and Show-Me Trips," box 2, CNF, IRRC; George S. James, Regional Forester, to Adolf Haugen, 24 June 1963, Haugen to John Van Bargen, Forest Supervisor, and Van Bargen to Haugen, 13 August 1963, all in "Special Use Permits-Adolf Haugen," box 46, CNF, IRRC.
22. Rev. G. C. Saunderson to Department of Agriculture, 6 August 1963, and Inspection of Norway Beach Summer Home Lots, 21 July 1974, and 1 October 1974, all in "Special Use Permits-Rev. G. C. Saunderson," box 47, CNF, IRRC; Report on the National Forest Recreation Resource Survey (Region 9), USFS, box 3, page 68, IRRC. On Star Island summer residents, see Ryan, *Star Island*.
23. Address by John Smrekar, 22 May 1964, University of Minnesota, "Friends of the Wilderness," box 15, USFS, IRRC; Haugen to Van Bargen and Van Bargen to Haugen, 13 August 1963, "Special Use Permits-Adolf Haugen," box 46, CNF, IRRC. Haugen wrote to the Forest Service in exasperation, "Understand that miserable stretch of road to where we interlopers seek solace is our responsibility—is this correct? This is rather difficult to comprehend since I have had to back into cabin entrances twice to allow campers and gear the right of way which I assume goes with their top priority."
24. *Grand Marais Pilot & Pictured Rocks Review*, 21 June 1985, cited in Karamanski, *The Pictured Rocks*. See chapter 2, "'The North Woods' and the Pictured Rocks: Economic Development through Preservation."
25. Karamanski, *The Pictured Rocks*, 44; Rothman, *Devil's Bargains*.
26. Wallace Stegner, Wilderness Letter, Stegner to David E. Pesonen, 3 December 1960, http://www.greenfoothills.org/about/WildernessLetter.html (accessed 17 July 2010).
27. Backes, *Canoe Country*, 44 and 55; Callicott and Nelson, eds., *The Great New Wilderness Debate*.
28. Backes, *Canoe Country*, 80, 109, 119.
29. Chester Wilson to Joseph Koschak, 4 June 1945, box 4, QSC, MHS.

30. Wilson to Jay H. Price, 9 July 1945, box 4, QSC, MHS.
31. Backes, *Canoe Country*, 109, 119, and 130. Grant Halladay, Paul Harvey, and Sigurd F. Olson, *Wilderness Canoe Country* (n.p., 1949), videocassette, MHS. On the film, see Minutes of President's Quetico-Superior Committee, 11 December 1948, folder 2, box 1, QSC, MHS.
32. Sig Olson, "Congress Holds Key to Development of Ontario-Minnesota Vacation Area," *Christian Science Monitor*, 22 March 1948, folder 2, box 1, QSC, MHS; Sig Olson to Marshall Elson, 18 March 1949, "1940–49," box 5, St. Louis County Club Records, MHS.
33. "The Wilderness Saved!," *Minneapolis Star*, 20 December 1949, folder 3, box 1, QSC, MHS.
34. Harold H. Martin, "Embattled Wilderness," reprint from *Saturday Evening Post*, "Correspondence and Misc. Papers, 1945–48," box 2, FOW, MHS.
35. Galen Pike to Regional Forester, 15 October 1946, and Ranger J. W. Trygg to Forest Supervisor, 15 October 1946, "Northern Great Lakes Area Council," box 13, USFS, IRRC. One study found forty-one resorts, twenty-two summer homes, and two year-round homes in the affected area. Of the forty-one resorts, thirty-one were on Basswood and Saganaga Lakes, one on Lac La Croix, two on Crooked Lake, and the rest on smaller lakes. *Plan of Management, Superior Roadless Areas, Superior National Forest*, 1950, "Correspondence and Misc. Papers, Maps, June 1954," box 2, and "Printed Material, Undated-1954," box 15, FOW, MHS.
36. Chester Wilson, "Wings over the Wilderness," *The Conservation Volunteer* 11 (Nov.-Dec. 1948), folder 2, box 1, QSC, MHS. Wilson later served, with Samuel Dana, on the ORRRC. Comments Pertaining to Mr. Joseph Perko's "Outline of Airplane Controversy," "Use of Airplanes-Policy, Regulation, Trespass, etc., 1954," box 20, USFS, IRRC; Minutes of Land Acquisition Priority Meeting regarding Superior Roadless Area, 8 November 1952, folder 4, box 1, QSC, MHS. Estimates suggested $332,000 was needed to purchase strategic resorts. The 1948 Thye-Blatnik Act directed the secretary of agriculture to acquire lands in areas "where in his opinion development or exploitation, or the potentialities for development or exploitation, impair or threaten to impair the unique qualities and natural features of the remaining wilderness canoe country." University of California Wildland Research Center, *Wilderness and Recreation*, 314.
37. Martin, "Embattled Wilderness," "Correspondence and Misc. Papers, 1945–48," box 2, FOW, MHS. Zupancich, Perko, and Skala led the contingent of Superior National Forest resort owners defying the federal government. For more, see box 35, USFS, IRRC. President Harry Truman, Executive Order no. 10092, "Establishing an Airspace Reservation over Certain Areas of the Superior National Forest in Minnesota," 17 December 1949, http://www.trumanlibrary.org/executiveorders (accessed 4 August 2011). The order went into effect in 1951.
38. Civil Action #1616, United States of America v. Joseph Perko and William Zupancich, 14–15 July 1955, pages 624–25, box 35, USFS, IRRC.
39. Quote appears in Joseph Perko to Mr. Morse, n.d., "Use of Airplanes-Policy, Regulation, Trespass, etc., 1953," box 20, USFS, IRRC; Perko to McCardle, 29 March 1954, "Use of Airplanes-Policy, Regulation, Trespass, etc., 1954," box 20, USFS, IRRC; Joe Perko to Guests, 15 February 1954, "Correspondence and Misc. Papers, Jan.–Feb. 1954," box 2, FOW, MHS; William Magie to Sigurd Olson, 16 January 1956, "Sigurd Olson, 1956," box 15, FOW, MHS.
40. William Magie to Paul Clement, 18 January 1955, "Paul Clement, 1949–64," box 12, FOW, MHS; Pronouncement from William Magie of Friends of the

Wilderness, 31 March 1953, folder 3, "Pamphlets Relating to the Arrowhead Region of Minnesota," MHS.

41. "Isolate and Exploit," roll 15, Superior National Forest Records, MHS; Sigurd Olson to Keith Denis, 1 October 1953, "Sigurd Olson, July–December, 1953," box 14, FOW, MHS.
42. *Ely Miner*, 23 July 1953, "Newspaper Clippings," box 17, FOW, MHS; Memo on Perko and Zupancich discussion with Forest Service Officials, January 28, 1952, "Use of Airplanes-Policy, Regulation, Trespass, etc., 1952," box 20, USFS, IRRC.
43. Searle, *Saving Quetico-Superior*, 170.
44. *Duluth News-Tribune*, 27 October 1953, "Newspaper Clippings," box 17, FOW, MHS.
45. Minutes from 17 November 1955 meeting, and Letter from William Essling, 4 May 1959, both in folder 9, box 1, QSC, MHS.
46. *Ely Miner*, 30 December 1949, and 29 June 1950, "Newspaper Clippings," box 17, FOW, MHS; Letter to Members, 24 January 1953, and Sigurd Olson to William Magie, 9 May 1953, "Sigurd Olson, January–June 1953," box 14, FOW, MHS.
47. Karl A. Danielson to Ely Chamber of Commerce, 27 March 1952, "Use of Airplanes-Policy, Regulation, Trespass, etc., 1952," box 20, USFS, IRRC.
48. Danielson to Stan Pechaver, 17 April 1952, USFS, IRRC; Sigurd Olson to Karl Danielson on meeting he had with Mr. Gandrieux, owner of Balsam Bay Resort, 16 April 1952, "Use of Airplanes-Policy, Regulation, Trespass, etc., 1952," box 20, USFS, IRRC.
49. On the August 28, 1948, *New Yorker* cover, see Sigurd Olson, "Airspace Reservations over Wilderness," *Sports Afield*, 1949, folder 1, box 6, QSC, MHS.
50. John Olson to Senator Hubert Humphrey, 4 February 1952, "Use of Airplanes-Policy, Regulation, Trespass, etc., 1952," box 20, USFS, IRRC.
51. Magie to Charles Kelly, 28 April 1955, "Charles Kelly, 1954–56," box 13, FOW, MHS.
52. Letter from Jean B. Raiken, 12 April 1959, "March–July 1959," box 7, FOW, MHS.
53. Outdoor Americans United, Brief Outlining Protest of Air Ban, Superior National Forest, 26 September 1950, "OAU, 1950–51," box 20, USFS, IRRC; Chester Wilson to Galen Pike, 10 March 1950, "OAU, 1950–51," box 20, USFS, IRRC.
54. Rom to *Minneapolis Tribune* editor, 22 September 1958, "September–December 1958," box 6, FOW, MHS; Rom to Frank Hubachek, 29 January 1951, "Frank Hubachek, 1949–53," box 12, FOW, MHS; Interview with William H. Rom, Interview A-96-3650, Ely Oral History Project, IRRC.
55. Hubachek to Rom, 12 March 1951, and Rom to Hubachek, 15 March 1951, both in "Frank Hubachek, 1949–53," box 12, FOW, MHS.
56. Rom to Magie, 20 January 1955, "Correspondence and Misc. Papers, January–February 1955," box 4, FOW, MHS; Magie to Rom, ca. April 1955, "Correspondence and Misc. Papers, March–April 1955," box 4, FOW, MHS.
57. Rom to Magie, 10 February 1959, "January–February 1959," box 6, FOW, MHS. Rom also corresponded with Forest Service officials. Rom to Lawrence Neff (Superior National Forest Supervisor), 28 January 1959, "January–February 1959," box 6, FOW, MHS; Rom to Don Ferguson, 12 May 1961, "March–July 1959," box 7, FOW, MHS; Rom to Neff, 5 March 1962, "Correspondence and Misc. Papers, January–March 1962," box 8, FOW, MHS.
58. Rom to Mrs. C. C. Sorensen, 28 February 1961, "January–February 1961," box 7, FOW, MHS. Sorensen had earlier written the Chamber of Commerce about

its position and received a letter back from Ted Wynn that prompted her to write Rom. Wynn to Mrs. C. C. Sorensen, n.d., "January–February 1961," box 7, FOW, MHS.

59. Rom to Magie, 6 April 1961, "April–May 1961," box 7, FOW, MHS.
60. "Friends of Wilderness Give the Answer to Ely," 3 November 1960, "Clippings 1960," box 18, FOW, MHS.
61. Response from Harold W. Griffin, President, Ely Chamber of Commerce, "Chamber Head Outlines 'Wilderness Bill' Stand," 17 November 1960, "Clippings 1960," box 18, FOW, MHS.
62. Letter from Donald Pakko in *Minneapolis Tribune*, 21 August 1960, "Clippings 1960," box 18, FOW, MHS.
63. Magie to Harold Griffin, "Friends of Wilderness Group Replies to Ely Chamber's Views on Roadless Area," *Mesabi Daily News*, 15 December 1960, "Clippings 1960," box 18, FOW, MHS; Magie to Griffin, 28 November 1960, "Friends of the Wilderness," box 15, USFS, IRRC; Fred C. Childers, "Sen. Humphrey Protests the Ely Miner Editorial," *Ely Miner*, 1 August 1957, "Clippings 1957," box 17, FOW, MHS.
64. Magie to Josiah Chase, 8 June 1957, "May–June 1957," box 6, FOW, MHS; Handwritten list of acreage and resorts remaining to be acquired (ca. July 1958), "July–August 1958," box 6, FOW, MHS.
65. Ted Wynn to Lawrence Neff, 13 February 1960, "Ely—Special Problem Area," box 13, USFS, IRRC.
66. Richard McArdle to Ted Wynn, 19 May 1960, "Ely—Special Problem Area," box 13, USFS, IRRC.
67. University of California Wildland Research Center, *Wilderness and Recreation*, 10, 145–51.
68. Arthur Carhart to J. Wesley White, 15 December 1964, and White to Carhart, 24 February 1965, both in "Carhart-Miscellaneous," box 15, USFS, IRRC. Carhart agreed with barring roads from the canoe country but labeled the BWCA an extremist measure, remarking, "I have not too much patience with the far-out wilderness group now rushing in to shout about making this a wilderness area without the sound of an axe or outboard motor." Backes, *Canoe Country*, 55–67. Backes describes Carhart's views on wilderness as "somewhat closer to those of northeastern Minnesota tourist promoters than to those held by leading wilderness proponents."
69. Arthur Carhart to William Vogt, 3 November 1964, and A. W. Greeley to Carhart, 20 November 1964, both in "Carhart-Miscellaneous," box 15, USFS, IRRC.
70. Report to U.S. Secretary of Agriculture by Boundary Waters Canoe Area Review Committee (Selke Report), "Subject Files, BWCA (2), George A. Selke Report, 15 December 1964," box 3, Presidents Quetico-Superior Committee Collection, MHS. For a BWCA chronological history, see http://www.friends-bwca.org/about/history/ (accessed 4 August 2011).
71. Address by John Smrekar, 22 May 1964, University of Minnesota, "Friends of the Wilderness," box 15, USFS, IRRC; Address by William H. Magie, 22 May 1964, University of Minnesota, "Friends of the Wilderness," box 15, USFS, IRRC.
72. Lucas, "Wilderness Perception and Use," 396.
73. John J. Chelesnik Letter to the *Ely Echo* editor, 26 September 1973, folder 3, "Newspaper Clippings and Magazine Articles, 1960–73," box 6, QSC, MHS; Proescholdt, Rapson, and Heinselman, *Troubled Waters*.
74. On the 1978 act, see http://www.friends-bwca.org/about/history/ (accessed 4 August 2011).

75. Bryan Cathcart to G. C. Wardrope, 17 January 1957, folder 4.19, "Memos-Minister 1956," box 106, RG 5-36, Correspondence of the Director of the Publicity Branch of the Department of Travel and Publicity, AO.
76. "Saving the Porcupine Mountains—Again and Again," *Michigan Environmental Report* 20 (October 2002).
77. U.S. Department of the Interior, National Park Service, *Record of Decision, Wilderness Study Final Environmental Impact Statement, Apostle Islands National Lakeshore, Wisconsin*, available online at www.nps.gov/apis; Stegner to Pesonen, 3 December 1960. On rewilding, see Cronon, "The Riddle of the Apostle Islands"; Cronon, "The Trouble with Wilderness, or, Getting Back to the Wrong Nature"; Feldman, *A Storied Wilderness.*
78. Nesper, *The Walleye War*, 45–105; Doherty, *Disputed Waters*; Nesper and Schendler, "The Politics of Cultural Revitalization and Intertribal Resource Management." Great Lakes Indian Fish and Wildlife Commission, "Ojibwe Treaty Rights," http://www.glifwc.org/TreatyRights/treatyrights.html (accessed 20 June 2011).
79. Explore Minnesota website, http://www.exploreminnesota.com (accessed 4 August 2011); "2002 Spring/Summer Seasonal Survey," Minnesota Office of Tourism, Minnesota Department of Trade and Economic Development website, http://www.dted.state.mn.us/04x03f.asp (accessed 7 July 2004). To view cached web pages from 2004, search the Internet Archive Wayback Machine: http://www.archive.org/.
80. Wisconsin Department of Tourism website, http://www.travelwisconsin.com (accessed 4 August 2011); Travel Wisconsin, "Travel Tracker—Who's Visiting Wisconsin Historic Sites?," http://agency.travelwisconsin.com/Research/MarketResearch_Active/historicsites2.shtm (accessed 7 July 2004); Wisconsin Department of Natural Resources website, "Boating in Wisconsin," http://www.dnr.state.wi.us/org/es/enforcement/safety/boatsaf.htm (accessed 7 July 2004). Alan Solomon, "The Lure of the North Woods," *Chicago Tribune*, 25 July 2004.
81. 2007 Wisconsin Travel Guide, http://comevisitwisconsin.com/pdf/2007_TRAVEL_GUIDE.pdf; Travel Wisconsin website, http://www.travelwisconsin.com (accessed 4 August 2011). Information comes from the main page and additional destination pages.
82. "Michigan's Hidden Treasures," http://travelmichigannews.org (accessed 7 July 2004); "Higher Gas Prices—Another Reason to Travel Michigan," http://travel.michigan.org (accessed 7 July 2004); "Pure Michigan," http://www.michigan.org/ (accessed 4 August 2011).
83. "Senator Carl Levin Announces Quincy Smelter Community Open House," 20 July 2009, http://www.epa.gov/Region5/cleanup/torchlake/index.htm (accessed 11 March 2012).

Bibliography

Unpublished Primary Sources

BENTLEY HISTORICAL LIBRARY, UNIVERSITY OF MICHIGAN, ANN ARBOR, MICHIGAN (BHL)

Bonifas Family Papers
Gordon Charles Papers
Edward C. Crafts Papers
James Oliver Curwood Papers
Samuel T. Dana Papers
Detroit News. Isle Royale Papers
Ben East Papers
East Michigan Tourist Association, Assorted Publications
Charles Follo Papers
Douglas Fulton Papers
Charles W. Garfield Papers
E. Genevieve Gillette Papers
Walter E. Hastings Papers
Albert Sidney Hazzard Papers
Paul A. Herbert Papers
Paul Herbert interview with Harry Gaines
Victor F. Lemmer Collection
Parrish S. Lovejoy Papers
Herman Lunden Papers
William Mershon Papers
Michigan Natural Areas Council Collection
Michigan United Conservation Clubs Records
Chase S. Osborn Papers
Penrod/Hiawatha Company, Records, 1950–97
Rood Family Papers
Filibert Roth Papers
Papers of Arthur William Stace, 1875–1950
Harold Titus Papers
Jack Van Coevering Papers
Frederick Wheeler Papers
G. Mennen Williams Papers
Jean Worth Papers
Leigh Jarvis Young Papers

COPPER COUNTRY HISTORICAL COLLECTIONS, MICHIGAN TECHNOLOGICAL UNIVERSITY, HOUGHTON, MICHIGAN (CCHC)

Calumet and Hecla Mining Companies Collection
Ben Chynowyth Collection
Copper Country Historical Collections Clippings Files
Grover Dillman Papers
Kenneth Dorman Papers
Records of Keweenaw County-Houghton County Road Commission
Keweenaw Historical Society Collection
Harold Putnam Collection

HENRY FORD MUSEUM AND GREENFIELD VILLAGE RESEARCH CENTER, DEARBORN, MICHIGAN

General Postcard Collection
Idlewild: Michigan's Harlem Renaissance Booklet
Travel Literature Collection

IRON RANGE RESEARCH CENTER, CHISHOLM, MINNESOTA (IRRC)

Chippewa National Forest Collection
City of Ely Records
Clippings Files
Ely Oral History Project
U.S. Forest Service Collection

LIBRARY OF MICHIGAN, LANSING, MICHIGAN

Pamphlet Collection and Vertical Files

MICHIGAN STATE UNIVERSITY, UNIVERSITY ARCHIVES AND HISTORICAL COLLECTIONS, EAST LANSING, MICHIGAN (MSU)

Edward C. Prophet Papers

MINNESOTA HISTORICAL SOCIETY, ST. PAUL, MINNESOTA (MHS)

G. C. Carlson, "History and Growth of the Tourist Business on Lake Vermilion," 1926
Collection of Conservation Printed Matter from Minnesota Organizations
Merril K. Cragun Papers, 1934–86
Roy E. Dunn Papers
Economic Development Department, Tourism Bureau, Public Information Division, Correspondence, 1947–54
Friends of the Wilderness Papers
Gooseberry Gatherings
Gunflint Gossips
Itasca State Park Guest Registers
Itasca State Park Oral History Project
Izaak Walton League Duluth Chapter Records
Emily Jensen Diary
Matthias Koll Papers
George Kratoska Papers
Minnesota Department of Conservation Records
Minnesota Department of Economic Development Records
Minnesota Emergency Conservation Committee Papers

Minnesota Environmental Issues Oral History Project
Minnesota Greatest Generation Oral History Project
Minnesota Resort Industry Oral History Project
Ernest C. Oberholtzer Papers
Ernest C. Oberholtzer Oral History Interviews
Sigurd F. Olson Papers
President's Quetico-Superior Committee Records
Quetico-Superior Council Records
Records of Ruttger Resorts
St. Louis County Club and Farm Bureau Association Papers, 1915–62
Fred Shadduck Diary
Sutherland Family Cabin Diary
Dawn E. Tornquist, Camp du Nord Scrapbook
Sam Traubshaw Photo Album
United States, Forest Service, Superior National Forest Records
Carl Warmington Papers
Chester Wilson Papers

NATIONAL ARCHIVES AND RECORDS ADMINISTRATION, CHICAGO, ILLINOIS (NARA-GL)

RG 75: Records of the Bureau of Indian Affairs, 1793–1989, Department of the Interior

NEWBERRY LIBRARY, SPECIAL COLLECTIONS, CHICAGO

Chicago, Burlington, and Quincy Railroad Company Collection
Rand McNally and Co. Map Collection

ARCHIVES OF ONTARIO, TORONTO, ONTARIO (AO)

Administrative Files of the Deputy Minister of Travel and Publicity
Correspondence of the Deputy Minister and Minister of Travel and Publicity
Correspondence of the Director of the Publicity Branch of the Department of Travel and Publicity Correspondence of the Minister of Tourism and Information
Department of Travel and Publicity Development Branch Records
Department of Travel and Publicity Reports and Publications
Deputy Minister of Travel and Publicity's United States Editors' Goodwill Tour of Ontario Correspondence
Development Branch Files of the Deputy Minister of Travel and Publicity
Dominion-Provincial Tourist Conferences Correspondence
Films of the United States Editors' Goodwill Tours of Ontario
Information Branch Files of the Deputy Minister of Travel and Publicity
Interdepartmental Correspondence of the Deputy Minister of Travel and Publicity
News releases, Speeches, and Broadcasts of the Minister of Tourism and Information
Records of the Director of the Publicity Branch of the Department of Tourism and Information
Tourism Development Branch Records
Tourism Promotion Photographs
Tourist Establishment Files
United States Correspondence of the Deputy Minister of Travel and Publicity
United States Editors' Goodwill Tour of Ontario Albums

WALTER REUTHER LIBRARY, WAYNE STATE UNIVERSITY, DETROIT, MICHIGAN

Olga Madar Collection
UAW Recreation Department Collection

STATE ARCHIVES OF MICHIGAN, LANSING, MICHIGAN (SAM)

East Michigan Tourist Association Papers, RG 77-1
Natural Resources Department Parks Division, Porcupine Mountains, 1925–74, RG94-106
Records of the Department of Commerce-Tourist Bureau, RG 77-96
Records of the Department of Conservation, Being the Records of the Michigan Tourist Council, RG 68-106
Records of the Department of Conservation, Executive Section, RG66-2-A
Records of the Executive Office, Harry Kelly, Governor, RG 42
Upper Peninsula Travel and Recreation Association Papers, RG79-74
West Michigan Tourist Association Papers RG80-94

WISCONSIN HISTORICAL SOCIETY ARCHIVES, MADISON, WISCONSIN (WHS)

William Aberg Papers
Board of Health, Hotel and Restaurant Index to Applications, Inspection Reports, and Fee Payments, 1932–43
John Serenus Bordner Papers
Campo Fiesta Collection
Frank Graass Collection
C. L. Harrington Papers
G. Arthur Johnson Collection
Oral History Interview with Norman Johnson
Lyle Kingston Papers
Joseph Mercedes Papers
Lewis Nagler Papers
Oral History Interview with Jennie Neubauer
Northern Great Lakes Area Council
Raymond Peabody Papers
Raymond J. Penn Papers
Alonzo Pond Papers
Ross' Teal Lake Lodge Collection
Ross' Teal Lake Lodge Photo Collection
Ernest Swift Papers
George Wehrwein Papers
Wisconsin Conservation Commission, Fred Fisher Papers
Wisconsin Conservation Department Photographic Record
Wisconsin Conservation Department Subject Files
Wisconsin Division of Economic Development Bureau of Commercial Recreation
Wisconsin Land Economic Inventory, Department of Agriculture Field Maps
Anthony Wise Collection

WISCONSIN HISTORICAL SOCIETY LIBRARY, MADISON, WISCONSIN

Pamphlet Collection

WISCONSIN HISTORICAL SOCIETY, ASHLAND AREA RESEARCH CENTER, ASHLAND, WISCONSIN (WHS-ARC)

Camp Manito-wish Collection
Camp Minocqua Records
Grant Cook Papers
J. Seymour Currey Collection
Mabel Sayner DeWitt Papers
Dillman's Sand Lake Lodge Records
Walter S. Fisher Papers
Four County Development Group Papers
Joseph F. Handlos Papers
Hayward Lakes Resort Association Records
Land O'Lakes Chamber of Commerce Papers
Herbert and Bert Warner Papers

WISCONSIN HISTORICAL SOCIETY, RESEARCH CENTER, STEVENS POINT, WISCONSIN

Philip A. MacDonald Papers
John Wesley White Papers

Published Sources

Akerman, James R. "Blazing a Well-Worn Path: Cartographic Commercialism, Highway Promotion, and Automobile Tourism in the United States, 1880–1930." *Cartographica* 30 (Spring 1993): 10–19.

———. "Selling Maps, Selling Highways: Rand McNally's 'Blazed Trails' Program." *Imago Mundi* 45 (1993): 77–89.

Alanen, Arnold R. *A Field Guide to the Architecture and Landscapes of Northeastern Minnesota*. Madison: Department of Landscape Architecture, University of Wisconsin Madison, 2000.

Allen, Donna. *Fringe Benefits: Wages or Social Obligation? An Analysis with Historical Perspectives from Paid Vacations*. Ithaca, N.Y.: Cornell University Press, 1964.

American Automobile Association. *Guide to Minnesota, Wisconsin, The Dakotas*. Washington, D.C.: American Automobile Association, 1943.

American Federation of Labor-Congress of Industrial Organizations (AFL-CIO). *American Federation of Labor: History, Encyclopedia, and Reference Book*. Washington, D.C.: AFL-CIO, 1960.

Aron, Cindy. *Working at Play: A History of Vacations in the United States*. New York: Oxford University Press, 1999.

Automobile Club of Michigan. *Upper Peninsula of Michigan as Seen by the Old AAA Traveler*. Detroit: Automobile Club of Michigan, 1940.

Auto Road Map Company. *Sportsman's and Automobile Map of the Upper Peninsula of Michigan*. Battle Creek: Auto Road Map Company, 1928.

Backes, David. *Canoe Country: An Embattled Wilderness*. Minocqua: Northword Press, 1991.

———. "Wilderness Visions: Arthur Carhart's 1922 Proposal for the Quetico Superior Wilderness." *Forest & Conservation History* 35 (1991): 128–37.

———, ed. *Spirit of the North: The Quotable Sigurd F. Olson*. Minneapolis and London: University of Minnesota Press, 2004.

Backes, David, and Sigurd F. Olson, eds. *The Meaning of Wilderness: Essential Articles and Speeches*. Minneapolis: University of Minnesota Press, 2001.

Baker-Seaton Realty Co. *Grandview Lodge, Gull Lake, Nisswa Minnesota*. Minneapolis: Baker-Seaton Realty Co., [1916?].

Baldwin, Donald N. *The Quiet Revolution: Grass Roots of Today's Wilderness Preservation Movement*. Boulder, Colo.: Pruett Publishing Company, 1972.

Balsam's. *The Balsams in the Big North Woods: In the Heart of America's Summer Playground*. Eagle River, Wis.: The Balsams, n.d.

Baranowski, Shelley, and Ellen Furlough, eds. *Being Elsewhere: Tourism, Consumer Culture, and Modern Identity in Modern Europe and North America*. Ann Arbor: University of Michigan Press, 2001.

Barnett, Le Roy. "Paper Trails: The Michigan Highway Map." *Michigan History* 83 (Nov./Dec. 1999): 18–23.

Barron, Hal S. *Mixed Harvest: The Second Great Transformation in the Rural North, 1870–1930*. Chapel Hill: University of North Carolina Press, 1997.

Bawden, Timothy. "Reinventing the Frontier: Tourism, Nature, and Environmental Change in Northern Wisconsin, 1880–1930." Ph.D. diss., University of Wisconsin-Madison, 2001.

Belasco, Warren. *Americans on the Road: From Autocamp to Motel, 1910–1945*. Cambridge, Mass.: MIT Press, 1979.

Bennett, James O'Donnell. *West Michigan's Flaming Forests*. Grand Rapids: West Michigan Tourist and Resort Association, 1935.

Bent's Camp. *Bent's Camp: A North Wisconsin Summer Resort, in the Heart of the Lake Region, the Recreational Grounds of the Middle West, Land O' Lakes, Wisconsin*. Vilas County, Wis.: The Camp, n.d.

Berger, Michael L. *The Devil Wagon in God's Country: The Automobile and Social Change in Rural America, 1893–1929*. Hamden, Conn.: Archon Books, 1979.

Birchwood Lodge. *Gertrude Doyle's Birchwood Lodge, Rhinelander, Wisconsin*. Rhinelander: The Lodge, [1940?].

Blackford, Mansel G. *Fragile Paradise: The Impact of Tourism on Maui, 1959–2000*. Lawrence: University Press of Kansas, 2001.

Blackmar, Elizabeth. "Going to the Mountains: A Social History." In *Resorts of the Catskills*, ed. Elizabeth Blackmar, Elizabeth Cromley, and John Margolies, 71–99. New York: St. Martins, 1978.

Blatchford Nick and Odell Rice, eds. *Camp Wipigaki: The First Fifty Years, A Collection of Recollections*. N.p.: R. R. Donnelley & Sons Co., 1972.

Bogue, Margaret Beattie. *Fishing the Great Lakes: An Environmental History, 1783–1933*. Madison: University of Wisconsin Press, 2000.

Bold, Christine. *The WPA Guides: Mapping America*. Jackson: University Press of Mississippi, 1999.

Boorstin, Daniel J. *The Image: A Guide to Pseudo-Events in America*. New York: Harper and Row, 1961.

Borchert, John, and Donald P. Yeager. *Atlas of Minnesota Resources and Settlement*. St. Paul: Minnesota State Planning Agency, 1968.

Boulder Junction Chamber of Commerce, *Boulder Junction, World's Greatest Musky Waters*. Boulder Junction Chamber of Commerce, Wis., [1940?].

B. F. Bowen and Co. *Bowen's Automobile and Sportsmen's Guide*. Indianapolis: B. F. Bowen and Co., 1916.

Breezy Point. *Fawcett's Breezy Point*. Pequot Lakes, Minn.: The Resort, [1924?].

Bromberg, Nicolette. *Wisconsin Then and Now: The Wisconsin Sesquicentennial Rephotography Project*. Madison: University of Wisconsin Press, 2001.

Brosnan, Kathleen A. *Uniting Mountain and Plain: Cities, Law, and Environmental Change along the Front Range*. Albuquerque: University of New Mexico Press, 2002.

Brown, Dona. *Inventing New England: Regional Tourism in the Nineteenth Century*. Washington, D.C.: Smithsonian Press, 1995.

Burlowe, Raleigh. "Changing Land Use and Policies: The Lake States." In *The Great Lakes Forest: An Environmental and Social History*, ed. Susan. L. Flader, 156–76. Minneapolis: University of Minnesota Press, 1983.

Burntside Lodge. *Burntside Lodge*. Ely: The Lodge, [1920?].

Call of the Open: Annual Vacation Section. St. Paul: *St. Paul Pioneer Press*, 1932, 1934, 1936, and 1939.

Callicott, J. Baird, and Michael P. Nelson, eds. *The Great New Wilderness Debate: An Expansive Collection of Writings Defining Wilderness from John Muir to Gary Snyder*. Athens: University of Georgia Press, 1998.

Carhart, Arthur. "Recreation in the Forests." *American Forestry* 26 (May 1920): 268–72.

———. "Vacation Opportunities in Your National Forests." *American Forestry* 26 (September 1920): 549–57.

———. "What Is Recreation's Next Step?" *American Forestry* 26 (September 1920): 593– 98.

———."Minimum Requirements in Recreation." *American Forestry* 28 (January 1922): 31–36.

———. "Producing the Recreation Commodity." *American Forestry* 28 (April 1922): 219–24.

———. "What Do Tourists Want?" *American Forestry* 29 (April 1923): 210–14.

Carner, Bettyann. "Rural Land Zoning in Vilas County, Wisconsin, 1933–1954—A Case History." Master's thesis, University of Chicago, 1955.

Carstensen, Vernon. *Farms or Forests: Evolution of a State Land Policy for Northern Wisconsin, 1850–1932*. Madison: Department of Agricultural Journalism, University of Wisconsin-Madison, 1984.

Cascade Lodge. *Cascade Lodge, Cascade State Park*. Grand Marais, Minn.: The Lodge, [1930?].

Cayton, Andrew R. L., and Susan E. Gray, eds. *The American Midwest: Essays on Regional History*. Bloomington: Indiana University Press, 2001.

Cayton, Andrew R. L., and Peter Onuf. *The Midwest and the Nation: Rethinking the History of an American Region*. Bloomington: Indiana University Press, 1990.

Chiang, Connie Y. *Shaping the Shoreline: Fisheries and Tourism on the Monterey Coast*. Seattle: University of Washington Press, 2008.

Chiarappa, Michael J., and Kristin Szylvian, eds. *Fish for All: An Oral History of Multiple Claims and Divided Sentiment on Lake Michigan*. East Lansing: Michigan State University Press, 2003.

Chicago and North Western Railway. *Hints to the Tourist: Where to Go, What It Costs, in the Enchanted Summerland*. Chicago: Rand McNally and Co., 1888.

———. *Lakes and Resorts of Northwest*. Chicago: Chicago and North Western Railway Passenger Dept., 1912.

———. *Summer Outings: Wisconsin, Michigan*. Chicago: Chicago and North Western Line, 1926.

Chicago Daily News Guide to Summer Resorts. Chicago: *Chicago Daily News*, 1921.

Chicago Great Western Railroad. *The Minnesota Lakes: The Land of Sky Blue Water*. Chicago: The Company, 1921.

Chicago, Milwaukee and St. Paul Railway Company. *Northern Wisconsin Lake Region, the Milwaukee Road*. Chicago: Chicago, Milwaukee and St. Paul Railway, n.d.

Chicago Motor Club. *Map of Northern Wisconsin Lakes Region*. Chicago: H. M. Gousha Co., 1939.

Clark, James I. "Cutover Problems: Colonization, Depression, Reforestation." *Chronicles of Wisconsin* 13 (1956): 3–20.

Clements, Kendrick A. "Herbert Hoover and Conservation, 1921–33." *American Historical Review* 89 (1984): 67–88.

———. *Hoover, Conservation, and Consumerism: Engineering the Good Life*. Lawrence: University Press of Kansas, 2000.

Cloverland Tourist's Guide. Menominee, Mich.: *Herald-Leader*, 1931.

Cocks, Catherine. *Doing the Town: The Rise of Urban Tourism in the United States, 1850–1915*. Berkeley: University of California Press, 2001.

Cohen, Lizabeth. *A Consumers' Republic: The Politics of Mass Consumption in Postwar America*. New York: Alfred A. Knopf, 2003.

———. *Making a New Deal: Industrial Workers in Chicago, 1919–1939*. Cambridge: Cambridge University Press, 1990.

Coleman, Annie Gilbert. *Ski Style: Sport and Culture in the Rockies*. Lawrence: University Press of Kansas, 2004.

Conard, Rebecca. *Places of Quiet Beauty: Parks, Preserves, and Environmentalism*. Iowa City: University of Iowa Press, 1997.

Coppe, Ivan. "Minnesota Opens Wide Her Gates: Ten Thousand Lakes Association Organized to Make Tourists Welcome." *Western Magazine* 11 (May 1918): 170–73.

Copper Country Vacationist League. *Ke-Wee-Naw Land in Lake Superior*. Houghton, Mich.: Copper Country Vacationist League, 1936–37.

———. *The Copper Country of Michigan: Keweenawland-Isle Royale*. Houghton, Mich.: Copper Country Vacationist League, 1938–1942, 1945, 1948.

———. *We Fell in Love with Keweenawland in Michigan's Famous Copper Country: Gateway to Isle Royale National Park*. Houghton, Mich.: Copper Country Vacationist League, 1956.

Cowie, Jefferson, and Joseph Heathcott, eds. *Beyond the Ruins: The Meanings of Deindustrialization*. Ithaca, N.Y.: ILR Press, 2003.

Crawford Lodge, *Crawford Lodge on Beautiful Lake GeGoKa*. Isabella, Minn.: S.V. Holmes Print. Co., [1921?].

Cronon, William. *Nature's Metropolis: Chicago and the Great West*. New York: W. W. Norton, 1991.

———. "The Trouble with Wilderness, or, Getting Back to the Wrong Nature." In *Uncommon Ground: Toward Reinventing Nature*, ed. William Cronon, 69–90. New York: W. W. Norton, 1995.

———. "The Riddle of the Apostle Islands." *Orion* (May/June 2003): 36–42.

———, ed. *Uncommon Ground: Toward Reinventing Nature*. New York: W. W. Norton, 1995.

Cross, Gary. *Time and Money: The Making of Consumer Culture*. London and New York: Routledge, 1993.

Culver, Lawrence. *The Frontier of Leisure: Southern California and the Shaping of Modern America*. New York: Oxford University Press, 2010.

Curtis, Kent. "Greening Anaconda: EPA, ARCO, and the Politics of Space in Postindustrial Montana." In *Beyond the Ruins: The Meanings of Deindustrialization*, ed. Jefferson Cowie and Joseph Heathcott, 91–111. Ithaca, N.Y.: Cornell University Press, 2003.

Dahlquist, Carol. *Then and Now, Camp du Nord: A Brief History*. Minnesota, 1978.

Dana, Samuel Trask. *Forest and Range Policy: Its Development in the United States*. New York: McGraw-Hill, 1956.

Danbom, David B. *Born in the Country: A History of Rural America*. Baltimore: Johns Hopkins University Press, 1995.

Danziger, Edmund J., Jr. *The Chippewas of Lake Superior*. Norman: University of Oklahoma Press, 1978.

Davis, Eleanor. *Recent Trends in Vacation Policies for Wage Earners*. Princeton, N.J.: Industrial Relations Section, Princeton University, 1935.

Davis, Mark. "Northern Choices: Rural Forest County in the 1920s," *Wisconsin Magazine of History* 79 (Autumn 1995): 3–31.

———. "Northern Choices: Rural Forest County in the 1920s," *Wisconsin Magazine of History* 79 (Winter 1995–96): 109–38.

———. "An Empire in Waiting: Northern Wisconsin's Lake Country, 1880–1940." Ph.D. diss., University of Wisconsin-Madison, 1997.

Dawson, Michael. *Selling British Columbia: Tourism and Consumer Culture, 1890–1970*. Vancouver: UBC Press, 2004.

Deloria, Philip J. *Playing Indian*. New Haven, Conn.: Yale University Press, 1998.

———. *Indians in Unexpected Places*. Lawrence: University Press of Kansas, 2004.

Dempsey, Dave. "'The Lady of the Parks,' Genevieve Gillette," *Michigan History* 85 (September/October 2001): 12–27.

———. *Ruin and Recovery: Michigan's Rise as a Conservation Leader*. Ann Arbor: University of Michigan Press, 2001.

DeSantis, Hugh. "The Democratization of Travel: The Travel Agent in American History." *Journal of American Culture* 1 (1978): 1–19.

Desmond, Jane. *Staging Tourism: Bodies on Display from Waikiki to Sea World*. Chicago: University of Chicago Press, 1999.

Detroit Lakes Civic and Commerce Association. *Detroit Lakes, Minnesota: 412 Lakes within 25 Miles*. Detroit Lakes: Civic & Commerce Association, 1937.

DeVisser, John, and Judy Thompson Ross. *Summer Cottages*. Toronto: Stoddart, 1991.

Dickinson and Gillespie, Inc., *Gull Lake Shores: The Land of Sunshine and Shade, Sand Beaches and Water*. Minneapolis: Dickinson and Gillespie, Inc., [1920?].

Dilworth, Leah. *Imagining Indians in the Southwest*. Washington, D.C.: Smithsonian Press, 1996.

Dispatch Printing Company Outing Department, *Outing Book*. *St. Paul Dispatch* and *St. Paul Pioneer Press*, 1915.

Doherty, Robert. *Disputed Waters: Native Americans and the Great Lakes Fishery*. Lexington: University Press of Kentucky, 1990.

Donnelly, Joseph M., ed. *Cloverland, the Upper Peninsula of Michigan: Its Romantic Past, Prosperous Present, Brilliant Future*. Ontonagon, Mich., 1914.

Doucette, Pauline, et al. *Oneida County: Centennial History Edition, 1887–1987*. Oneida County, Wis.: Oneida County Board of Supervisors, 1987.

Douglas Lodge. *Douglas Lodge, Itasca State Park: Minnesota's Own*. Minnesota: The Lodge, [1930?].

Drache, Hiram M. *Taming the Wilderness: The Northern Border Country, 1910–1939*. Danville, Ill.: Interstate Publishers, 1992.

Dubinsky, Karen. *Second Greatest Disappointment: Honeymooning and Tourism at Niagara Falls*. New Brunswick, N.J.: Rutgers University Press, 1999.

Duke, Richard D. *Some Notes on Planning for Tourism in Michigan's Upper Peninsula*. East Lansing: Institute for Community Development and Services, Michigan State University, 1962.

Duluth & Iron Range Railroad Company. *Lakes and Streams of Northern Minnesota*. Duluth: Duluth & Iron Range Railroad Company, 1914.

———. *The Playground of a Nation in the Arrowhead Country: Via the Vermilion Route*. Duluth: Duluth & Iron Range Railroad Company, 1926.

Dunn, Michael, III. *Wisconsin's Northwoods: Vilas and Oneida Counties*. Madison: Tamarack Press, 1978.

East, Dennis, II. "Water Power and Forestry in Wisconsin: Issues of Conservation, 1890–1915." Ph.D. diss., University of Wisconsin-Madison, 1971.

East Michigan Tourist Association. *East Michigan Blue Book*. Bay City: East Michigan Tourist Association, 1937, 1939, 1940, 1942–45.

——. *East Michigan Tourist Guide*. Bay City: East Michigan Tourist Association, 1932 and 1934.

Ebasco Services Incorporated and Michigan Economic Development Commission. *Engineering Study of the Economic Resources of the Michigan Upper Peninsula*. New York: Ebasco Services, Inc., 1953.

Eckert, Kathryn Bishop. *Buildings of Michigan*. New York: Oxford University Press, 1993.

Elliott, Kennell M. *History of the Nicolet National Forest, 1928–1976*. Washington, D.C.: Forest Service, U.S. Department of Agriculture, 1977.

Ely, Richard T., and George S. Wehrwein. *Land Economics*. New York: MacMillan Co., 1940.

Ely Commercial Club. *Ely, Minnesota, The Playground of a Nation*. Ely: The Club, 1932.

——. *Ely: Where the Wilderness Begins, Heart of Superior National Forest, Minnesota Arrowhead Country*. Ely: The Club, 1940.

Espeseth, Edmund C. "Lodestar in the Northland." *Wisconsin Magazine of History* 36 (1952): 23–27, 56.

——. "Early Vilas County—Cradle of an Industry." *Wisconsin Magazine of History* 37 (1953): 27–34, 51–54.

Feldman, James. *A Storied Wilderness: Rewilding the Apostle Islands*. Seattle: University of Washington Press, 2011.

——. "The View from Sand Island: Reconsidering the Peripheral Economy, 1880–1940." *Western Historical Quarterly* 35 (Autumn 2004): 285–308.

Fenton, John H. *Midwest Politics*. New York: Holt, Rinehart and Winston, 1966.

Fine, Isadore. *Wisconsin Vacation Recreation Papers*. Madison: University of Wisconsin School of Commerce, Bureau of Business Research and Service, 1960.

Fine, Isadore V., and E. E. Werner. *The Wisconsin Vacationer*. Madison: University of Wisconsin School of Commerce, Bureau of Business Research and Service, 1960.

Fine, Isadore V., Ralph B. Hovind, and Philip H. Lewis Jr. *The Lake Superior Region Recreational Potential: Preliminary Report*. Madison: Wisconsin Department of Resource Development, 1962.

Fine, Lisa M. "Rights of Men, Rites of Passage: Hunting and Masculinity at REO Motors of Lansing, Michigan, 1945–1975." *Journal of Social History* (2000): 805–23.

——. *The Story of Reo Joe: Work, Kin, and Community in Autotown, U.S.A*. Philadelphia: Temple University Press, 2004.

Flader, Susan L. *Thinking Like a Mountain: Aldo Leopold and the Evolution of an Ecological Attitude toward Deer, Wolves, and Forests*. Columbia: University of Missouri Press, 1974.

——, ed. *The Great Lakes Forest: An Environmental and Social History*. Minneapolis: University of Minnesota Press, 1983.

Flader, Susan L., and J. Baird Callicott, eds. *The River of the Mother of God and Other Essays by Aldo Leopold*. Madison: University of Wisconsin Press, 1991.

Flink, James J. *The Car Culture*. Cambridge, Mass.: MIT Press, 1976.

——. *The Automobile Age*. Cambridge, Mass.: MIT Press, 1988.

Foster, Mark S. "In the Face of 'Jim Crow': Prosperous Blacks and Vacations, Travel, and Outdoor Leisure, 1890–1945." *Journal of Negro History* 84 (1999): 130–49.

Fox, Richard, and T. J. Jackson Lears, eds. *Culture of Consumption*. New York: Pantheon, 1983.

Francaviglia, Richard V. *Hard Places: Reading the Landscape of America's Historic Mining Districts*. Iowa City: University of Iowa Press, 1991.

Franklin, Dixie Lee. "Cloverland, My Cloverland." In *A Most Superior Land: Life in the Upper Peninsula of Michigan*, comp. David M. Frimodig, 84–91. Lansing, Mich.: Two Peninsula Press, 1983.

Frimodig, David M., comp. *A Most Superior Land: Life in the Upper Peninsula of Michigan*. Lansing, Mich.: Two Peninsula Press, 1983.

Gale, Kendra, and Thomas P. Gale. *Isle Royale: A Photographic History*. Houghton, Mich.: Isle Royale Natural History Association, 1995.

Gawboy, Carl, Aguar, Jyring & Whiteman, and U.S. Bureau of Indian Affairs. *Tourist and Recreational Resources, Lac du Flambeau Indian Reservation, Wisconsin*. Duluth: The Firm, 1964.

———. *Tourist and Recreational Resources, Lac Court Oreilles Indian Reservation, Wisconsin*. Duluth: The Firm, 1965.

———. *Tourist and Recreational Resources, Wisconsin Indian Reservations*. Duluth: The Firm, 1965.

Geismar, Leo M. *Upper Peninsula of Michigan*. Marquette, Mich.: Upper Peninsula Development Bureau, 1920.

Glad, Paul W. *The History of Wisconsin: War, a New Era, and Depression, 1914–1940*. Madison: State Historical Society of Wisconsin, 1990.

Goc, Michael J. *Reflections of Lac du Flambeau: An Illustrated History of Lac du Flambeau, Wisconsin, 1745–1995*. Friendship, Wis.: New Past Press, 1995.

Goin, Peter, and Elizabeth Raymond. "Recycled Landscapes: Mining's Legacies in the Mesabi Iron Range." In *Technologies of Landscape: From Reaping to Recycling*, ed. David Nye, 267–83. Amherst: University of Massachusetts Press, 1999.

Gottlieb, Robert. *Forcing the Spring: The Transformation of the American Environmental Movement*. Washington, D.C.: Island Press, 1993.

Gough, Robert J. "Richard T. Ely and the Development of the Wisconsin Cutover." *Wisconsin Magazine of History* 75: 1 (1991): 3–38.

———. *Farming the Cutover: A Social History of Northern Wisconsin, 1900–1940*. Lawrence: University Press of Kansas, 1997.

———. "Defining a Region: Logging, Farming, and Tourism in Northern Wisconsin, 1870–1940." *Voyageur* 24: 1 (Summer/Fall 2007): 42–52.

Grand Marais Chamber of Commerce. *Come See: The Gunflint Trail*. Grand Marais: Chamber of Commerce, 1938.

Graves, Henry S. *A Policy of Forestry for the Nation*. Washington, D.C.: U.S. Department of Agriculture, Government Printing Office, 1918.

———. "A Crisis in National Recreation." *American Forestry* 26 (1920): 391–400.

Gregg, Sara M. *Managing the Mountains: Land Use Planning, the New Deal, and the Creation of a Federal Landscape in Appalachia*. New Haven, Conn.: Yale University Press, 2010.

Groves, Theodore. *Land of the Tamarack: Up-North Wisconsin*. Berkeley, Calif.: North Atlantic Books, 1986.

Gunn, Clare A. *Planning Better Vacation Accommodations*. East Lansing: Michigan State College, Cooperative Extension Service, Agricultural Experiment Station, 1952.

———. *A Study of Changes in Buildings for Tourists and Resorters in Michigan*. East Lansing: Michigan State College of Agriculture and Applied Science, 1952.

———. *Planning Winter Sports Areas*. East Lansing: Cooperative Extension Service, 1958.

Gunn, Clare A., and David J. Luck. *Winter Resorts in Michigan: A Survey and Appraisal*. East Lansing: Bureau of Business Research, Michigan State College, 1954.

Hackett, J. D. "Vacation with Pay for Factory Workers." *Survey* (1920): 626–27.

Hamilton, Charles F., ed. *Our Hiawatha Land*. Chicago: Lyons and Carnahan, 1940.

Harrington, C. L. "The Trail Ahead—How to Put Forestry in Wisconsin on a Sound Basis." *American Forestry* (December 1922): 712–15.

Harris, Neil. "On Vacation." In *Resorts of the Catskills*, ed. Elizabeth Blackmar, Elizabeth Cromley, and John Margolies, 101–8. New York: St. Martins, 1979.

Harrison, Blake. *The View from Vermont: Tourism and the Making of an American Rural Landscape*. Burlington, Vt.: University Press of New England, 2006.

Hart, John Fraser. "Resort Areas in Wisconsin." *Geographical Review* 74 (1982): 192–217.

———. *The Rural Landscape*. Baltimore: Johns Hopkins University Press, 1998.

Harvey, Mark. *A Symbol of Wilderness: Echo Park and the American Conservation Movement*. Albuquerque: University of New Mexico Press, 1994.

———. "Sound Politics: Wilderness, Recreation, and Motors in the Boundary Waters, 1945–1964." *Minnesota History* 58: 3 (Fall 2002): 130–45.

———. *Wilderness Forever: Howard Zahniser and the Path to the Wilderness Act*. Seattle: University of Washington Press, 2005.

Haswell, Susan O., and Arnold Alanen. "Colonizing the Cutover: Wisconsin's Progressive-Era Experiments in Rural Planning." *Landscape Journal* 14 (1995): 171–89.

Hays, Samuel P. *Conservation and the Gospel of Efficiency: The Progressive Conservation Movement, 1880–1920*. Cambridge, Mass.: Harvard University Press, 1959.

———. "Human Choice in the Great Lakes Wildlands." In *The Great Lakes Forest: An Environmental and Social History*, ed. Susan L. Flader, 295–318. Minneapolis: University of Minnesota Press, 1983.

———. "From the History of the City to the History of Urbanized Society." *Journal of Urban History* 19 (1993): 3–25.

Hedrick, Wilbur O. *Recreational Use of Northern Michigan Cutover Lands*. East Lansing: Michigan State College of Agriculture and Applied Science, Agricultural Experiment Station, 1934.

Heinen, Tom. "Hitting the Road for the *Journal*," *Once-A-Year Magazine*. Milwaukee: Milwaukee Press Club, 1998.

Henry, W. A. *Northern Wisconsin: A Hand-Book for the Homeseeker*. Madison: Democratic Printing Co., State Printer, 1896.

Heritage Research, Ltd., and Wisconsin Historical Society. *Historical/Architectural Resources Survey, Historic Resorts of Vilas County*. Menomonee Falls, Wis.: Heritage Research, 2004.

Higbie, Frank Tobias. *Indispensable Outcasts: Hobo Workers and Community in the American Midwest, 1880–1930*. Urbana: University of Illinois Press, 2003.

High, Steven. *Industrial Sunset: The Making of North America's Rust Belt, 1969–1984*. Toronto: University of Toronto Press, 2003.

Hirsch, Jerrold. *Portrait of America: A Cultural History of the Federal Writers' Project*. Chapel Hill: University of North Carolina Press, 2003.

Hirt, Paul W. *A Conspiracy of Optimism: Management of the National Forests since World War Two*. Lincoln: University of Nebraska Press, 1994.

Hoagland, Alison K. *Mine Towns: Buildings for Workers in Michigan's Copper Country*. University of Minnesota Press, 2010.

Holway, C. P. "How a State Publicity Campaign Popularized Conservation." *Public Opinion Quarterly* 1 (1937): 140–43.

———. *How to Profit from the Tourist Business*. Milwaukee: Jay Rathburn, 1949.

Horowitz, Daniel. *The Morality of Spending: Attitudes toward the Consumer Society in America, 1875–1940*. Baltimore: Johns Hopkins University Press, 1985.

Huffman, Thomas R. *Protectors of the Land and Water: Environmentalism in Wisconsin, 1961–1968*. Chapel Hill: University of North Carolina Press, 1994.

Hummon, David. "Tourist Worlds: Tourist Advertising, Ritual, and American Culture." *Sociological Quarterly* 29 (1988): 179–202.

"Industrial and Labor Conditions: Vacations with Pay for Wage Earners." *Monthly Labor Review* (1935): 1494–97.

In the Arrowhead Country of Northern Minnesota: Where Industry and Recreation Go Hand in Hand. Duluth, 1925.

IXL Creative. *Best of the Lure of the Land of Hiawatha: A 30s Compilation, Michigan's Upper Peninsula*. Hermansville, Mich.: IXL Creative, 1996.

Jackson, Kenneth. *Crabgrass Frontier: The Suburbanization of the United States*. New York: Oxford University Press, 1985.

Jacoby, Karl. "Class and Environmental History: Lessons from the 'War in the Adirondacks.'" *Environmental History* 2 (1997): 324–42.

———. *Crimes against Nature: Squatters, Poachers, Thieves, and the Hidden History of American Conservation*. Berkeley: University of California Press, 2001.

Jakle, John. *The Tourist: Travel in Twentieth-Century North America*. Lincoln: University of Nebraska Press, 1985.

Jamerson, William. *Winter Wonderland: Michigan's Golden Age of Skiing*. Traverse City, Mich.: Forgotten Films and Video, 1995. Videocassette.

Jasen, Patricia. *Wild Things: Nature, Culture, and Tourism in Ontario 1790–1914*. Toronto: University of Toronto Press, 1995.

Johnson, Benjamin Heber. "Conservation, Subsistence, and Class at the Birth of the Superior National Forest." *Environmental History* 4 (1999): 80–99.

Johnson, Hugh Albert. "Recreational Land Use Problems of the Highland Lake Region of Northern Wisconsin." Master's thesis, University of Wisconsin-Madison, 1941.

Johnson, Iven V. *Johnson's Weblake Resort: Along the Pines of Wisconsin, Welcomes You*. Danbury, Wis.: Iven V. Johnson, 1931.

Johnson, Robert. *Tour Guide of Minnesota*. St. Paul: Department of Business Research and Development, 1949.

Jones, George O., and Norman S. McVean. *History of Lincoln, Oneida and Vilas Counties Wisconsin*. Minneapolis: H. C. Cooper, Jr. & Co., 1924.

Judd, Richard W. "Reshaping Maine's Landscape: Rural Culture, Tourism, and Conservation, 1890–1929." *Journal of Forest History* 32 (1988): 180–90.

———. *Common Lands, Common People: The Origins of Conservation in Northern New England*. Cambridge, Mass.: Harvard University Press, 1997.

Kalt, Brian C. *Sixties Sandstorm: The Fight over Establishment of a Sleeping Bear Dunes National Lakeshore, 1961–1970*. East Lansing: Michigan State University Press, 2001.

Karamanski, Theodore J. *Deep Woods Frontier: A History of Logging in Michigan*. Detroit: Wayne State University Press, 1989.

———. *The Pictured Rocks: An Administrative History of Pictured Rocks National Lakeshore*. Omaha: Midwest Regional Office, U.S. Department of the Interior, National Park Service, 1995.

Kates, James. *Planning a Wilderness: Regenerating the Great Lakes Cutover Region*. Minneapolis: University of Minnesota Press, 2001.

Klingle, Matthew. "Spaces of Consumption in Environmental History." *History and Theory* 42 (2003).

Kneipp, L. F. "Forest Recreation Comes of Age." *American Forests and Forest Life* 36 (July 1930): 415–18.

———. "Recreational Use of the National Forests." *Journal of Forestry* 28 (1930): 618–25.

Koch, John N. "Touching Every Forty: John Bordner and the Wisconsin Land Economic Inventory." *Wisconsin Magazine of History* 89: 4 (2005–06): 14–25.

Korn, Claire. *Yesterday through Tomorrow: Michigan State Parks*. East Lansing: Michigan State University Press, 1989.

Koshar, Rudy "'What Ought to Be Seen': Tourists' Guidebooks and National Identities in Modern Germany and Europe." *Journal of Contemporary History* 33 (1998): 323–40.

Krog, Carl E. "'Organizing the Production of Leisure': Herbert Hoover and the Conservation Movement of the 1920s." *Wisconsin Magazine of History* 67 (1984): 199–218.

Laabs, Joyce. *A Collection of Northwoods Nostalgia from the Pages of the Lakeland Times*. Sun Prairie, Wis.: Royle Publishing, 1978.

Lake, Ivan Clyde. *Minocqua: A Brief History of the Island City*. Minocqua, Wis.: Ivan Clyde Lake, 1931.

Lakeland Color Press. *Minnesota's Greatest Lake District*. Brainerd, Minn.: Lakeland Color Press, 1940.

Lakeland Times. The First 100 Years: Minocqua-Woodruff, 1888–1988. Minocqua, Wis.: Lakeland Times, 1988.

Lakota Resort. *Lakota Resort*. Conover, Wis.: N. Langerman, n.d.

The Land of Ten Thousand Lakes over Jefferson Highway Minnesota. N.p., 1920 and 1922.

Landis, Paul H. *Three Iron Mining Towns: A Study in Cultural Change*. Ann Arbor: Edwards Brothers, 1938.

Lankton, Larry. *Cradle to Grave: Life, Work, and Death at the Lake Superior Copper Mines*. New York: Oxford University Press, 1991.

———. *Beyond the Boundaries: Life and Landscape at the Lake Superior Copper Mines, 1840–1875*. New York: Oxford University Press, 1997.

———. *Hollowed Ground: Copper Mining and Community Building on Lake Superior, 1840s–1990s*. Detroit: Wayne State Press, 2010.

Lanning, Victor H. *The Wisconsin Tourist: A Study of the Resort and Recreation Business of Wisconsin, 1949*. Madison: University of Wisconsin, 1950.

Larson, Agnes M. *The White Pine Industry in Minnesota: A History*. Minneapolis: University of Minnesota Press, [1949] 2007.

Larson, Herbert F. *Be-wa-bic Country: The Story of the Menominee Iron Range in the Upper Peninsula of Michigan*. New York: Carlton Press, 1963.

Larson, Paul Clifford. *A Place at the Lake*. Afton, Minn.: Afton Historical Society Press, 1998.

Lass, William E. *Minnesota: A History*. New York: W. W. Norton & Company, 1998.

Lears, Jackson. *No Place of Grace: Antimodernism and the Transformation of American Culture, 1880–1920*. Chicago: University of Chicago Press, 1983.

———. *Fables of Abundance: A Cultural History of Advertising in America*. New York: Basic Books, 1994.

Leopold, Aldo. "The Wilderness and Its Place in Forest Recreational Policy." *Journal of Forestry* 19 (1921): 718–21.

———. *A Sand County Almanac, with Other Essays on Conservation from Round River*. New York: Oxford, 1966.

Lost Lake Resort. *Ed Gabe's Lost Lake Resort: A Famous Summer Hotel in Northern Wisconsin's Charming Lakeland, Sayner, Wisconsin*. Sayner: The Resort, [1920?].

Limerick, Patricia Nelson. "Seeing and Being Seen: Tourism in the American West." In *Over the Edge: Remapping the American West*, ed. Valerie J. Matsumoto and Blake Allmendinger, 15–31. Berkeley: University of California Press, 1999.

Linn, Walter. *Visiting the Land of Hiawatha*. Chicago, 1932.

Lovejoy, P. S. "Michigan's Fight for Forests." *American Forestry* 28 (December 1922): 749–53.

———. "In the Name of Development." *American Forestry* 29 (July 1923): 387–93, 447.

Lucas, Robert C. "Wilderness Perception and Use: The Example of the Boundary Waters Canoe Area." *Natural Resources Journal* 3 (1964): 394–411.

MacCannell, Dean. *The Tourist: A New Theory of the Leisure Class*. 3rd ed. Berkeley: University of California Press, 1999.

Madison, James H., ed. *Heartland: Comparative Histories of Midwestern States*. Bloomington: Indiana University Press, 1988.

Magnaghi, Russell. *An Outline History of Michigan's Upper Peninsula with Bibliography*. Marquette, Mich.: Belle Fontaine Press, 1997.

Maher, Neil. "A New Deal Body Politic: Landscape, Labor, and the Civilian Conservation Corps." *Environmental History* 7 (2002): 435–61.

———. *Nature's New Deal: The Civilian Conservation Corps and the Roots of the American Environmental Movement*. New York: Oxford, 2008.

"Making Money for the State: Ten Thousand Lakes of Minnesota Association Has Justified Its Creation and Existence." *Western Magazine* 17 (January 1921): 11–13.

The Manitowish Lodge. N.p., 1906, 1908, 1909, 1911, and 1913.

Manitowish Waters Association. *Vacation on the Manitowish Waters on U.S. 51*. Manitowish, Wis.: Manitowish Waters Association, [1920?].

Manitowish Waters Chamber of Commerce. *Vacation Days Are Happy Days*. Manitowish Waters, Wis.: Manitowish Waters Chamber of Commerce, 1936 and 1938.

Manuel, Jeffrey T. "Developing Resources: Industry, Policy, and Memory on the Post Industrial Iron Range." Ph.D. diss., University of Minnesota, 2009.

Marchand, Roland. *Advertising the American Dream: Making Way for Modernity, 1920–1940*. Berkeley: University of California Press, 1985.

Marling, Karal Ann. *Colossus of Roads: Myth and Symbol along the American Highway*. Minneapolis: University of Minnesota Press, 1984.

Marple, Eldon M. *A History of the Hayward Lakes Region through the Eyes of the Visitor Who Came and Stayed*. Hayward, Wis.: Chicago Bay Grafix, 1976.

Marshall, Robert. *The People's Forests*. New York: Harrison Smith and Robert Haas, 1933.

Martin, C. Brenden. *Tourism in the Mountain South: A Double-Edged Sword*. Knoxville: University of Tennessee Press, 2007.

Martin, J. F. *Clef Camp, Grand Rapids, Minnesota on Lake Pokegama*. Grand Rapids: The Camp, 1927.

Martin, John Bartlow. *Call It North Country: The Story of Upper Michigan*. New York: A. A. Knopf, 1944.

Mason Lake Resort. *Mason Lake Resort, Incorporated, Fifield, Wis.: One of the Finest Natural Beauty Spots in Upper Wisconsin, Pike, Bass and Muskellunge Fishing*. Park Falls, Wis.: Herald Print, 1921.

———. *Recreation at Mason Lake Resort, Northern Wisconsin*. Fifield: H. Boyd and Sons, 1925.

Masse, Benjamin J. "Vacations with Pay." *America* XCV3 (1956): 315.

McGregor, F. H. *Shingwauk Resort*. Aitkin, Minn.: The Resort, [1930?].

McIntosh, Robert W. "Wildland Planning Procedures with Emphasis on Recreational Land Use in the Tahquamenon-Pictured Rocks Region, Upper Peninsula of Michigan." Ph.D. diss., University of Michigan, 1955.

Mead and Hunt, Inc. *"Land of Silver Lakes and Streams": Survey of Resorts and Boathouses Oneida County, Wisconsin*. Madison: Mead and Hunt, 1998.

Meyer, Roy W. *Everyone's Country Estate: A History of Minnesota's State Parks*. St. Paul: Minnesota Historical Society Press, 1991.

Michigan Department of Conservation. *The Biennial Report of the Department of Conservation of the State of Michigan*. Lansing: The Department, 1922–68.
——. *A Program for the Purchase of a Recreation Area in the Porcupine Mountains*. Lansing: The Department, 1943.
——. *The Porcupine Mountain State Park: A Progress Report*. Lansing: The Department, 1947.
——. *Forty Years of Conservation*. Lansing: Department of Conservation, 1961.
Michigan Department of Natural Resources. *History of Hunting and Trapping License Sales, 1895–1969*. Lansing: The Department, 1970.
——. *Managing Michigan's Natural Resources: A Historical Overview of the Department of Natural Resources*. Lansing: The Bureau, 1991.
Michigan Highway Department. *Official Michigan Highway Map*. Lansing: The Department,1934–38.
Michigan Public Domain Commission and Michigan Immigration Commission. *Michigan: Agricultural, Horticultural, and Industrial Advantages*. N.p.: Immigration Publication, 1914.
Michigan Tourist and Resort Association. *West Michigan Vacation Directory*. Grand Rapids: Michigan Tourist and Resort Association, 1925, 1929, 1931, 1933, 1934, 1936–38.
——. *Annual Report of the President and Secretary*. N.p.: The Association, 1929.
——. *Western Michigan Automobile Road Map of the Resort Sections*. Grand Rapids: Michigan Tourist and Resort Association, 1930.
——. *Carefree Days in West Michigan*. Grand Rapids: Michigan Tourist and Resort Association, 1939–41, 1943–45.
Michigan Tourist Council. *Annual Report*. Lansing: The Council, 1965.
Michigan's Charms Now Surround You: Ahead Lies the Land of Hiawatha. Sault Ste. Marie, Mich.: Chamber of Commerce, 1930.
Miller, Char. *Gifford Pinchot and the Making of Modern Environmentalism*. Washington, D.C.: Island Press, 2001.
Miller, Dana H. *The Iron Range Resources and Rehabilitation Board*. Eveleth, Minn.: Iron Range Resources and Rehabilitation Board, 1991.
Mills, Charles M. *Vacations for Industrial Workers*. New York: Ronald Press, 1927.
Milwaukee Journal Tour Club Road Map of Wisconsin. Milwaukee: The Journal Co., 1924 and 1930.
Minneapolis Civic and Commerce Association, Publicity Bureau. *Vacation Days: A Complete Guide to the Hotels, Resorts and Vacation Places in Minnesota Land of Ten Thousand Lakes*. Minneapolis: Civic and Commerce Association, 1923–25.
Minneapolis Public Schools. *A Summer Vacation Guide: Nature and Science*. Minneapolis: The Schools, 1937.
Minnesota Arrowhead Association. *The Minnesota Arrowhead Country: Follow the Arrows to the Arrowhead*. Duluth: Minnesota Arrowhead Association, 1926.
——. *Main Highways and Some By-ways Duluth*. Duluth: The Association, 1928.
——. *Lake Superior International Highway*. Duluth: Minnesota Arrowhead Association, Fort William Civic Tourist Bureau and Port Arthur Chamber of Commerce, 1929.
——. *Report on Tourist Business for the 1929 Season*. Duluth: The Association, 1929.
——. *Tourist Guide and Map of Minnesota Arrowhead Country*. Duluth: The Association, 1929.
——. *Annual Tourist Report, 1930–1931*. Duluth: The Association, 1931.
——. *Annual Report*. Duluth: The Association, 1931, 1941–46.
——. *President's Report*. Duluth: The Association, 1936–38.
——. *Minnesota Arrowhead Country: Hotel and Resort Directory*. Duluth: The Association, 1938.

———. *Map of the Famous Minnesota Arrowhead Country*. Duluth: Minnesota Arrowhead Association, 1939.
———. *Publicity Program*. Duluth: The Association, 1939.
———. *Minnesota Arrowhead Country and Canadian Lakehead Visitor Directory*. Duluth: Minnesota Arrowhead Association, 1952, 1957, 1958, 1960, and 1961.
———. *Report on Activities at Annual Meeting and Luncheon*. Duluth: The Association, September 25, 1953, and September 16, 1955.
———. *M.A.A. Vacation-Travel Survey*. Duluth, 1958.
Minnesota Board of Immigration. *Minnesota: The Land of Opportunity*. St. Paul: State Bureau of Immigration, 1919.
———. *Northeastern Minnesota: Land of Certainties*. Minneapolis: Great West Printing Co., 1919.
———. *Northwestern Minnesota: A Wonderful Agricultural Section*. Minneapolis: Great West Printing Co., 1925.
Minnesota Commission of Conservation. *Biennial Report of the Commission of Conservation*. St. Paul: Minnesota Commission of Conservation, 1932.
Minnesota Department of Business Research and Development. *Steps to Better Vacations in Minnesota: A Survey of Minnesota's Vacation Industry*. St. Paul: Department of Business Research and Development, 1949.
Minnesota Department of Conservation. *Biennial Report*. St. Paul: Minnesota Department of Conservation, 1934–60.
Minnesota Department of Highways. *Minnesota Trunk Highways*. Minneapolis: The Department, 1928.
———. *1934 Condition Map of Minnesota Trunk Highways: Showing National and State Markings*. St. Paul: Minnesota Department of Highways, 1934.
Minnesota Department of Transportation. *Official Road Map of Minnesota*. St. Paul: Minnesota Department of Transportation, 1940.
Minnesota State Board of Immigration. *Map of Minnesota: The Land of Opportunities*. St. Paul: Minnesota State Board of Immigration and McGill-Warner Co., 1925.
Minnesota State Planning Board. *Report of the Minnesota State Planning Board*. St. Paul: Minnesota State Planning Board, 1938.
Minnesota Tourist Bureau. *Fisher's Marvelous Minnesota Manual for 1937*. St. Paul: Fisher Publisher Co., 1937.
———. *Marvelous Minnesota*. St. Paul: Minnesota Tourist Bureau, 1937.
———. *Minnesota Has Everything*. St. Paul: Minnesota Tourist Bureau, 1940.
Minnesota's Greatest Lake District. Brainerd: Lakeland Color Press, 1940.
Minocqua District Resort Association. *"Wisconsin for Muskies": The World's Most Concentrated Lake Region*. Minocqua, Wis.: Minocqua District Resort Association, [1935?].
Mitman, Gregg. "Hay Fever Holiday: Health, Leisure, and Place in Gilded-Age America." *Bulletin of the History of Medicine* 77 (2003): 600–635.
Montrie, Chad. *Making a Living: Work and Environment in the United States*. Chapel Hill: University of North Carolina Press, 2008.
Morrissey, Katherine G. *Mental Territories: Mapping the Inland Empire*. Ithaca, N.Y.: Cornell University Press, 1997.
Nasaw, David. *Going Out: The Rise and Fall of Public Amusements*. New York: Basic Books, 1993.
Nash, Roderick. *Wilderness and the American Mind*. 3rd ed. New Haven, Conn.: Yale University Press, 1982.
National Automobile Chamber of Commerce. *Facts and Figures of, by, and for the Automobile Industry*. New York: National Automobile Chamber of Commerce, 1919–72.

National Industrial Conference Board. *Vacations with Pay for Wage Earners*. New York: National Industrial Conference Board, 1935.

Nelson, Daniel. *Farm and Factory: Workers in the Midwest, 1880–1990*. Bloomington: Indiana University Press, 1995.

Nesper, Larry. *The Walleye War: The Struggle for Ojibwe Spearfishing and Treaty Rights*. Lincoln: University of Nebraska Press, 2002.

———. "Simulating Culture: Being Indian for Tourists in Lac du Flambeau's Wa-Swa-Gon Indian Bowl." *Ethnohistory* 50 (Summer 2003): 447–72.

Nesper, Larry, and James H. Schendler. "The Politics of Cultural Revitalization and Intertribal Resource Management: The Great Lakes Indian Fish and Wildlife Commission and the States of Wisconsin, Michigan, and Minnesota." In *Native Americans and the Environment: Perspectives on the Ecological Indian*, ed. Michael E. Harkin and David Rich Lewis, 277–303. Lincoln: University of Nebraska Press, 2007.

Neth, Mary. *Preserving the Family Farm: Women, Community and the Foundations of Agribusiness in the Midwest, 1900–1940*. Baltimore: Johns Hopkins Press, 1995.

———. "Seeing the Midwest with Peripheral Vision: Identities, Narratives, and Region." In *The American Midwest: Essays on Regional History*, ed. Andrew R. L. Cayton and Susan E. Gray, 27–48. Bloomington: Indiana University Press, 2001.

Norkunas, Martha. *The Politics of Public Memory: Tourism, History, and Ethnicity in Monterey, California*. Albany: State University of New York Press, 1993.

Northern Great Lakes Area Council. *Progress Report of a United Tourist Program in the Northern Great Lakes Area of Ontario, Minnesota, Wisconsin, Michigan*. Sarnia, Ontario: The Council, 1949.

Northern Minnesota Publishing Company. *The Long Bow Country of Minnesota*. Hackensack, Minn.: Northern Minnesota Pub. Co., 1938.

Northern Wisconsin Land of Lakes. Minocqua, Wis.: Art Dorwin's Sportswear, 1952.

Nute, Grace Lee. *Lake Superior*. Indianapolis: Bobbs-Merrill, 1944.

Nye, David. *Electrifying America: Social Meanings of a New Technology, 1880–1940*. Cambridge, Mass.: MIT Press, 1990.

Oberholtzer, Ernest. "A Lakeland Archipelago." *American Forests and Forest Life* 35 (September 1929): 547–50, 588.

———. "The Ancient Game of Grab: How the Resources of the Ontario Minnesota Border Lakes Are Vanishing into Thin Air." *American Forests and Forest Life* 35 (October 1929): 631–35, 644.

———. "A University of the Wilderness: The Proposal to Perpetuate by Treaty the Ontario-Minnesota Border Lakes." *American Forests and Forest Life* 35 (November 1929): 689–93, 700.

Olsenius, Richard. *Minnesota Travel Companion: A Guide to History along Minnesota's Highways*. Minneapolis: University of Minnesota Press, 2001.

Ontonagon County Board of Supervisors. *Ontonagon County: The Cloverfield of Cloverland*. Ontonagon, Mich.: Board of Supervisors, 1915.

Ostergren, Robert C., and Thomas R. Vale, eds. *Wisconsin Land and Life*. Madison: University of Wisconsin Press, 1997.

Ottawa Tourist Association. *The Vacation Guide: The Key to the Realm of Sports, to the Kingdom of Fishermen in Hiawatha Land*. Iron River, Mich.: The Association, 1942.

Outdoor Recreation Resources Review Commission. *A Progress Report to the President and to the Congress*. Washington, D.C.: The Commission, 1961.

———. *Outdoor Recreation for America*. Washington, D.C.: U.S. Government Printing Office, 1962.

Oxbo Resort. *Oxbo, Resort on the Flambeau: The Heart of Wisconsin's Vacation Land*. Draper, Wis.: The Resort, 1932.

Paddock, Joe. *Keeper of the Wild: The Life of Ernest Oberholtzer*. St. Paul: Minnesota Historical Society Press, 2001.

Paris, Leslie. *Children's Nature: The Rise of the American Summer Camp*. New York: NYU Press, 2008.

Paylin, Jolie. *Cutover Country: Jolie's Story*. Ames: Iowa State University Press, 1976.

Peiss, Kathy. *Cheap Amusements: Working Women and Leisure in Turn-of-the-Century New York*. Philadelphia: Temple University Press, 1986.

Phillips, Sarah. *This Land, This Nation: Conservation, Rural America and the New Deal*. Cambridge: Cambridge University Press, 2007.

Pike, Galen W. "Recreation Plans for Superior National Forest." *Journal of Forestry* (1953): 508–11.

Pinchot, Gifford. *The Fight for Conservation*. New York: Doubleday Page and Co., 1910.

Planets. *The Planets, Planets, Wisconsin: A Vacation Resort in Wisconsin's Land O' Lakes*. Crandon, Wis.: Planets, n.d.

The Playground of a Nation: The Arrowhead Country of Northern Minnesota, Where Industry and Recreation Go Hand in Hand. Duluth, 1925.

Proescholdt, Kevin, Rip Rapson, and Miron L. Heinselman. *Troubled Waters: The Fight for the Boundary Waters Canoe Area Wilderness*. St. Cloud: North Star Press, 1995.

Pugh, Grace. "Vacations with Pay." *Survey* (1923): 435–36.

Radford, Gail. "From Municipal Socialism to Public Authorities: Institutional Factors in the Shaping of American Public Enterprise." *Journal of American History* 90: 3 (December 2003): 863–90.

Rae, John B. *The Road and Car in American Life*. Cambridge, Mass.: MIT Press, 1975.

Rand McNally and Company. *Official 1923 Auto Trails Map District No. 9 Minnesota, W. Wisconsin*. Chicago: Rand McNally and Company, 1923.

———. *Official 1924 Auto Trails Map Cloverland and Vicinity*. Chicago: Rand McNally and Company, 1924.

Reiger, John F. *American Sportsmen and the Origins of Conservation*. 3rd ed. Corvallis: Oregon State Press, 2000.

Reinhardt, Hazel H. "Social Adjustments to a Changing Environment." In *The Great Lakes Forest: An Environmental and Social History*, ed. Susan L. Flader, 205–19. Minneapolis and Santa Cruz: University of Minnesota Press and Forest History Society, 1983.

Report of the Minister of Travel and Publicity, Province of Ontario. Toronto: Printer to the King's Most Excellent Majesty, 1946–51.

Report of the Minister of Travel and Publicity, Province of Ontario. Toronto: Printer to the Queen's Most Excellent Majesty, 1956, 1957, and 1960.

Reynolds, Terry S. "'Quite an Experiment': A Mining Company's Attempt to Promote Agriculture on Michigan's Upper Peninsula, 1895–1915." *Agricultural History* 80 (Winter 2006): 64–98.

Robbins, William G. *American Forestry: A History of National, State, and Private Cooperation*. Lincoln: University of Nebraska Press, 1985.

———. *Landscapes of Promise: The Oregon Story, 1800–1940*. Seattle: University of Washington Press, 1997.

———. *Landscapes of Conflict: The Oregon Story, 1940–2000*. Seattle: University of Washington Press, 2004.

Rome, Adam. *The Bulldozer in the Countryside: Suburban Sprawl and the Rise of American Environmentalism*. Cambridge: Cambridge University Press, 2001.

Rosenzweig, Roy. *Eight Hours for What We Will: Workers and Leisure in an Industrial City, 1870–1920*. Cambridge: Cambridge University Press, 1983.

Roth, Filibert. *On the Forestry Conditions in Wisconsin*. Madison: The State, 1898.

Rothman, Hal K. "'A Regular Ding-Dong Fight': Agency Culture and Evolution in the NPS-USFS Dispute, 1916–1937." *Western Historical Quarterly* 20 (May 1989): 141–61.

———. *Devil's Bargains: Tourism in the Twentieth-Century American West*. Lawrence: University Press of Kansas, 1998.

Rowlands, Walter A. "County Zoning for Agriculture, Forestry, and Recreation in Wisconsin." *Journal of Land and Public Utility Economics* 9 (1933): 272–82.

———. "The Great Lakes Cutover Region." In *Regionalism in America*, ed. Merrill Jensen, 331–46. Madison: University of Wisconsin Press, 1951.

Rugh, Susan Sessions. *Are We There Yet? The Golden Age of Family Vacations*. Lawrence: University Press of Kansas, 2008.

Ryan, Carol Crawford. "Saving Star Island: Land Use, Local Economy, and Community Interaction in Northern Minnesota." *Minnesota History* 48 (1982): 108–18.

———. *Star Island: A Minnesota Summer Community*. St. Paul: Pogo Press, 2000.

St. Louis County Club. *The Vacation Land Supreme amid the Pines and Lakes of Northern Minnesota*. Duluth, 1921.

———. *Sportland of the North: Cool Minnesota Arrowhead Country*. Duluth: St. Louis County Club, 1936.

Schmaltz, Norman J. "Cutover Land Crusade: The Michigan Forest Conservation Movement, 1899–1931." Ph.D. diss., University of Michigan, 1972.

———. "P. S. Lovejoy: Michigan's Cantankerous Conservationist." *Journal of Forest History* (April 1975): 72–81.

———. "Michigan's Land Economic Survey." *Agricultural History* 52 (1978): 229–46.

———. "The Land Nobody Wanted: The Dilemma of Michigan's Cutover Lands." *Michigan History* 67 (1983): 32–40.

Schultz, Elizabeth. *Shoreline: Seasons at the Lake*. East Lansing: Michigan State University Press, 2001.

Searle, Newell. "Minnesota National Forest: The Politics of Compromise, 1898–1908." *Minnesota History* (Fall 1971): 242–57.

———. "Minnesota Forestry Comes of Age: Christopher C. Andrews, 1895–1911." *Forest History* (July 1973): 14–25.

———. *Saving Quetico-Superior: A Land Set Apart*. St. Paul: Minnesota Historical Society Press, 1977.

Sears, John F. *Sacred Places: American Tourist Attractions in the 19th Century*. New York: Oxford University Press, 1989.

70-155 Advancement Association Information Bureau. *The Lake Region*. Eagle River, Wis.: 70-155 Advancement Association Information Bureau, [1930?].

Shaffer, Marguerite S. *See America First: Tourism and National Identity, 1880–1940*. Washington, D.C.: Smithsonian Press, 2001.

Shave, Ed. "Why Is Minnesota Losing the Race for Travel and Industry Dollars? A Report on the Critical Challenge Facing Minnesotans." Minneapolis: *Minneapolis Star and Tribune*, 1950.

Shorewood Vista. *Blaesing's Shorewood Vista: A Typical "Dude Ranch," Completely Modern in the Heart of the Nation's Greatest Vacation Land, A Resort We Know You Will Like, Rhinelander, Wisconsin*. Rhinelander: Shorewood Vista, n.d.

Shortridge, James. *The Middle West: Its Meaning in American Culture*. Lawrence: University Press of Kansas, 1989.

Sielaff, Richard O. *The Economics of Outdoor Recreation in the Upper Midwest*.

Duluth: University of Minnesota-Duluth Social Sciences Research Fund, 1963. 285

Sielaff, Richard O., and Glenn O. Gronseth. *A Look at Employment in Minnesota Resorts for 1961*. Duluth: Minnesota Department of Employment Security, 1961.

Silfverston, Carl. *This Minnesota Arrowhead Country: A Guidebook for Vacationists*. Duluth, 1947.

Sommer, Barbara W. *Hard Work and a Good Deal: The Civilian Conservation Corps in Minnesota*. St. Paul: Minnesota Historical Society Press, 2008.

Southeastern Michigan Tourist and Publicity Association. *Beautiful Michigan*. Detroit: Southeastern Michigan Tourist and Publicity Association, 1930.

Souvenir of Northern Michigan: In the Land of Hiawatha. Milwaukee: E. C. Kropp Co., n.d.

Sparhawk, William N., and Warren D. Brush. *Economic Aspects of Forest Destruction in Northern Michigan*. Washington, D.C.: U.S. Department of Agriculture, 1929.

Spence, Mark. *Dispossessing the Wilderness: Indian Removal and the Making of the National Parks*. New York: Oxford University Press, 1999.

Spooner Chamber of Commerce. *I'd Sooner Go to Spooner: Heart of Wisconsin's Indian Head Country*. Spooner: Spooner Chamber of Commerce, 1941.

Stace, Arthur W. *Touring the Coasts of Michigan*. Ann Arbor: Booth Newspapers Inc., 1938.

Starnes, Richard D., ed. *Southern Journeys: Tourism, History, and Culture in the Modern South*. Tuscaloosa: University of Alabama Press, 2003.

Steinberg, Theodore. *Down to Earth: Nature's Role in American History*. New York: Oxford, 2002.

Steiner, Jesse. *Americans at Play: Recent Trends in Recreation and Leisure Time Activities*. New York and London: McGraw-Hill, 1933.

———. "Challenge of the New Leisure." *Recreation* 27 (1934): 517–22.

———. *Research Memorandum on Recreation in the Depression*. New York: Social Science Research Council, 1937.

Stenlund, Milt. *Burntside Lake, The Early Days, 1880–1920*. Ely, Minn.: Ely-Winton Historical Society, 1986.

Stephenson, Isaac. *The Story of Cloverland*. Delta County, Mich.: I. Stephenson Co., 1910.

———. *Recollections of a Long Life, 1829–1915*. Chicago: Donnelley Company, 1915.

Stoll, Albert, Jr. "Isle Royale: An Unspoiled and Little Known Wonderland of the North." *American Forests and Forest Life* 32 (July 1926): 457–59, 512.

Stoltenberg, Carl H. "Rural Zoning in Minnesota: An Appraisal." *Land Economics* (May 1954): 153–63.

Stroud, Ellen Frances. "The Return of the Forest: Urbanization and Reforestation in the Northeastern United States." Ph.D. diss., Columbia University, 2001.

Summers, Gregory. *Consuming Nature: Environmentalism in the Fox River Valley, 1850–1950*. Lawrence: University Press of Kansas, 2006.

Sutter, Paul. "'A Blank Spot on the Map': Aldo Leopold, Wilderness, and the U.S. Forest Service Recreational Policy, 1909–1924." *Western Historical Quarterly* 29 (1998): 187–214.

———. *Driven Wild: How the Fight against Automobiles Launched the Modern Wilderness Movement*. Seattle: University of Washington Press, 2002.

Symon, Charles A., ed. *Alger County: A Centennial History*. Munising, Mich.: Bayshore Press, 1986.

Teaford, Jon C. *Cities of the Heartland: The Rise and Fall of the Industrial Midwest*. Bloomington: Indiana University Press, 1993.

———. *The Rise of the States: Evolution of American State Government*. Baltimore: Johns Hopkins University Press, 2002.

Ten Thousand Lakes–Greater Minnesota Association. *Minnesota: Land of Ten Thousand Lakes*. St. Paul: McGill-Warner, 1928.

———. *Come to Minnesota: You'll Do Better on a Minnesota Farm*. St. Paul: The Association, 1929 and 1930.

———. *Annual Report*. St. Paul, 1929–32.

———. *The Minnesota Book*. St. Paul: The Association, 1929–32.

———. *Minnesota: Land of Ten Thousand Lakes*. St. Paul: McGill-Warner, 1931.

Ten Thousand Lakes of Minnesota Association. *Annual Report*. St. Paul: The Association, 1918, 1919, 1923, 1925, 1926, 1928.

———. *Minnesota Canoe Trails*. St. Paul, 1918.

———. *Proceedings of the Conference of Northwest Tourist Association Secretaries in Saint Paul, Minnesota, November 20–21, 1919*. St. Paul: Ten Thousand Lakes of Minnesota Association, 1919.

———. *A Report to the Members of the 10,000 Lakes of Minnesota Association*. St. Paul: Corning, 1919.

———. *Minnesota: The Land of Ten Thousand Lakes*. St. Paul: Ten Thousand Lakes of Minnesota Association, 1926.

———. *Recreation Days*. St. Paul: Ten Thousand Lakes of Minnesota Association, 1927–28.

Thompson, William F. *The History of Wisconsin: Continuity and Change, 1940–1965*. Madison: State Historical Society of Wisconsin Press, 1988.

Three Lakes Wisconsin Resort Association. *For Health, for Recreation, for Sports on Land and Water: Three Lakes, Wisconsin*. Three Lakes: Three Lakes Wisconsin Resort Association, [1940?].

Thurner, Arthur. *Strangers and Sojourners: A History of Michigan's Keweenaw Peninsula*. Detroit: Wayne State University Press, 1994.

Tingdale Bros. *The North Woods Are Calling You*. Minneapolis: Tingdale Bros., Inc., [1920?].

Titus, Harold. *Timber*. Cambridge, Mass.: Small, Maynard and Company, 1922.

———. "Michigan, Onward!" *American Forestry* 29 (July 1923): 400.

———. "Two Decades of Wisconsin Forestry." *Wisconsin Magazine of History* 30 (1946): 187–91.

Toftey, Adolph A. *Cook County, Minnesota: Nature's Gift to the Arrowhead Country*. Minnesota, 1920 and 1930.

Tornes, Elizabeth, ed. *Memories of Lac du Flambeau Elders*. Madison: Center for the Study of Upper Midwestern Cultures, 2004.

"Tourist and Resort Services for Michigan: Suggestions for Prospective Operators," Circular R-101. East Lansing: Michigan State College, Extension Service and Agricultural Experiment Station, 1946.

Trachtenberg, Alan. *Shades of Hiawatha: Staging Indians, Making Americans, 1880–1930*. New York: Hill and Wang, 2004.

Treuer, Robert. *Voyageur Country: The Story of Minnesota's National Park*. Minneapolis: University of Minnesota Press, 1998.

Turner, James Morton. "From Woodcraft to 'Leave No Trace': Wilderness, Consumerism, and Environmentalism in Twentieth Century America." *Environmental History* 7 (2002): 462–84.

Tweed, William C. *Recreation Site Planning and Improvement in the National Forests, 1891–1942*. Washington, D.C.: U.S. Department of Agriculture, Forest Service, 1981.

U.S. Congress. Senate. Committee on Interior and Insular Affairs. *Outdoor Recreation Resources Commission: Hearing before the Committee on Interior and Insular Affairs*. 85th Cong., 1st sess., May 15, 1957.

———. *Outdoor Recreation Act of 1962: Hearings before the Senate Committee on Interior and Insular Affairs*. 87th Cong., 2nd sess., May 10–11, 1962.

U.S. Department of Agriculture. *National Forests in Michigan*. Washington, D.C.: Government Printing Office, 1941.

U.S. Department of the Interior, National Park Service. *Our Fourth Shore: Great Lakes Shoreline Recreation Area Survey*. Washington, D.C.: U.S. Department of the Interior, National Park Service, 1959.

U.S. Forest Service. *A Vacation Land of Lakes and Woods: The Superior National Forest*. Washington, D.C.: Government Printing Office, 1919.

U.S. National Park Service. *Isle Royale National Park, Michigan*. Chicago: Gunthorp Warren Print. Co., 1942.

U.S. Natural Resources Board, Land Planning Committee. *Supplementary Report of the Land Planning Committee to the National Resources Board, 1935–1942*. New York: Arno Press, 1972.

U.S. Railroad Administration. *The Northern Lakes: Wisconsin, Minnesota, Upper Michigan, Iowa, Illinois*. Chicago: U.S. Railroad Administration, 1919.

U.S. Senate, Committee on Public Works. *Opportunities for Development in Michigan's Upper Peninsula*. Washington, D.C.: Government Printing Office, 1962.

University of California Wildland Research Center. *Wilderness and Recreation—A Report on Resources, Values, and Problems. Report to the ORRRC*. Washington, D.C.: Government Printing Office, 1962.

Upper Michigan Ahoy Vacationist!. [Michigan], 1930.

Upper Peninsula Development Bureau (UPDB). *Seven Million Fertile Acres in the Upper Peninsula of Michigan*. Marquette: UPDB, 1911.

———. *Homes and Farms in the Upper Peninsula of Michigan*. N.p.: UPDB, [1911?].

———. *Cloverland in Clovertime: Touring through Picturesque Upper Peninsula of Michigan*. Marquette: UPDB, 1917.

———. *Cloverland: Upper Peninsula of Michigan, The Tourist's Paradise*. Marquette: UPDB, 1920, 1923, and 1930.

———. *Land of Hiawatha: Upper Peninsula of Michigan, The Tourist's Paradise*. Marquette: UPDB, 1929.

———. *Land of Hiawatha, Upper Peninsula of Michigan: The Playground of the Nation*. Marquette: UPDB, 1930.

———. *Land of Hiawatha*. Marquette: UPDB, 1934.

———. *Lure of the Land of Hiawatha: Michigan's Upper Peninsula*. Marquette: UPDB, 1936.

———. *Lure of the Land of Hiawatha*. Marquette: UPDB, 1937.

———. *Lured by the Land of Hiawatha*. Marquette: UPDB, 1938.

———. *Lure Book of Michigan's Upper Peninsula*. Marquette: UPDB, 1939–52.

———. *The Winter Lure of Michigan's Upper Peninsula*. Marquette: UPDB, 1949.

———. *The Lure of Michigan's Upper Peninsula*. Marquette: UPDB, 1953–58.

Vacation Days: A Guide to the Advertised Summer Resorts of Minnesota and Wisconsin. Minneapolis: *Minneapolis Journal*, 1918–22.

Vacationland in Northern Minnesota: In the Land O'Pines. Pequot, Minn.: Benn A. Wagner, 1933.

"Vacations for Factory Workers." *Factory* May 1 (1921): 1086–87.

"Vacations with Pay for Production Workers." *Monthly Labor Review* (July 1926): 35–36.

"Vacations with Pay for Wage Earners." *Monthly Labor Review* (May 1926): 1–7.

Valliere, Leon, Jr. "A Brief History of the Waaswaaganing Ojibweg," In *Memories of Lac du Flambeau Elders*, ed. Elizabeth Tornes, 9–59. Madison: Center for the Study of Upper Midwestern Cultures, 2004.

Van Slyck, Abigail. *A Manufactured Wilderness: Summer Camps and the Shaping of American Youth, 1890–1960*. Minneapolis: University of Minnesota Press, 2006.

Vermilion Boat and Outing Co. *Beautiful Lake Vermilion: In the Pine Forests of Northern Minnesota*. Tower, Minn.: Vermilion Boat and Outing Co., 1914.

W. A. Fisher Company. *Ely: Map of Resort and Canoe Area*. Virginia, Minn.: W.A. Fisher Co., 1944.

Walsh, Eileen Patricia. "The Last Resort: Northern Minnesota Tourism and the Integration of Rural and Urban Worlds, 1900–1950." Ph.D. diss., University of Minnesota, 1994.

Warren, Louis S. *The Hunter's Game: Poachers and Conservationists in 20th Century America*. New Haven, Conn.: Yale University Press, 1997.

Waugh, Frank. *Recreation Uses on the National Forests*. Washington, D.C.: U.S. Department of Agriculture, Government Printing Office, 1918.

Wehrwein, George S., and Hugh A. Johnson. "A Recreation Livelihood Area." *Journal of Land and Public Utility Economics* 19: 2 (May 1943): 193–206.

Wehrwein, George S., and Kenneth H. Parsons. *Recreation as a Land Use*. Madison: University of Wisconsin-Madison Agricultural Experiment Station, 1932.

Where to Go? A Guide to the Leading Summer Resorts of Minnesota and Wisconsin. Minneapolis: *Minneapolis Tribune*, 1916.

White, Richard. "'Are You an Environmentalist or Do You Work for a Living?': Work and Nature." In *Uncommon Ground: Toward Reinventing Nature*, ed. William Cronon, 171–85. New York: W. W. Norton, 1995.

Whiteley, Harry. *A Post War Public Works Program for Conservation and Recreation for the State of Michigan*. Lansing: Michigan Department of Conservation, 1944.

Whiteshield, C. F. *Cloverland Echoes*. Marquette, Mich.: Guelff Print Co., 1923.

Wilderness Outfitters, Inc. *Basswood Lake Fishing Lodge Located on the Canadian Border: America's Finest Game Fishing*. Ely, Minn.: Wilderness Outfitters, [1930?].

Williams, Michael. *Americans and Their Forests: A Historical Geography*. Cambridge: Cambridge University Press, 1989.

Wilson, F. G. "Zoning for Forestry and Recreation: Wisconsin's Pioneer Role." *Wisconsin Magazine of History* 41 (Winter 1957–58): 102–6.

———. *E. M. Griffith and the Early Story of Wisconsin Forestry (1903–1915)*. Madison: Wisconsin Department of Natural Resources, 1982.

Wingerd, Mary Lethert. *North Country: The Making of Minnesota*. Minneapolis: University of Minnesota Press, 2010.

Winks, Robin W. *Laurance S. Rockefeller: Catalyst for Conservation*. Washington, D.C.: Island Press, 1997.

Wisconsin Cartographers' Guild. *Wisconsin's Past and Present: A Historical Atlas*. Madison: University of Wisconsin Press, 1998.

Wisconsin Committee on Land Use and Forestry. *Forest Land Use in Wisconsin*. Madison: Executive Office, 1932.

Wisconsin Conservation Commission. *Biennial Reports of the Wisconsin Conservation Commission*. Madison: The Department, 1915–56.

Wisconsin Conservation Department, Recreational Publicity Division. *Follow the Birds to Vacation Land, Wisconsin*. Madison: Wisconsin Conservation Department, Recreational Publicity Division, 1936.

Wisconsin Heart O'Lakes: Where the Nation Finds Recreation. Rhinelander: Heart O'Lakes Association, 1934–35, 1937–39.

Wisconsin Heart O' The Lakes Association. *Visit Wisconsin's Beautiful "Heart o' the Lakes": A Perfect Vacation Paradise: World's Most Concentrated Lake Region*. Rhinelander: Heart o' the Lakes Association, n.d.

Wisconsin Indian Head Country. *Call o' the Lakes*. Rice Lake, Wis.: Rice Lake Publishing Co., 1932–37.

———. *Wisconsin Indian Head Country: Vacation Edition of the Call o' the Lakes.* Chippewa Falls: Chippewa Printery, 1942.

Wisconsin Land & Lumber Company. *Blaney Park in Upper Michigan: The Playground of Paul Bunyan.* Blaney Park, Mich.: Wisconsin Land & Lumber Company, n. d.

Wisconsin State Planning Board. *The Cutover Region of Wisconsin: Report of Conditions and Recommendations for Rehabilitation.* Madison: Wisconsin State Planning Board, 1939.

———. *A Recreational Plan for Vilas County.* Madison: Wisconsin State Planning Board, 1941.

Wisconsin State Planning Board and Conservation Commission. *A Park, Parkway and Recreational Area Plan.* Madison: Wisconsin State Planning Board and Conservation Commission, 1939.

Witzig, Fred T. *Eighty Years in the Making: A Legislative History of Voyageurs National Park.* Minnesota: National Park Service, Voyageurs National Park, 2000.

———. *Voyageurs National Park: The Battle to Create Minnesota's National Park.* Minneapolis: University of Minnesota Press, 2004.

Woodward, David, et al. *Cultural Map of Wisconsin: A Cartographic Portrait of the State.* Madison: University of Wisconsin Press, 1996.

Work Projects Administration in the State of Wisconsin. *Wisconsin: A Guide to the Badger State.* New York: Duell, Sloan and Pearce, 1941.

Works Progress Administration in the State of Minnesota, *Minnesota: A State Guide.* New York: Viking, 1938.

Writers' Program of the Work Projects Administration in the State of Michigan. *Michigan: A Guide to the Wolverine State.* New York: Oxford University Press, 1941.

Writers' Program of the Work Projects Administration in the State of Michigan. *Michigan's Upper Peninsula: Its Places and People.* Lansing, 1940.

Writers' Program of the Work Projects Administration in the State of Minnesota. *The Minnesota Arrowhead Country.* Chicago: Albert Whitman and Co., 1941.

Writers' Program of the Work Projects Administration in the State of Minnesota. *The WPA Guide to the Minnesota Arrowhead Country.* St. Paul: Minnesota Historical Society Press, 1988.

Yorke, Douglas A., and John Margolies. *Hitting the Road: The Art of the American Road Map.* San Francisco: Chronicle Books, 1996.

Index

THE LURE OF THE NORTH WOODS

Aaron Shapiro, a Chicago native and North Woods visitor since his youth, is assistant professor of history at Auburn University. He previously served as national historian for the USDA Forest Service in Washington, D.C., and as assistant director of the Scholl Center for Family and Community History at Chicago's Newberry Library.